Shojo Beat

Kaze Hikaru

17

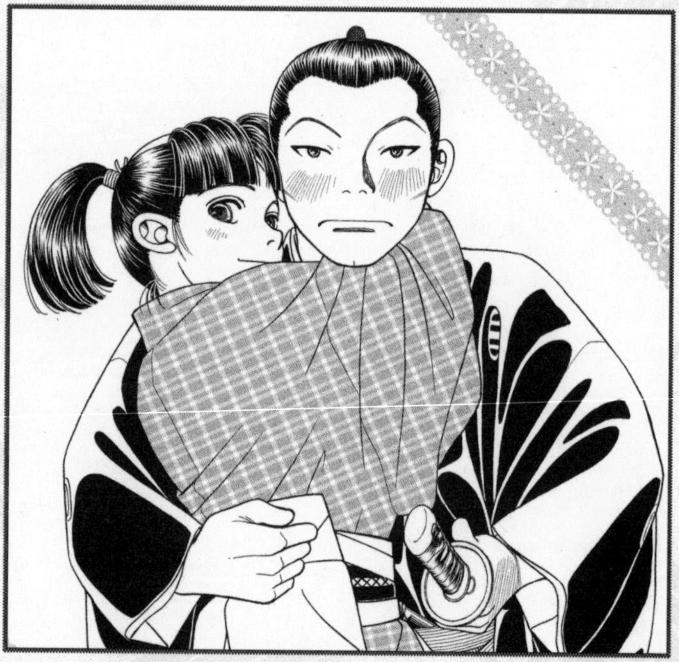

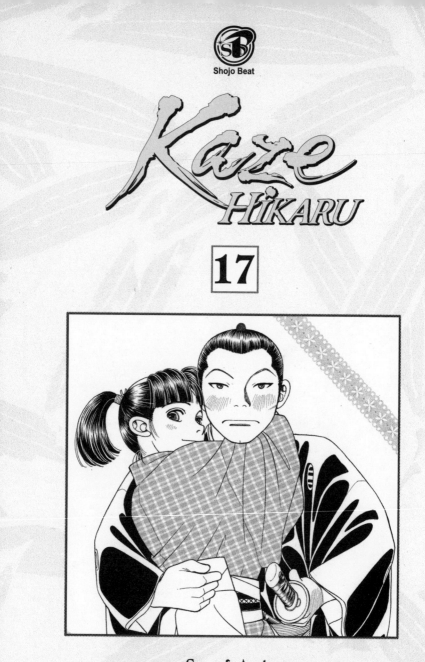

Story & Art by

Taeko Watanabe

Contents

Story Thus Far

It is the end of the Bakufu era, the third year of Bunkyu (1863) in Kyoto. The Shinsengumi is a band of warriors formed to protect the shogun.

Tominaga Sei, the daughter of a former Bakufu *bushi*, joined the Shinsengumi disguised as a boy by the name of Kamiya Seizaburo to avenge her father and brother. She has continued her training under the only person in the Shinsengumi who knows her true identity, Okita Soji, and she aspires to become a true *bushi*.

Sei learns that the father she believed never cared about his family had in fact deeply loved them all. It prompts her to wonder whether a man needs a warm home to return to.

Meanwhile, Okita entertains a marriage proposal on Kondo's orders. During the meeting, Okita is struck by the sight of a girl in a bright blue kimono. It is in fact Sei dressed as a girl. When she is assaulted by violent men, Saito Sensei comes to her rescue disguised as a normal townsman.

Characters

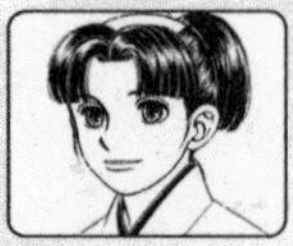

Tominaga Sei
She disguises herself as a boy to enter the Mibu-Roshi. She trains under Soji, aspiring to become a true *bushi*. But secretly, she is in love with Soji.

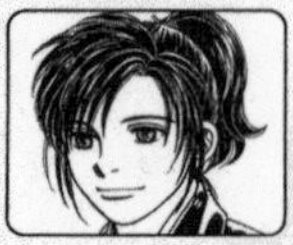

Okita Soji
Assistant vice captain of the Shinsengumi, and licensed master of the Ten'nen Rishin-Ryu. He supports the troop alongside Kondo and Hijikata and guides Seizaburo with a kind yet firm hand.

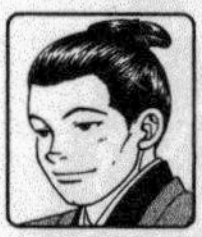

Kondo Isami
Captain of the Shinsengumi and fourth grandmaster of the Ten'nen Rishin-ryu. A passionate, warm and well-respected leader.

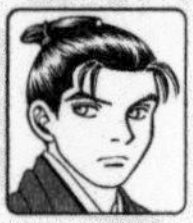

Hijikata Toshizo
Vice captain of the Shinsengumi. He commands both the group and himself with a rigid strictness. He is also known as the "Oni vice captain."

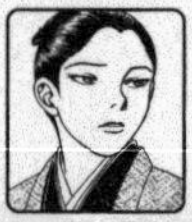

Ito Kashitaro
Councillor of the Shinsengumi. A skilled swordsman yet also an academic with anti-Bakufu sentiments, he plots to sway the direction of the troop.

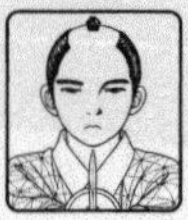

Saito Hajime
Assistant vice captain. He was a friend of Sei's older brother. Sei is attached to him in place of her lost brother.

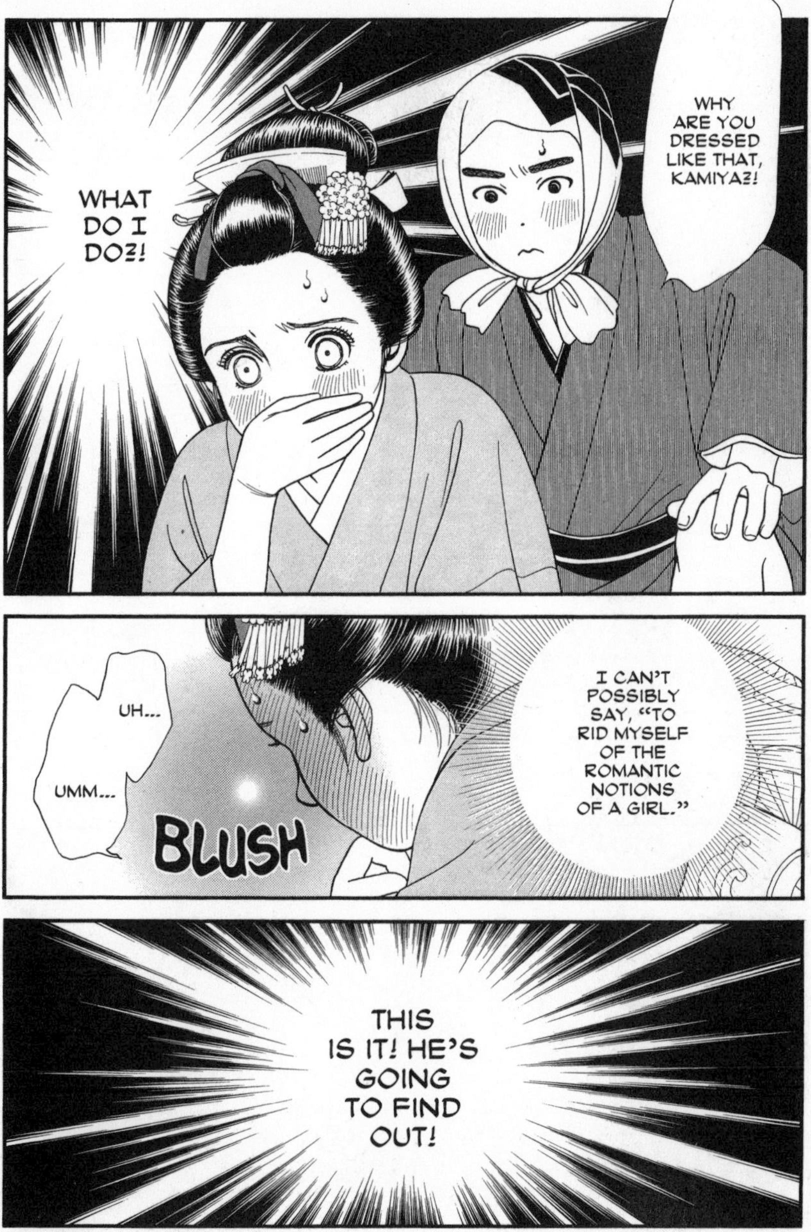
WHY ARE YOU DRESSED LIKE THAT, KAMIYA?!
WHAT DO I DO?!
I CAN'T POSSIBLY SAY, "TO RID MYSELF OF THE ROMANTIC NOTIONS OF A GIRL."
UH...
UMM...
BLUSH
THIS IS IT! HE'S GOING TO FIND OUT!

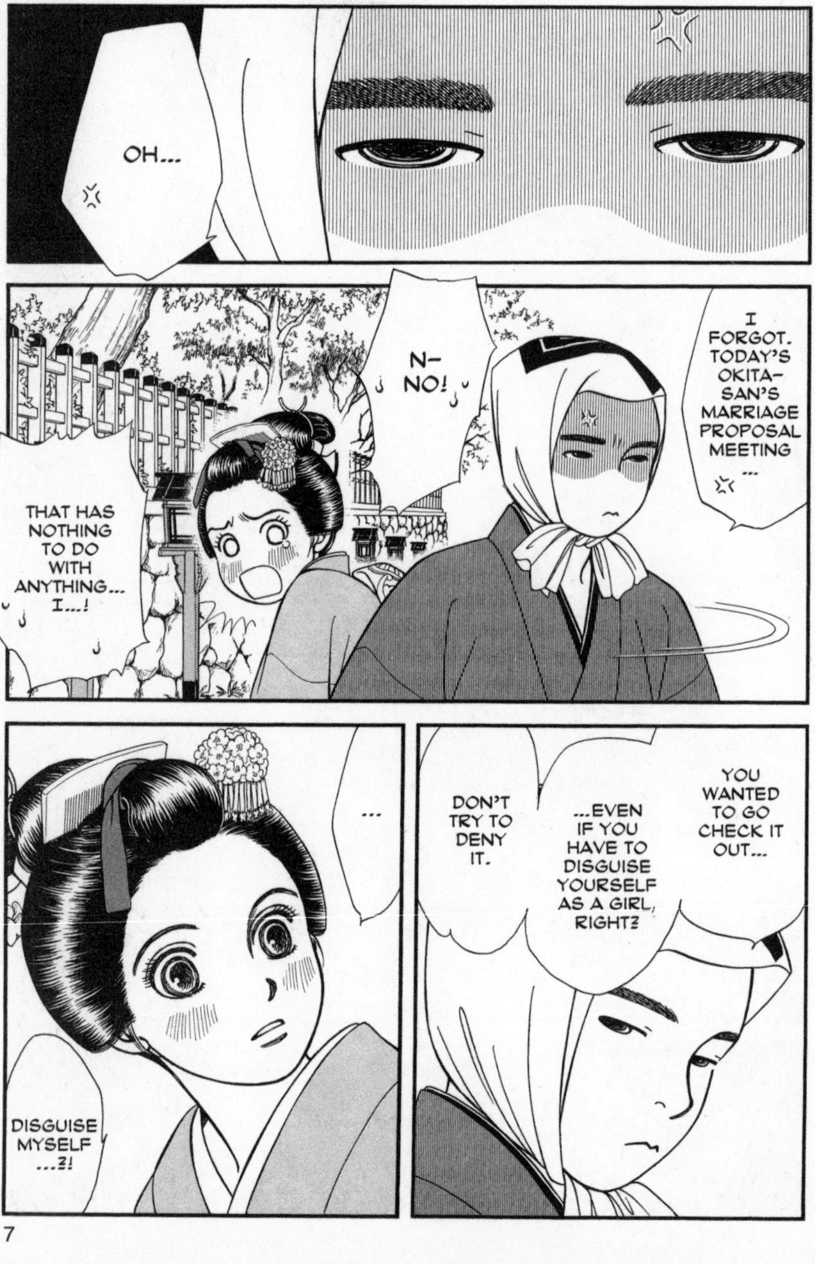
OH...
I FORGOT. TODAY'S OKITA-SAN'S MARRIAGE PROPOSAL MEETING ...
N-NO!
THAT HAS NOTHING TO DO WITH ANYTHING... I...!
YOU WANTED TO GO CHECK IT OUT...
...EVEN IF YOU HAVE TO DISGUISE YOURSELF AS A GIRL, RIGHT?
DON'T TRY TO DENY IT.
...
DISGUISE MYSELF ...?!

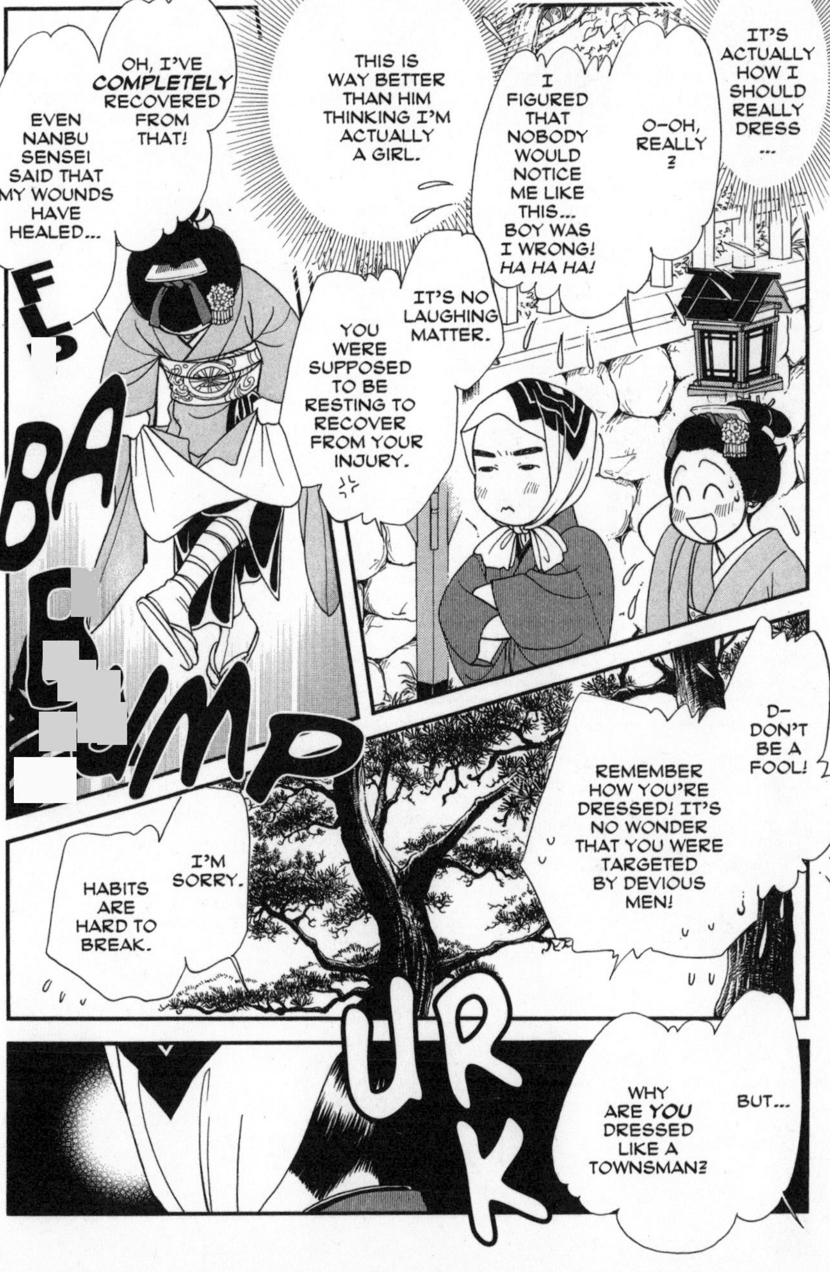
IT'S ACTUALLY HOW I SHOULD REALLY DRESS...
O-OH, REALLY?
I FIGURED THAT NOBODY WOULD NOTICE ME LIKE THIS... BOY WAS I WRONG! *HA HA HA!*
THIS IS WAY BETTER THAN HIM THINKING I'M ACTUALLY A GIRL.
IT'S NO LAUGHING MATTER.
YOU WERE SUPPOSED TO BE RESTING TO RECOVER FROM YOUR INJURY.
OH, I'VE **COMPLETELY** RECOVERED FROM THAT!
EVEN NANBU SENSEI SAID THAT MY WOUNDS HAVE HEALED...
D-DON'T BE A FOOL!
REMEMBER HOW YOU'RE DRESSED! IT'S NO WONDER THAT YOU WERE TARGETED BY DEVIOUS MEN!
I'M SORRY.
HABITS ARE HARD TO BREAK.
URK
BUT...
WHY ARE **YOU** DRESSED LIKE A TOWNSMAN?

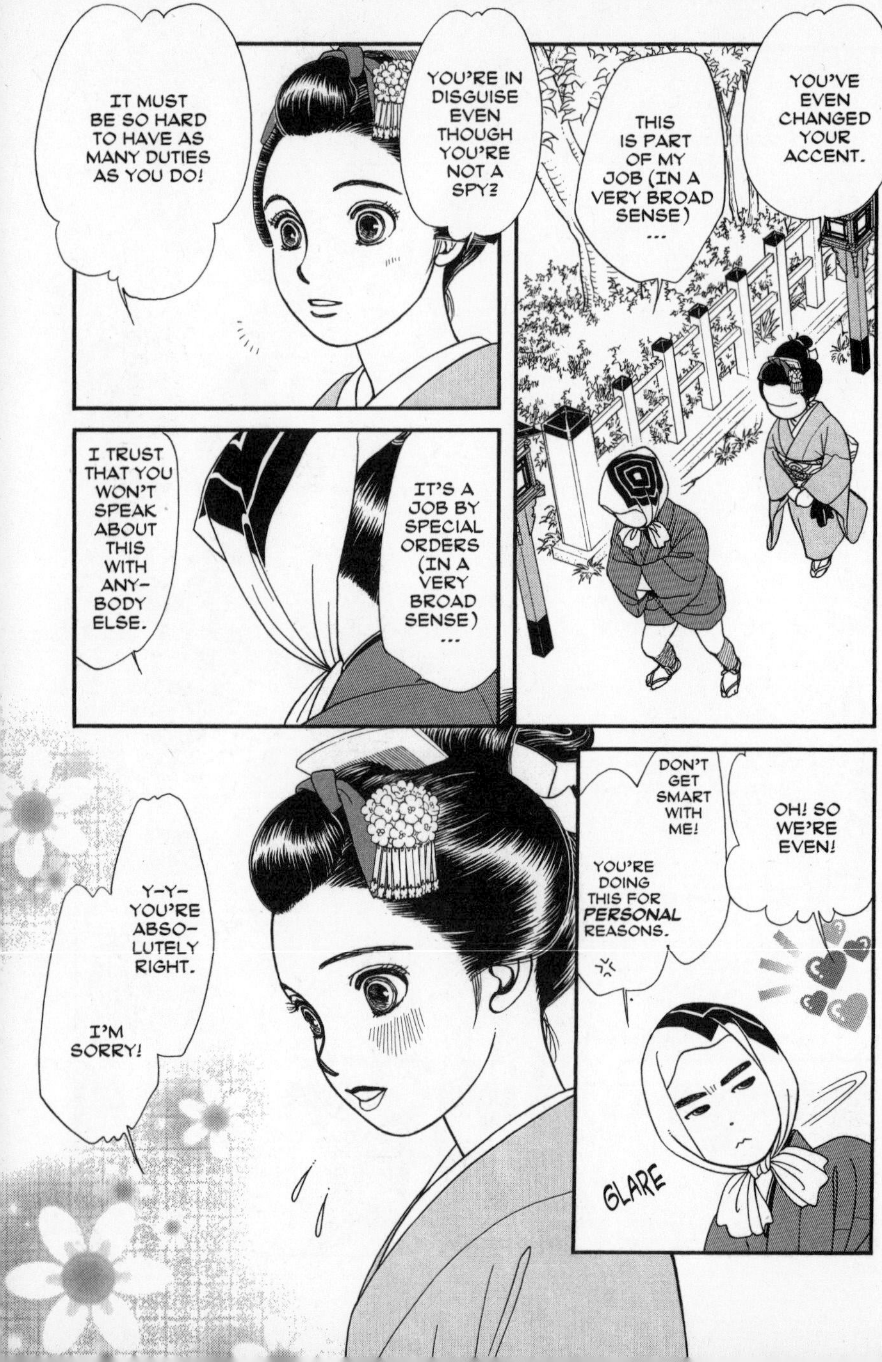
YOU'VE EVEN CHANGED YOUR ACCENT.
THIS IS PART OF MY JOB (IN A VERY BROAD SENSE)...
YOU'RE IN DISGUISE EVEN THOUGH YOU'RE NOT A SPY?
IT MUST BE SO HARD TO HAVE AS MANY DUTIES AS YOU DO!
IT'S A JOB BY SPECIAL ORDERS (IN A VERY BROAD SENSE)...
I TRUST THAT YOU WON'T SPEAK ABOUT THIS WITH ANY-BODY ELSE.
OH! SO WE'RE EVEN!
DON'T GET SMART WITH ME!
YOU'RE DOING THIS FOR PERSONAL REASONS.
GLARE
Y-Y-YOU'RE ABSO-LUTELY RIGHT.
I'M SORRY!

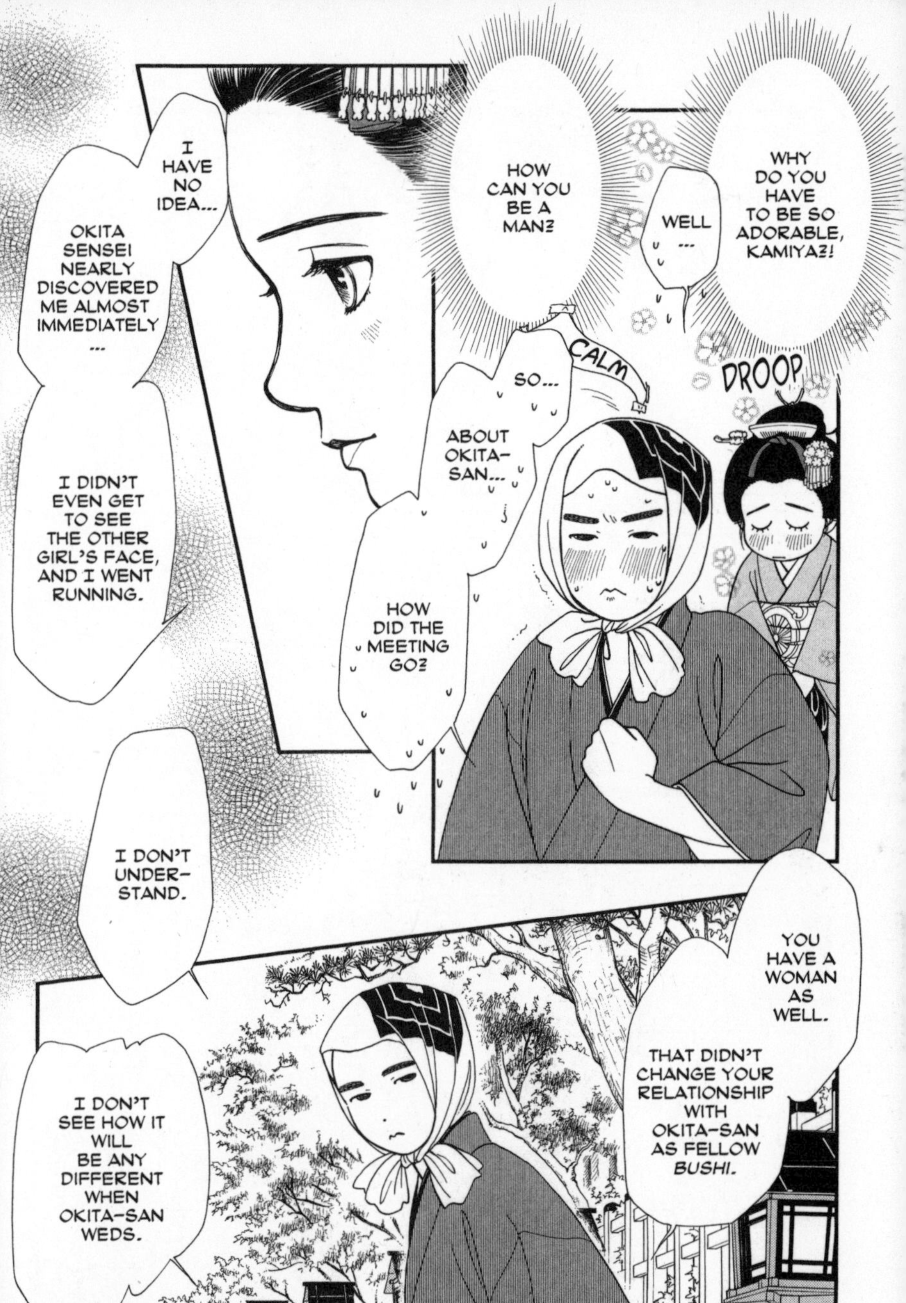
WHY DO YOU HAVE TO BE SO ADORABLE, KAMIYA?!
HOW CAN YOU BE A MAN?
WELL...
DROOP
CALM
SO... ABOUT OKITA-SAN... HOW DID THE MEETING GO?
I HAVE NO IDEA... OKITA SENSEI NEARLY DISCOVERED ME ALMOST IMMEDIATELY...
I DIDN'T EVEN GET TO SEE THE OTHER GIRL'S FACE, AND I WENT RUNNING.
I DON'T UNDER-STAND.
YOU HAVE A WOMAN AS WELL. THAT DIDN'T CHANGE YOUR RELATIONSHIP WITH OKITA-SAN AS FELLOW *BUSHI*.
I DON'T SEE HOW IT WILL BE ANY DIFFERENT WHEN OKITA-SAN WEDS.

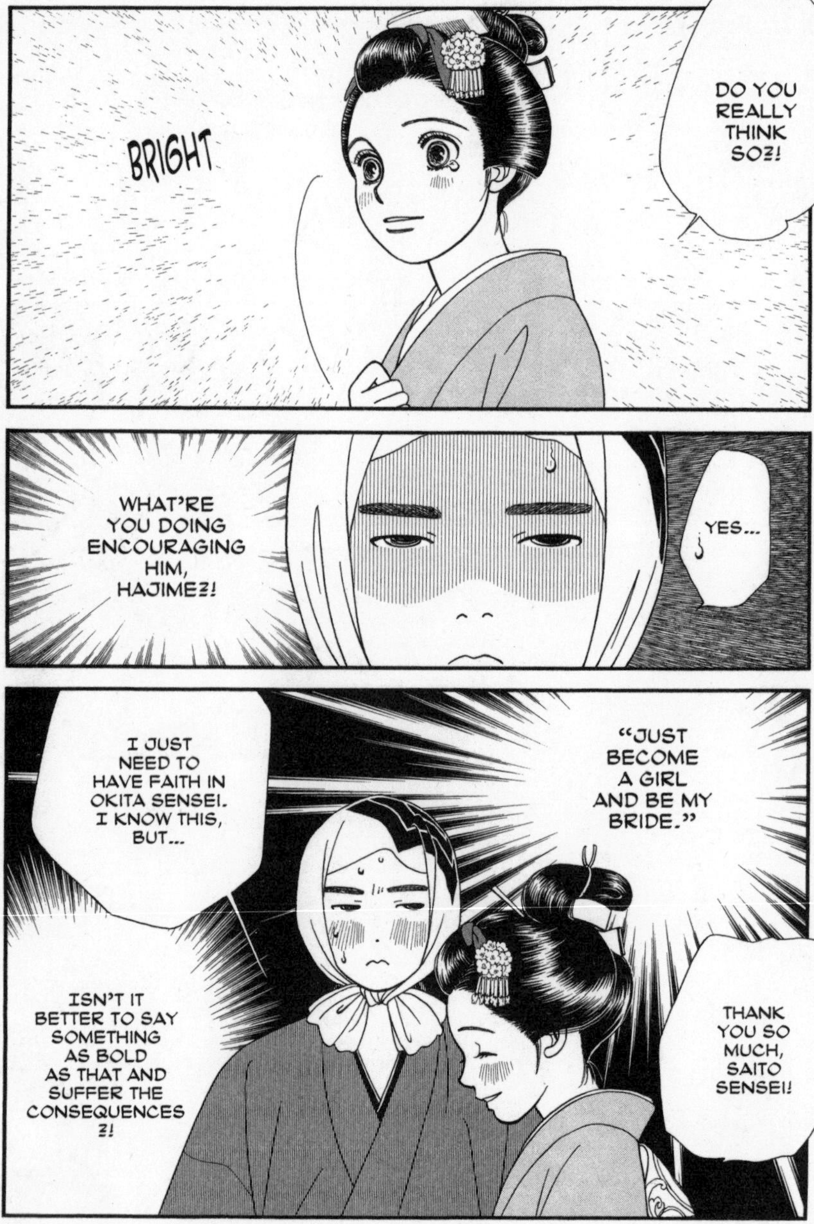
DO YOU REALLY THINK SO?!
BRIGHT
YES...
WHAT'RE YOU DOING ENCOURAGING HIM, HAJIME?!
"JUST BECOME A GIRL AND BE MY BRIDE."
I JUST NEED TO HAVE FAITH IN OKITA SENSEI. I KNOW THIS, BUT...
THANK YOU SO MUCH, SAITO SENSEI!
ISN'T IT BETTER TO SAY SOMETHING AS BOLD AS THAT AND SUFFER THE CONSEQUENCES?!

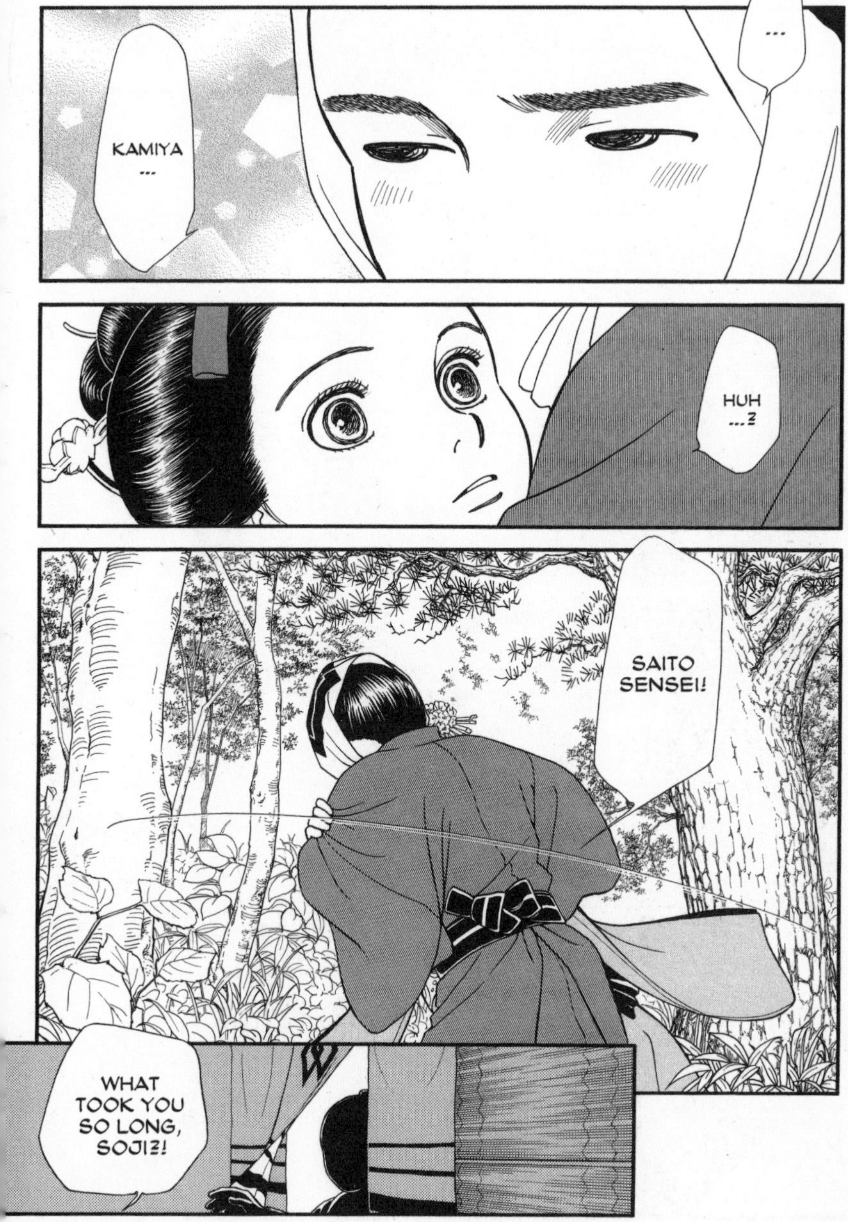
...
KAMIYA ...
HUH ...?
SAITO SENSEI!
WHAT TOOK YOU SO LONG, SOJI?!

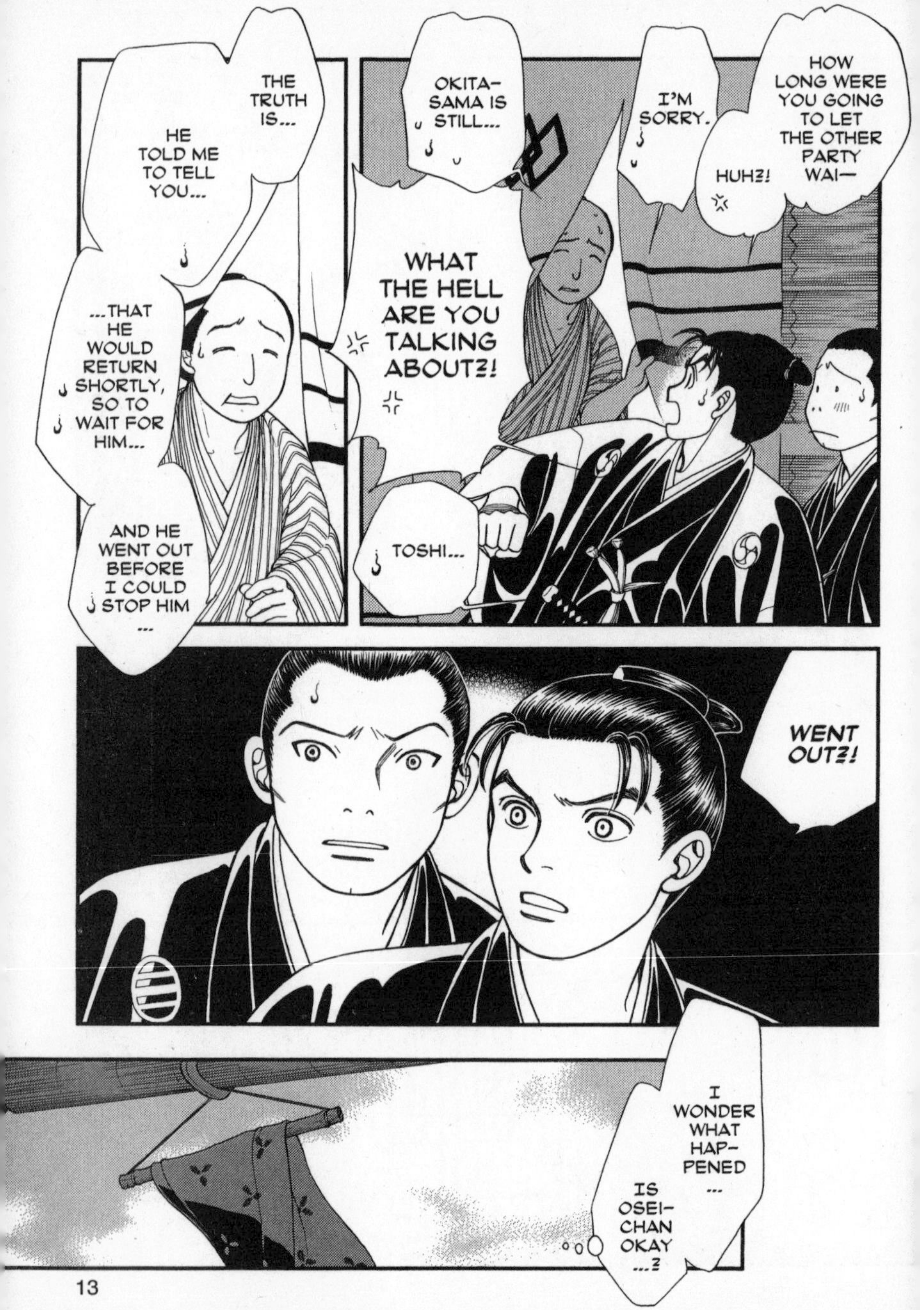
HOW LONG WERE YOU GOING TO LET THE OTHER PARTY WAI—
HUH?!
I'M SORRY.
OKITA-SAMA IS STILL...
WHAT THE HELL ARE YOU TALKING ABOUT?!
TOSHI...
THE TRUTH IS...
HE TOLD ME TO TELL YOU...
...THAT HE WOULD RETURN SHORTLY, SO TO WAIT FOR HIM...
AND HE WENT OUT BEFORE I COULD STOP HIM...
WENT OUT?!
I WONDER WHAT HAPPENED...
IS OSEI-CHAN OKAY...?

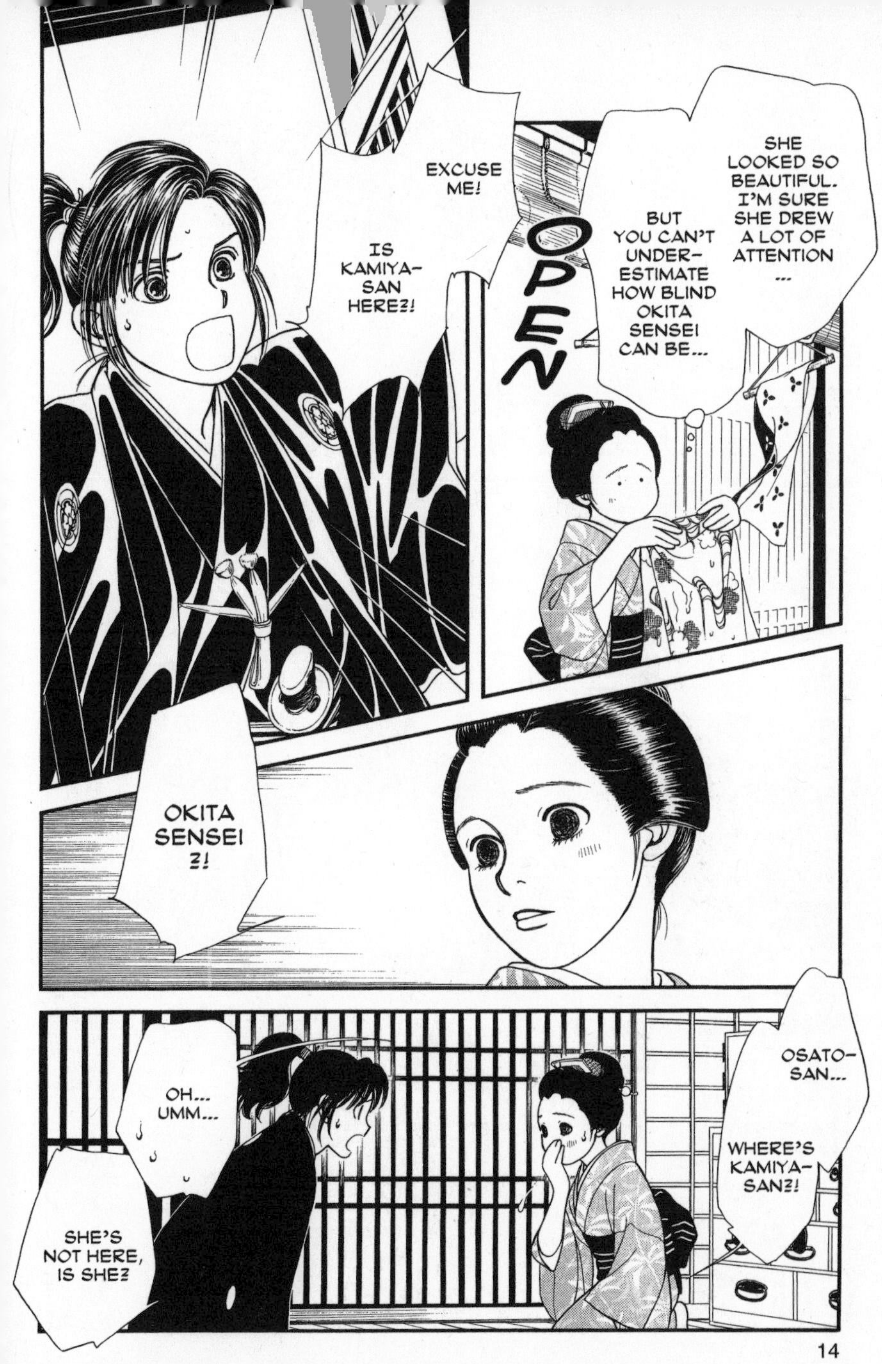
SHE LOOKED SO BEAUTIFUL. I'M SURE SHE DREW A LOT OF ATTENTION...
BUT YOU CAN'T UNDER-ESTIMATE HOW BLIND OKITA SENSEI CAN BE...
OPEN
EXCUSE ME!
IS KAMIYA-SAN HERE?!
OKITA SENSEI?!
OSATO-SAN...
WHERE'S KAMIYA-SAN?!
OH... UMM...
SHE'S NOT HERE, IS SHE?

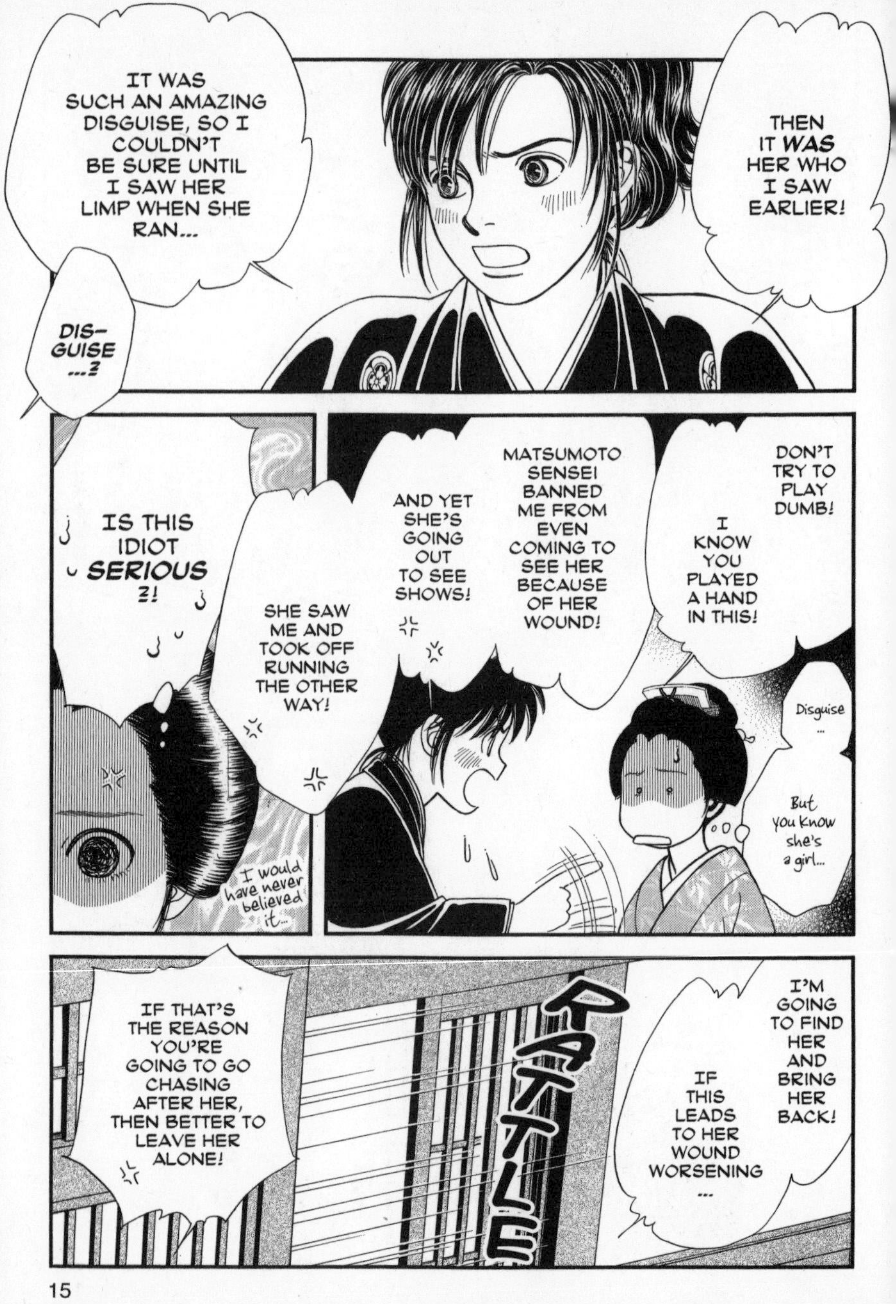
THEN IT WAS HER WHO I SAW EARLIER!
IT WAS SUCH AN AMAZING DISGUISE, SO I COULDN'T BE SURE UNTIL I SAW HER LIMP WHEN SHE RAN...
DIS-GUISE ...?
DON'T TRY TO PLAY DUMB!
I KNOW YOU PLAYED A HAND IN THIS!
MATSUMOTO SENSEI BANNED ME FROM EVEN COMING TO SEE HER BECAUSE OF HER WOUND!
AND YET SHE'S GOING OUT TO SEE SHOWS!
SHE SAW ME AND TOOK OFF RUNNING THE OTHER WAY!
Disguise...
But you know she's a girl...
IS THIS IDIOT SERIOUS?!
I would have never believed it...
I'M GOING TO FIND HER AND BRING HER BACK!
IF THIS LEADS TO HER WOUND WORSENING...
RATTLE
IF THAT'S THE REASON YOU'RE GOING TO GO CHASING AFTER HER, THEN BETTER TO LEAVE HER ALONE!

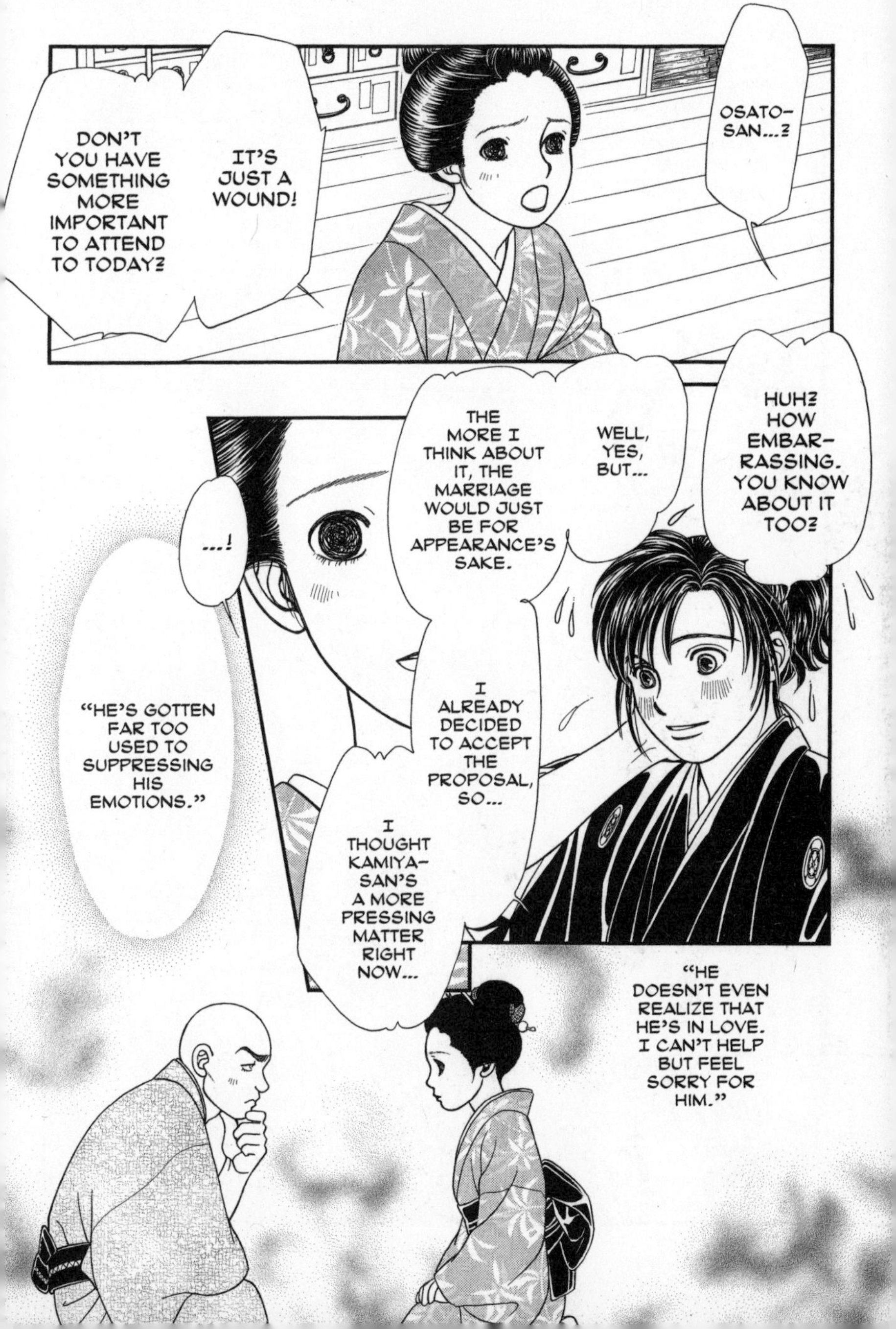
OSATO-SAN...?
IT'S JUST A WOUND!
DON'T YOU HAVE SOMETHING MORE IMPORTANT TO ATTEND TO TODAY?
HUH? HOW EMBARRASSING. YOU KNOW ABOUT IT TOO?
WELL, YES, BUT...
THE MORE I THINK ABOUT IT, THE MARRIAGE WOULD JUST BE FOR APPEARANCE'S SAKE.
I ALREADY DECIDED TO ACCEPT THE PROPOSAL, SO...
I THOUGHT KAMIYA-SAN'S A MORE PRESSING MATTER RIGHT NOW...
...!
"HE'S GOTTEN FAR TOO USED TO SUPPRESSING HIS EMOTIONS."
"HE DOESN'T EVEN REALIZE THAT HE'S IN LOVE. I CAN'T HELP BUT FEEL SORRY FOR HIM."

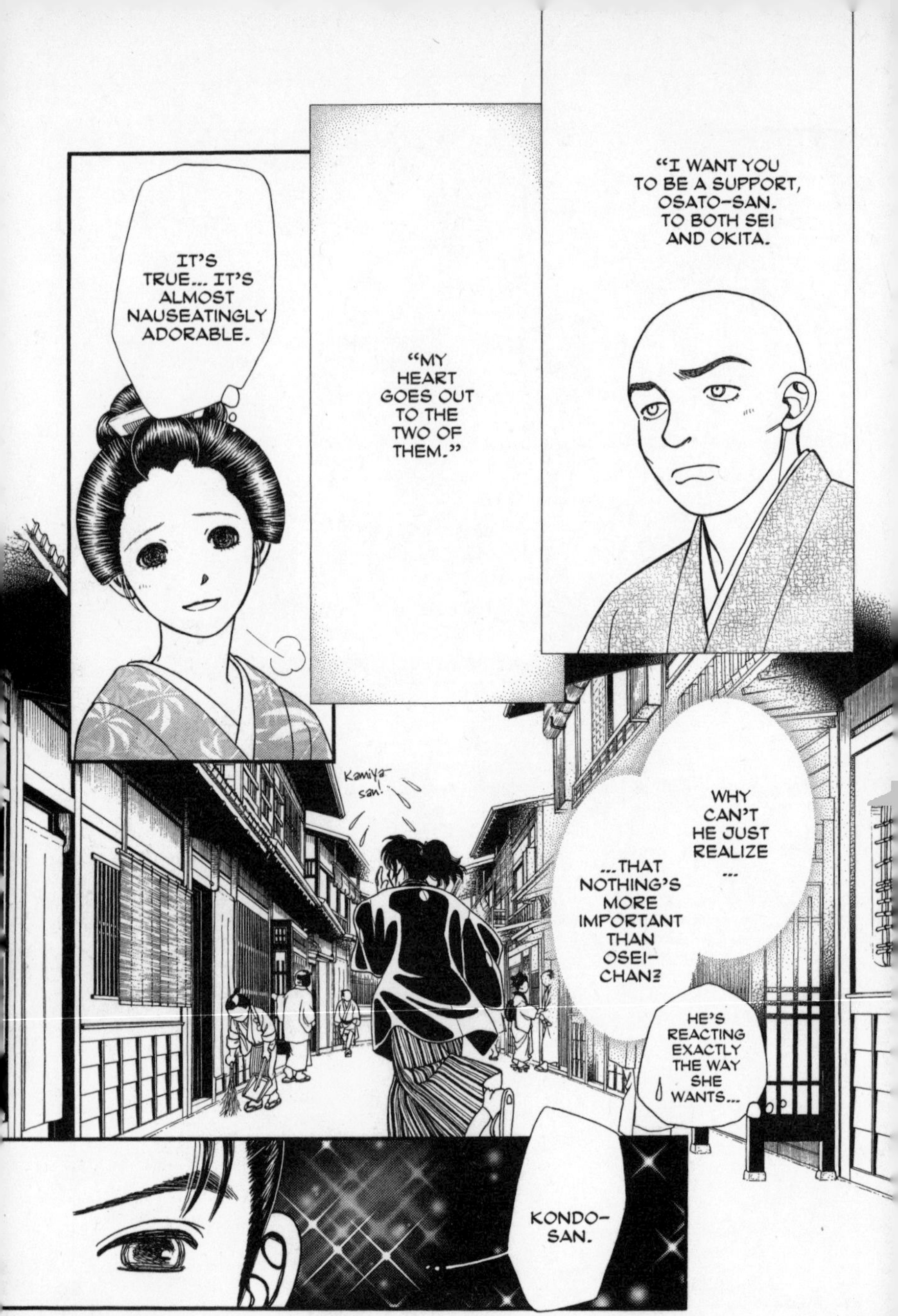
"I WANT YOU TO BE A SUPPORT, OSATO-SAN. TO BOTH SEI AND OKITA.
"MY HEART GOES OUT TO THE TWO OF THEM."
IT'S TRUE... IT'S ALMOST NAUSEATINGLY ADORABLE.
WHY CAN'T HE JUST REALIZE ...
...THAT NOTHING'S MORE IMPORTANT THAN OSEI-CHAN?
Kamiya-san!
HE'S REACTING EXACTLY THE WAY SHE WANTS...
KONDO-SAN.

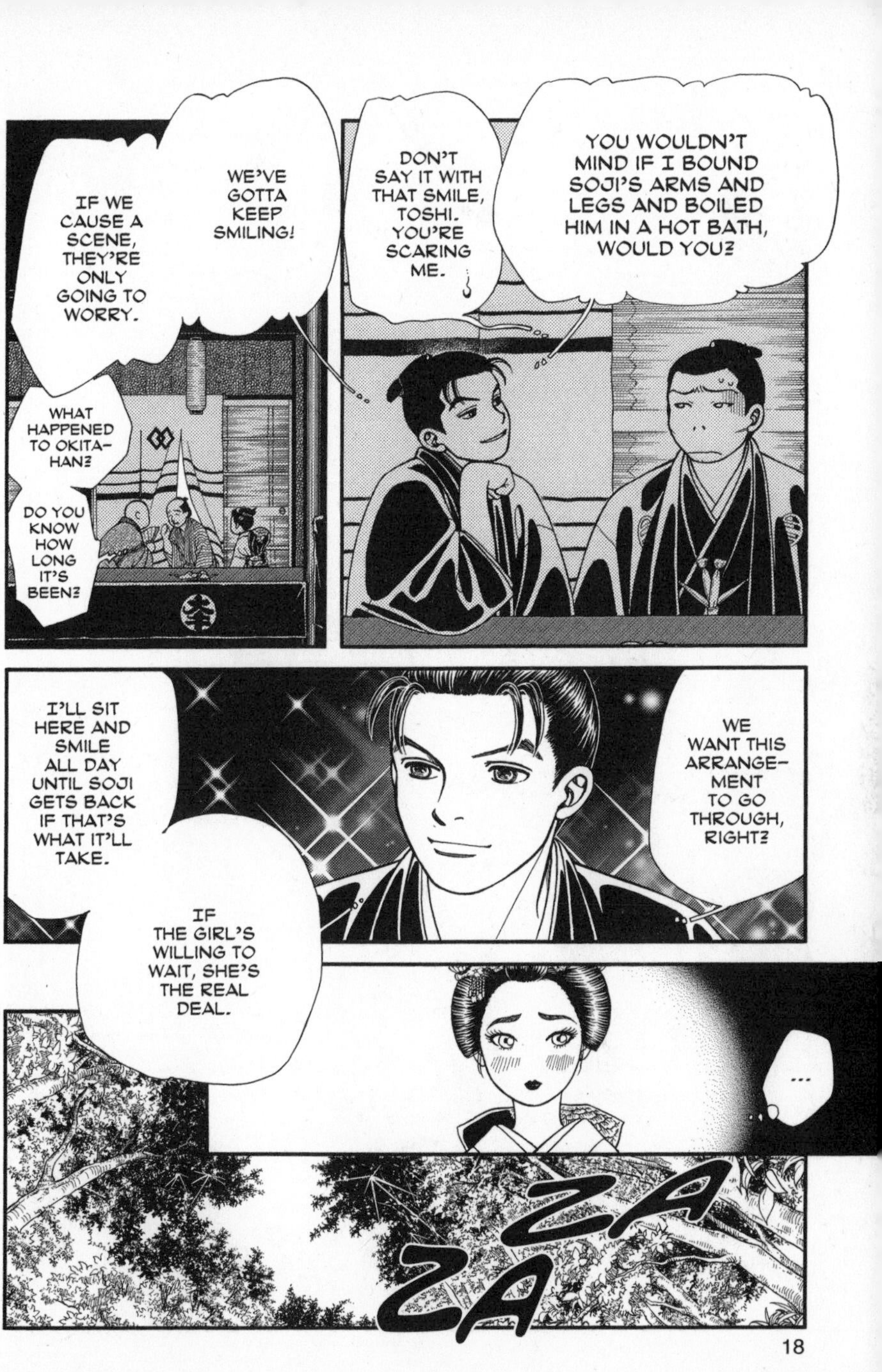
YOU WOULDN'T MIND IF I BOUND SOJI'S ARMS AND LEGS AND BOILED HIM IN A HOT BATH, WOULD YOU?
DON'T SAY IT WITH THAT SMILE, TOSHI. YOU'RE SCARING ME.
WE'VE GOTTA KEEP SMILING!
IF WE CAUSE A SCENE, THEY'RE ONLY GOING TO WORRY.
WHAT HAPPENED TO OKITA-HAN?
DO YOU KNOW HOW LONG IT'S BEEN?
WE WANT THIS ARRANGEMENT TO GO THROUGH, RIGHT?
I'LL SIT HERE AND SMILE ALL DAY UNTIL SOJI GETS BACK IF THAT'S WHAT IT'LL TAKE.
IF THE GIRL'S WILLING TO WAIT, SHE'S THE REAL DEAL.
...
ZA
ZA

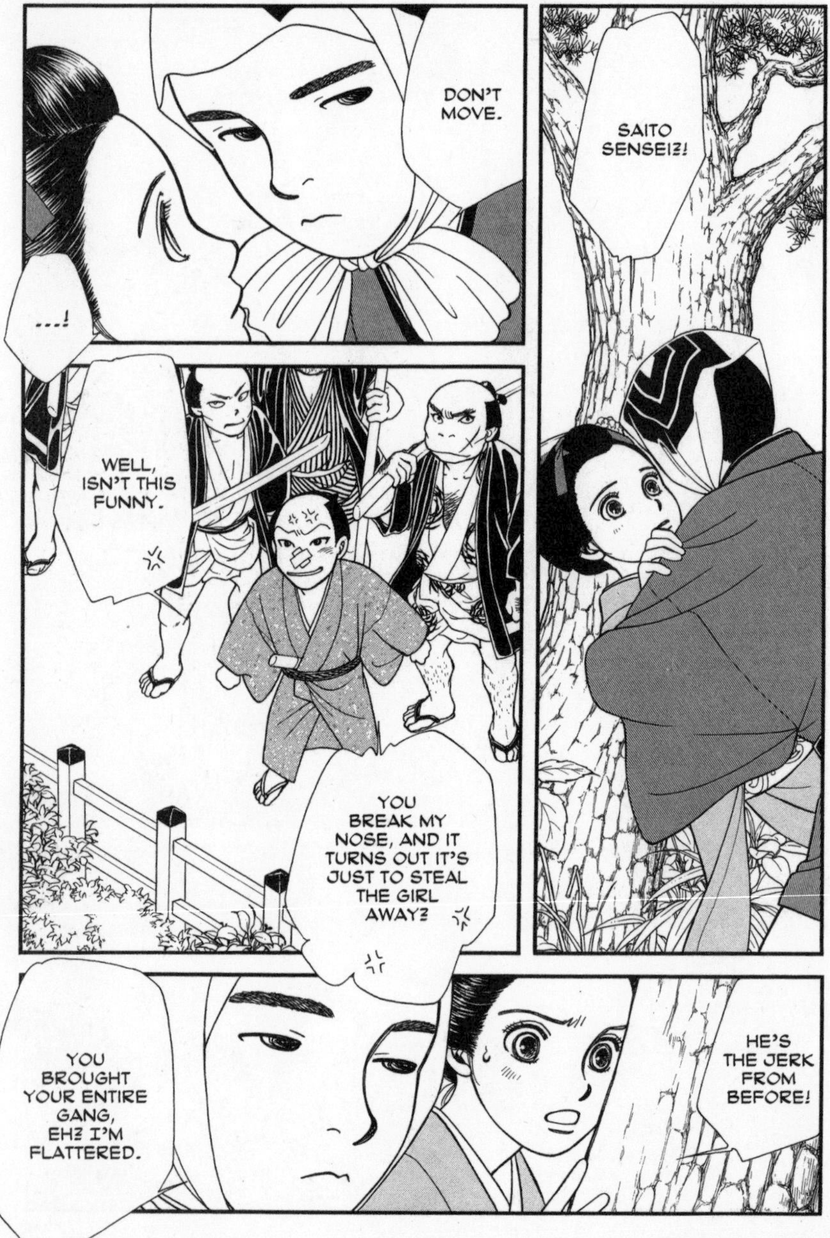
SAITO SENSEI?!
DON'T MOVE.
...!
WELL, ISN'T THIS FUNNY.
YOU BREAK MY NOSE, AND IT TURNS OUT IT'S JUST TO STEAL THE GIRL AWAY?
HE'S THE JERK FROM BEFORE!
YOU BROUGHT YOUR ENTIRE GANG, EH? I'M FLATTERED.

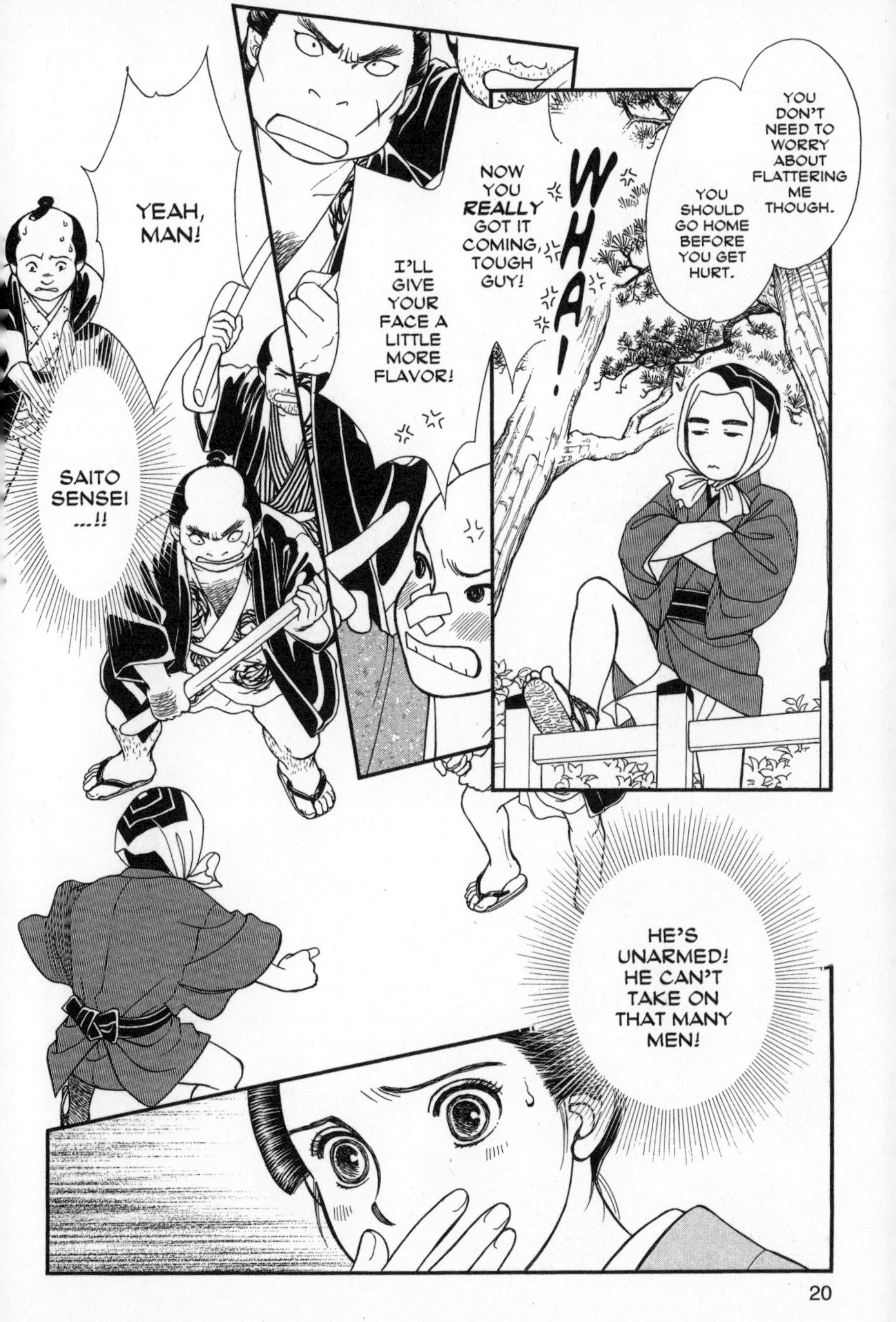
YOU DON'T NEED TO WORRY ABOUT FLATTERING ME THOUGH.
YOU SHOULD GO HOME BEFORE YOU GET HURT.
WHA!
NOW YOU REALLY GOT IT COMING, TOUGH GUY!
I'LL GIVE YOUR FACE A LITTLE MORE FLAVOR!
YEAH, MAN!
SAITO SENSEI ...!!
HE'S UNARMED! HE CAN'T TAKE ON THAT MANY MEN!

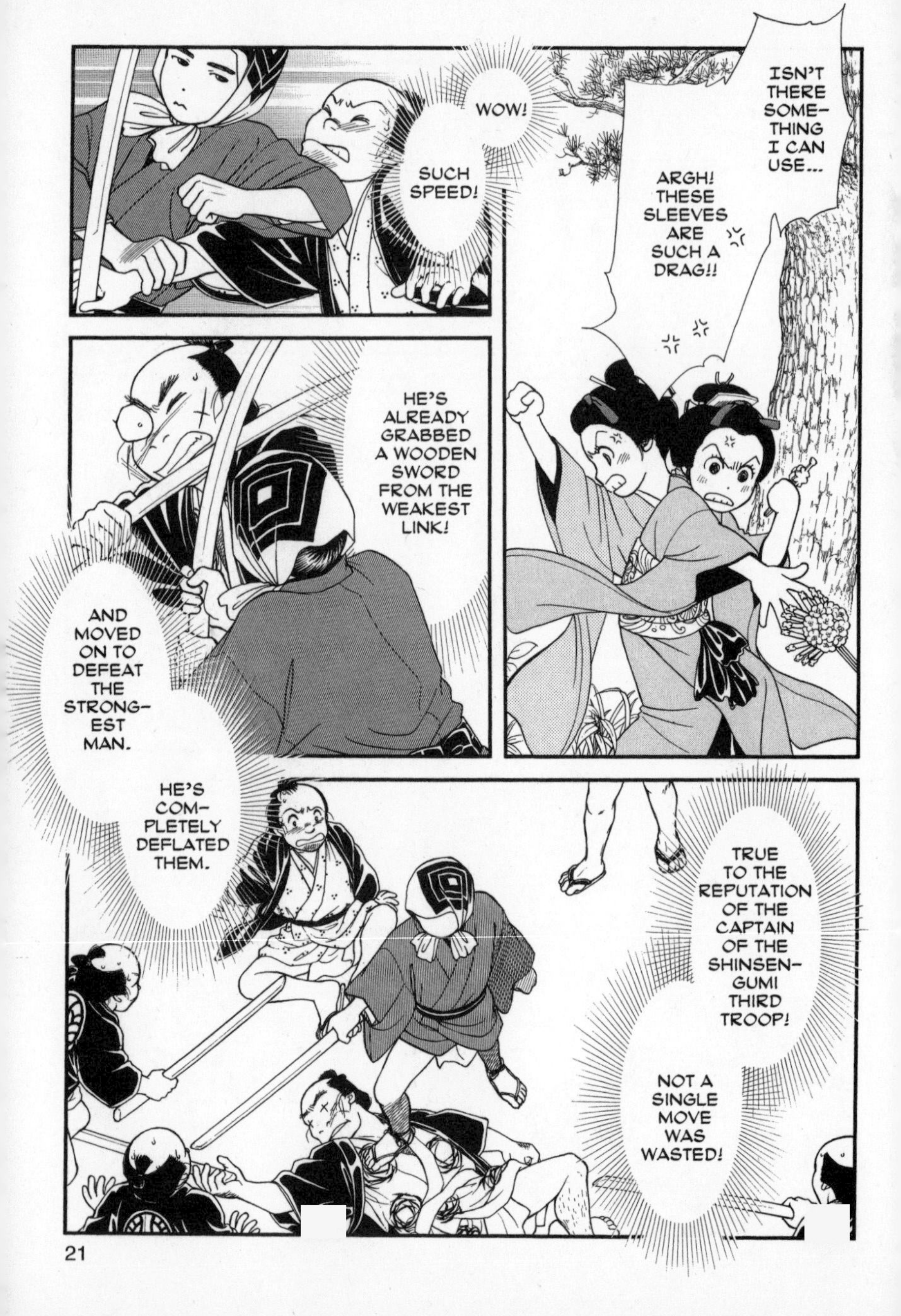
ISN'T THERE SOMETHING I CAN USE...
ARGH! THESE SLEEVES ARE SUCH A DRAG!!
WOW!
SUCH SPEED!
HE'S ALREADY GRABBED A WOODEN SWORD FROM THE WEAKEST LINK!
AND MOVED ON TO DEFEAT THE STRONGEST MAN.
TRUE TO THE REPUTATION OF THE CAPTAIN OF THE SHINSENGUMI THIRD TROOP!
HE'S COMPLETELY DEFLATED THEM.
NOT A SINGLE MOVE WAS WASTED!

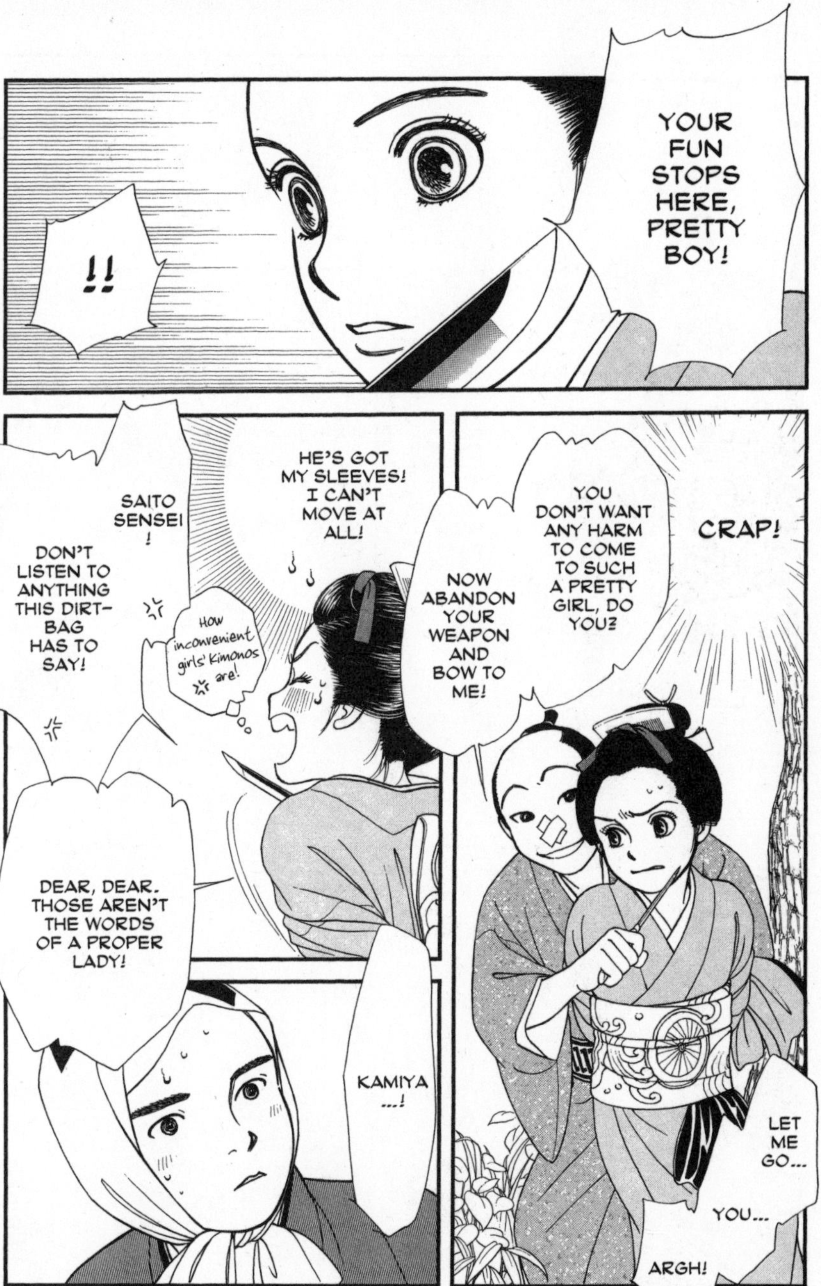
YOUR FUN STOPS HERE, PRETTY BOY!
!!
CRAP!
YOU DON'T WANT ANY HARM TO COME TO SUCH A PRETTY GIRL, DO YOU?
NOW ABANDON YOUR WEAPON AND BOW TO ME!
LET ME GO...
YOU...
ARGH!
HE'S GOT MY SLEEVES! I CAN'T MOVE AT ALL!
SAITO SENSEI!
How inconvenient girls' kimonos are!
DON'T LISTEN TO ANYTHING THIS DIRT-BAG HAS TO SAY!
DEAR, DEAR. THOSE AREN'T THE WORDS OF A PROPER LADY!
KAMIYA...!

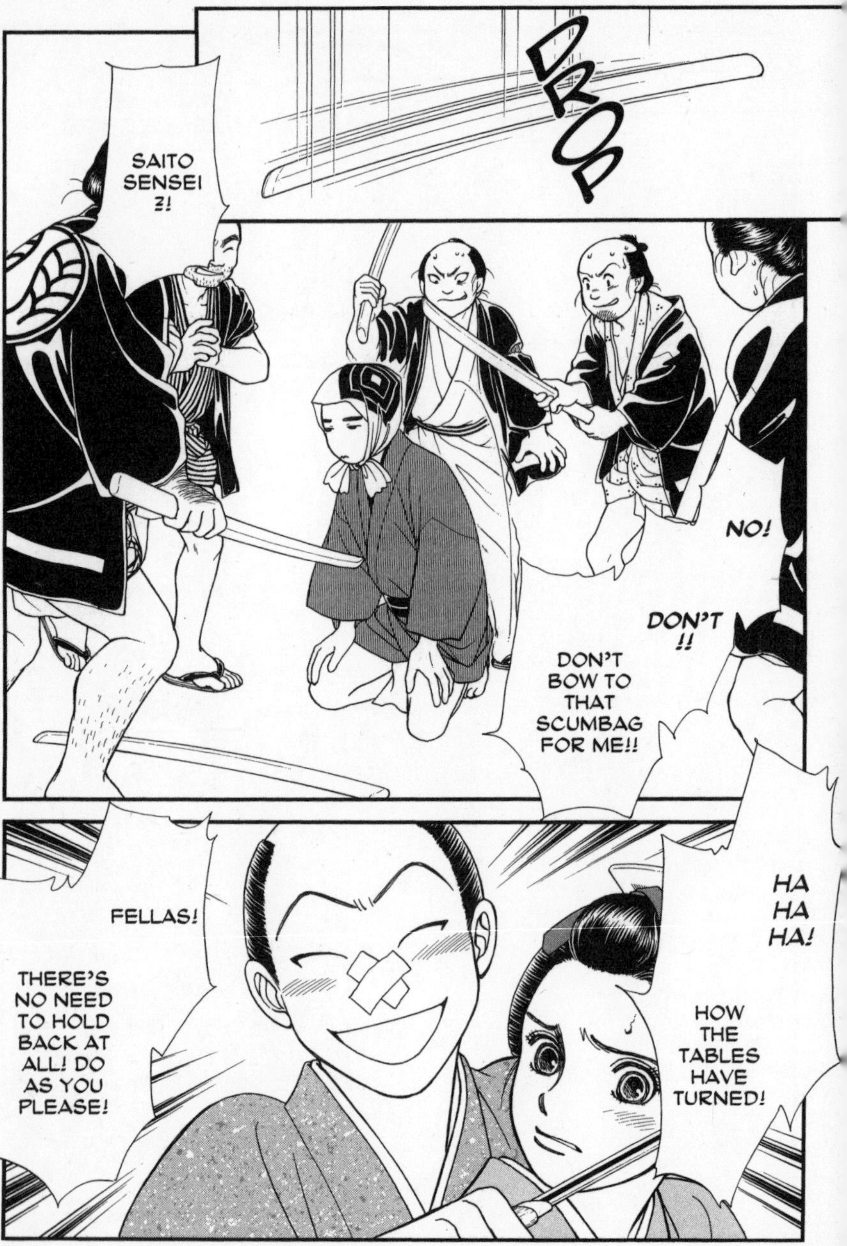
DROP
SAITO SENSEI?!
NO!
DON'T!!
DON'T BOW TO THAT SCUMBAG FOR ME!!
HA HA HA!
HOW THE TABLES HAVE TURNED!
FELLAS!
THERE'S NO NEED TO HOLD BACK AT ALL! DO AS YOU PLEASE!

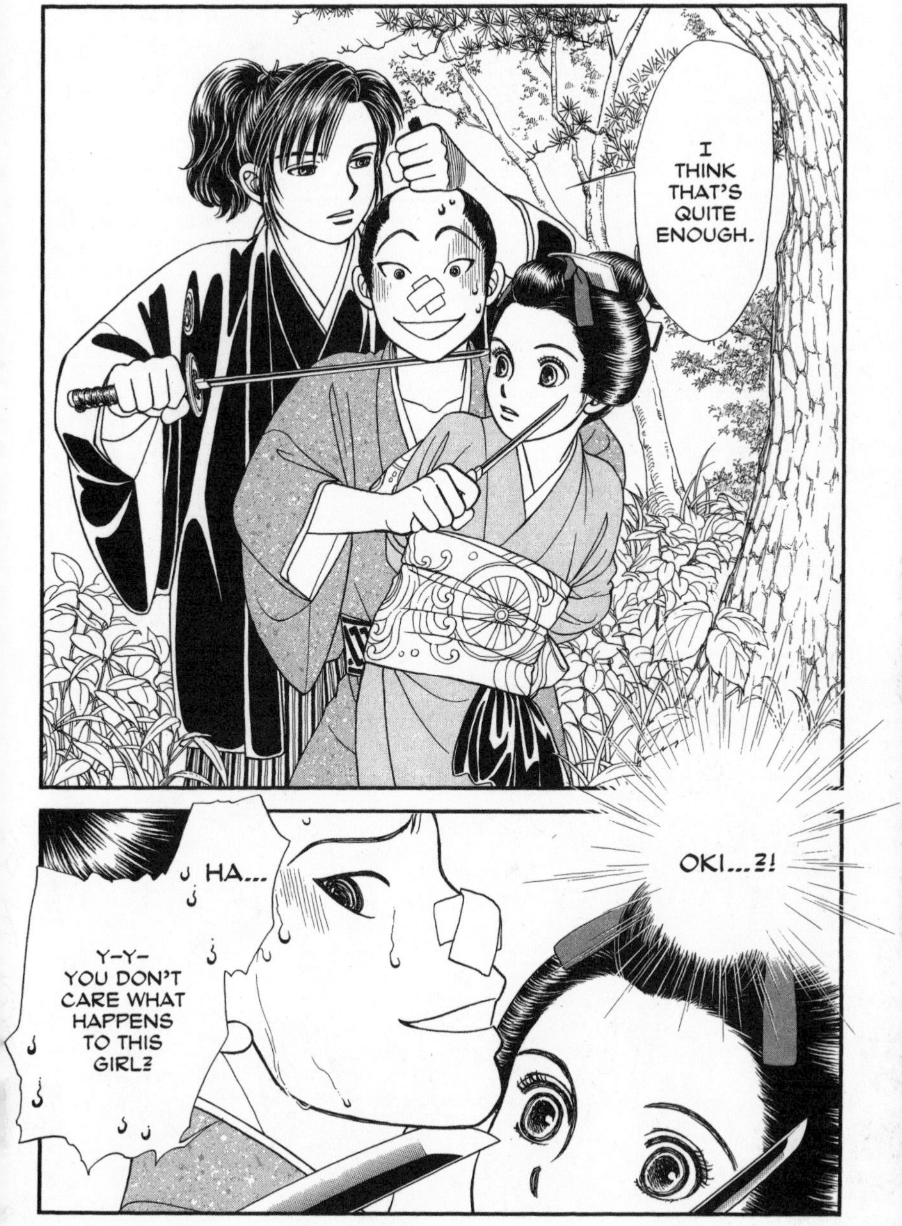
I THINK THAT'S QUITE ENOUGH.
OKI...?!
HA...
Y-Y- YOU DON'T CARE WHAT HAPPENS TO THIS GIRL?

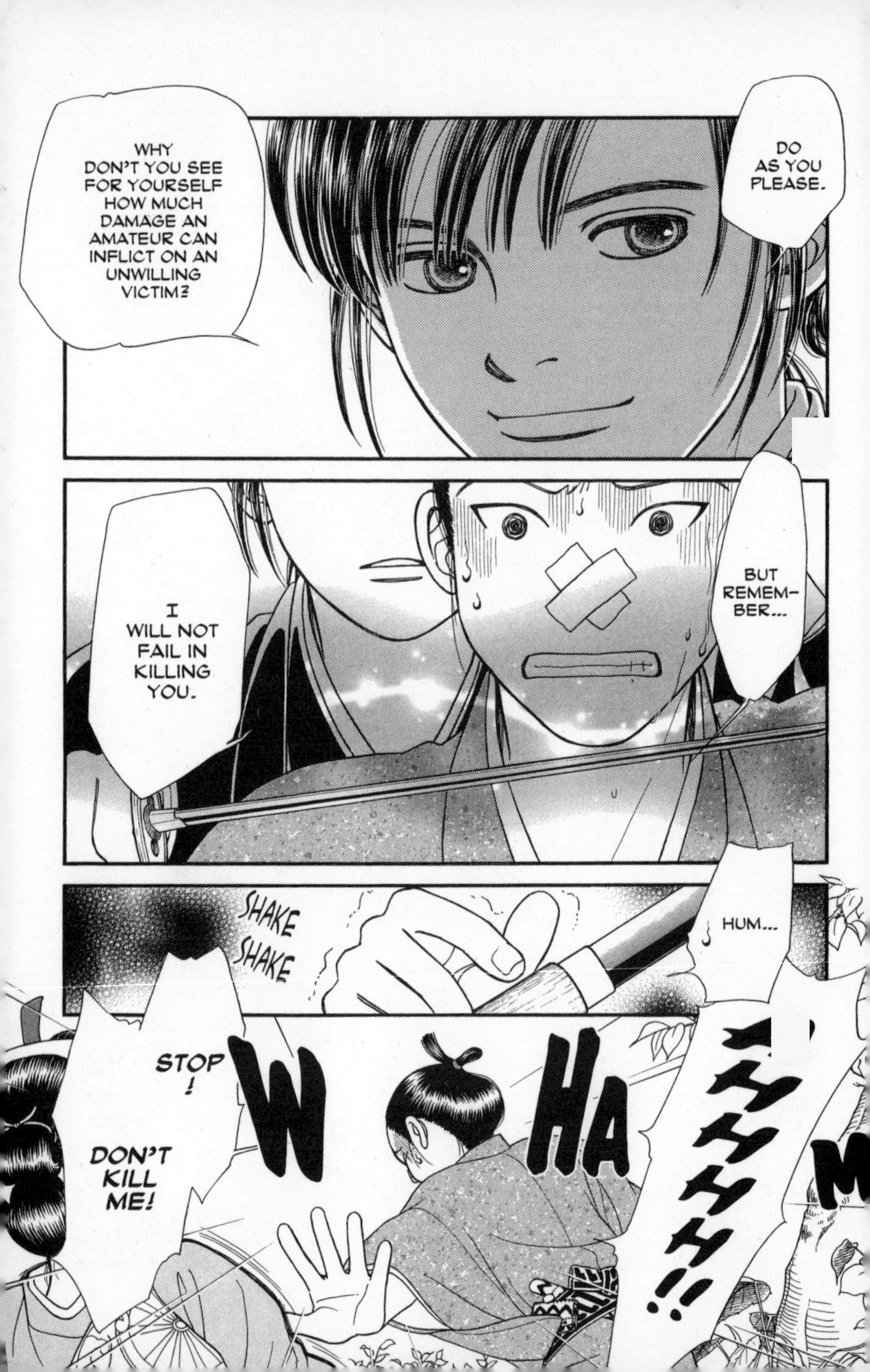
DO AS YOU PLEASE.
WHY DON'T YOU SEE FOR YOURSELF HOW MUCH DAMAGE AN AMATEUR CAN INFLICT ON AN UNWILLING VICTIM?
BUT REMEMBER...
I WILL NOT FAIL IN KILLING YOU.
HUM...
SHAKE SHAKE
W HA M
STOP!
DON'T KILL ME!

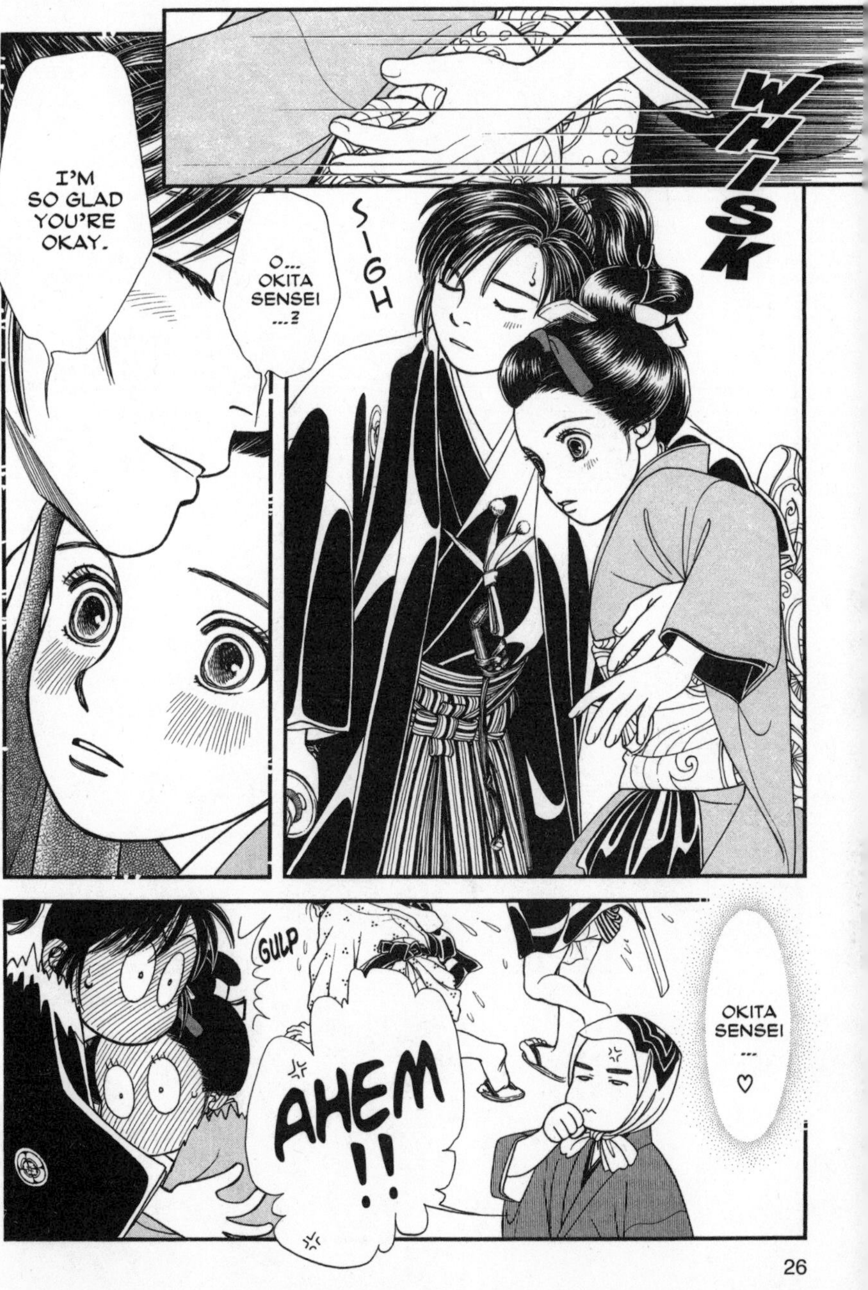
WHISK
O... OKITA SENSEI ...?
SIGH
I'M SO GLAD YOU'RE OKAY.
OKITA SENSEI ... ♡
AHEM !!
GULP

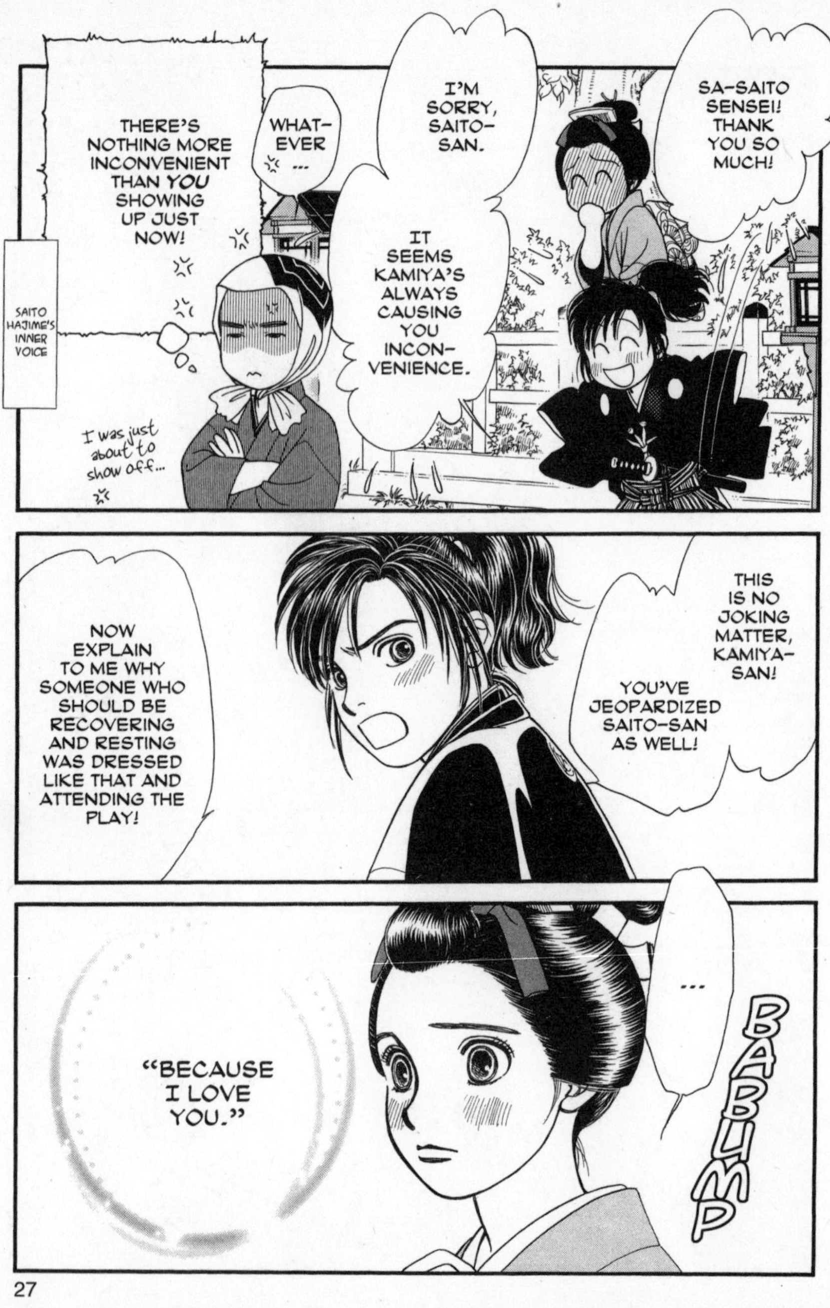
SA-SAITO SENSEI! THANK YOU SO MUCH!
I'M SORRY, SAITO-SAN.
IT SEEMS KAMIYA'S ALWAYS CAUSING YOU INCON-VENIENCE.
WHAT-EVER ...
THERE'S NOTHING MORE INCONVENIENT THAN *YOU* SHOWING UP JUST NOW!
SAITO HAJIME'S INNER VOICE
I was just about to show off...
THIS IS NO JOKING MATTER, KAMIYA-SAN!
YOU'VE JEOPARDIZED SAITO-SAN AS WELL!
NOW EXPLAIN TO ME WHY SOMEONE WHO SHOULD BE RECOVERING AND RESTING WAS DRESSED LIKE THAT AND ATTENDING THE PLAY!
...
BABUMP
"BECAUSE I LOVE YOU."

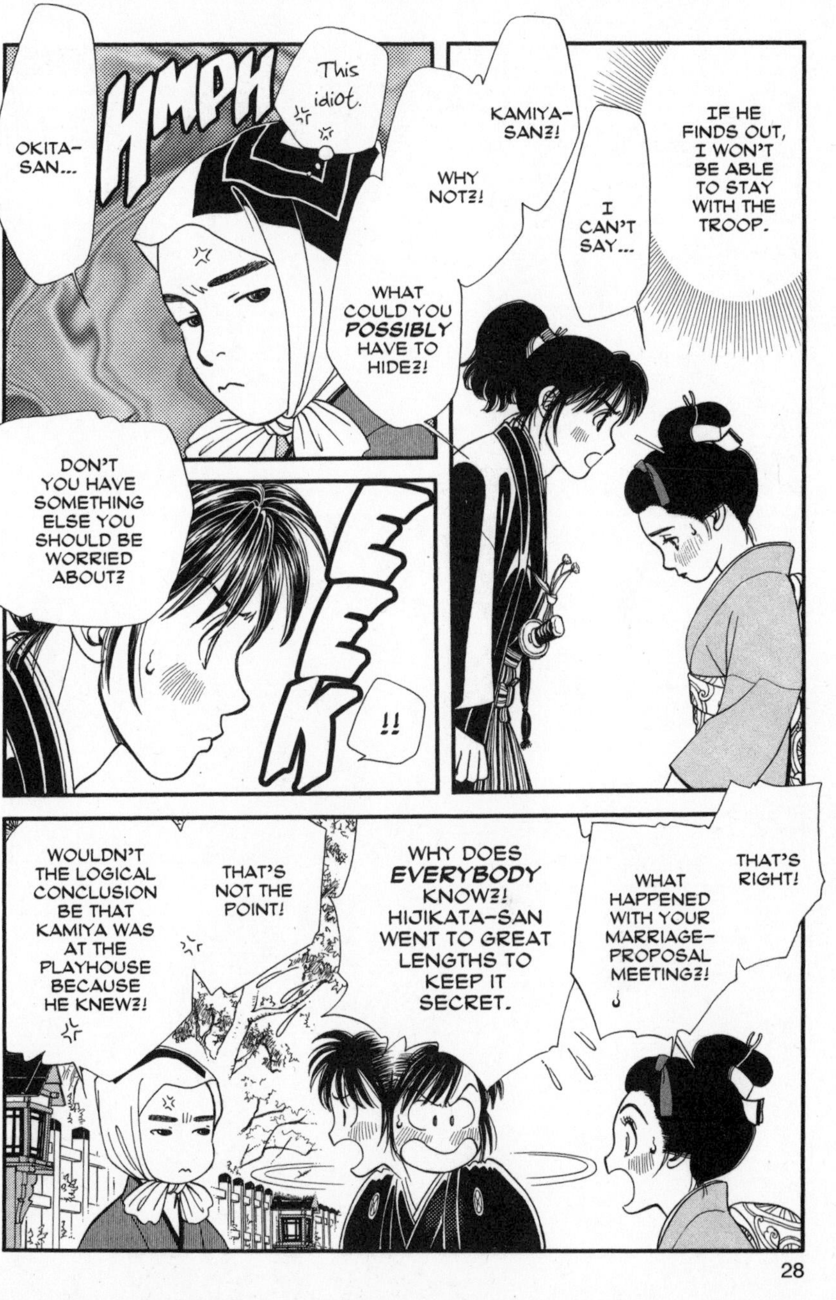
IF HE FINDS OUT, I WON'T BE ABLE TO STAY WITH THE TROOP.
I CAN'T SAY...
KAMIYA-SAN?!
WHY NOT?!
WHAT COULD YOU *POSSIBLY* HAVE TO HIDE?!
This idiot.
HMPH
OKITA-SAN...
DON'T YOU HAVE SOMETHING ELSE YOU SHOULD BE WORRIED ABOUT?
EEEK
!!
THAT'S RIGHT!
WHAT HAPPENED WITH YOUR MARRIAGE-PROPOSAL MEETING?!
WHY DOES *EVERYBODY* KNOW?! HIJIKATA-SAN WENT TO GREAT LENGTHS TO KEEP IT SECRET.
THAT'S NOT THE POINT!
WOULDN'T THE LOGICAL CONCLUSION BE THAT KAMIYA WAS AT THE PLAYHOUSE BECAUSE HE KNEW?!

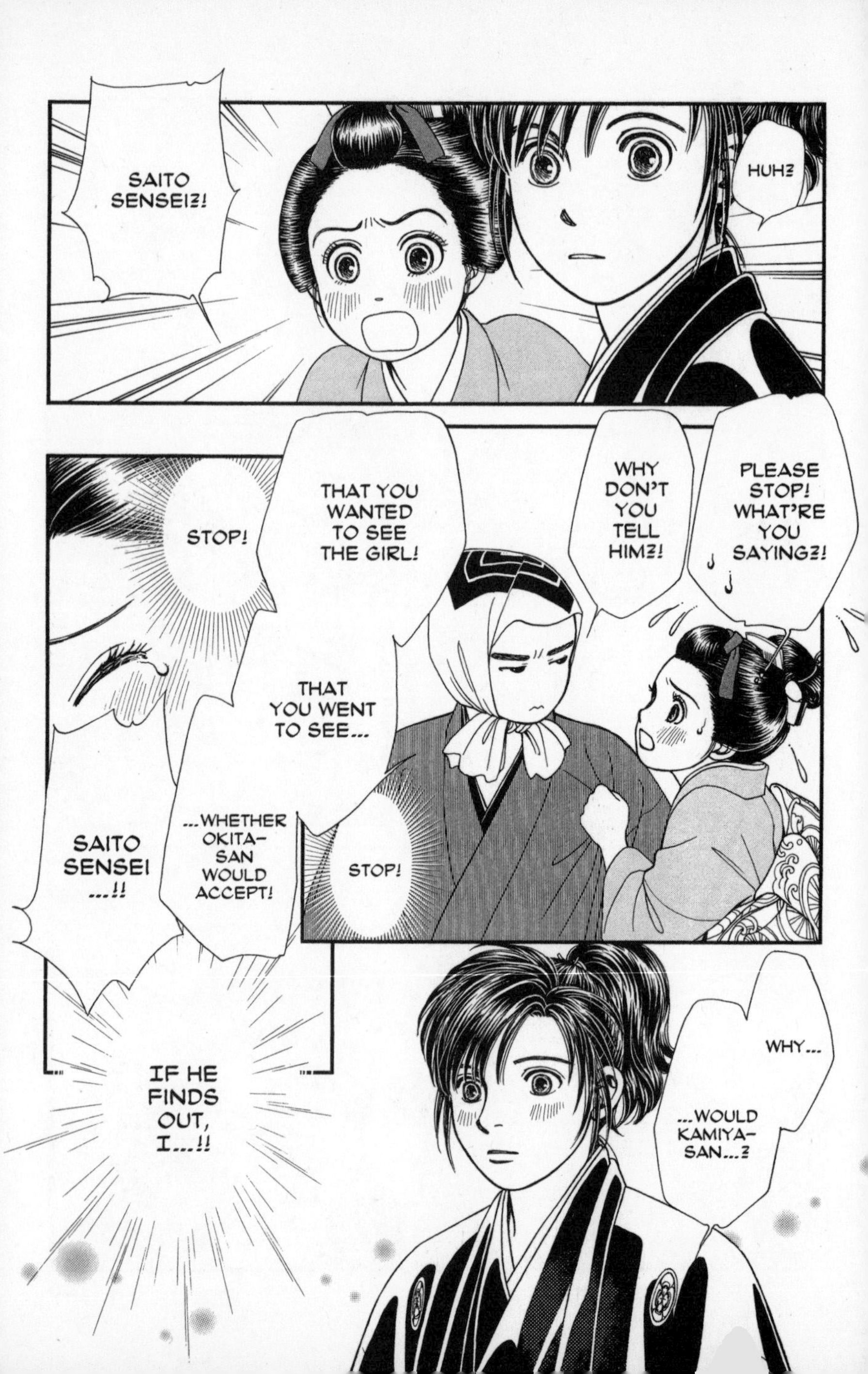
HUH?
SAITO SENSEI?!
PLEASE STOP! WHAT'RE YOU SAYING?!
WHY DON'T YOU TELL HIM?!
THAT YOU WANTED TO SEE THE GIRL!
STOP!
THAT YOU WENT TO SEE...
STOP!
...WHETHER OKITA-SAN WOULD ACCEPT!
WHY...
...WOULD KAMIYA-SAN...?
SAITO SENSEI...!!
IF HE FINDS OUT, I...!!

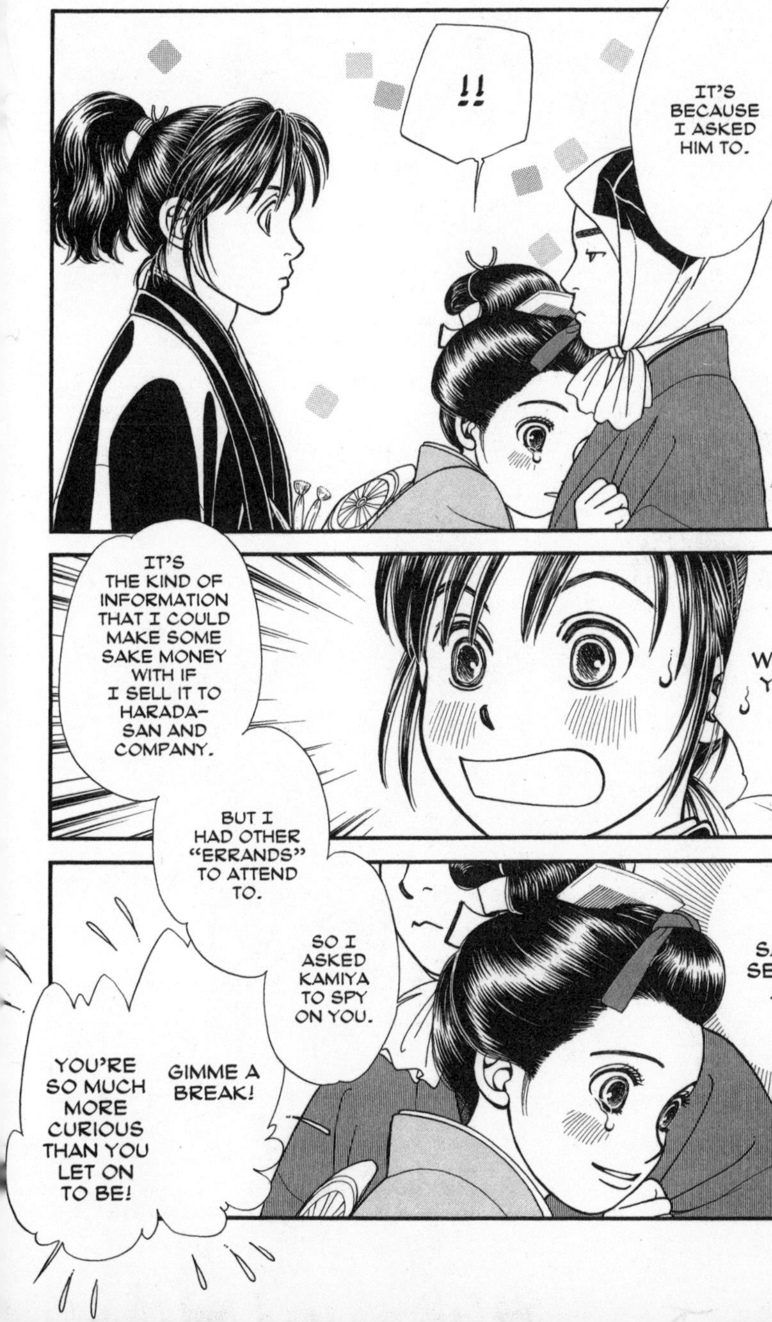
IT'S BECAUSE I ASKED HIM TO.
!!
WHAT?! YOU?!
IT'S THE KIND OF INFORMATION THAT I COULD MAKE SOME SAKE MONEY WITH IF I SELL IT TO HARADA-SAN AND COMPANY.
BUT I HAD OTHER "ERRANDS" TO ATTEND TO.
SO I ASKED KAMIYA TO SPY ON YOU.
SAITO SENSEI ...!!
GIMME A BREAK!
YOU'RE SO MUCH MORE CURIOUS THAN YOU LET ON TO BE!

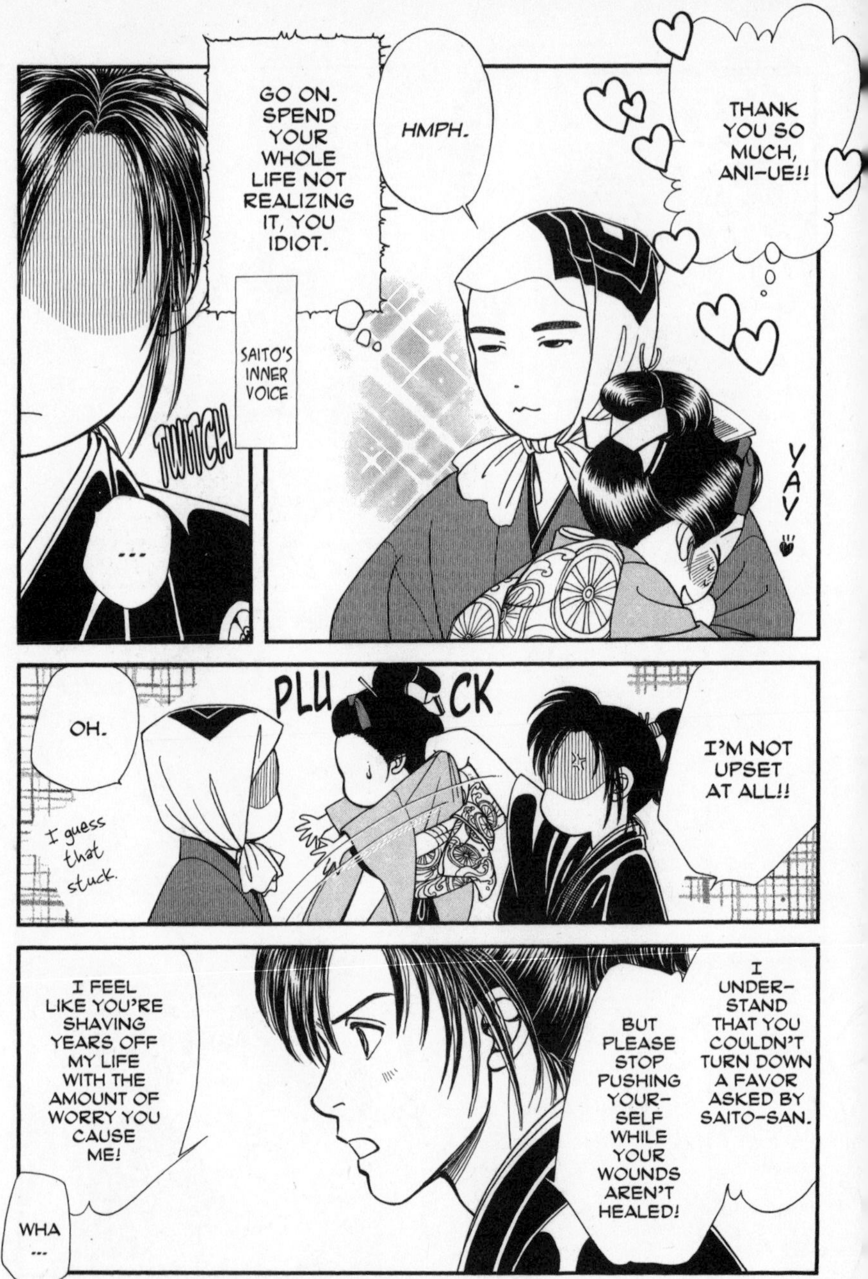
THANK YOU SO MUCH, ANI-UE!!
HMPH.
GO ON. SPEND YOUR WHOLE LIFE NOT REALIZING IT, YOU IDIOT.
SAITO'S INNER VOICE
YAY
TWITCH
...
I'M NOT UPSET AT ALL!!
PLUCK
OH.
I guess that stuck.
I UNDER-STAND THAT YOU COULDN'T TURN DOWN A FAVOR ASKED BY SAITO-SAN.
BUT PLEASE STOP PUSHING YOUR-SELF WHILE YOUR WOUNDS AREN'T HEALED!
I FEEL LIKE YOU'RE SHAVING YEARS OFF MY LIFE WITH THE AMOUNT OF WORRY YOU CAUSE ME!
WHA...

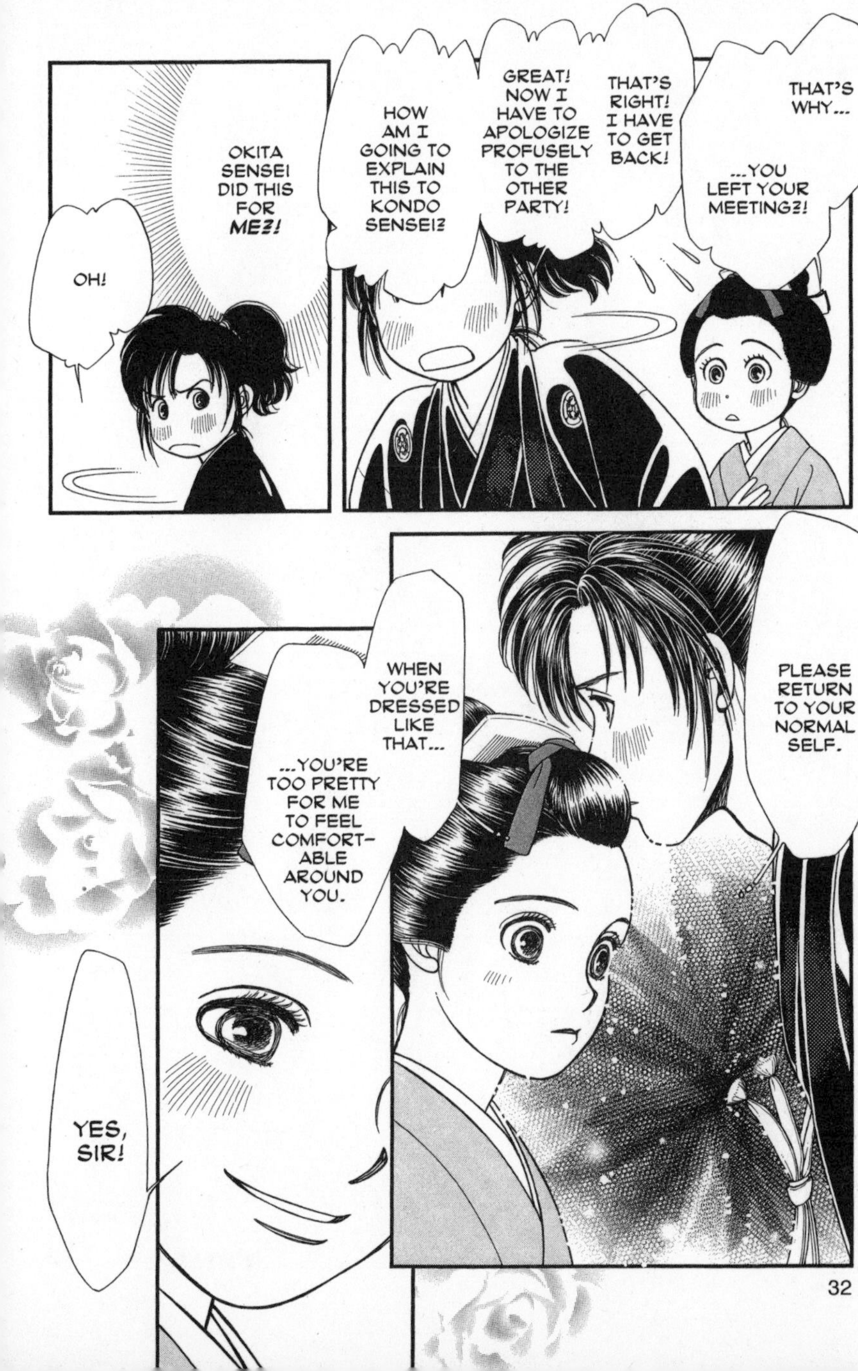
THAT'S WHY...
...YOU LEFT YOUR MEETING?!
THAT'S RIGHT! I HAVE TO GET BACK!
GREAT! NOW I HAVE TO APOLOGIZE PROFUSELY TO THE OTHER PARTY!
HOW AM I GOING TO EXPLAIN THIS TO KONDO SENSEI!?
OKITA SENSEI DID THIS FOR ME?!
OH!
PLEASE RETURN TO YOUR NORMAL SELF.
WHEN YOU'RE DRESSED LIKE THAT...
...YOU'RE TOO PRETTY FOR ME TO FEEL COMFORTABLE AROUND YOU.
YES, SIR!

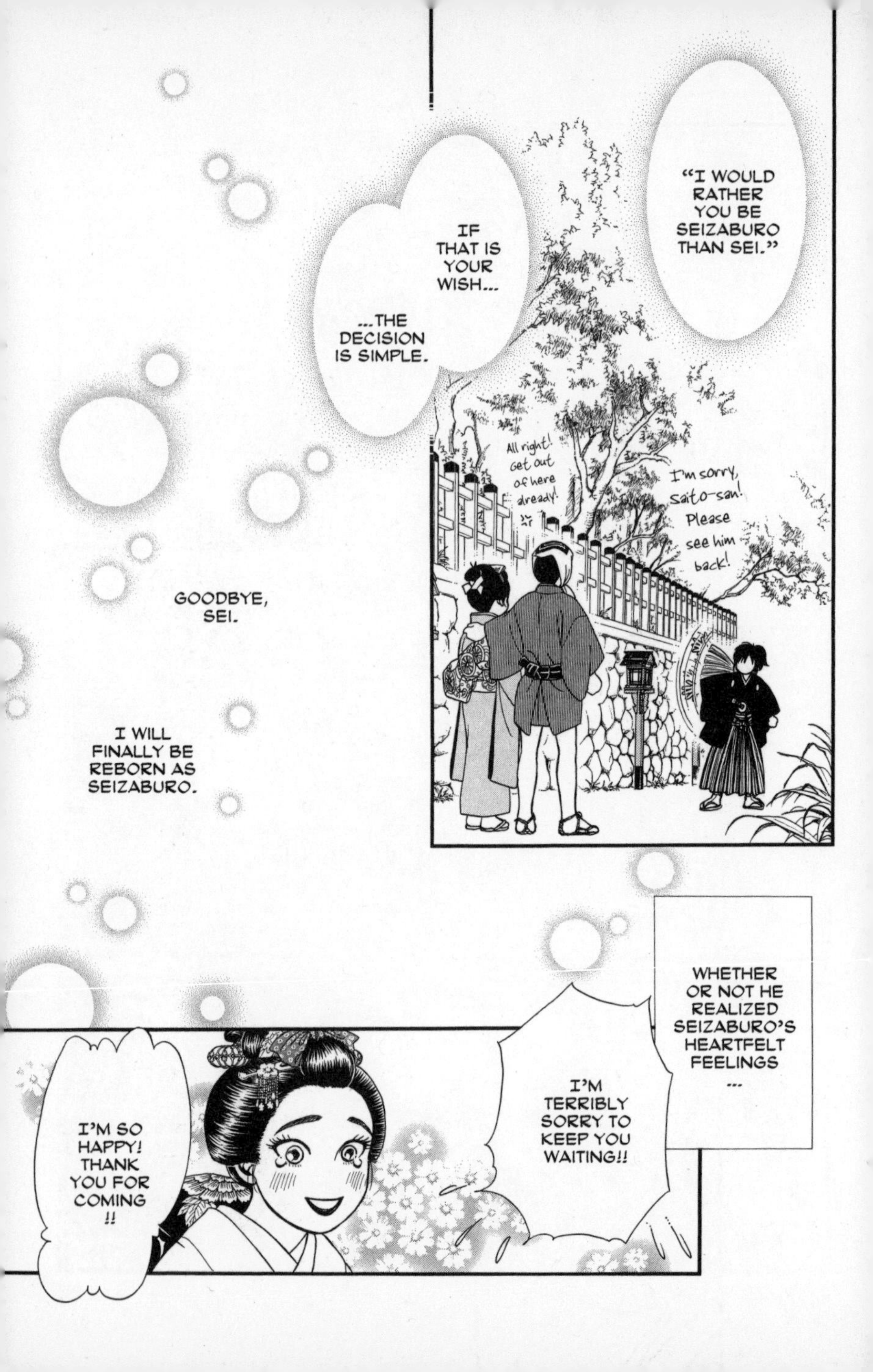
"I WOULD RATHER YOU BE SEIZABURO THAN SEI."
IF THAT IS YOUR WISH...
...THE DECISION IS SIMPLE.
I'm sorry, Saito-san! Please see him back!
All right! Get out of here already!
GOODBYE, SEI.
I WILL FINALLY BE REBORN AS SEIZABURO.
WHETHER OR NOT HE REALIZED SEIZABURO'S HEARTFELT FEELINGS ...
I'M TERRIBLY SORRY TO KEEP YOU WAITING!!
I'M SO HAPPY! THANK YOU FOR COMING!!

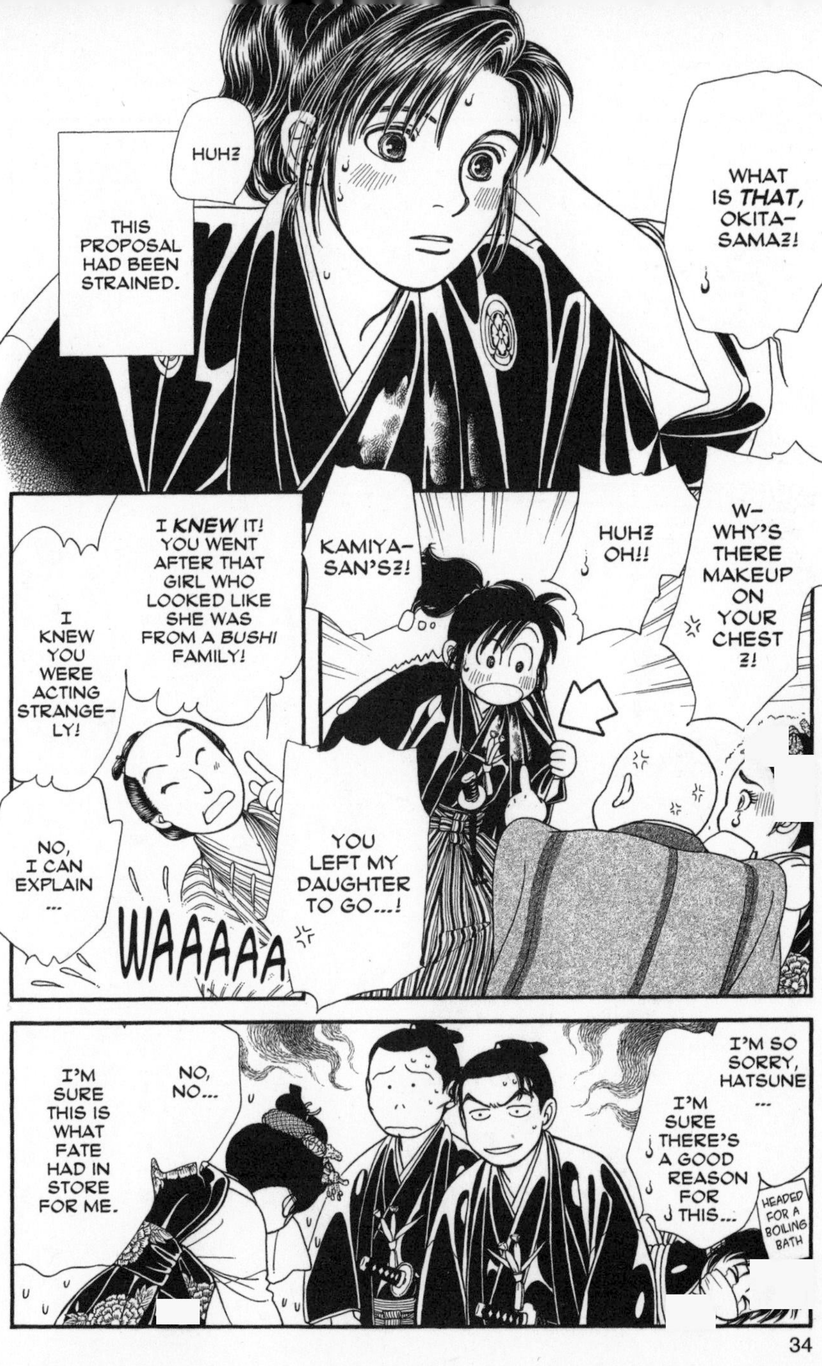
WHAT IS *THAT*, OKITA-SAMA?!
HUH?
THIS PROPOSAL HAD BEEN STRAINED.
W— WHY'S THERE MAKEUP ON YOUR CHEST?!
HUH? OH!!
KAMIYA-SAN'S?!
YOU LEFT MY DAUGHTER TO GO...!
I *KNEW* IT! YOU WENT AFTER THAT GIRL WHO LOOKED LIKE SHE WAS FROM A *BUSHI* FAMILY!
I KNEW YOU WERE ACTING STRANGE-LY!
NO, I CAN EXPLAIN ...
WAAAAA
HEADED FOR A BOILING BATH
I'M SO SORRY, HATSUNE ...
I'M SURE THERE'S A GOOD REASON FOR THIS...
NO, NO...
I'M SURE THIS IS WHAT FATE HAD IN STORE FOR ME.

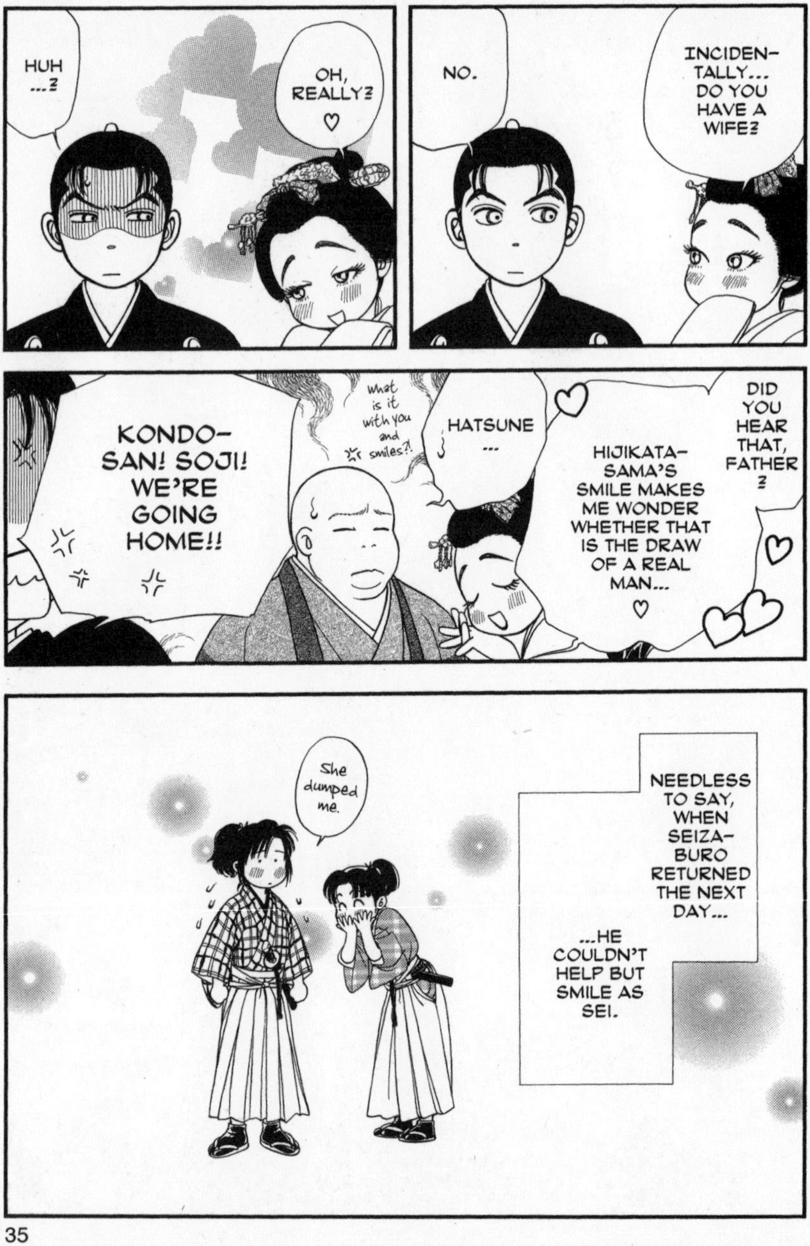
INCIDENTALLY... DO YOU HAVE A WIFE?
NO.
OH, REALLY? ♡
HUH ...?
DID YOU HEAR THAT, FATHER?
HIJIKATA-SAMA'S SMILE MAKES ME WONDER WHETHER THAT IS THE DRAW OF A REAL MAN... ♡
HATSUNE ...
What is it with you and smiles?!
KONDO-SAN! SOJI! WE'RE GOING HOME!!
NEEDLESS TO SAY, WHEN SEIZABURO RETURNED THE NEXT DAY...
...HE COULDN'T HELP BUT SMILE AS SEI.
She dumped me.

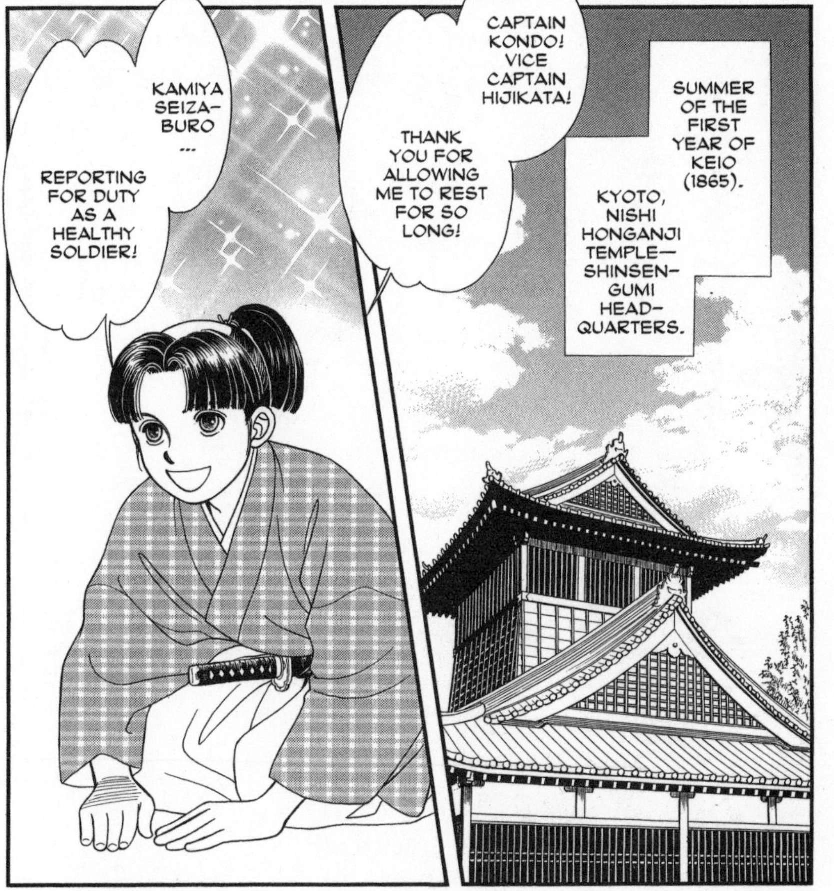
SUMMER OF THE FIRST YEAR OF KEIO (1865).
KYOTO, NISHI HONGANJI TEMPLE— SHINSEN-GUMI HEAD-QUARTERS.
CAPTAIN KONDO! VICE CAPTAIN HIJIKATA!
THANK YOU FOR ALLOWING ME TO REST FOR SO LONG!
KAMIYA SEIZA-BURO ...
REPORTING FOR DUTY AS A HEALTHY SOLDIER!

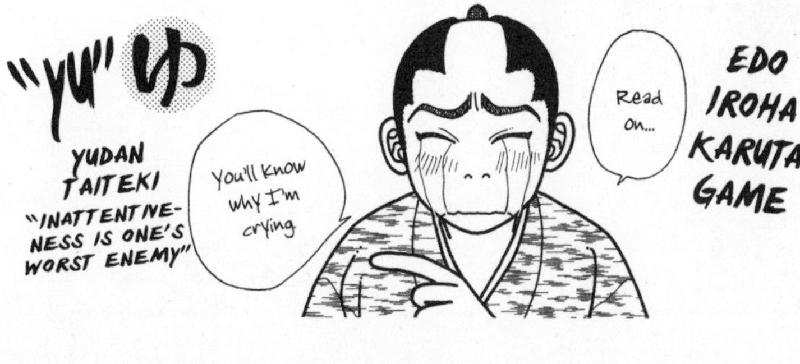
EDO IROHA KARUTA GAME
Read on...
You'll know why I'm crying
"YU" ゆ
YUDAN TAITEKI
"INATTENTIVE-NESS IS ONE'S WORST ENEMY"

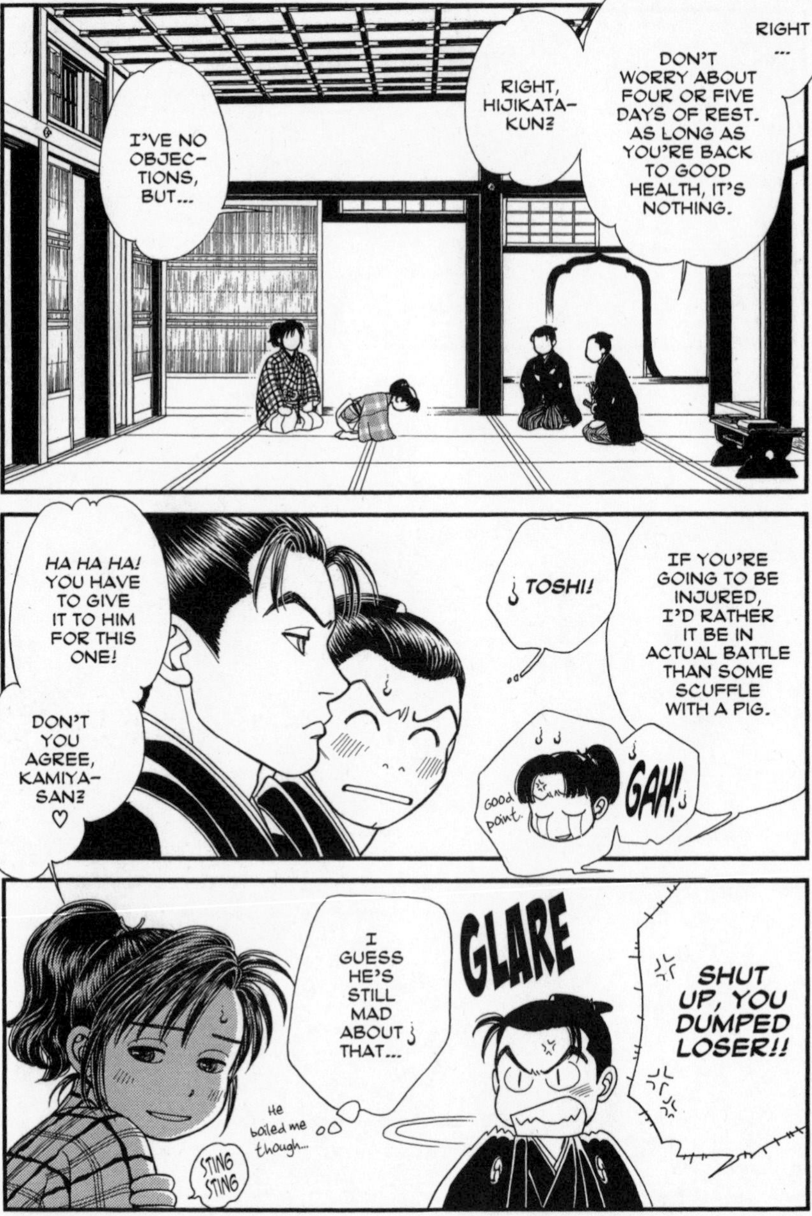
RIGHT ...
DON'T WORRY ABOUT FOUR OR FIVE DAYS OF REST. AS LONG AS YOU'RE BACK TO GOOD HEALTH, IT'S NOTHING.
RIGHT, HIJIKATA-KUN?
I'VE NO OBJECTIONS, BUT...
IF YOU'RE GOING TO BE INJURED, I'D RATHER IT BE IN ACTUAL BATTLE THAN SOME SCUFFLE WITH A PIG.
TOSHI!
GAH!
Good point.
HA HA HA! YOU HAVE TO GIVE IT TO HIM FOR THIS ONE!
DON'T YOU AGREE, KAMIYA-SAN? ♡
SHUT UP, YOU DUMPED LOSER!!
GLARE
I GUESS HE'S STILL MAD ABOUT THAT...
He boiled me though...
STING STING

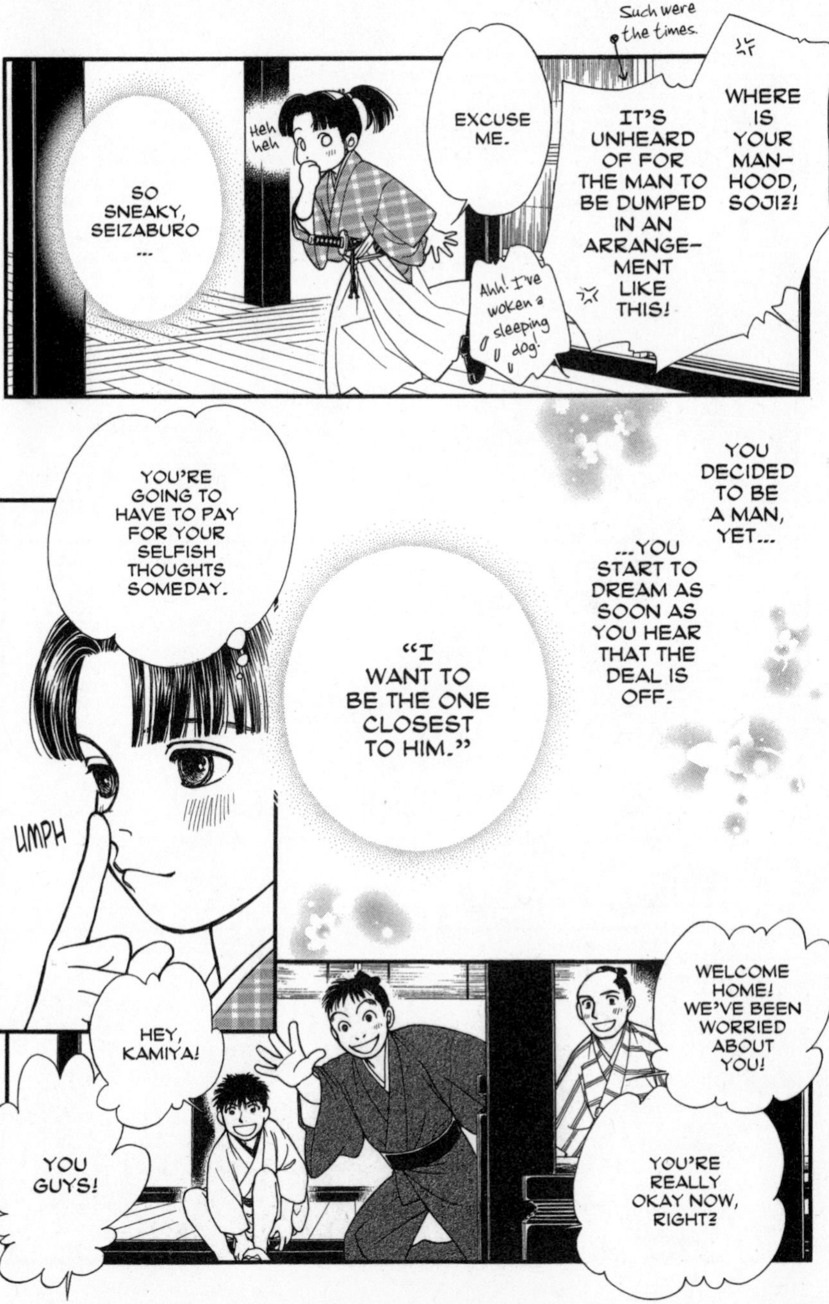
Such were the times.
WHERE IS YOUR MAN-HOOD, SOJI?!
IT'S UNHEARD OF FOR THE MAN TO BE DUMPED IN AN ARRANGE-MENT LIKE THIS!
EXCUSE ME.
Ahh! I've woken a sleeping dog!
Heh heh
SO SNEAKY, SEIZABURO ...
YOU DECIDED TO BE A MAN, YET...
...YOU START TO DREAM AS SOON AS YOU HEAR THAT THE DEAL IS OFF.
“I WANT TO BE THE ONE CLOSEST TO HIM.”
YOU'RE GOING TO HAVE TO PAY FOR YOUR SELFISH THOUGHTS SOMEDAY.
UMPH
WELCOME HOME! WE'VE BEEN WORRIED ABOUT YOU!
YOU'RE REALLY OKAY NOW, RIGHT?
HEY, KAMIYA!
YOU GUYS!

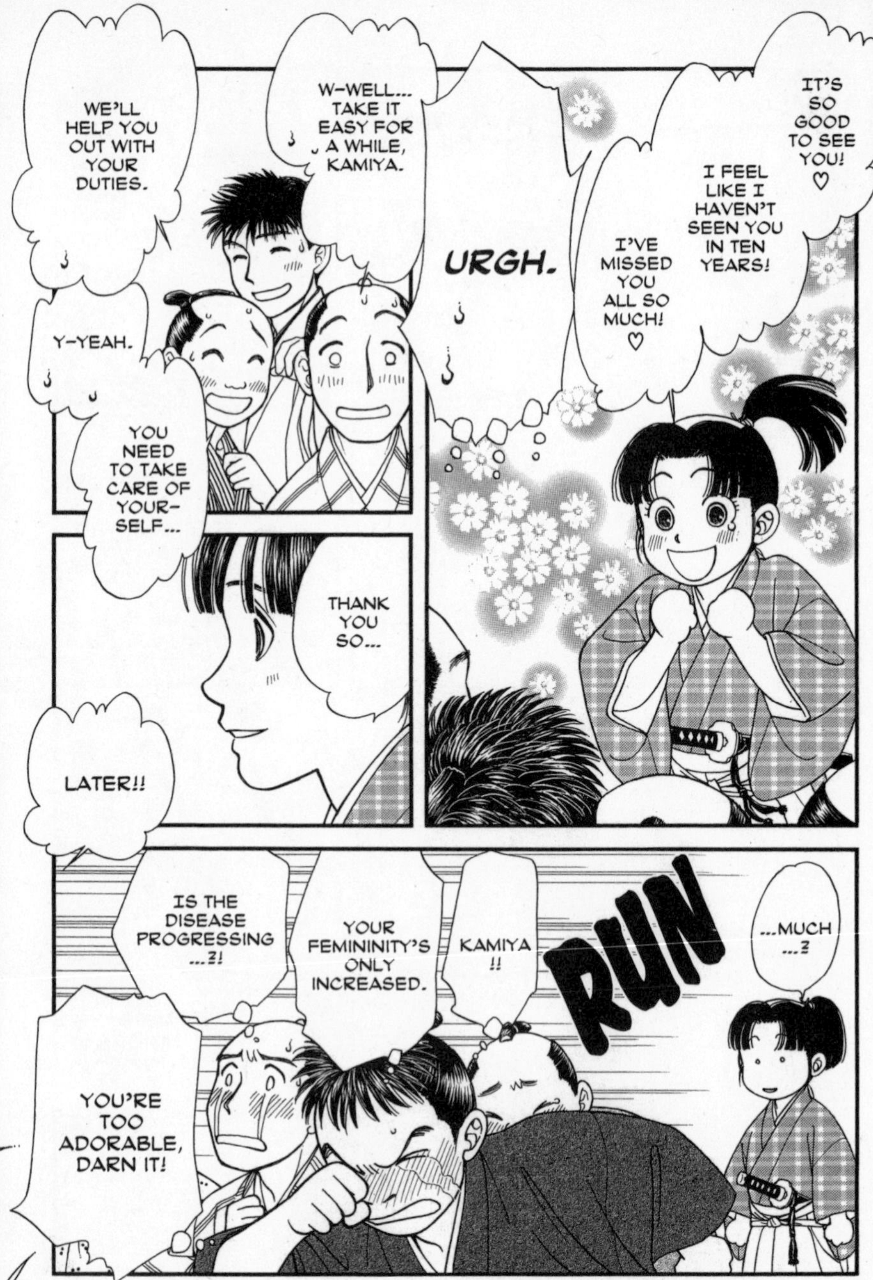
IT'S SO GOOD TO SEE YOU! ♡
I FEEL LIKE I HAVEN'T SEEN YOU IN TEN YEARS!
I'VE MISSED YOU ALL SO MUCH! ♡
URGH.
W-WELL... TAKE IT EASY FOR A WHILE, KAMIYA.
WE'LL HELP YOU OUT WITH YOUR DUTIES.
Y-YEAH.
YOU NEED TO TAKE CARE OF YOUR-SELF...
THANK YOU SO...
LATER!!
...MUCH ...?
RUN
KAMIYA !!
YOUR FEMININITY'S ONLY INCREASED.
IS THE DISEASE PROGRESSING ...?!
YOU'RE TOO ADORABLE, DARN IT!

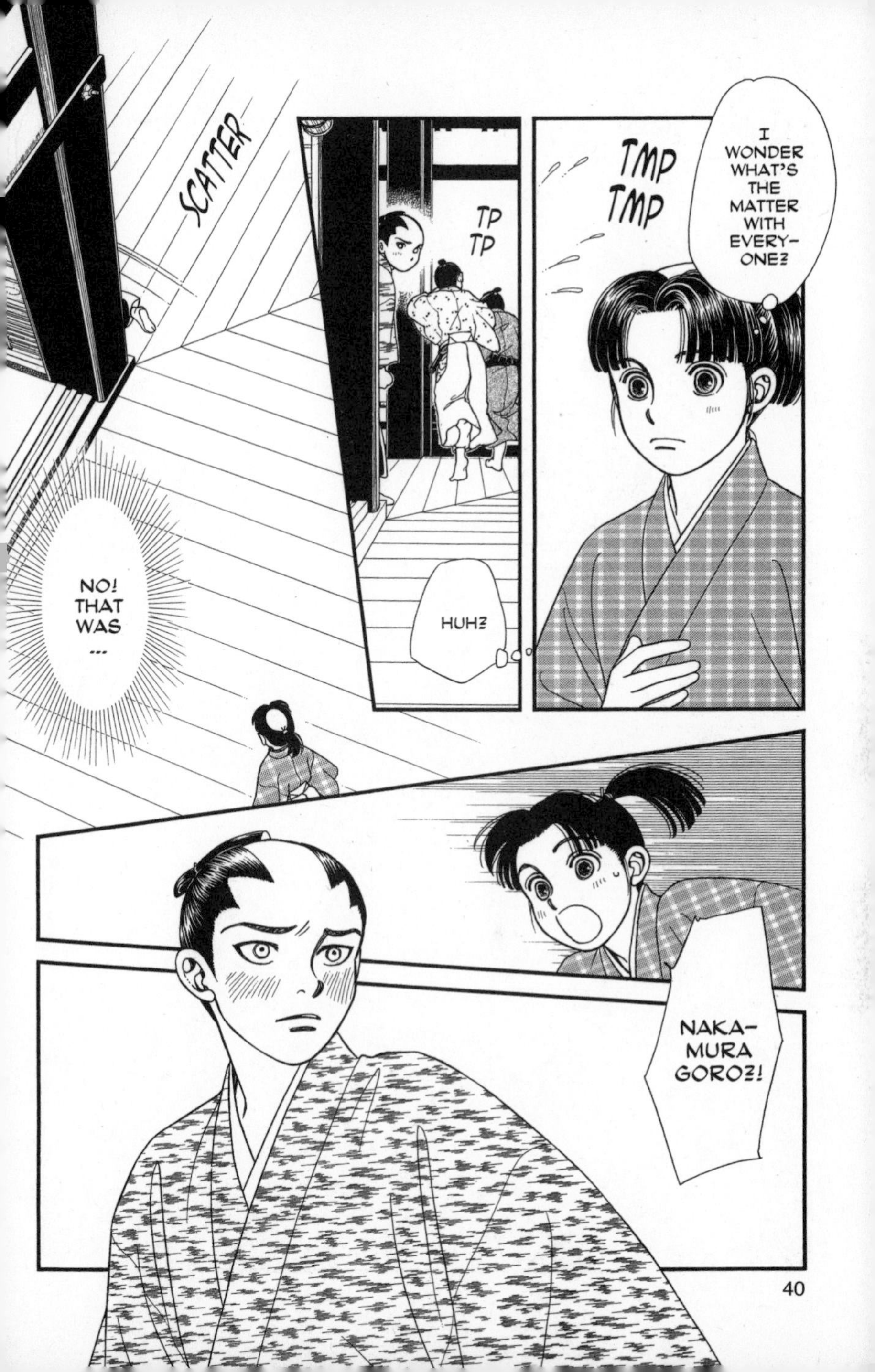
I WONDER WHAT'S THE MATTER WITH EVERY-ONE?
TMP TMP
TP TP
HUH?
SCATTER
NO! THAT WAS ...
NAKA-MURA GORO?!

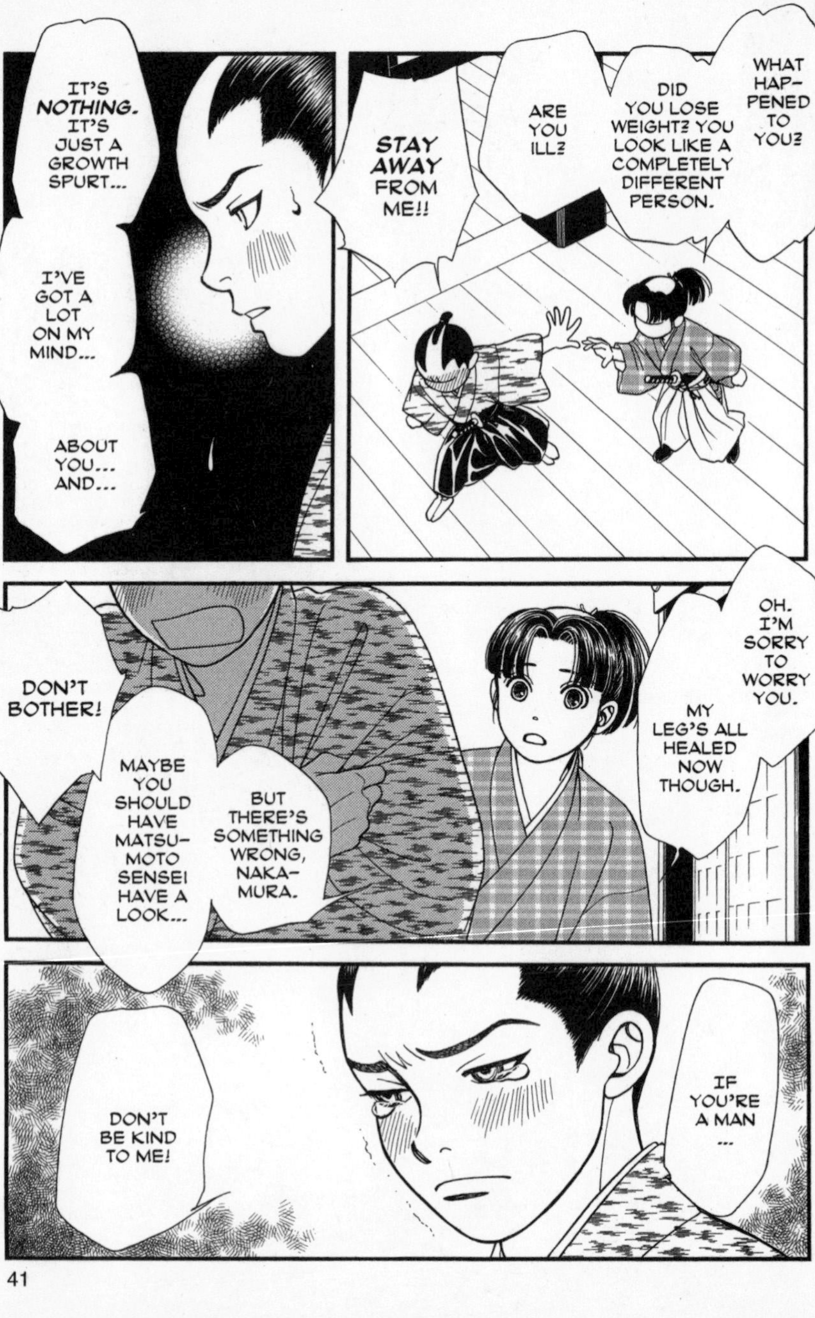
WHAT HAPPENED TO YOU?
DID YOU LOSE WEIGHT? YOU LOOK LIKE A COMPLETELY DIFFERENT PERSON.
ARE YOU ILL?
STAY AWAY FROM ME!!
IT'S NOTHING. IT'S JUST A GROWTH SPURT...
I'VE GOT A LOT ON MY MIND...
ABOUT YOU... AND...
OH. I'M SORRY TO WORRY YOU.
MY LEG'S ALL HEALED NOW THOUGH.
BUT THERE'S SOMETHING WRONG, NAKAMURA.
MAYBE YOU SHOULD HAVE MATSUMOTO SENSEI HAVE A LOOK...
DON'T BOTHER!
IF YOU'RE A MAN ...
DON'T BE KIND TO ME!

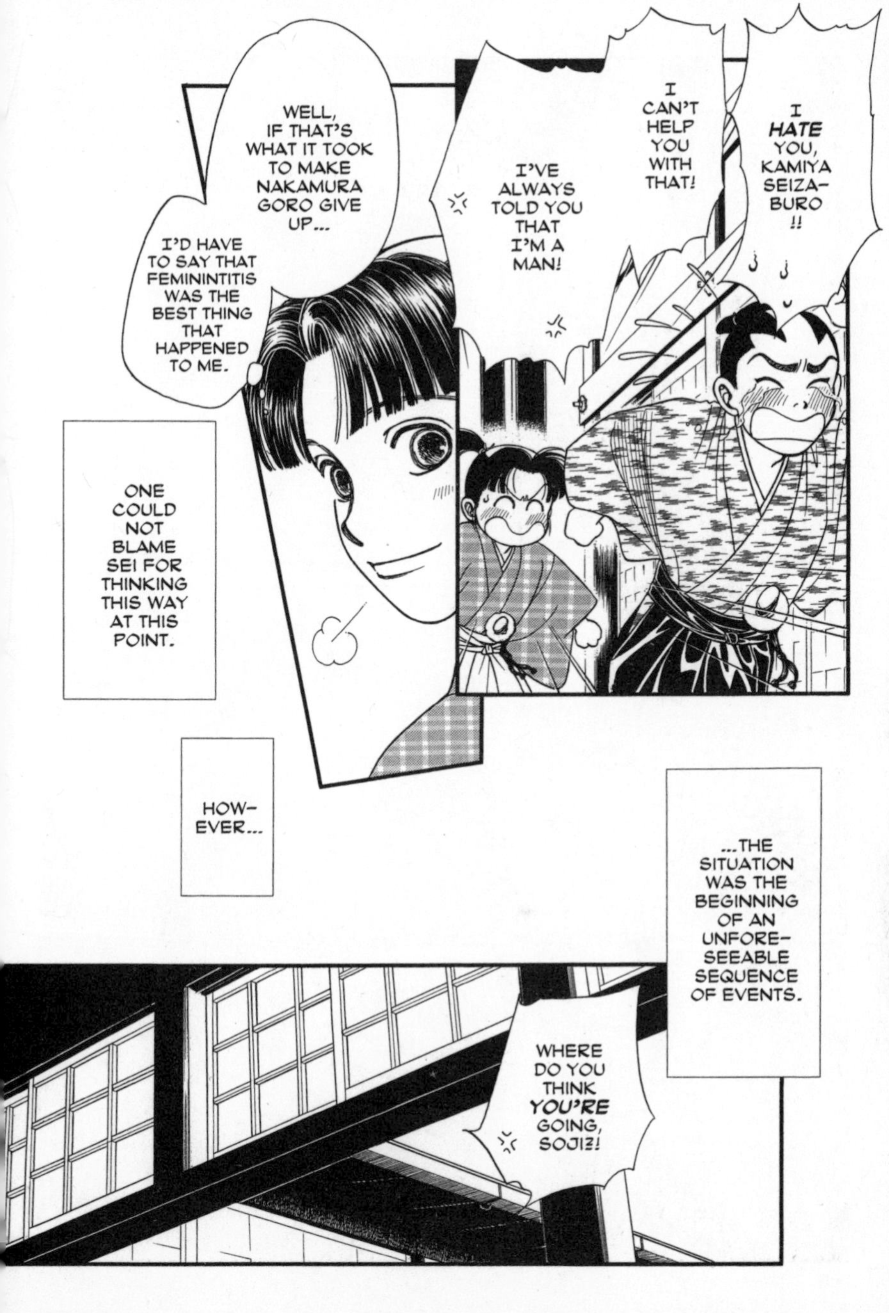
I *HATE* YOU, KAMIYA SEIZABURO!!
I CAN'T HELP YOU WITH THAT!
I'VE ALWAYS TOLD YOU THAT I'M A MAN!
WELL, IF THAT'S WHAT IT TOOK TO MAKE NAKAMURA GORO GIVE UP...
I'D HAVE TO SAY THAT FEMININTITIS WAS THE BEST THING THAT HAPPENED TO ME.
ONE COULD NOT BLAME SEI FOR THINKING THIS WAY AT THIS POINT.
HOW-EVER...
...THE SITUATION WAS THE BEGINNING OF AN UNFORE-SEEABLE SEQUENCE OF EVENTS.
WHERE DO YOU THINK *YOU'RE* GOING, SOJI!?

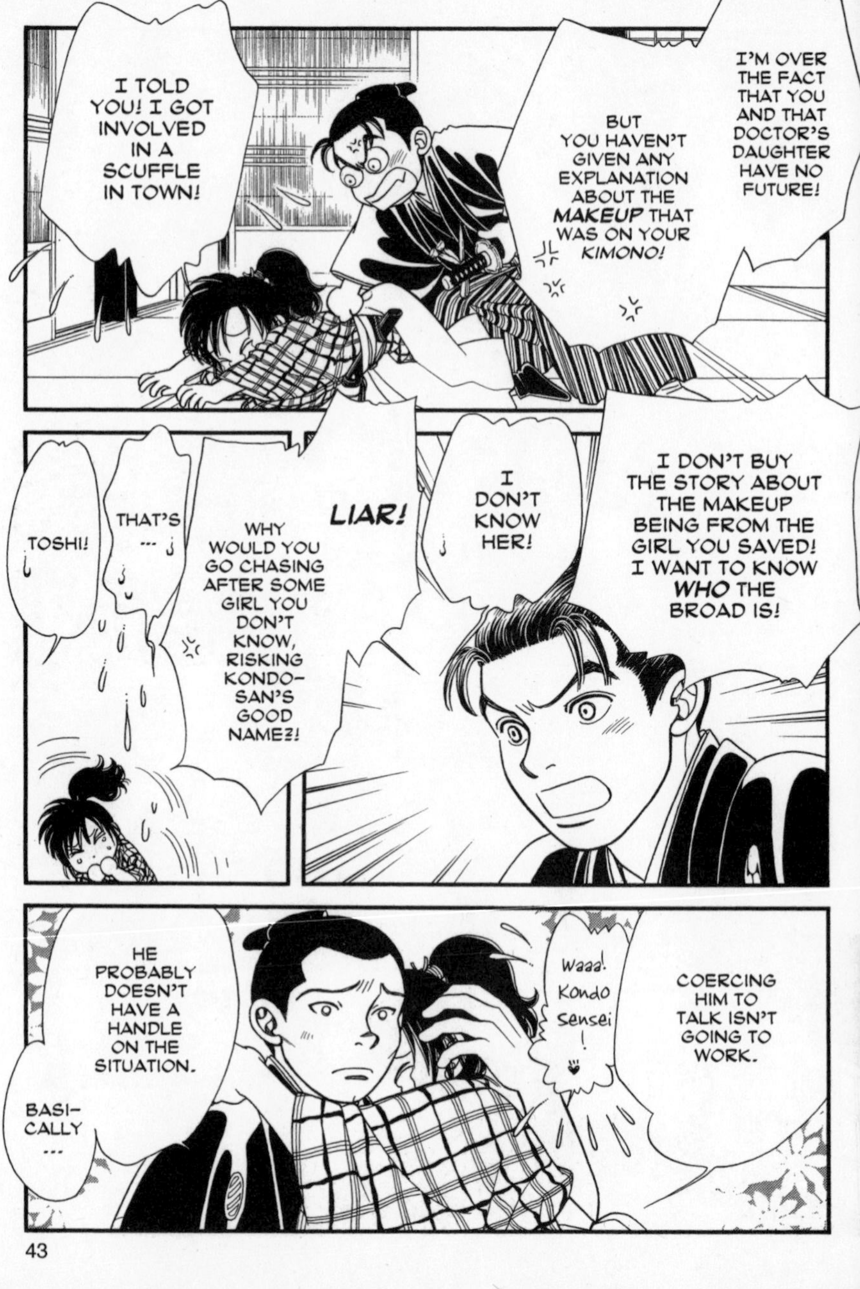
I'M OVER THE FACT THAT YOU AND THAT DOCTOR'S DAUGHTER HAVE NO FUTURE!
BUT YOU HAVEN'T GIVEN ANY EXPLANATION ABOUT THE *MAKEUP* THAT WAS ON YOUR *KIMONO!*
I TOLD YOU! I GOT INVOLVED IN A SCUFFLE IN TOWN!
I DON'T BUY THE STORY ABOUT THE MAKEUP BEING FROM THE GIRL YOU SAVED! I WANT TO KNOW *WHO* THE BROAD IS!
I DON'T KNOW HER!
LIAR!
WHY WOULD YOU GO CHASING AFTER SOME GIRL YOU DON'T KNOW, RISKING KONDO-SAN'S GOOD NAME?!
THAT'S ...
TOSHI!
COERCING HIM TO TALK ISN'T GOING TO WORK.
Waaa! Kondo Sensei!
HE PROBABLY DOESN'T HAVE A HANDLE ON THE SITUATION.
BASI-CALLY ...

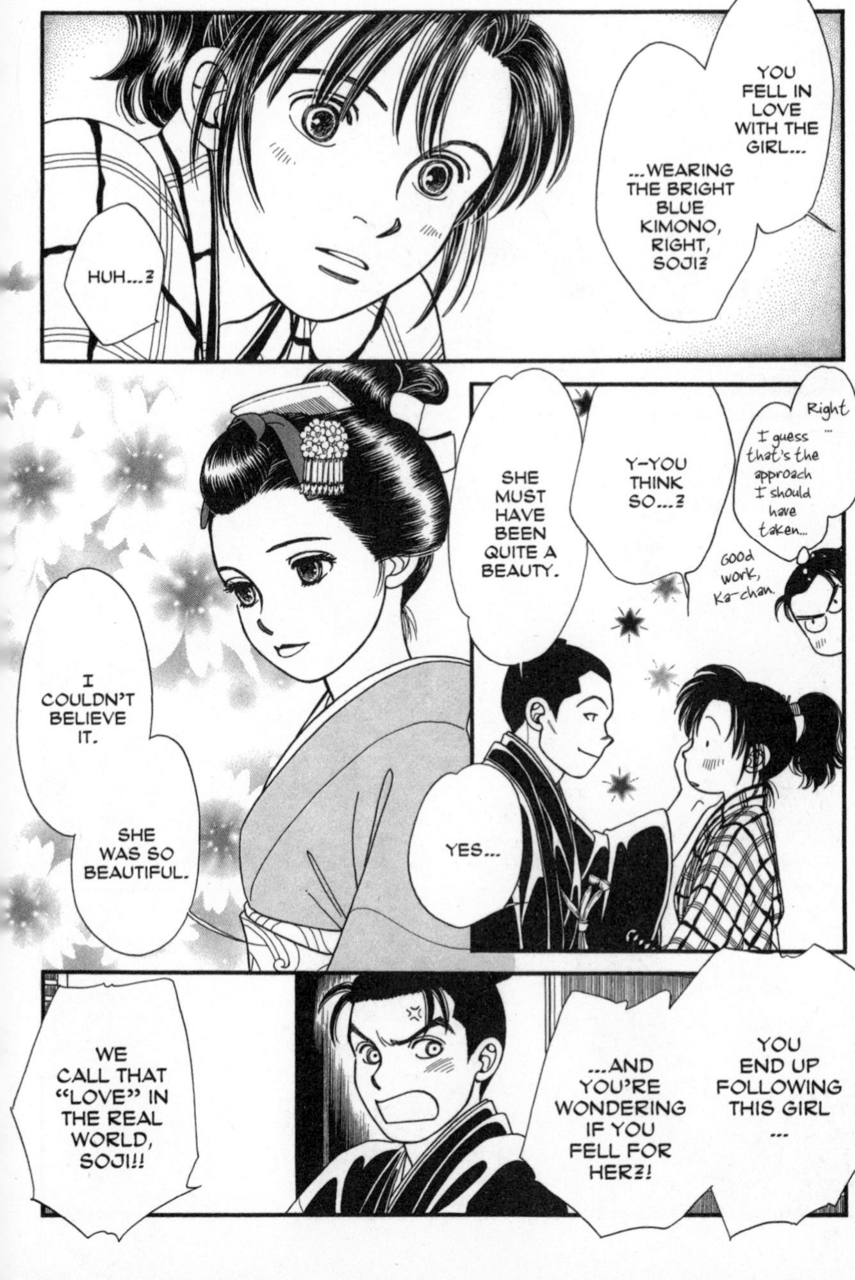
YOU FELL IN LOVE WITH THE GIRL...
...WEARING THE BRIGHT BLUE KIMONO, RIGHT, SOJI?!
HUH...?
Right... I guess that's the approach I should have taken...
Good work, Ka-chan.
Y-YOU THINK SO...?
SHE MUST HAVE BEEN QUITE A BEAUTY.
YES...
I COULDN'T BELIEVE IT.
SHE WAS SO BEAUTIFUL.
YOU END UP FOLLOWING THIS GIRL...
...AND YOU'RE WONDERING IF YOU FELL FOR HER?!
WE CALL THAT "LOVE" IN THE REAL WORLD, SOJI!!

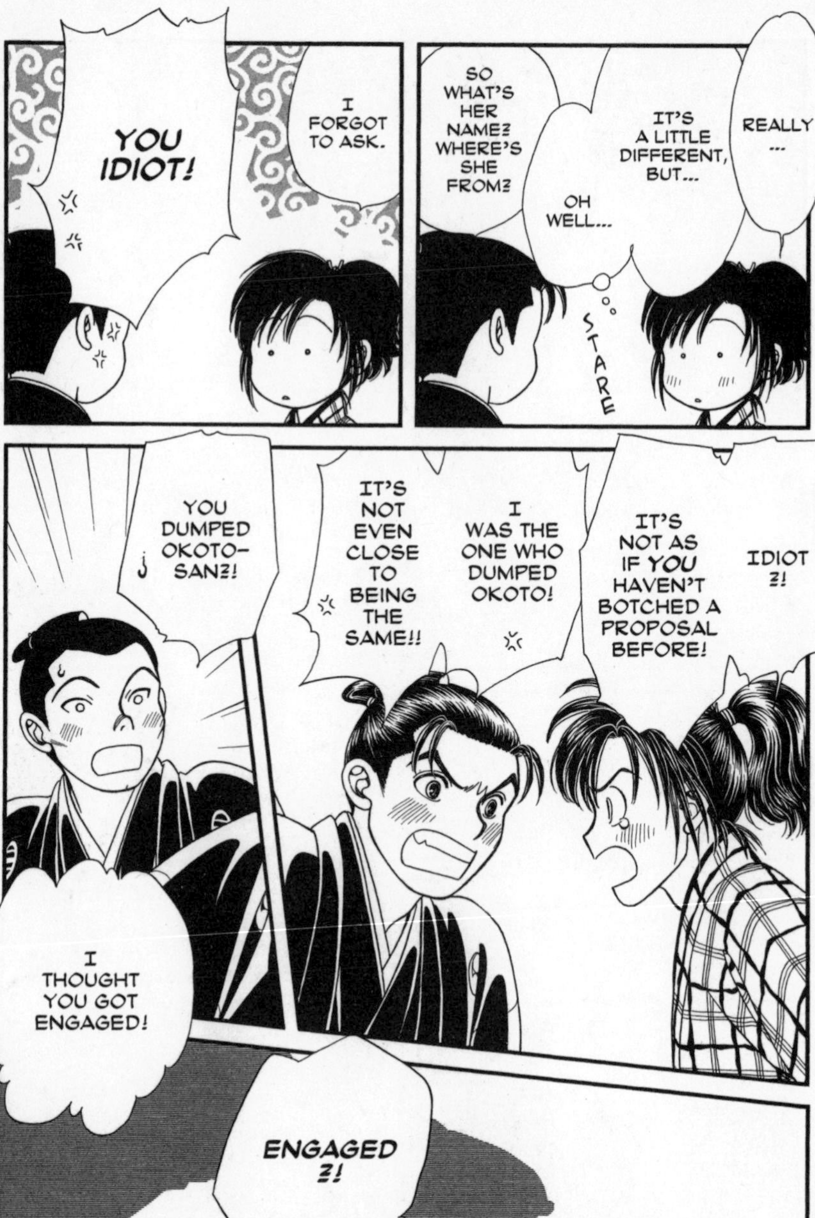
REALLY ...
IT'S A LITTLE DIFFERENT, BUT...
OH WELL...
STARE
SO WHAT'S HER NAME? WHERE'S SHE FROM?
I FORGOT TO ASK.
YOU IDIOT!
IDIOT ?!
IT'S NOT AS IF YOU HAVEN'T BOTCHED A PROPOSAL BEFORE!
I WAS THE ONE WHO DUMPED OKOTO!
IT'S NOT EVEN CLOSE TO BEING THE SAME!!
YOU DUMPED OKOTO-SAN?!
I THOUGHT YOU GOT ENGAGED!
ENGAGED ?!

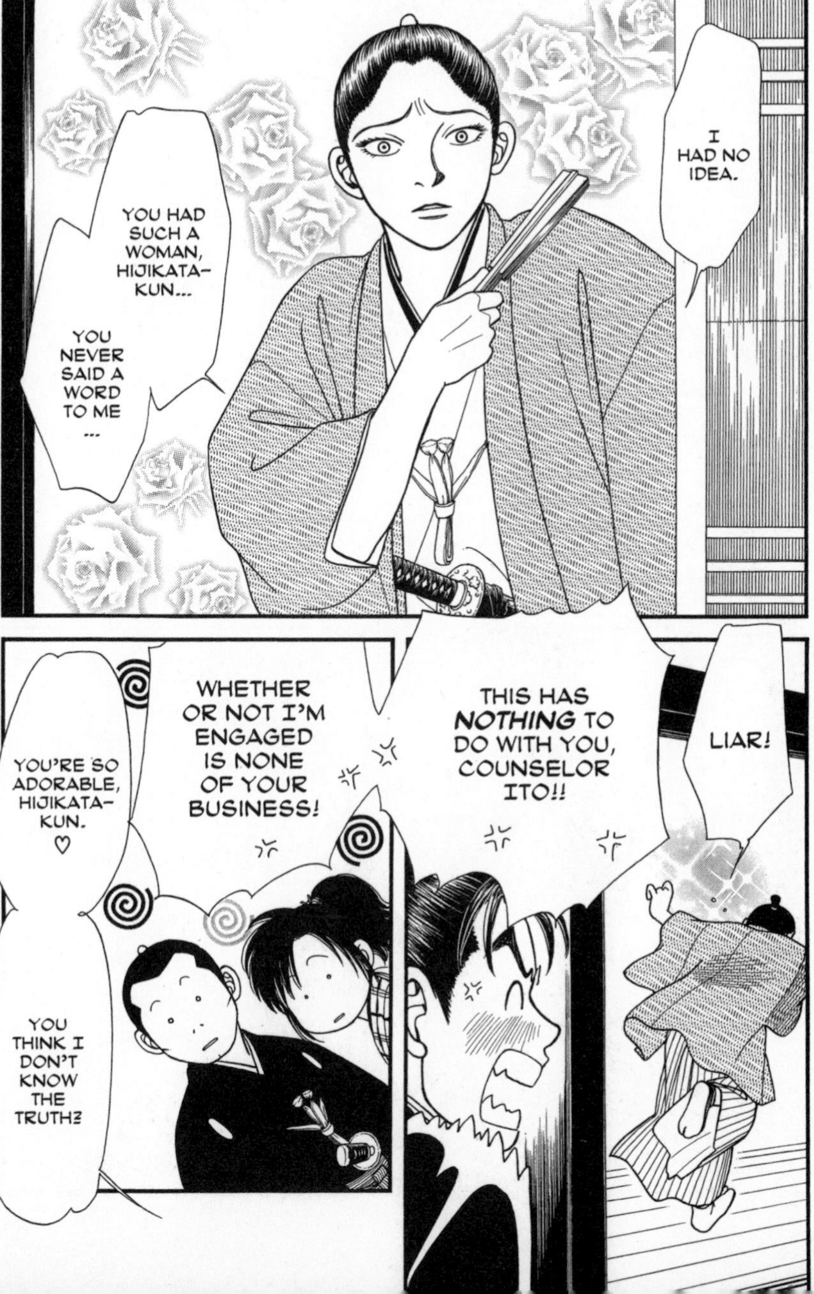
I HAD NO IDEA.
YOU HAD SUCH A WOMAN, HIJIKATA-KUN...
YOU NEVER SAID A WORD TO ME ...
LIAR!
THIS HAS NOTHING TO DO WITH YOU, COUNSELOR ITO!!
WHETHER OR NOT I'M ENGAGED IS NONE OF YOUR BUSINESS!
YOU'RE SO ADORABLE, HIJIKATA-KUN. ♡
YOU THINK I DON'T KNOW THE TRUTH?

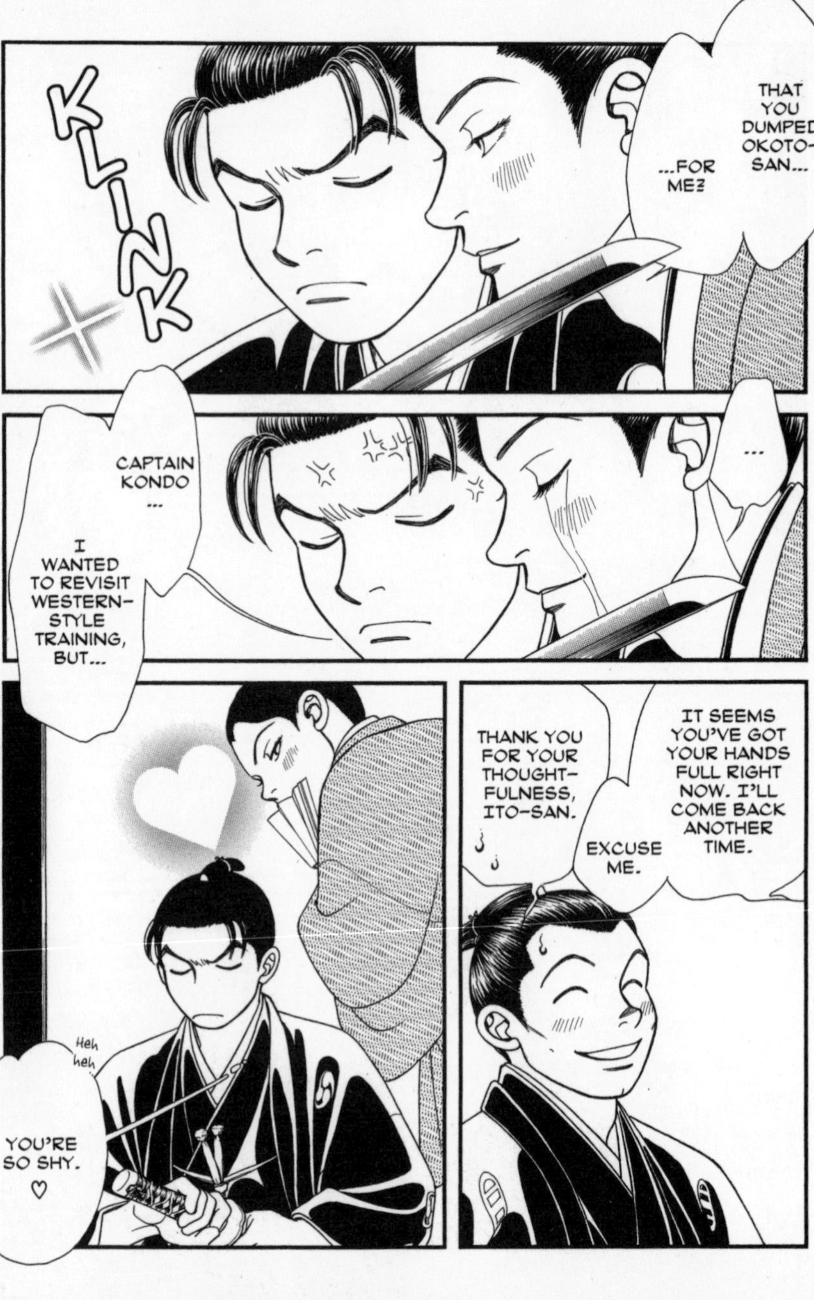
KLINK
THAT YOU DUMPED OKOTO-SAN...
...FOR ME?
...
CAPTAIN KONDO ...
I WANTED TO REVISIT WESTERN-STYLE TRAINING, BUT...
IT SEEMS YOU'VE GOT YOUR HANDS FULL RIGHT NOW. I'LL COME BACK ANOTHER TIME.
EXCUSE ME.
THANK YOU FOR YOUR THOUGHTFULNESS, ITO-SAN.
Heh heh
YOU'RE SO SHY. ♡

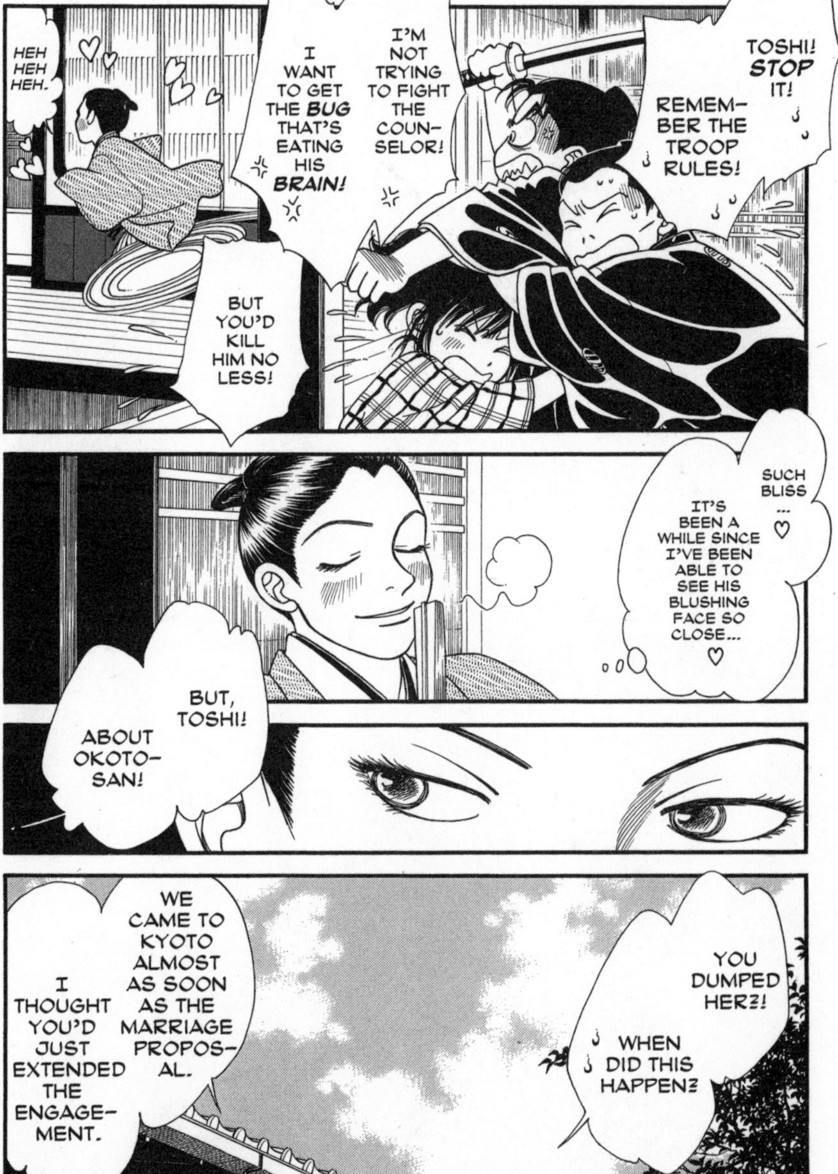

TOSHI! **STOP** IT!
REMEMBER THE TROOP RULES!
I'M NOT TRYING TO FIGHT THE COUNSELOR!
I WANT TO GET THE **BUG** THAT'S EATING HIS **BRAIN!**
BUT YOU'D KILL HIM NO LESS!
HEH HEH HEH.
SUCH BLISS... ♡
IT'S BEEN A WHILE SINCE I'VE BEEN ABLE TO SEE HIS BLUSHING FACE SO CLOSE... ♡
BUT, TOSHI!
ABOUT OKOTO-SAN!
YOU DUMPED HER?!
WHEN DID THIS HAPPEN?
WE CAME TO KYOTO ALMOST AS SOON AS THE MARRIAGE PROPOSAL.
I THOUGHT YOU'D JUST EXTENDED THE ENGAGEMENT.

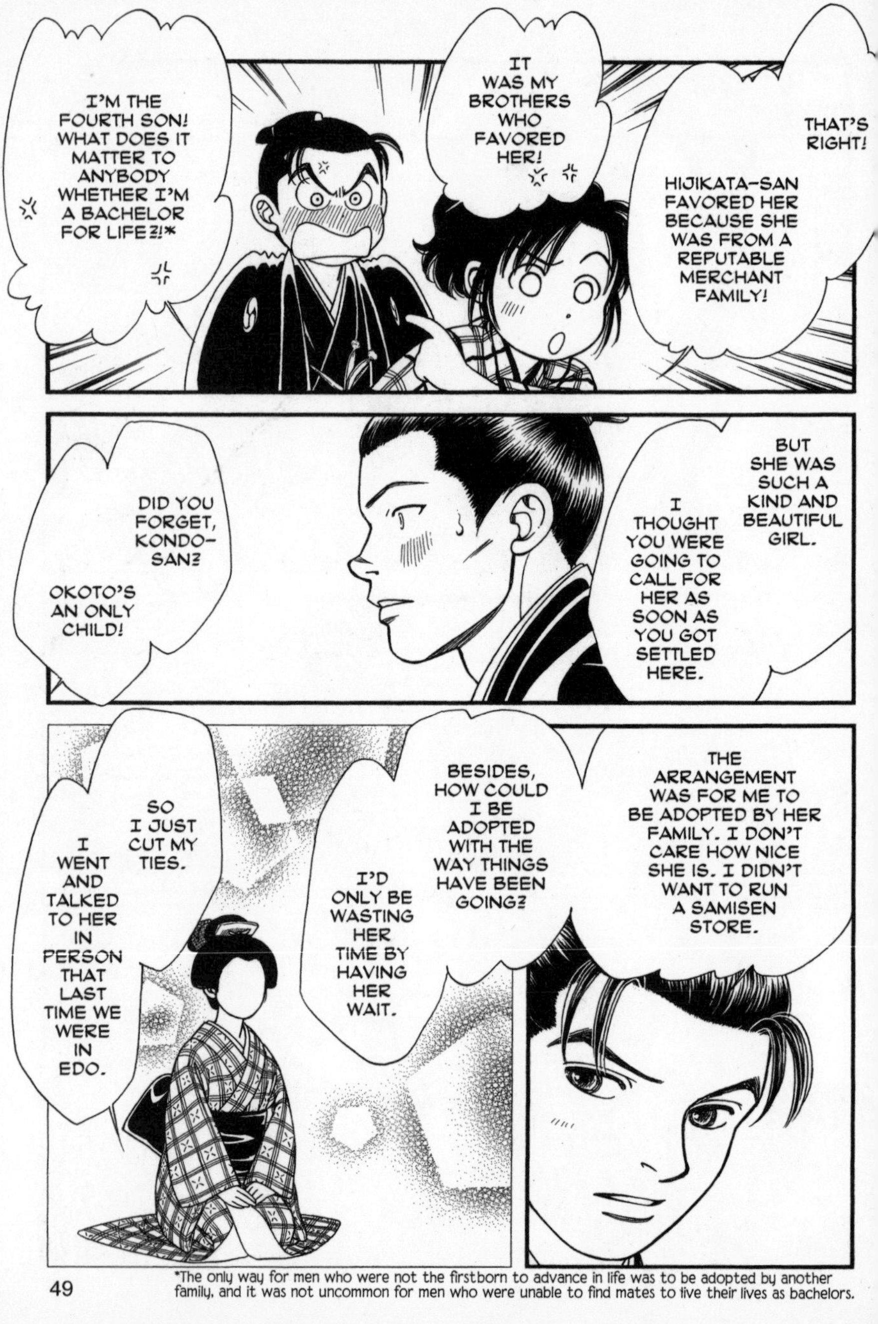
THAT'S RIGHT!
HIJIKATA-SAN FAVORED HER BECAUSE SHE WAS FROM A REPUTABLE MERCHANT FAMILY!
IT WAS MY BROTHERS WHO FAVORED HER!
I'M THE FOURTH SON! WHAT DOES IT MATTER TO ANYBODY WHETHER I'M A BACHELOR FOR LIFE?!*
BUT SHE WAS SUCH A KIND AND BEAUTIFUL GIRL.
I THOUGHT YOU WERE GOING TO CALL FOR HER AS SOON AS YOU GOT SETTLED HERE.
DID YOU FORGET, KONDO-SAN?
OKOTO'S AN ONLY CHILD!
THE ARRANGEMENT WAS FOR ME TO BE ADOPTED BY HER FAMILY. I DON'T CARE HOW NICE SHE IS. I DIDN'T WANT TO RUN A SAMISEN STORE.
BESIDES, HOW COULD I BE ADOPTED WITH THE WAY THINGS HAVE BEEN GOING?
I'D ONLY BE WASTING HER TIME BY HAVING HER WAIT.
SO I JUST CUT MY TIES.
I WENT AND TALKED TO HER IN PERSON THAT LAST TIME WE WERE IN EDO.

*The only way for men who were not the firstborn to advance in life was to be adopted by another family, and it was not uncommon for men who were unable to find mates to live their lives as bachelors.

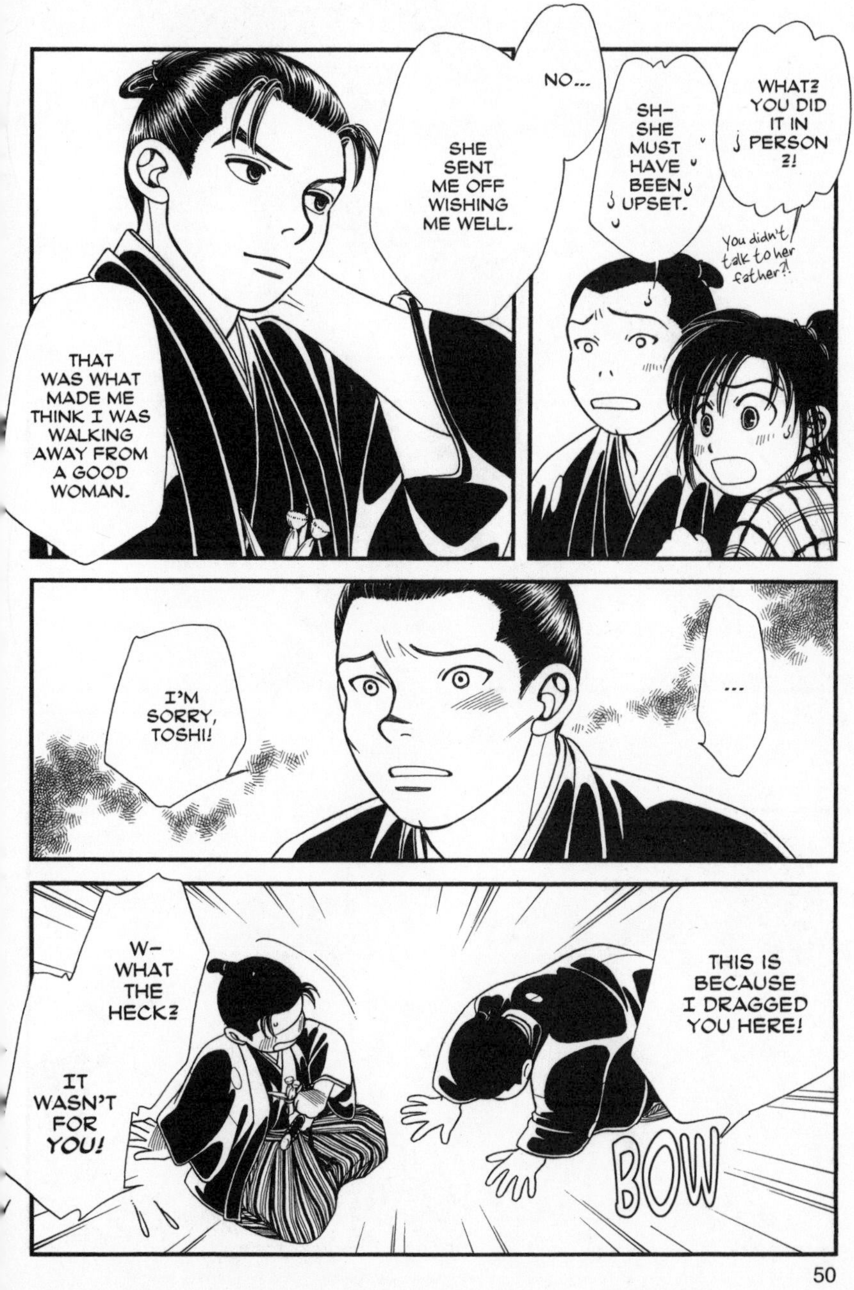
WHAT? YOU DID IT IN PERSON?!
You didn't talk to her father?!
SH-SHE MUST HAVE BEEN UPSET.
NO...
SHE SENT ME OFF WISHING ME WELL.
THAT WAS WHAT MADE ME THINK I WAS WALKING AWAY FROM A GOOD WOMAN.
...
I'M SORRY, TOSHI!
THIS IS BECAUSE I DRAGGED YOU HERE!
BOW
W-WHAT THE HECK?
IT WASN'T FOR *YOU*!

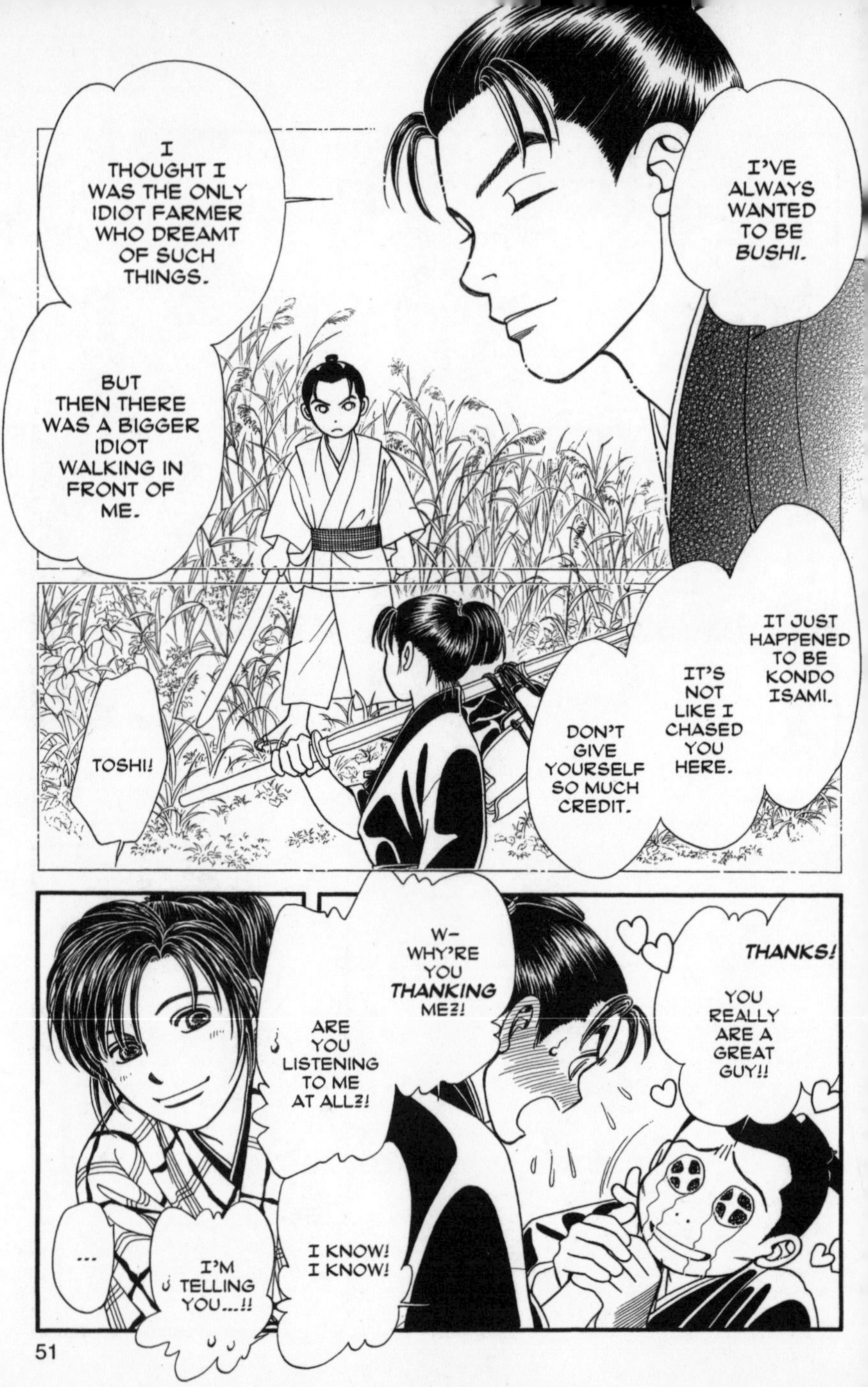
I'VE ALWAYS WANTED TO BE *BUSHI*.
I THOUGHT I WAS THE ONLY IDIOT FARMER WHO DREAMT OF SUCH THINGS.
BUT THEN THERE WAS A BIGGER IDIOT WALKING IN FRONT OF ME.
IT JUST HAPPENED TO BE KONDO ISAMI.
IT'S NOT LIKE I CHASED YOU HERE.
DON'T GIVE YOURSELF SO MUCH CREDIT.
TOSHI!
THANKS!
YOU REALLY ARE A GREAT GUY!!
W-WHY'RE YOU ***THANKING*** ME?!
ARE YOU LISTENING TO ME AT ALL?!
I KNOW! I KNOW!
I'M TELLING YOU...!!
...

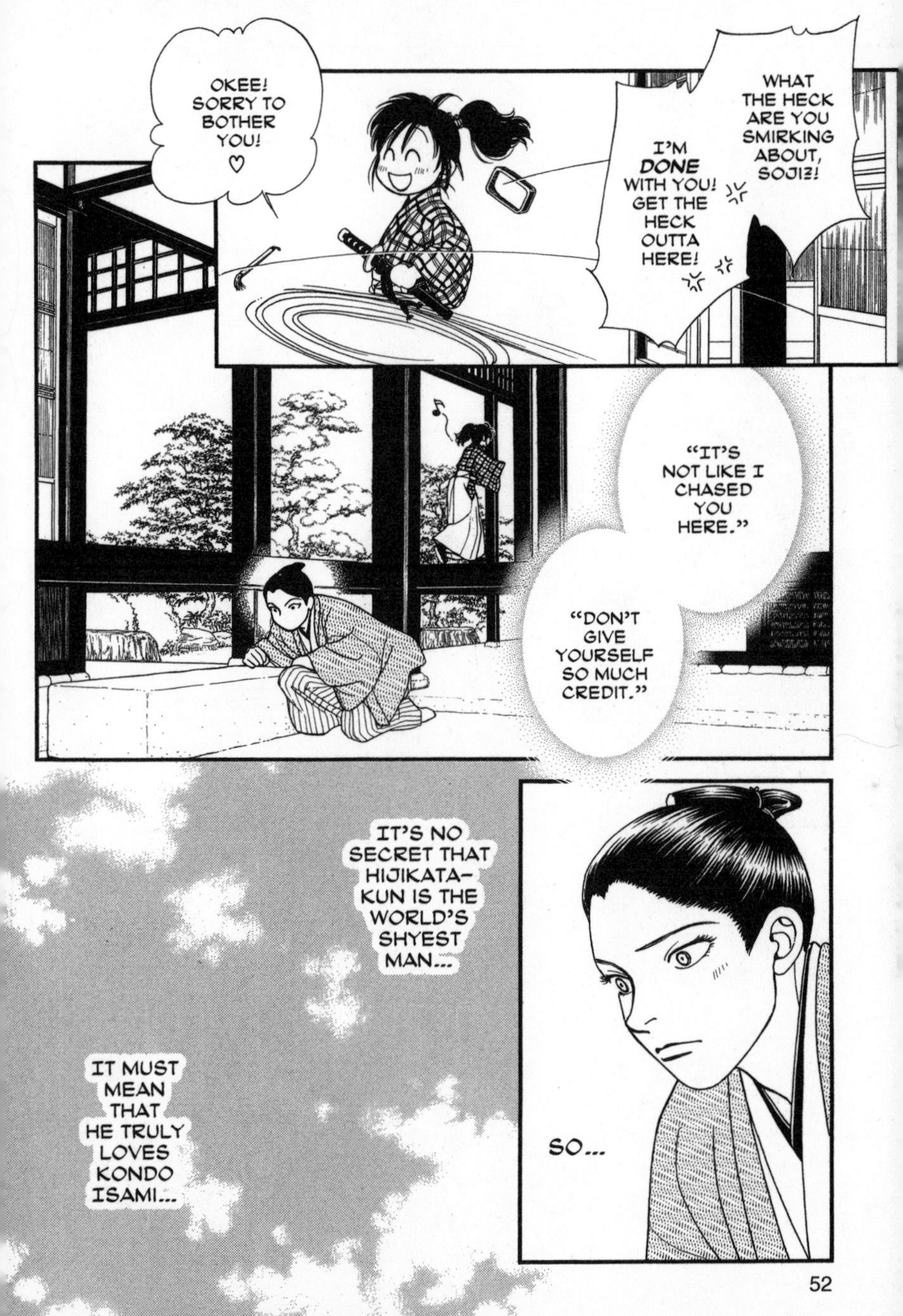
WHAT THE HECK ARE YOU SMIRKING ABOUT, SOJI?!
I'M **DONE** WITH YOU! GET THE HECK OUTTA HERE!
OKEE! SORRY TO BOTHER YOU! ♡
"IT'S NOT LIKE I CHASED YOU HERE."
"DON'T GIVE YOURSELF SO MUCH CREDIT."
SO...
IT'S NO SECRET THAT HIJIKATA-KUN IS THE WORLD'S SHYEST MAN...
IT MUST MEAN THAT HE TRULY LOVES KONDO ISAMI...

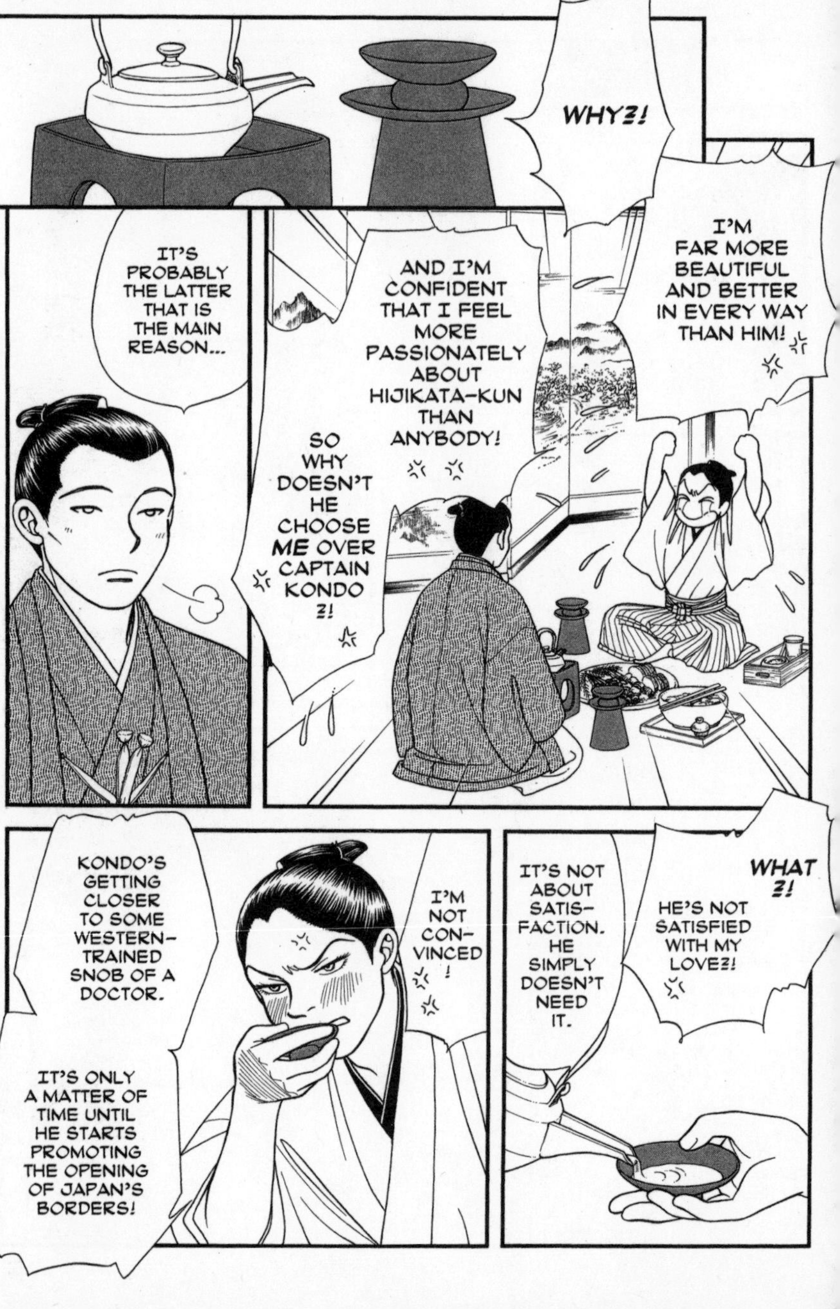
WHY?!
I'M FAR MORE BEAUTIFUL AND BETTER IN EVERY WAY THAN HIM!
AND I'M CONFIDENT THAT I FEEL MORE PASSIONATELY ABOUT HIJIKATA-KUN THAN ANYBODY!
SO WHY DOESN'T HE CHOOSE ME OVER CAPTAIN KONDO?!
IT'S PROBABLY THE LATTER THAT IS THE MAIN REASON...
WHAT?! HE'S NOT SATISFIED WITH MY LOVE?!
IT'S NOT ABOUT SATISFACTION. HE SIMPLY DOESN'T NEED IT.
I'M NOT CONVINCED!
KONDO'S GETTING CLOSER TO SOME WESTERN-TRAINED SNOB OF A DOCTOR.
IT'S ONLY A MATTER OF TIME UNTIL HE STARTS PROMOTING THE OPENING OF JAPAN'S BORDERS!

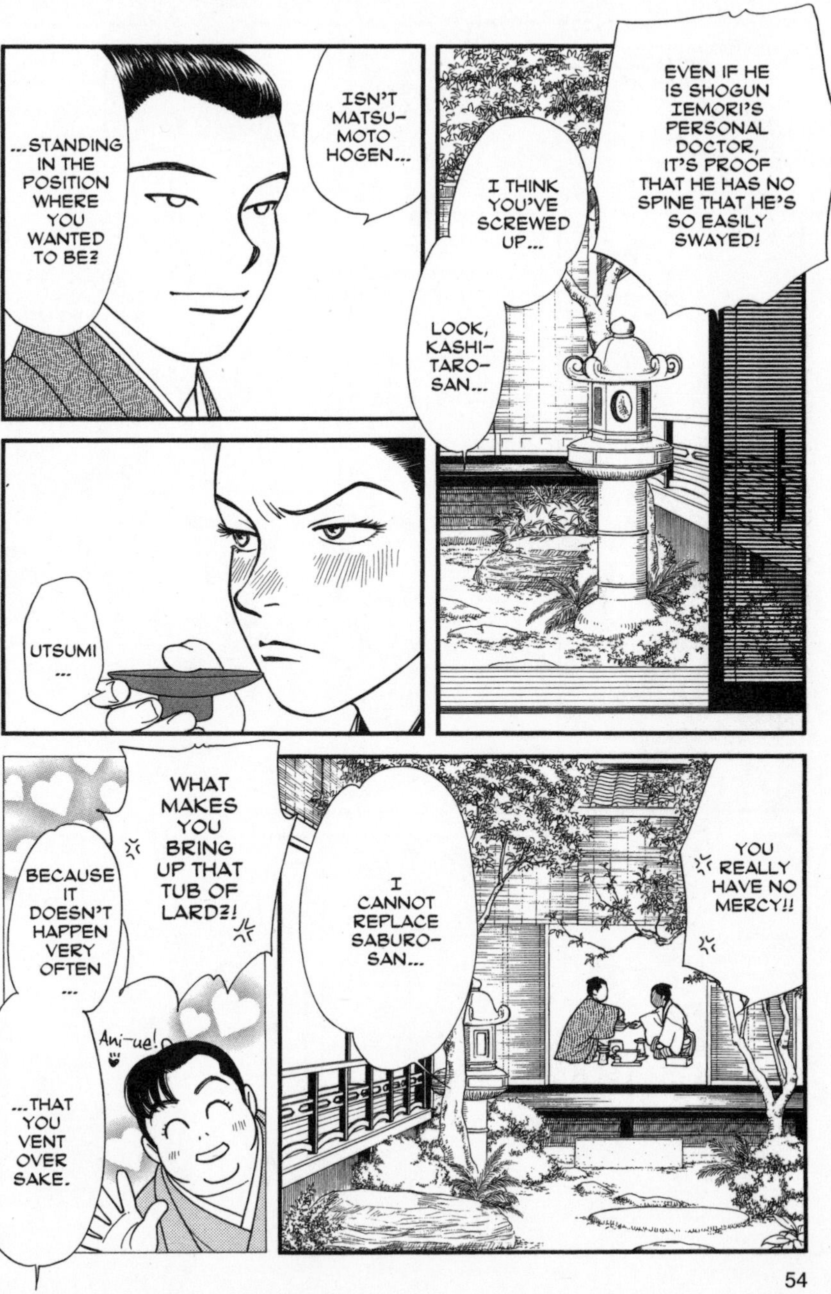
EVEN IF HE IS SHOGUN IEMORI'S PERSONAL DOCTOR, IT'S PROOF THAT HE HAS NO SPINE THAT HE'S SO EASILY SWAYED!
I THINK YOU'VE SCREWED UP...
LOOK, KASHITARO-SAN...
ISN'T MATSUMOTO HOGEN...
...STANDING IN THE POSITION WHERE YOU WANTED TO BE?
UTSUMI ...
YOU REALLY HAVE NO MERCY!!
I CANNOT REPLACE SABURO-SAN...
WHAT MAKES YOU BRING UP THAT TUB OF LARD?!
BECAUSE IT DOESN'T HAPPEN VERY OFTEN ...
Ani-ue!
...THAT YOU VENT OVER SAKE.

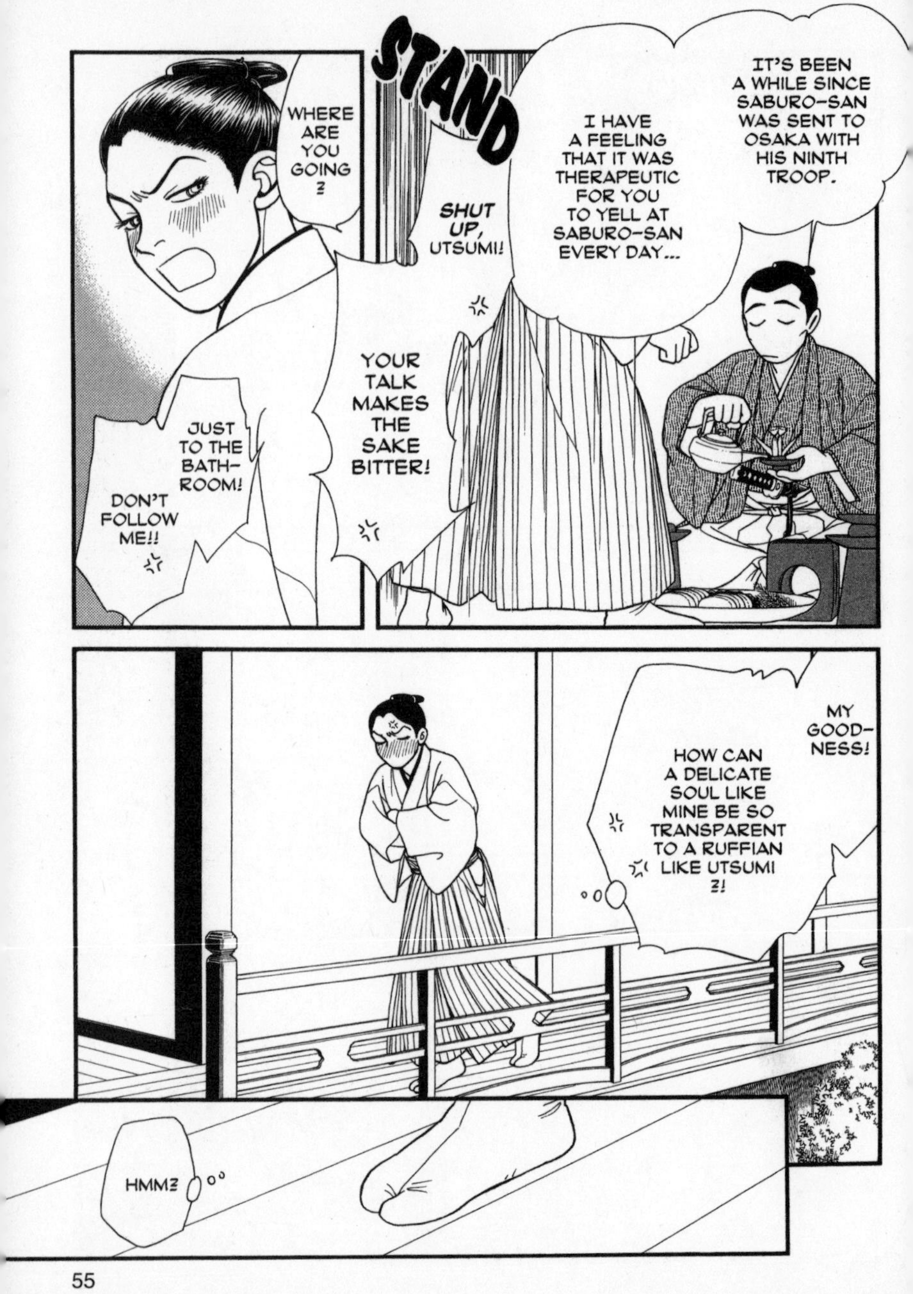
IT'S BEEN A WHILE SINCE SABURO-SAN WAS SENT TO OSAKA WITH HIS NINTH TROOP.
I HAVE A FEELING THAT IT WAS THERAPEUTIC FOR YOU TO YELL AT SABURO-SAN EVERY DAY...
STAND
SHUT UP, UTSUMI!
YOUR TALK MAKES THE SAKE BITTER!
WHERE ARE YOU GOING?
JUST TO THE BATH-ROOM!
DON'T FOLLOW ME!!
MY GOOD-NESS!
HOW CAN A DELICATE SOUL LIKE MINE BE SO TRANSPARENT TO A RUFFIAN LIKE UTSUMI?!
HMM?

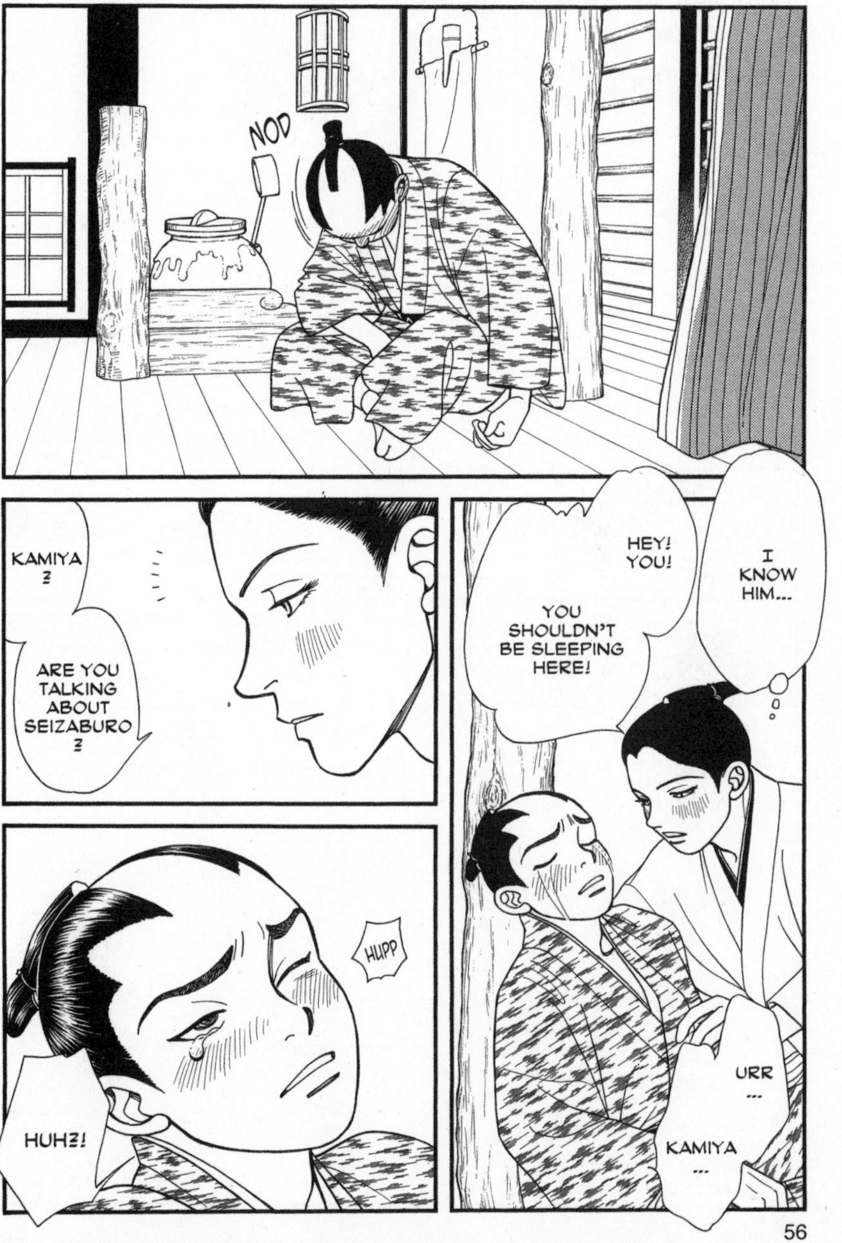
NOD
I KNOW HIM...
HEY! YOU!
YOU SHOULDN'T BE SLEEPING HERE!
URR...
KAMIYA...
KAMIYA?
ARE YOU TALKING ABOUT SEIZABURO?
HUPP
HUH?!

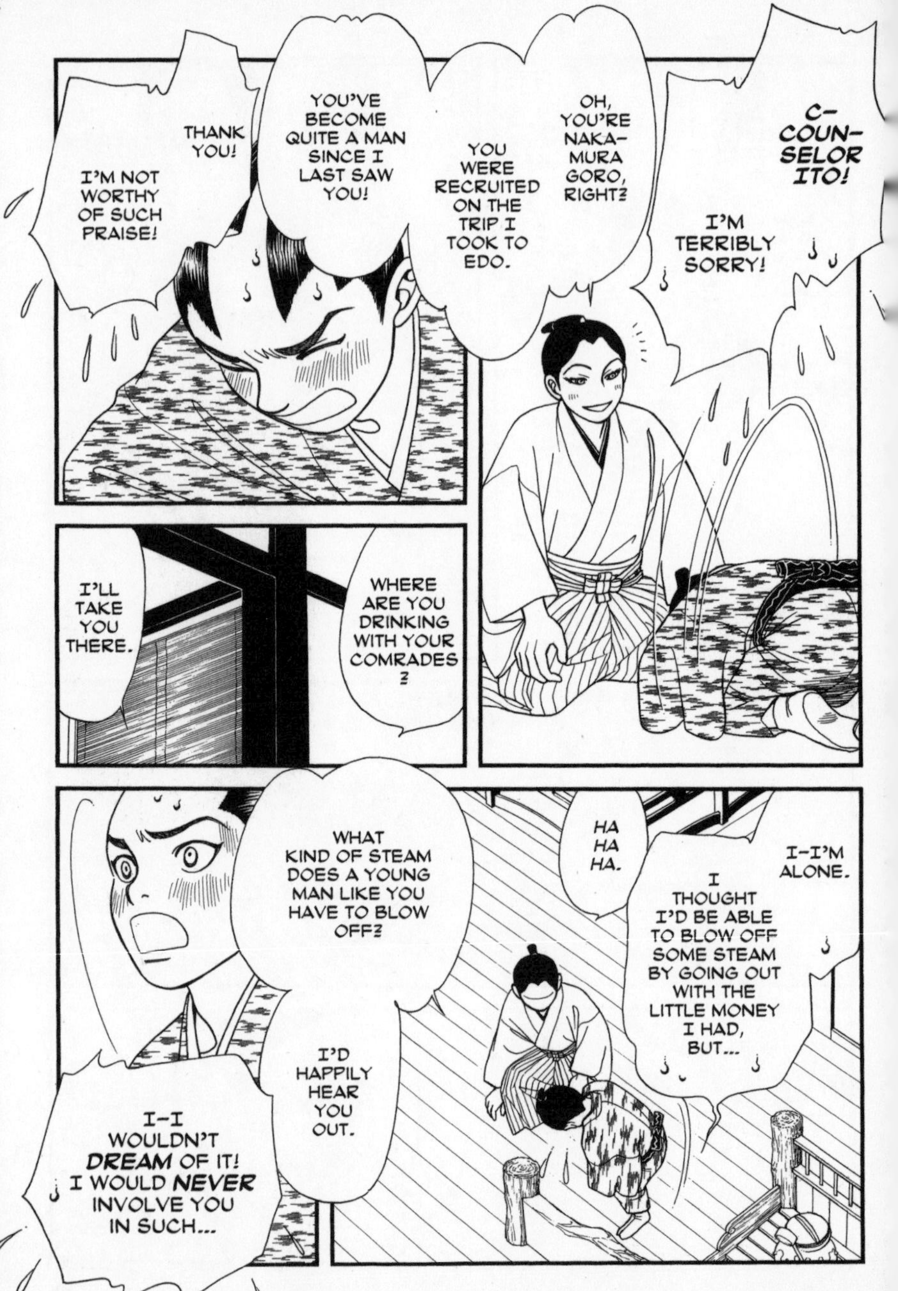
C-COUNSELOR ITO!
I'M TERRIBLY SORRY!
OH, YOU'RE NAKAMURA GORO, RIGHT?
YOU WERE RECRUITED ON THE TRIP I TOOK TO EDO.
YOU'VE BECOME QUITE A MAN SINCE I LAST SAW YOU!
THANK YOU!
I'M NOT WORTHY OF SUCH PRAISE!
WHERE ARE YOU DRINKING WITH YOUR COMRADES?
I'LL TAKE YOU THERE.
I-I'M ALONE.
I THOUGHT I'D BE ABLE TO BLOW OFF SOME STEAM BY GOING OUT WITH THE LITTLE MONEY I HAD, BUT...
HA HA HA.
WHAT KIND OF STEAM DOES A YOUNG MAN LIKE YOU HAVE TO BLOW OFF?
I'D HAPPILY HEAR YOU OUT.
I-I WOULDN'T ***DREAM*** OF IT! I WOULD ***NEVER*** INVOLVE YOU IN SUCH...

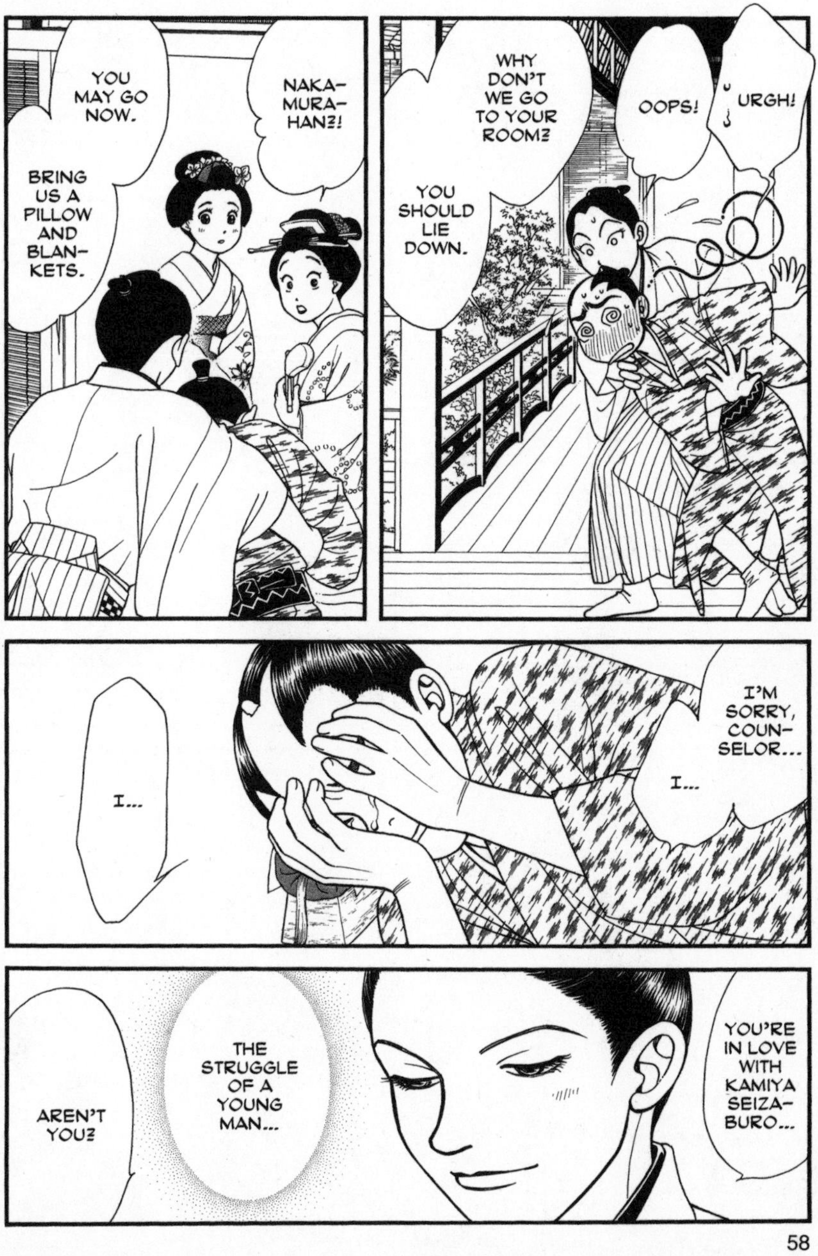
URGH!
OOPS!
WHY DON'T WE GO TO YOUR ROOM?
YOU SHOULD LIE DOWN.
NAKA-MURA-HAN?!
YOU MAY GO NOW.
BRING US A PILLOW AND BLAN-KETS.
I'M SORRY, COUN-SELOR...
I...
I...
YOU'RE IN LOVE WITH KAMIYA SEIZA-BURO...
THE STRUGGLE OF A YOUNG MAN...
AREN'T YOU?

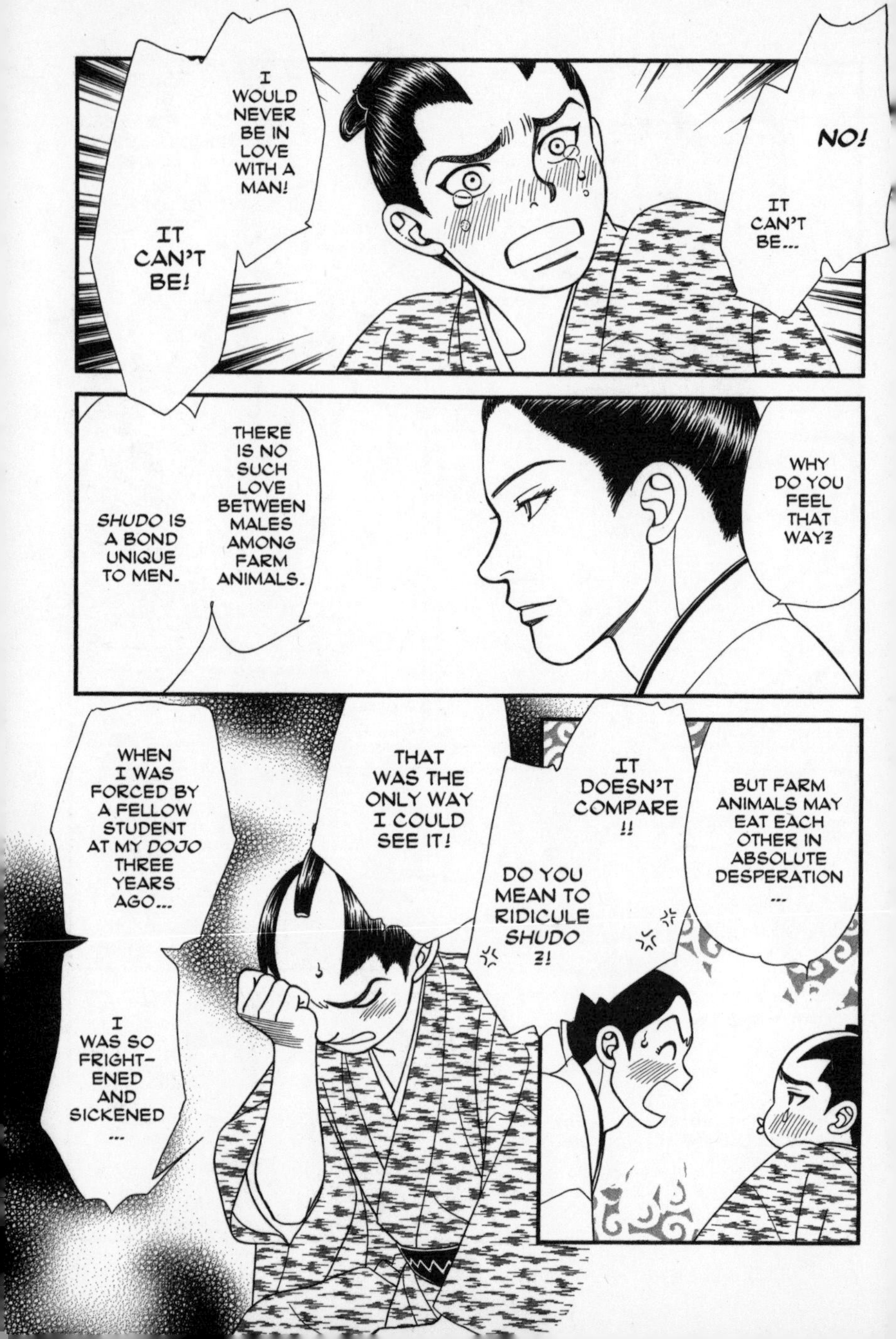
NO!
IT CAN'T BE...
I WOULD NEVER BE IN LOVE WITH A MAN!
IT CAN'T BE!
WHY DO YOU FEEL THAT WAY?
THERE IS NO SUCH LOVE BETWEEN MALES AMONG FARM ANIMALS.
SHUDO IS A BOND UNIQUE TO MEN.
BUT FARM ANIMALS MAY EAT EACH OTHER IN ABSOLUTE DESPERATION ...
IT DOESN'T COMPARE !!
DO YOU MEAN TO RIDICULE *SHUDO* ?!
THAT WAS THE ONLY WAY I COULD SEE IT!
WHEN I WAS FORCED BY A FELLOW STUDENT AT MY *DOJO* THREE YEARS AGO...
I WAS SO FRIGHT-ENED AND SICKENED ...

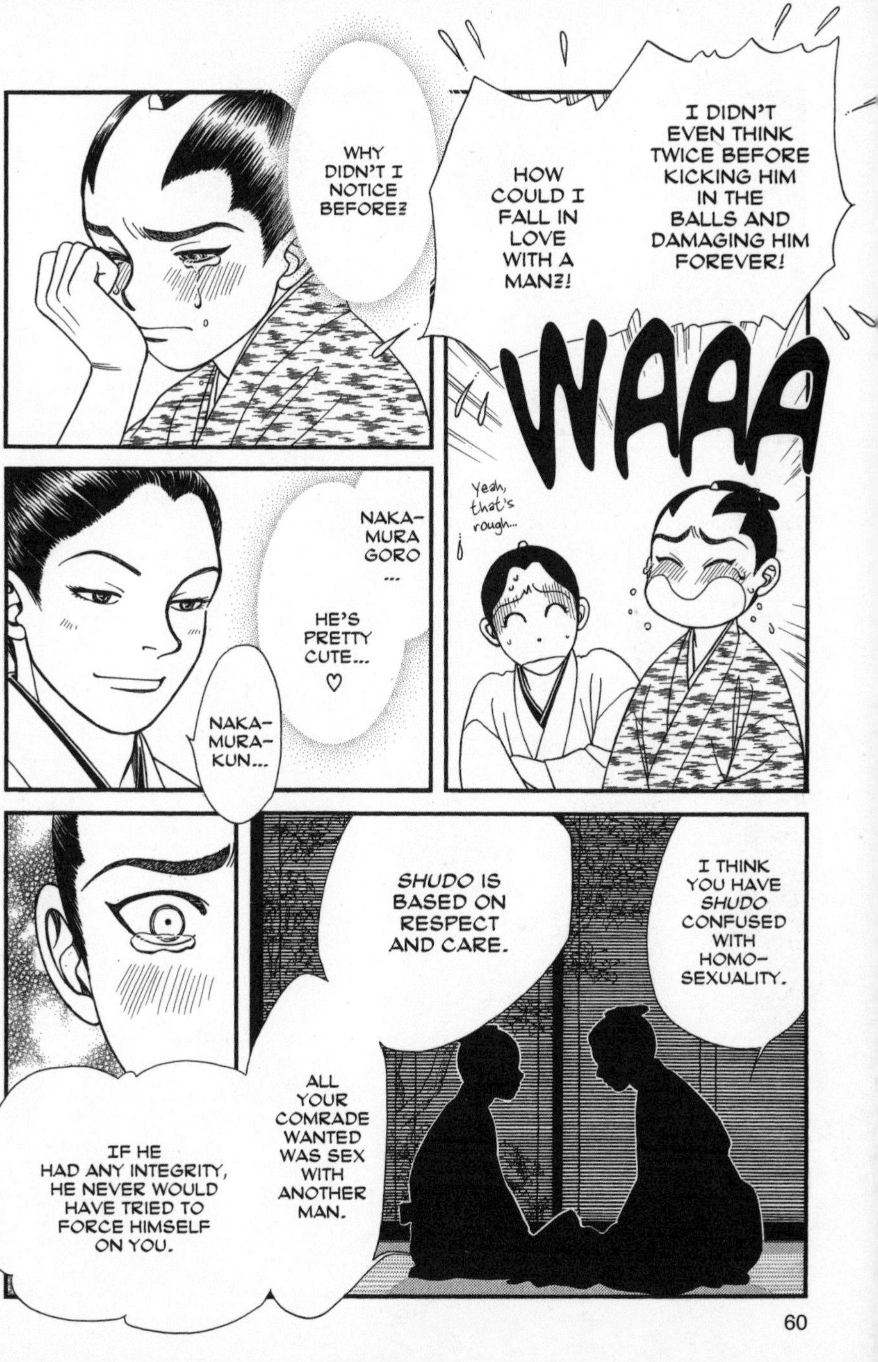
I DIDN'T EVEN THINK TWICE BEFORE KICKING HIM IN THE BALLS AND DAMAGING HIM FOREVER!
HOW COULD I FALL IN LOVE WITH A MAN?!
WAAA
Yeah, that's rough...
WHY DIDN'T I NOTICE BEFORE?
NAKAMURA GORO...
HE'S PRETTY CUTE... ♡
NAKAMURA-KUN...
I THINK YOU HAVE *SHUDO* CONFUSED WITH HOMOSEXUALITY.
SHUDO IS BASED ON RESPECT AND CARE.
ALL YOUR COMRADE WANTED WAS SEX WITH ANOTHER MAN.
IF HE HAD ANY INTEGRITY, HE NEVER WOULD HAVE TRIED TO FORCE HIMSELF ON YOU.

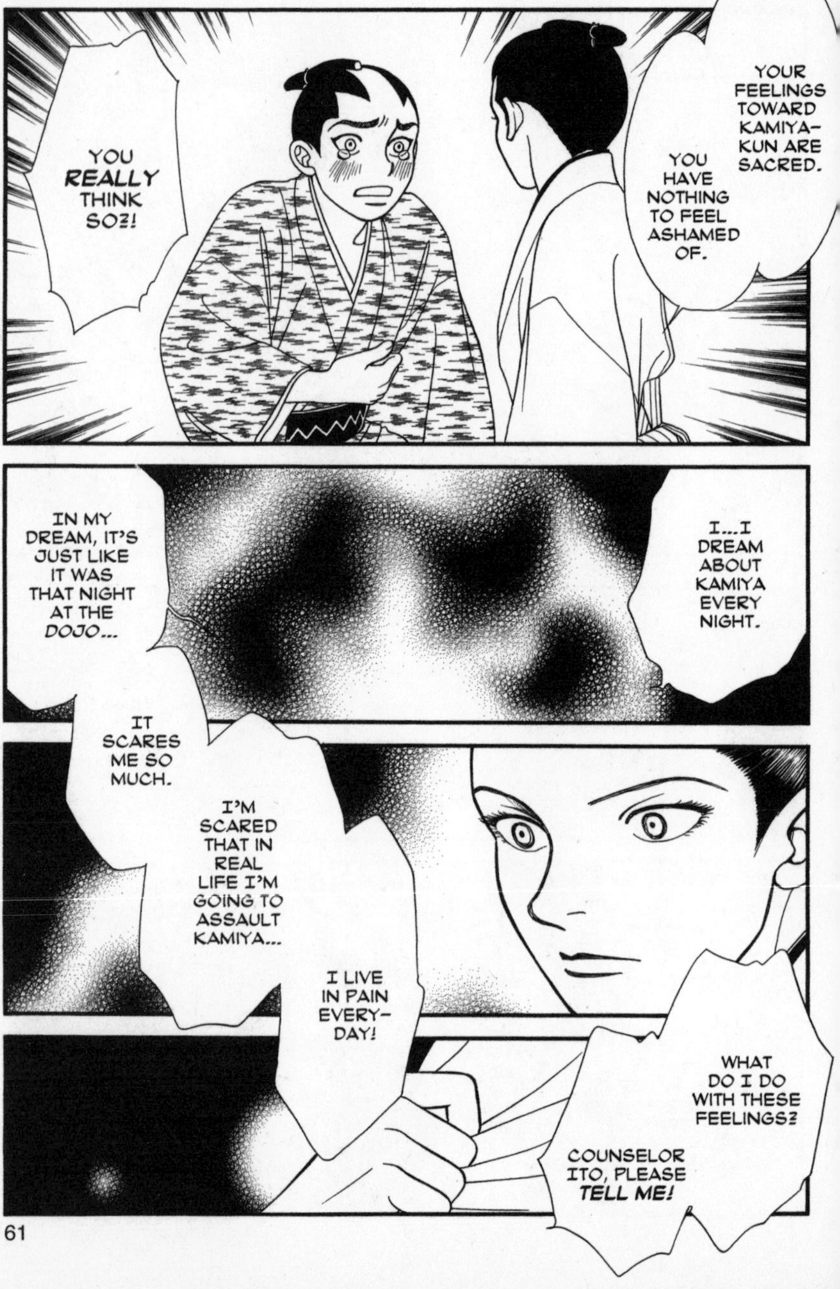
YOUR FEELINGS TOWARD KAMIYA-KUN ARE SACRED.
YOU HAVE NOTHING TO FEEL ASHAMED OF.
YOU REALLY THINK SO?!
I...I DREAM ABOUT KAMIYA EVERY NIGHT.
IN MY DREAM, IT'S JUST LIKE IT WAS THAT NIGHT AT THE DOJO...
IT SCARES ME SO MUCH.
I'M SCARED THAT IN REAL LIFE I'M GOING TO ASSAULT KAMIYA...
I LIVE IN PAIN EVERY-DAY!
WHAT DO I DO WITH THESE FEELINGS?
COUNSELOR ITO, PLEASE TELL ME!

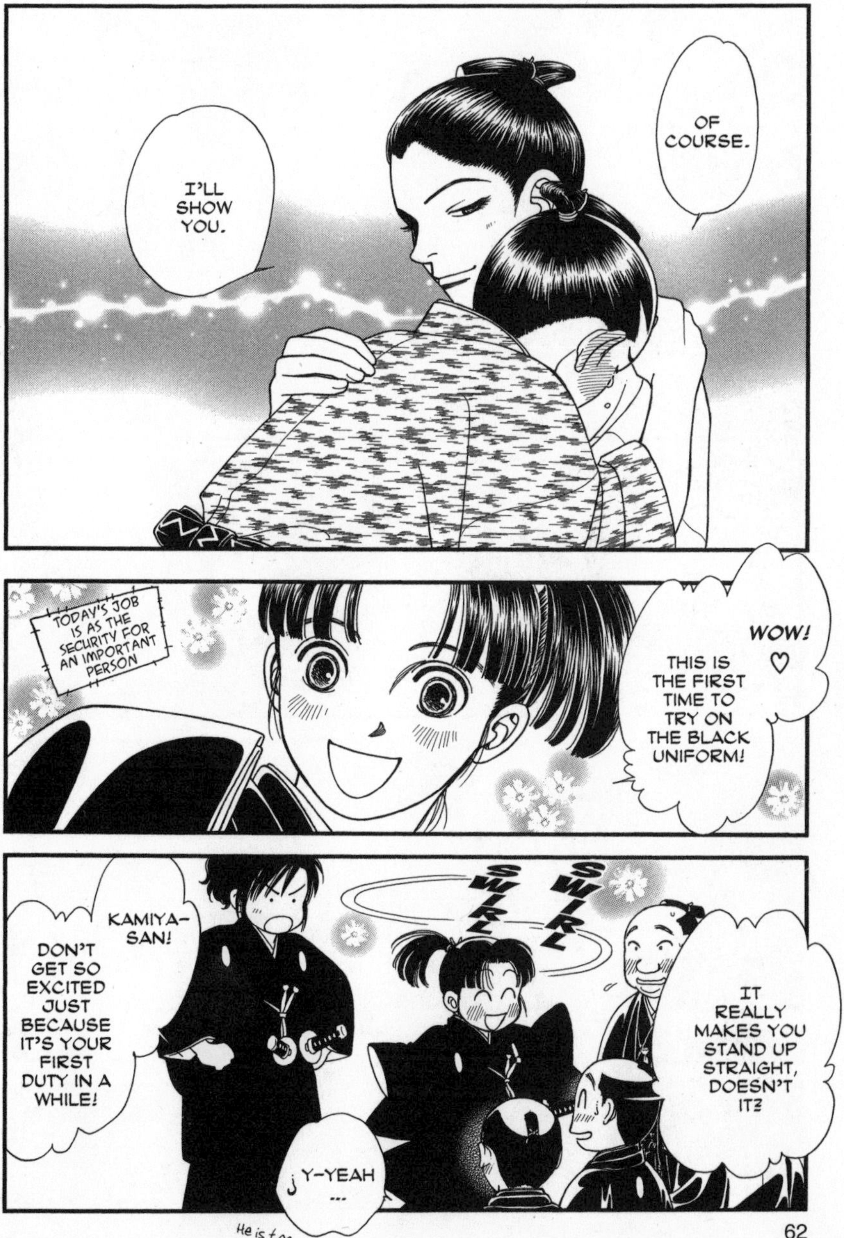
OF COURSE.
I'LL SHOW YOU.
WOW! ♡
THIS IS THE FIRST TIME TO TRY ON THE BLACK UNIFORM!
TODAY'S JOB IS AS THE SECURITY FOR AN IMPORTANT PERSON
IT REALLY MAKES YOU STAND UP STRAIGHT, DOESN'T IT?
SWIRL
SWIRL
KAMIYA-SAN!
DON'T GET SO EXCITED JUST BECAUSE IT'S YOUR FIRST DUTY IN A WHILE!
Y-YEAH ...

He is too cute...

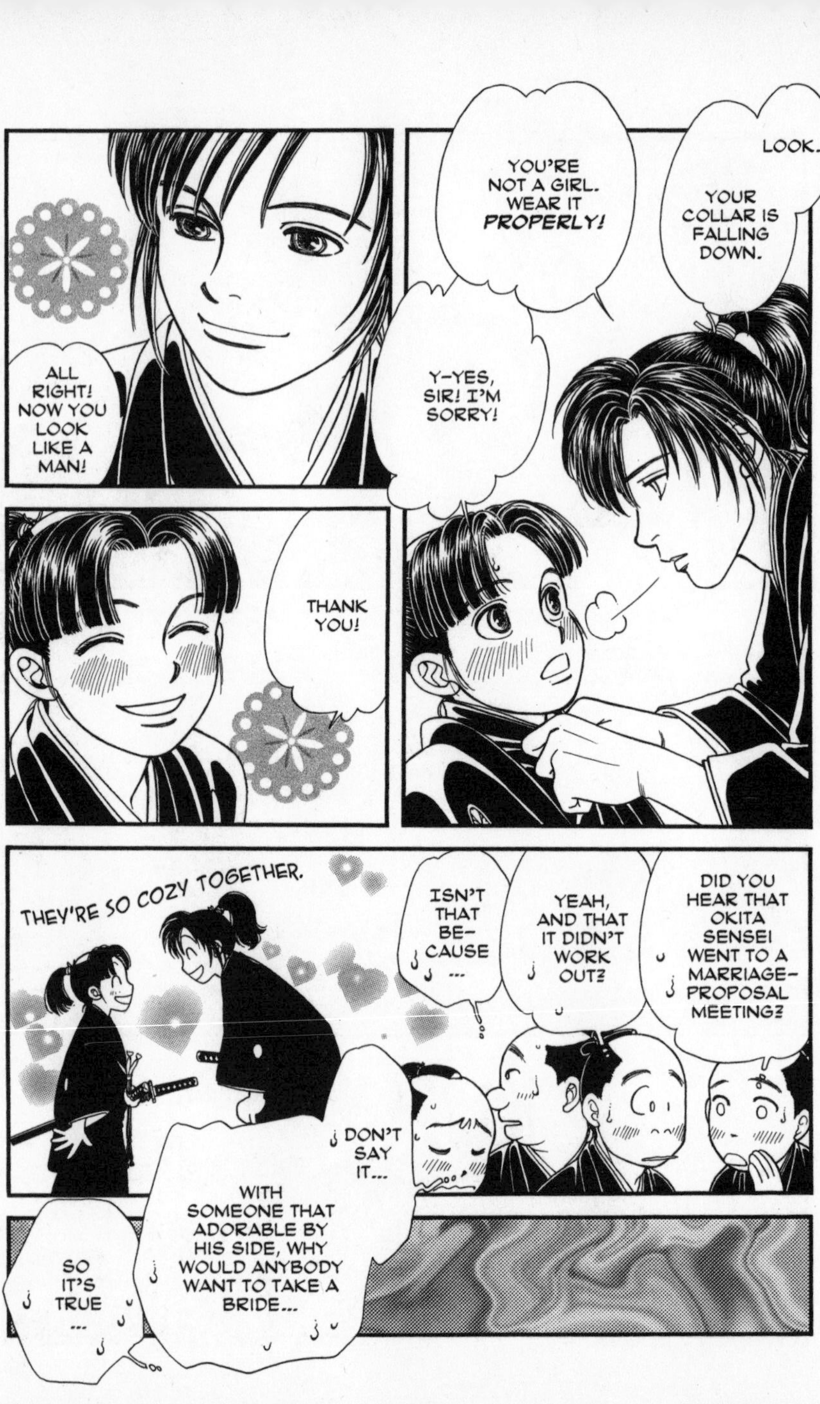
LOOK.
YOUR COLLAR IS FALLING DOWN.
YOU'RE NOT A GIRL. WEAR IT *PROPERLY!*
Y-YES, SIR! I'M SORRY!
ALL RIGHT! NOW YOU LOOK LIKE A MAN!
THANK YOU!
DID YOU HEAR THAT OKITA SENSEI WENT TO A MARRIAGE-PROPOSAL MEETING?
YEAH, AND THAT IT DIDN'T WORK OUT?
ISN'T THAT BE-CAUSE ...
THEY'RE SO COZY TOGETHER.
DON'T SAY IT...
WITH SOMEONE THAT ADORABLE BY HIS SIDE, WHY WOULD ANYBODY WANT TO TAKE A BRIDE...
SO IT'S TRUE ...

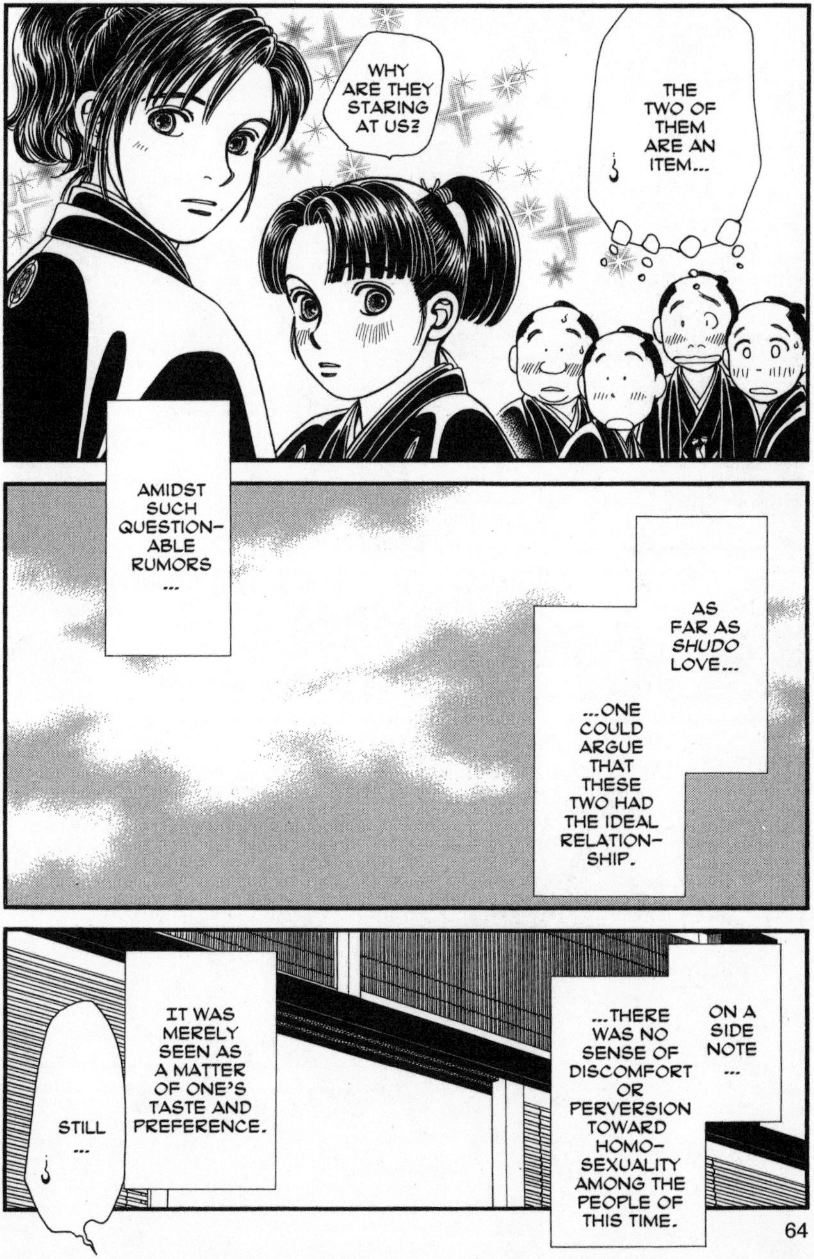
THE TWO OF THEM ARE AN ITEM...
WHY ARE THEY STARING AT US?
AMIDST SUCH QUESTIONABLE RUMORS...
AS FAR AS *SHUDO* LOVE...
...ONE COULD ARGUE THAT THESE TWO HAD THE IDEAL RELATIONSHIP.
ON A SIDE NOTE...
...THERE WAS NO SENSE OF DISCOMFORT OR PERVERSION TOWARD HOMOSEXUALITY AMONG THE PEOPLE OF THIS TIME.
IT WAS MERELY SEEN AS A MATTER OF ONE'S TASTE AND PREFERENCE.
STILL...

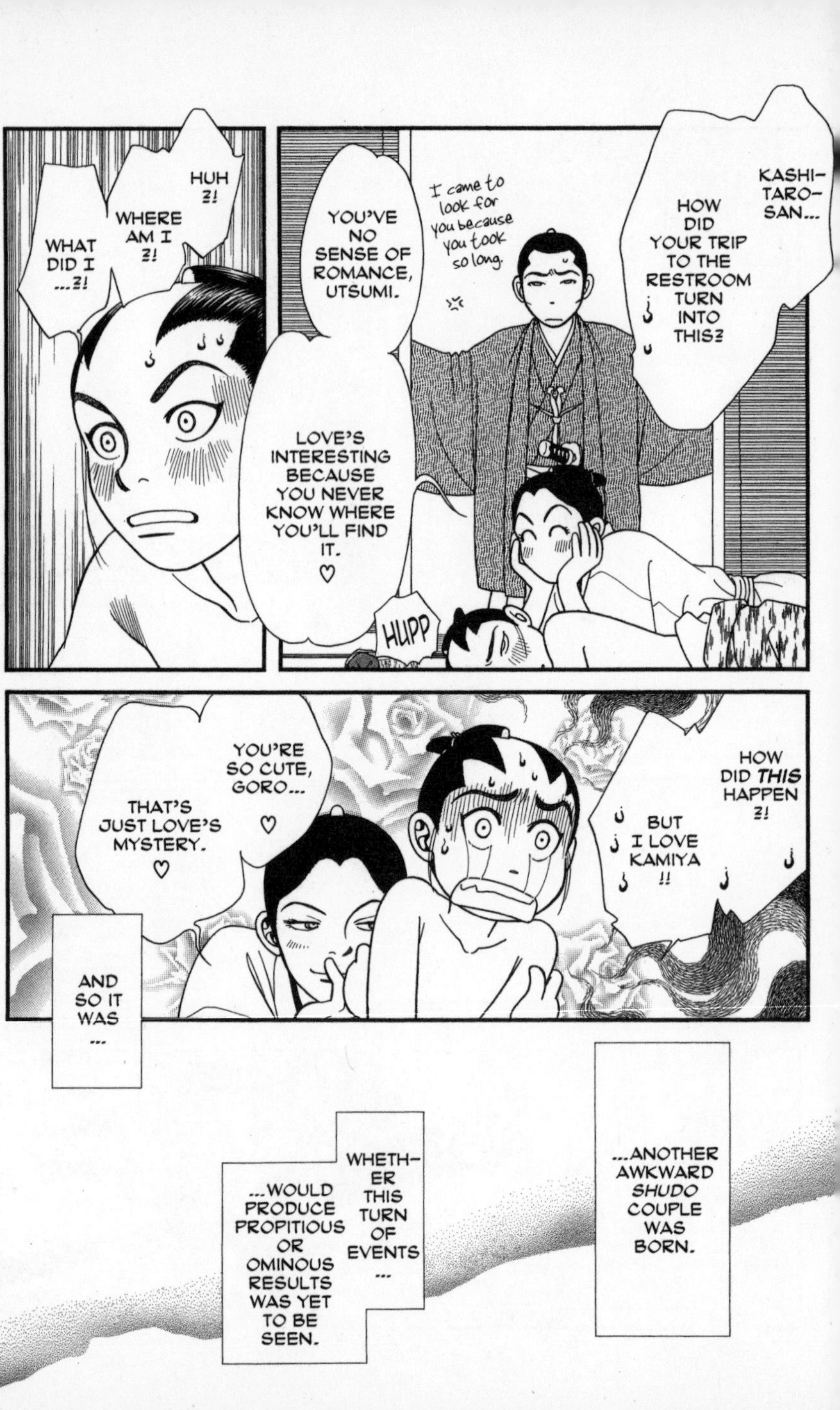
KASHI-TARO-SAN...
HOW DID YOUR TRIP TO THE RESTROOM TURN INTO THIS?
I came to look for you because you took so long.
YOU'VE NO SENSE OF ROMANCE, UTSUMI.
LOVE'S INTERESTING BECAUSE YOU NEVER KNOW WHERE YOU'LL FIND IT. ♡
HUPP
HUH ?!
WHERE AM I ?!
WHAT DID I ...?!
HOW DID THIS HAPPEN ?!
BUT I LOVE KAMIYA !!
YOU'RE SO CUTE, GORO... ♡
THAT'S JUST LOVE'S MYSTERY. ♡
AND SO IT WAS ...
...ANOTHER AWKWARD SHUDO COUPLE WAS BORN.
WHETH-ER THIS TURN OF EVENTS ...
...WOULD PRODUCE PROPITIOUS OR OMINOUS RESULTS WAS YET TO BE SEEN.

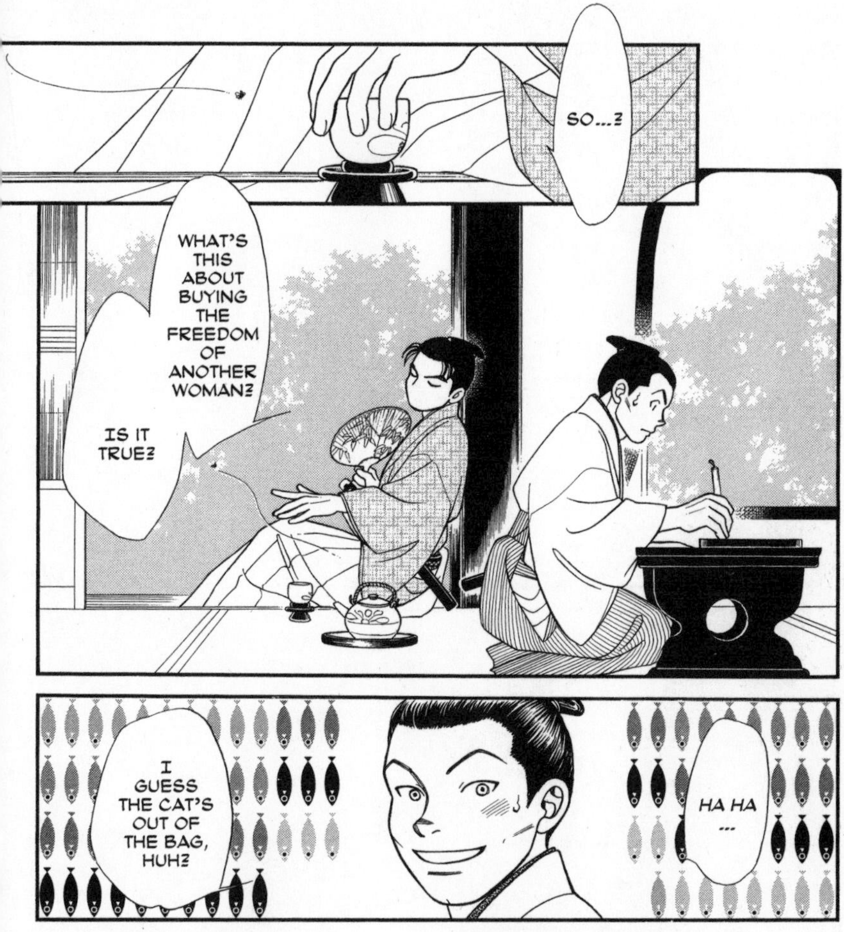
SO...?
WHAT'S THIS ABOUT BUYING THE FREEDOM OF ANOTHER WOMAN?
IS IT TRUE?
HA HA ...
I GUESS THE CAT'S OUT OF THE BAG, HUH?

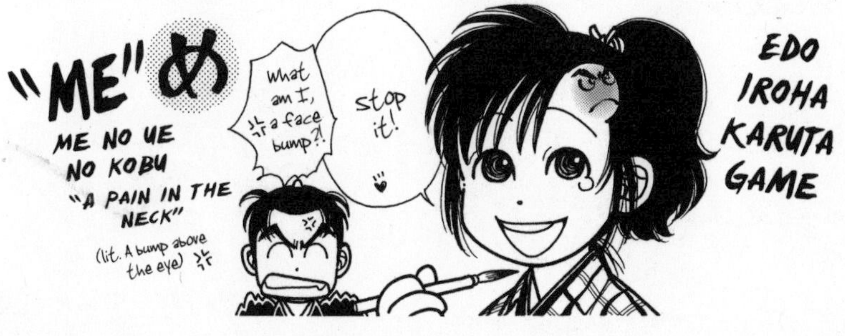
EDO IROHA KARUTA GAME
stop it!
What am I, a face bump?!
"ME" め
ME NO UE NO KOBU
"A PAIN IN THE NECK"
(lit. A bump above the eye)

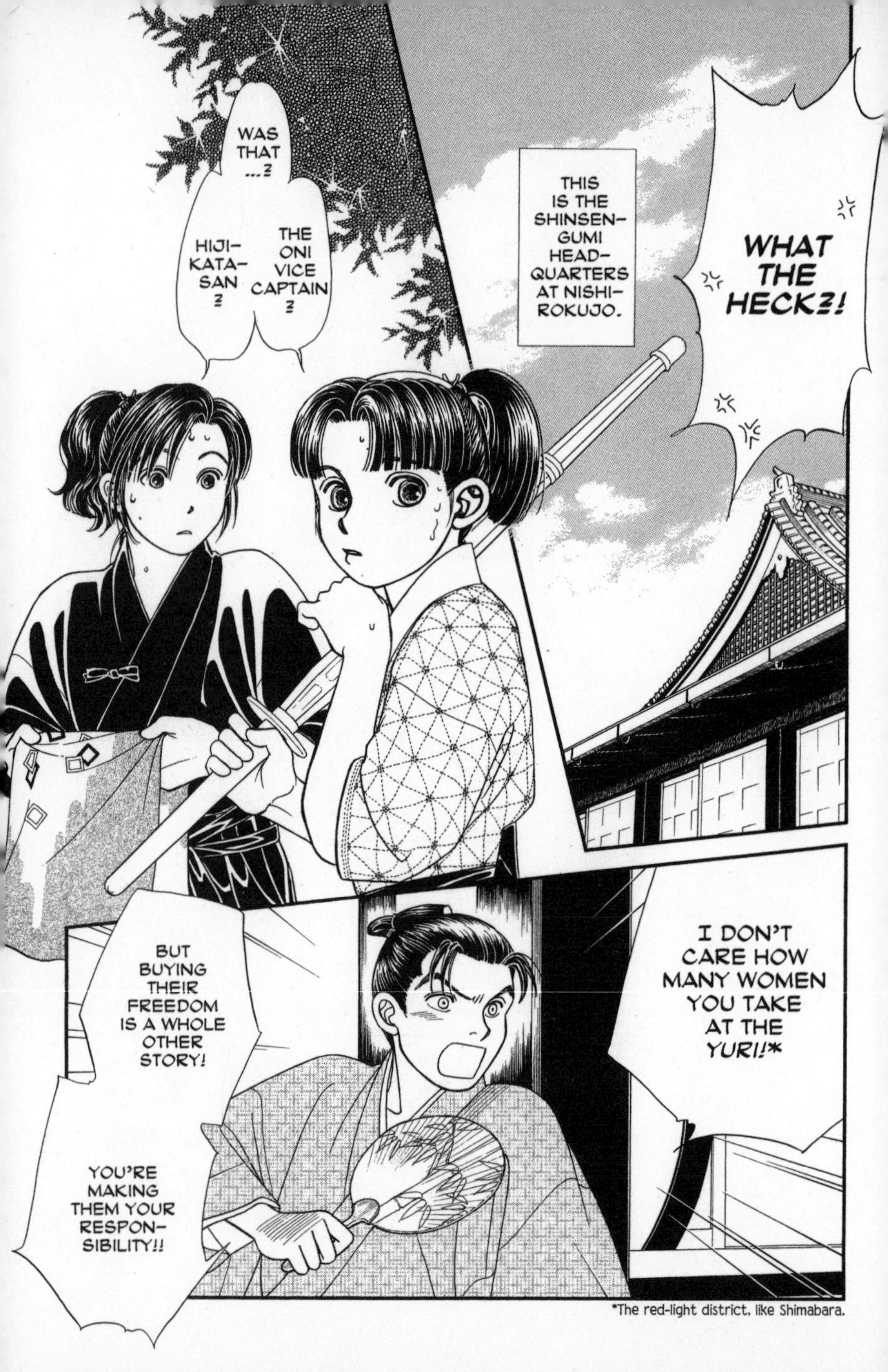
WHAT THE HECK?!
THIS IS THE SHINSEN-GUMI HEAD-QUARTERS AT NISHI-ROKUJO.
WAS THAT ...?
THE ONI VICE CAPTAIN?
HIJI-KATA-SAN?
I DON'T CARE HOW MANY WOMEN YOU TAKE AT THE *YURI!**
BUT BUYING THEIR FREEDOM IS A WHOLE OTHER STORY!
YOU'RE MAKING THEM YOUR RESPON-SIBILITY!!

*The red-light district, like Shimabara.

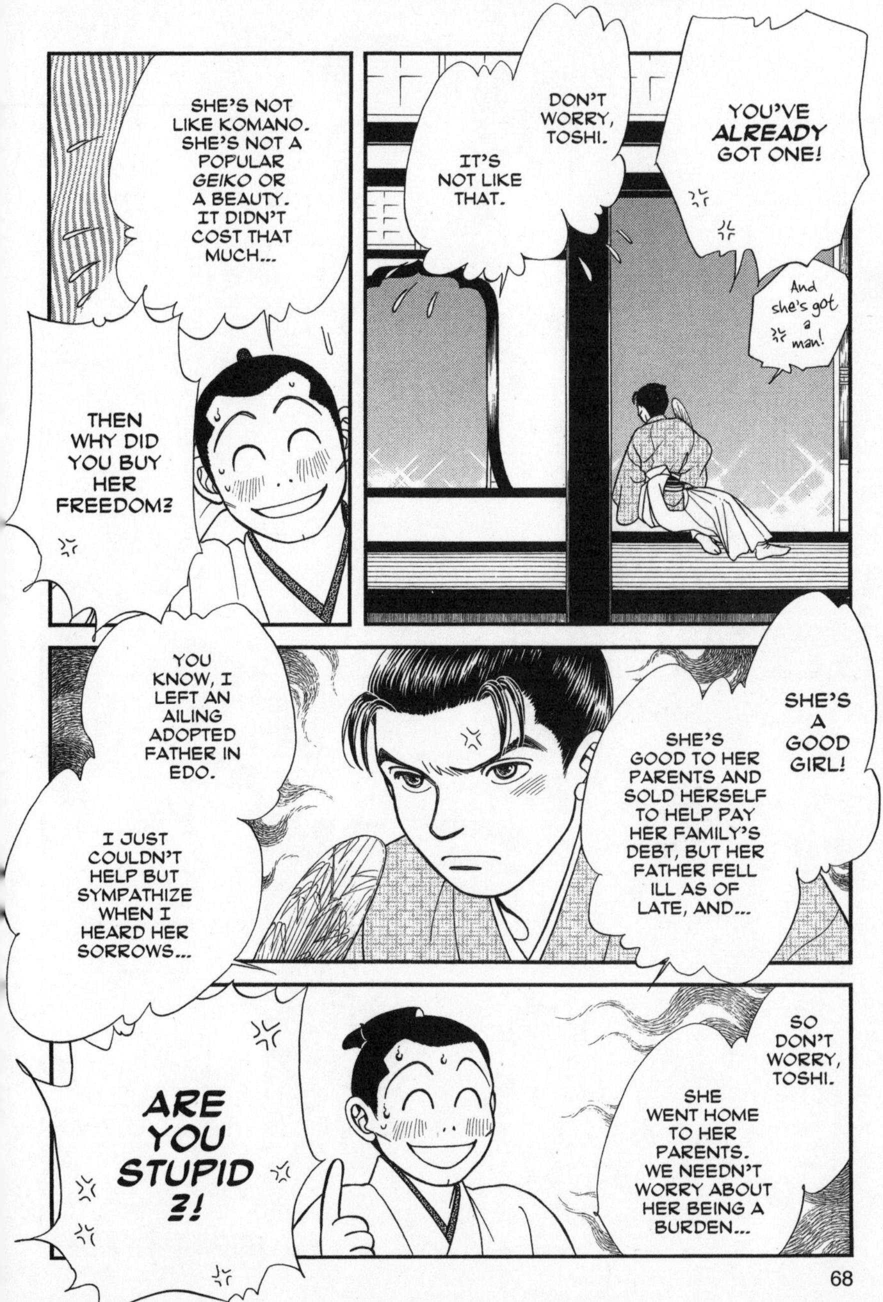
YOU'VE ALREADY GOT ONE!
And she's got a man!
DON'T WORRY, TOSHI.
IT'S NOT LIKE THAT.
SHE'S NOT LIKE KOMANO. SHE'S NOT A POPULAR GEIKO OR A BEAUTY. IT DIDN'T COST THAT MUCH...
THEN WHY DID YOU BUY HER FREEDOM?
SHE'S A GOOD GIRL!
SHE'S GOOD TO HER PARENTS AND SOLD HERSELF TO HELP PAY HER FAMILY'S DEBT, BUT HER FATHER FELL ILL AS OF LATE, AND...
YOU KNOW, I LEFT AN AILING ADOPTED FATHER IN EDO.
I JUST COULDN'T HELP BUT SYMPATHIZE WHEN I HEARD HER SORROWS...
SO DON'T WORRY, TOSHI.
SHE WENT HOME TO HER PARENTS. WE NEEDN'T WORRY ABOUT HER BEING A BURDEN...
ARE YOU STUPID?!

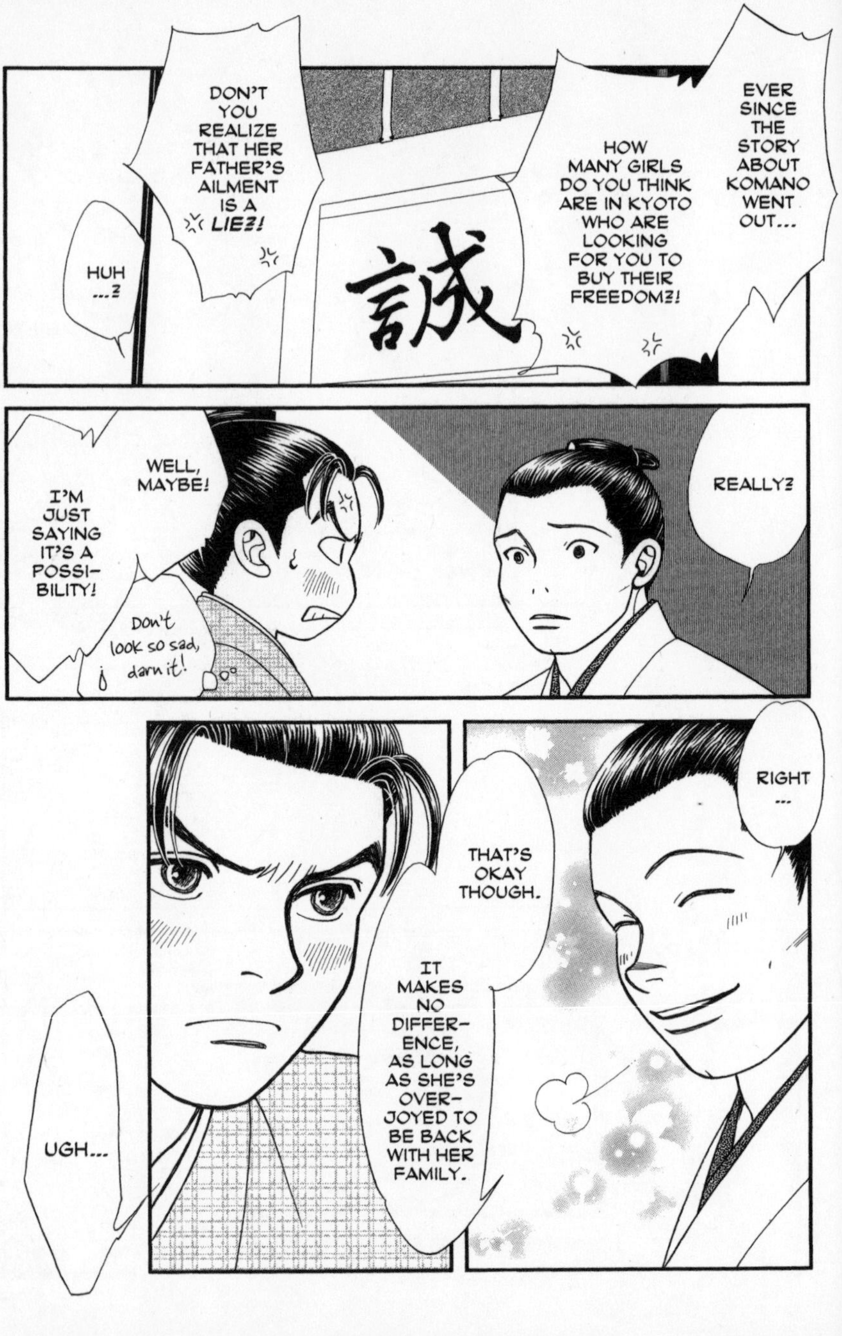
EVER SINCE THE STORY ABOUT KOMANO WENT OUT...
HOW MANY GIRLS DO YOU THINK ARE IN KYOTO WHO ARE LOOKING FOR YOU TO BUY THEIR FREEDOM?!
誠
DON'T YOU REALIZE THAT HER FATHER'S AILMENT IS A LIE?!
HUH...?
REALLY?
WELL, MAYBE!
I'M JUST SAYING IT'S A POSSIBILITY!
Don't look so sad, darn it!
RIGHT...
THAT'S OKAY THOUGH.
IT MAKES NO DIFFERENCE, AS LONG AS SHE'S OVERJOYED TO BE BACK WITH HER FAMILY.
UGH...

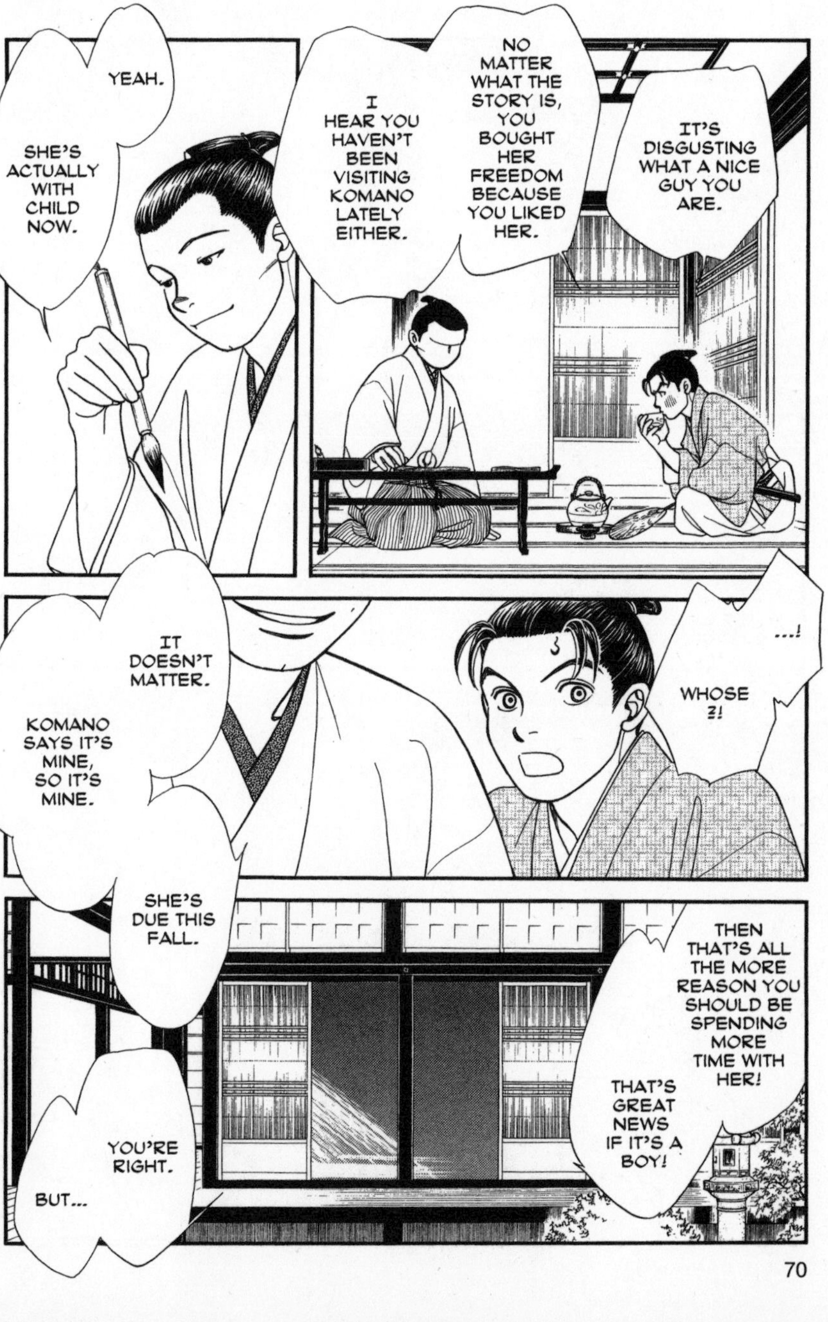
IT'S DISGUSTING WHAT A NICE GUY YOU ARE.
NO MATTER WHAT THE STORY IS, YOU BOUGHT HER FREEDOM BECAUSE YOU LIKED HER.
I HEAR YOU HAVEN'T BEEN VISITING KOMANO LATELY EITHER.
YEAH.
SHE'S ACTUALLY WITH CHILD NOW.
...!
WHOSE ?!
IT DOESN'T MATTER.
KOMANO SAYS IT'S MINE, SO IT'S MINE.
SHE'S DUE THIS FALL.
THAT'S GREAT NEWS IF IT'S A BOY!
THEN THAT'S ALL THE MORE REASON YOU SHOULD BE SPENDING MORE TIME WITH HER!
YOU'RE RIGHT.
BUT...

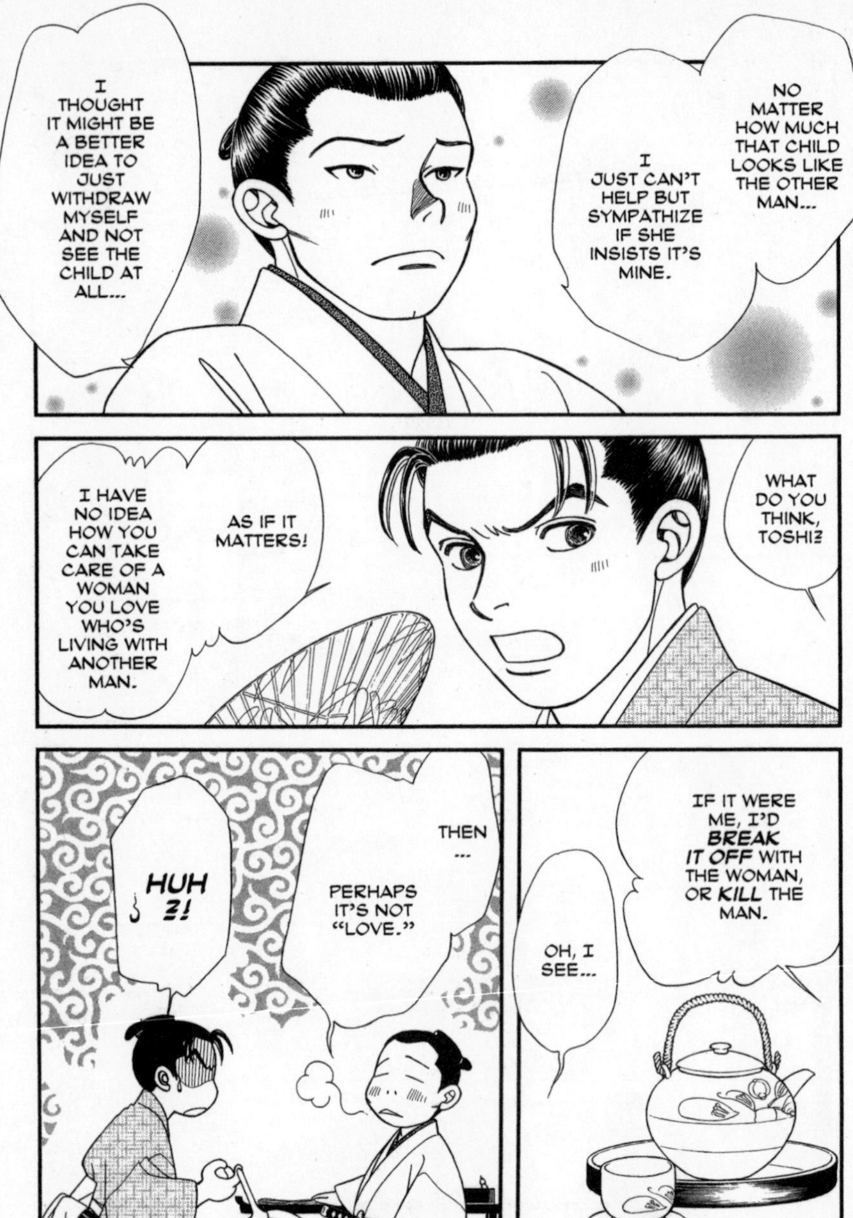
NO MATTER HOW MUCH THAT CHILD LOOKS LIKE THE OTHER MAN...
I JUST CAN'T HELP BUT SYMPATHIZE IF SHE INSISTS IT'S MINE.
I THOUGHT IT MIGHT BE A BETTER IDEA TO JUST WITHDRAW MYSELF AND NOT SEE THE CHILD AT ALL...
WHAT DO YOU THINK, TOSHI?
AS IF IT MATTERS!
I HAVE NO IDEA HOW YOU CAN TAKE CARE OF A WOMAN YOU LOVE WHO'S LIVING WITH ANOTHER MAN.
IF IT WERE ME, I'D *BREAK IT OFF* WITH THE WOMAN, OR *KILL* THE MAN.
OH, I SEE...
THEN ...
PERHAPS IT'S NOT "LOVE."
HUH ?!

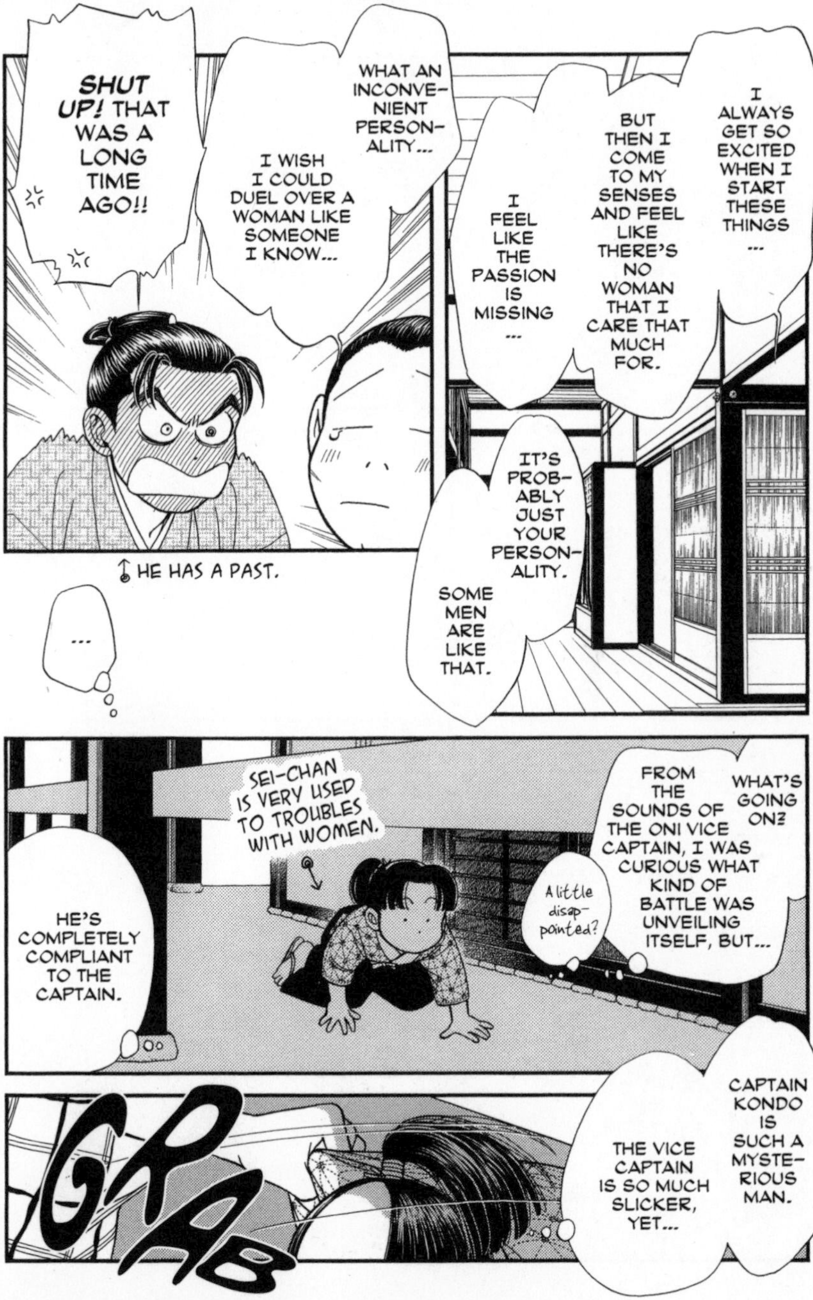
I ALWAYS GET SO EXCITED WHEN I START THESE THINGS...
BUT THEN I COME TO MY SENSES AND FEEL LIKE THERE'S NO WOMAN THAT I CARE THAT MUCH FOR.
I FEEL LIKE THE PASSION IS MISSING...
IT'S PROBABLY JUST YOUR PERSONALITY.
SOME MEN ARE LIKE THAT.
WHAT AN INCONVENIENT PERSONALITY...
I WISH I COULD DUEL OVER A WOMAN LIKE SOMEONE I KNOW...
SHUT UP! THAT WAS A LONG TIME AGO!!
HE HAS A PAST.
...
WHAT'S GOING ON?
FROM THE SOUNDS OF THE ONI VICE CAPTAIN, I WAS CURIOUS WHAT KIND OF BATTLE WAS UNVEILING ITSELF, BUT...
A little disap-pointed?
SEI-CHAN IS VERY USED TO TROUBLES WITH WOMEN.
HE'S COMPLETELY COMPLIANT TO THE CAPTAIN.
CAPTAIN KONDO IS SUCH A MYSTERIOUS MAN.
THE VICE CAPTAIN IS SO MUCH SLICKER, YET...
GRAB

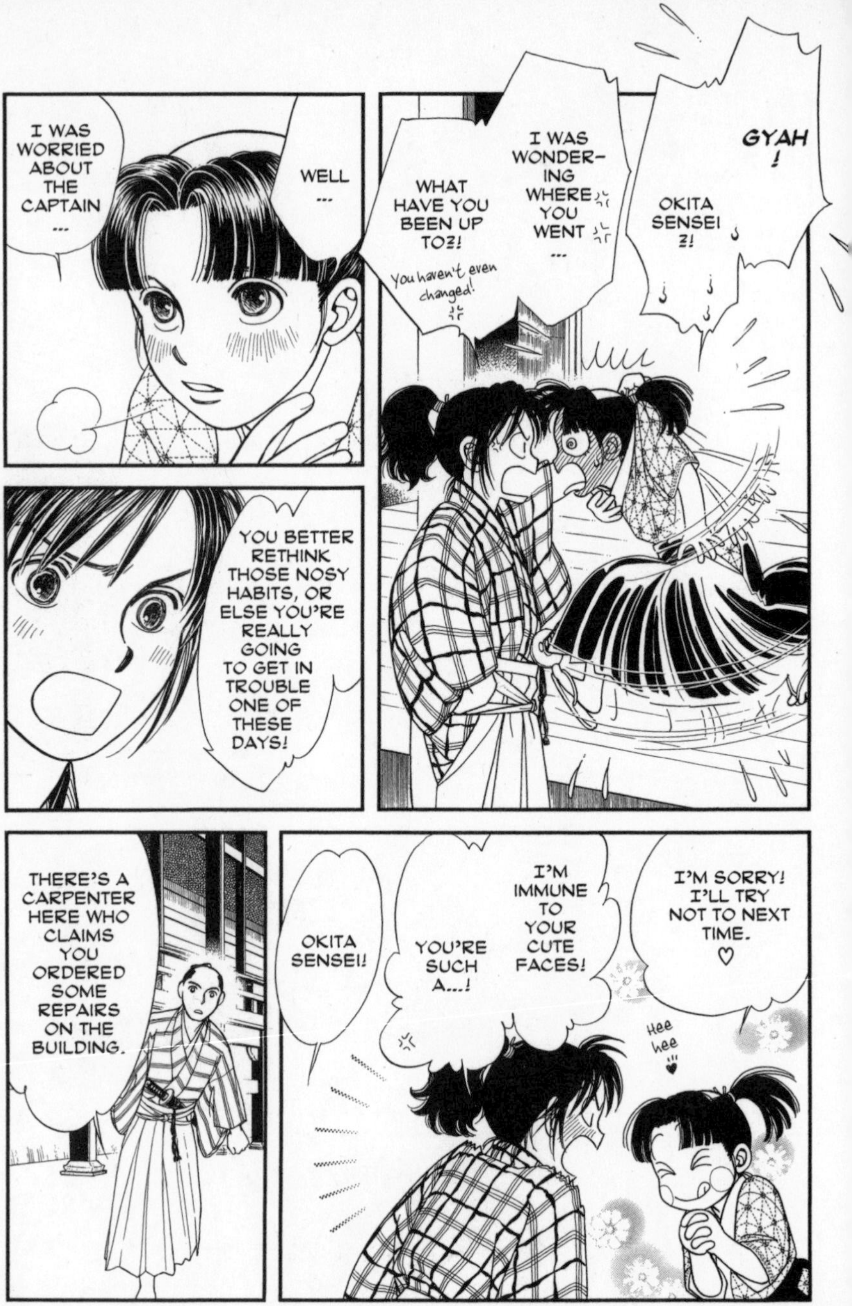
GYAH!
OKITA SENSEI?!
I WAS WONDERING WHERE YOU WENT...
WHAT HAVE YOU BEEN UP TO?!
You haven't even changed!
WELL...
I WAS WORRIED ABOUT THE CAPTAIN...
YOU BETTER RETHINK THOSE NOSY HABITS, OR ELSE YOU'RE REALLY GOING TO GET IN TROUBLE ONE OF THESE DAYS!
I'M SORRY! I'LL TRY NOT TO NEXT TIME. ♡
Hee hee
I'M IMMUNE TO YOUR CUTE FACES!
YOU'RE SUCH A...!
OKITA SENSEI!
THERE'S A CARPENTER HERE WHO CLAIMS YOU ORDERED SOME REPAIRS ON THE BUILDING.

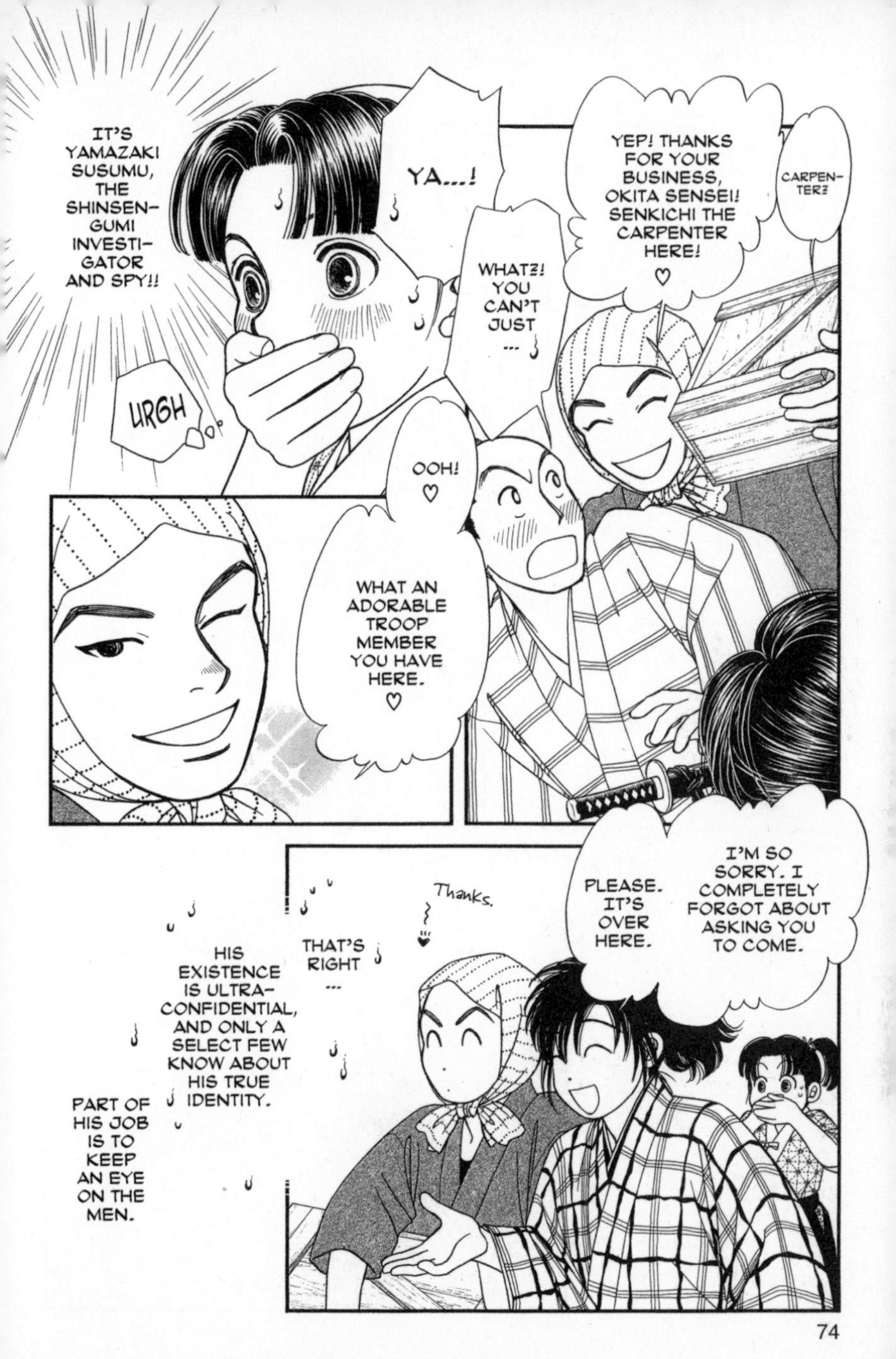

YEP! THANKS FOR YOUR BUSINESS, OKITA SENSEI! SENKICHI THE CARPENTER HERE! ♡
CARPENTER?
YA...!
WHAT?! YOU CAN'T JUST ---
IT'S YAMAZAKI SUSUMU, THE SHINSEN-GUMI INVESTI-GATOR AND SPY!!
URGH
OOH! ♡
WHAT AN ADORABLE TROOP MEMBER YOU HAVE HERE. ♡
I'M SO SORRY. I COMPLETELY FORGOT ABOUT ASKING YOU TO COME.
PLEASE. IT'S OVER HERE.
Thanks.
THAT'S RIGHT ---
HIS EXISTENCE IS ULTRA-CONFIDENTIAL, AND ONLY A SELECT FEW KNOW ABOUT HIS TRUE IDENTITY.
PART OF HIS JOB IS TO KEEP AN EYE ON THE MEN.

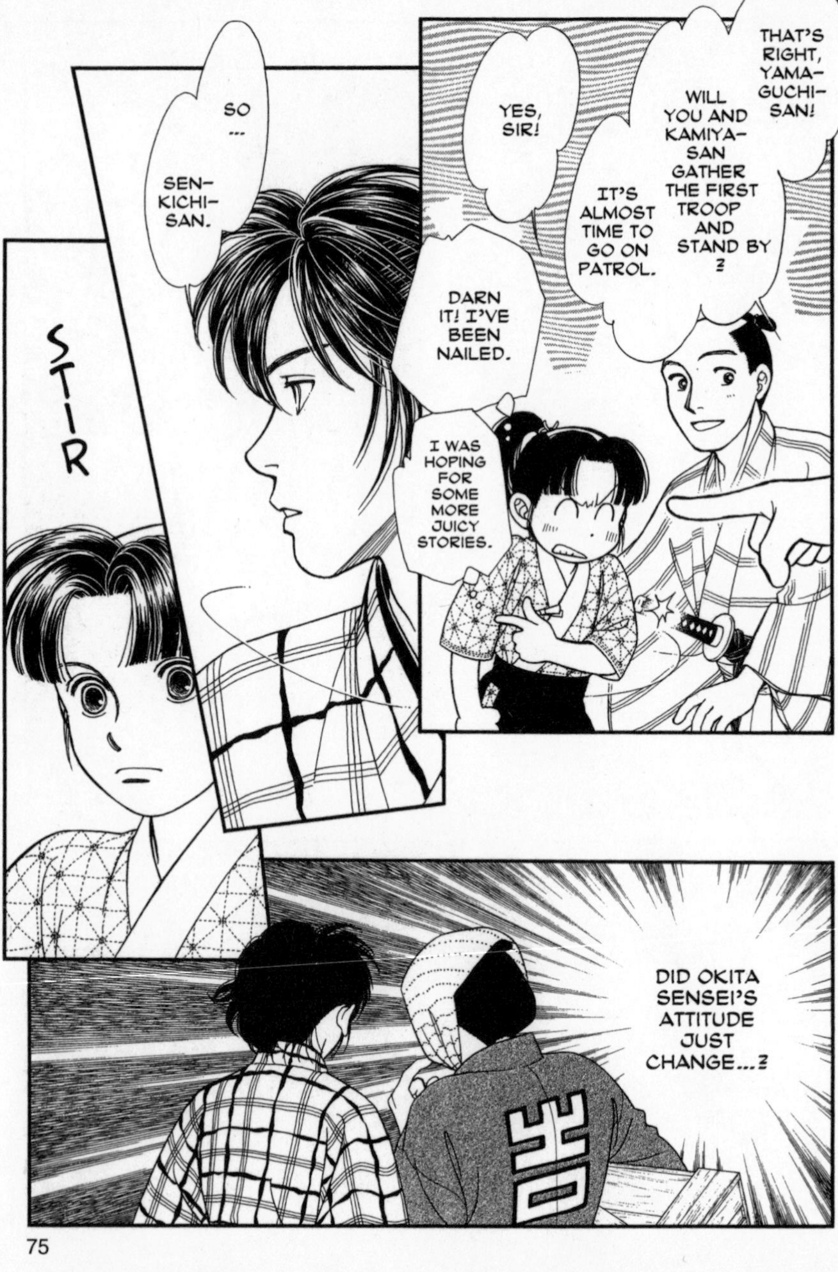
THAT'S RIGHT, YAMAGUCHI-SAN!
WILL YOU AND KAMIYA-SAN GATHER THE FIRST TROOP AND STAND BY?
IT'S ALMOST TIME TO GO ON PATROL.
YES, SIR!
DARN IT! I'VE BEEN NAILED.
I WAS HOPING FOR SOME MORE JUICY STORIES.
SO ... SEN-KICHI-SAN.
STIR
DID OKITA SENSEI'S ATTITUDE JUST CHANGE...?

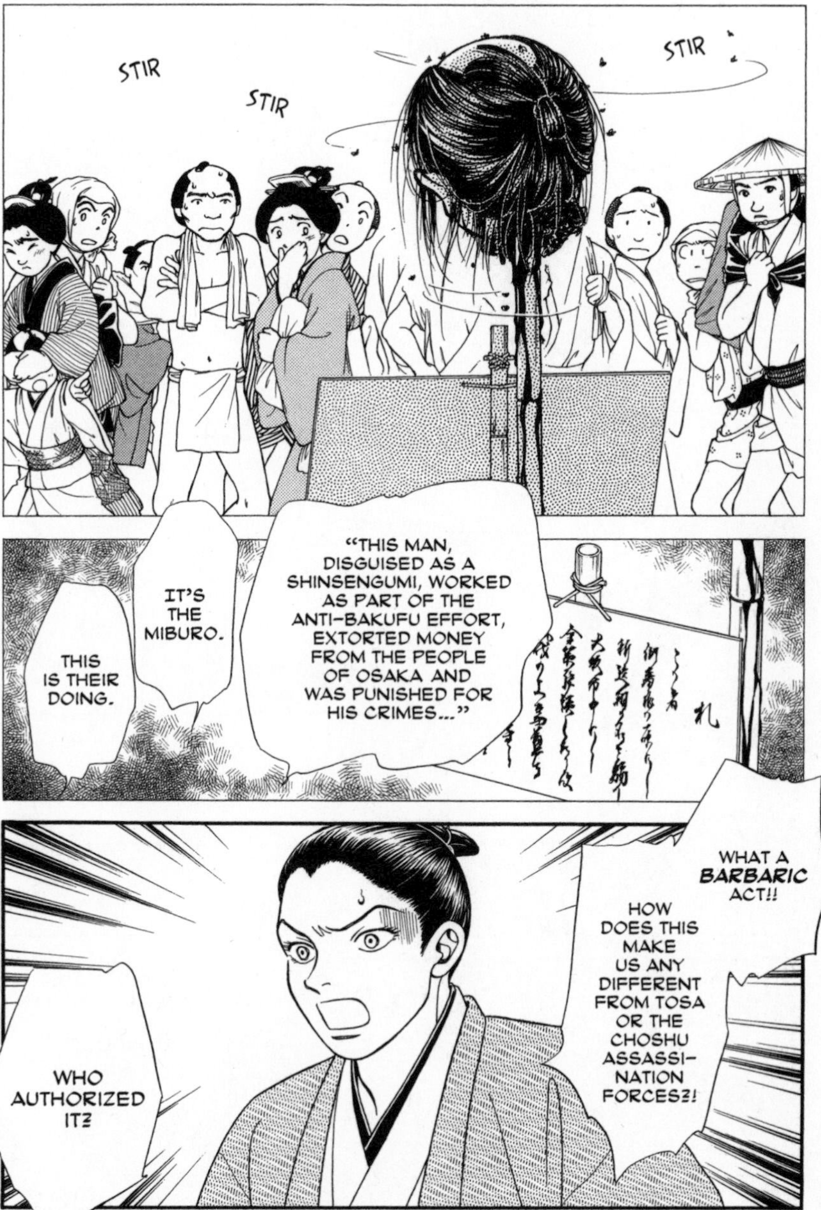
STIR
STIR
STIR
"THIS MAN, DISGUISED AS A SHINSENGUMI, WORKED AS PART OF THE ANTI-BAKUFU EFFORT, EXTORTED MONEY FROM THE PEOPLE OF OSAKA AND WAS PUNISHED FOR HIS CRIMES..."
IT'S THE MIBURO.
THIS IS THEIR DOING.
WHAT A **BARBARIC** ACT!!
HOW DOES THIS MAKE US ANY DIFFERENT FROM TOSA OR THE CHOSHU ASSASSI-NATION FORCES?!
WHO AUTHORIZED IT?

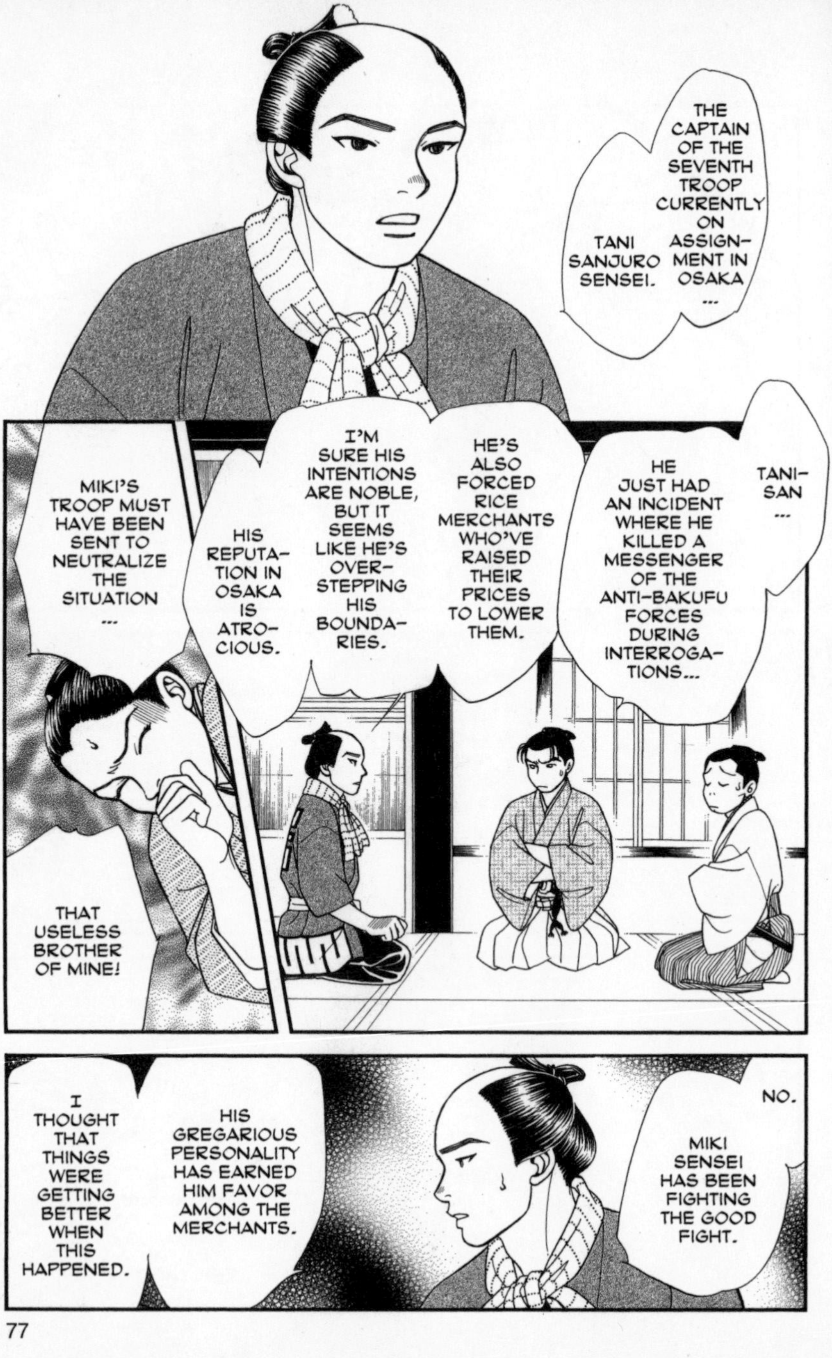
THE CAPTAIN OF THE SEVENTH TROOP CURRENTLY ON ASSIGNMENT IN OSAKA ...
TANI SANJURO SENSEI.
TANI-SAN ...
HE JUST HAD AN INCIDENT WHERE HE KILLED A MESSENGER OF THE ANTI-BAKUFU FORCES DURING INTERROGA-TIONS...
HE'S ALSO FORCED RICE MERCHANTS WHO'VE RAISED THEIR PRICES TO LOWER THEM.
I'M SURE HIS INTENTIONS ARE NOBLE, BUT IT SEEMS LIKE HE'S OVER-STEPPING HIS BOUNDA-RIES.
HIS REPUTA-TION IN OSAKA IS ATRO-CIOUS.
MIKI'S TROOP MUST HAVE BEEN SENT TO NEUTRALIZE THE SITUATION ...
THAT USELESS BROTHER OF MINE!
NO.
MIKI SENSEI HAS BEEN FIGHTING THE GOOD FIGHT.
HIS GREGARIOUS PERSONALITY HAS EARNED HIM FAVOR AMONG THE MERCHANTS.
I THOUGHT THAT THINGS WERE GETTING BETTER WHEN THIS HAPPENED.

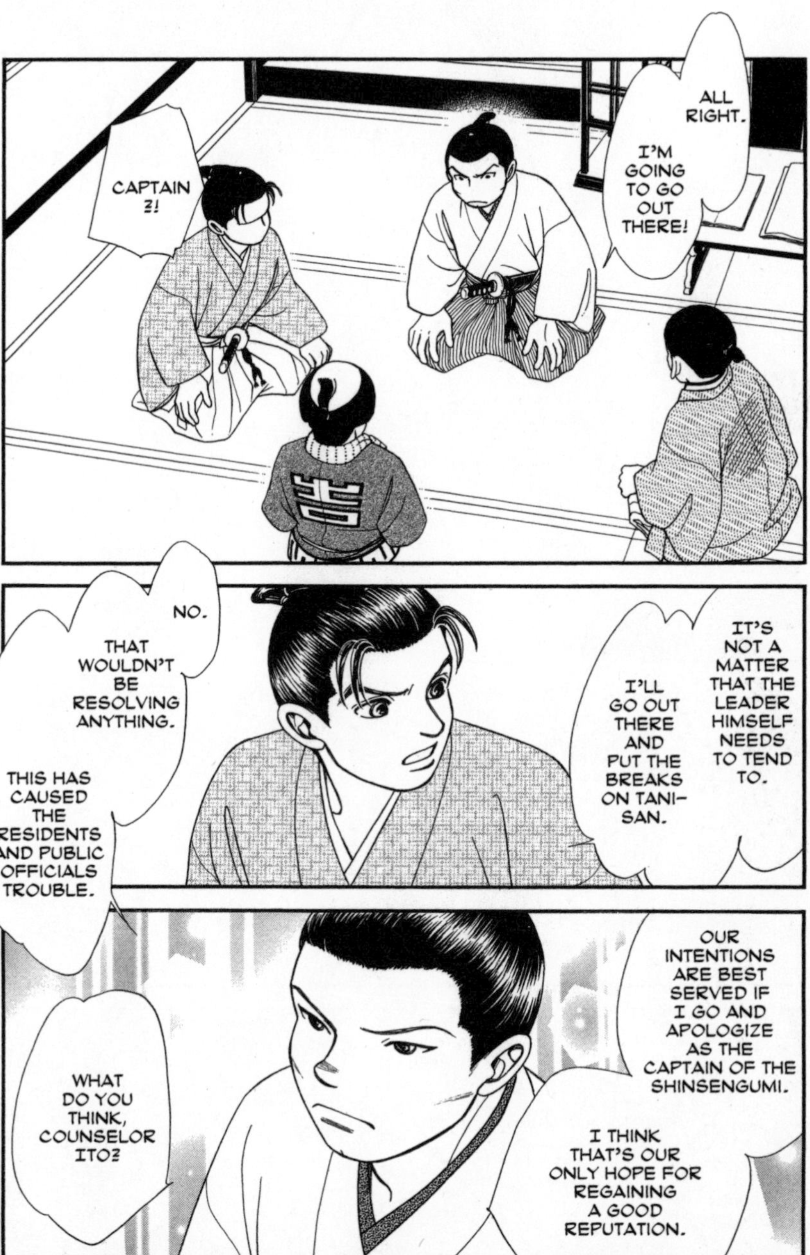
ALL RIGHT.
I'M GOING TO GO OUT THERE!
CAPTAIN?!
IT'S NOT A MATTER THAT THE LEADER HIMSELF NEEDS TO TEND TO.
I'LL GO OUT THERE AND PUT THE BREAKS ON TANI-SAN.
NO.
THAT WOULDN'T BE RESOLVING ANYTHING.
THIS HAS CAUSED THE RESIDENTS AND PUBLIC OFFICIALS TROUBLE.
OUR INTENTIONS ARE BEST SERVED IF I GO AND APOLOGIZE AS THE CAPTAIN OF THE SHINSENGUMI.
I THINK THAT'S OUR ONLY HOPE FOR REGAINING A GOOD REPUTATION.
WHAT DO YOU THINK, COUNSELOR ITO?

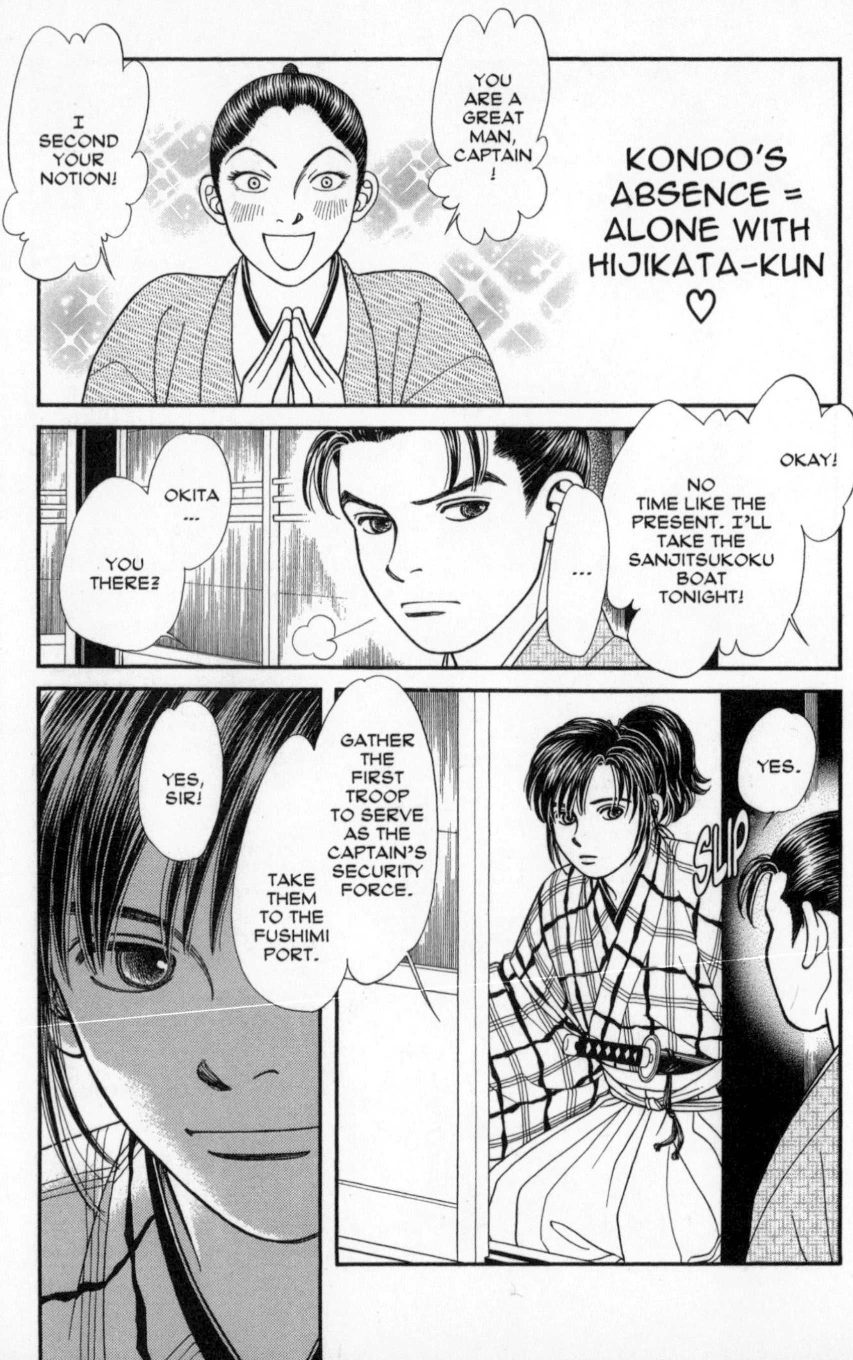
KONDO'S ABSENCE = ALONE WITH HIJIKATA-KUN ♡
YOU ARE A GREAT MAN, CAPTAIN!
I SECOND YOUR NOTION!
OKAY!
NO TIME LIKE THE PRESENT. I'LL TAKE THE SANJITSUKOKU BOAT TONIGHT!
...
OKITA ...
YOU THERE?
YES.
SLIP
GATHER THE FIRST TROOP TO SERVE AS THE CAPTAIN'S SECURITY FORCE.
TAKE THEM TO THE FUSHIMI PORT.
YES, SIR!

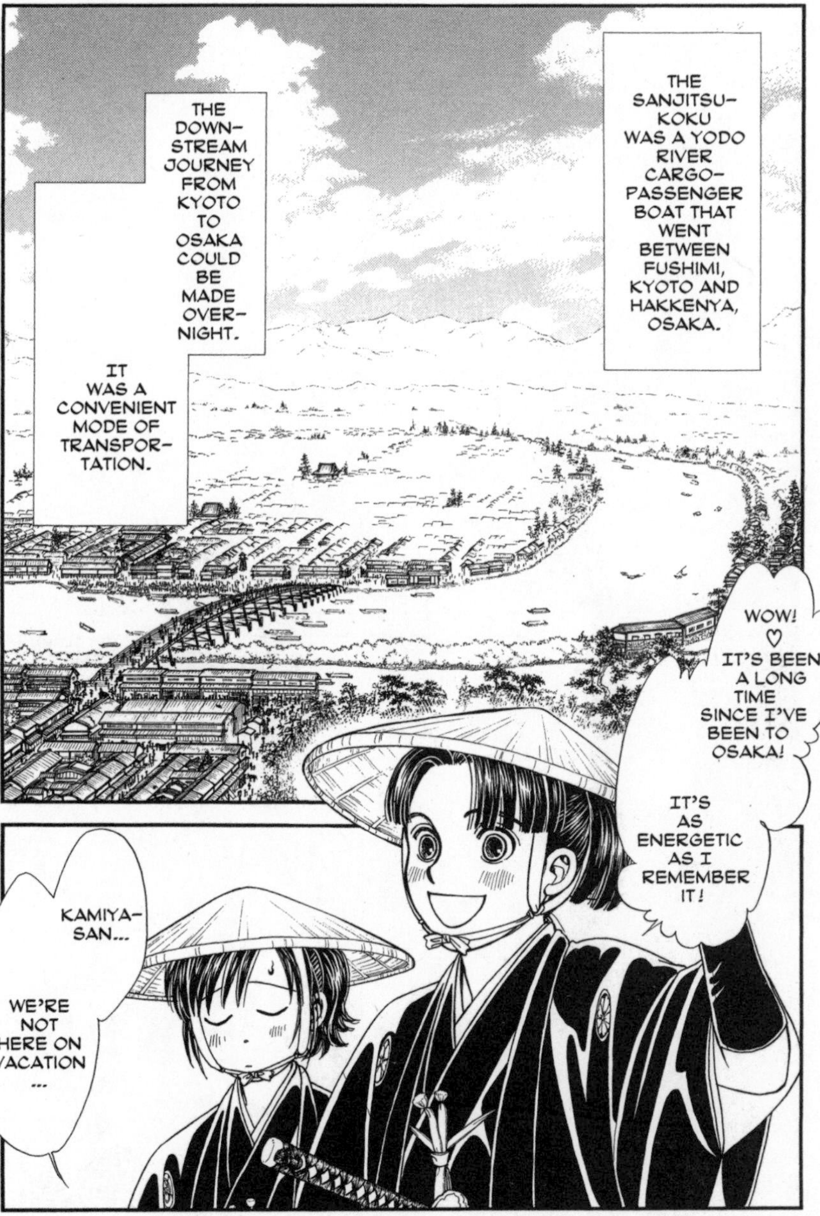
THE SANJITSU-KOKU WAS A YODO RIVER CARGO-PASSENGER BOAT THAT WENT BETWEEN FUSHIMI, KYOTO AND HAKKENYA, OSAKA.
THE DOWN-STREAM JOURNEY FROM KYOTO TO OSAKA COULD BE MADE OVER-NIGHT.
IT WAS A CONVENIENT MODE OF TRANSPOR-TATION.
WOW! ♡ IT'S BEEN A LONG TIME SINCE I'VE BEEN TO OSAKA!
IT'S AS ENERGETIC AS I REMEMBER IT!
KAMIYA-SAN...
WE'RE NOT HERE ON VACATION ...

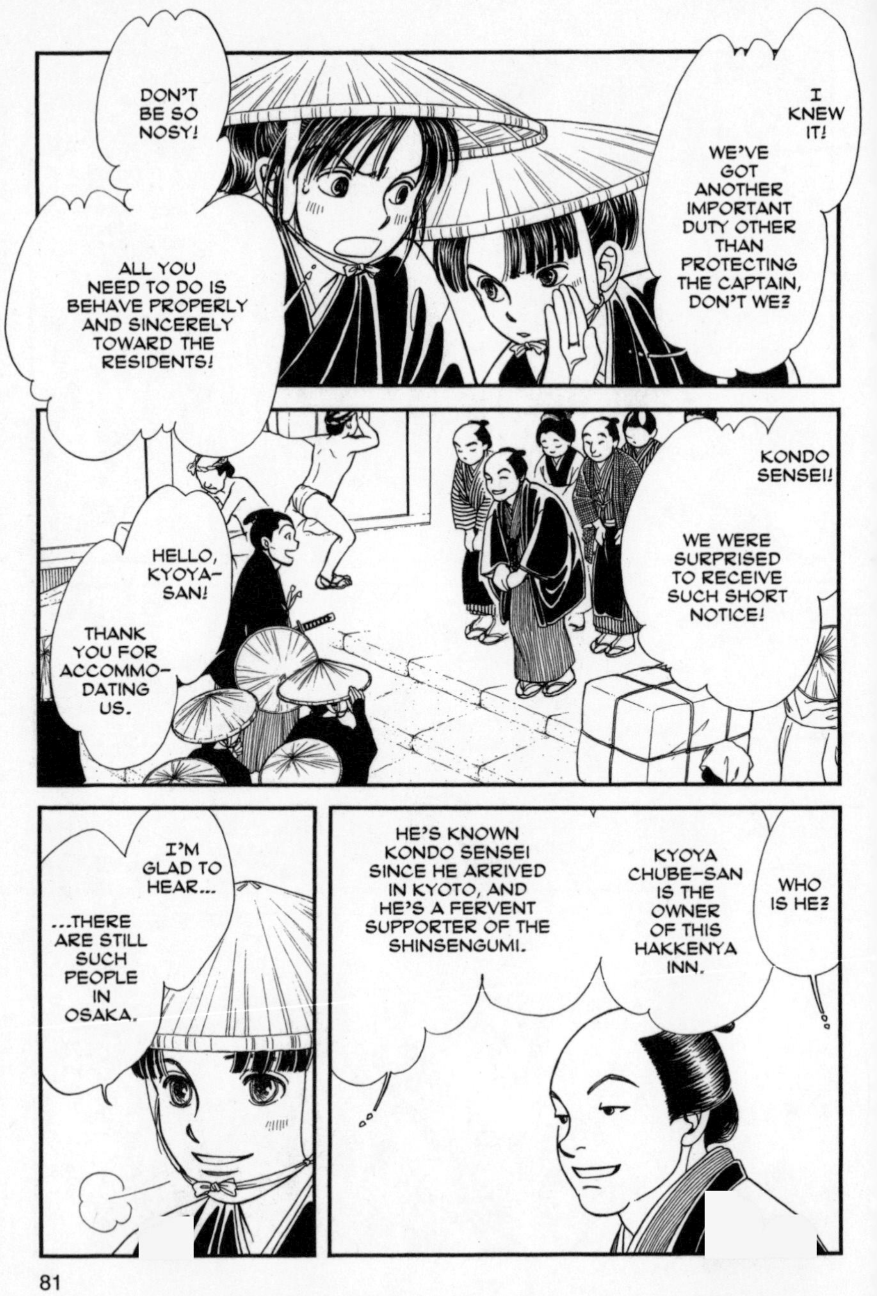
I KNEW IT!
WE'VE GOT ANOTHER IMPORTANT DUTY OTHER THAN PROTECTING THE CAPTAIN, DON'T WE?
DON'T BE SO NOSY!
ALL YOU NEED TO DO IS BEHAVE PROPERLY AND SINCERELY TOWARD THE RESIDENTS!
KONDO SENSEI!
WE WERE SURPRISED TO RECEIVE SUCH SHORT NOTICE!
HELLO, KYOYA-SAN!
THANK YOU FOR ACCOMMODATING US.
WHO IS HE?
KYOYA CHUBE-SAN IS THE OWNER OF THIS HAKKENYA INN.
HE'S KNOWN KONDO SENSEI SINCE HE ARRIVED IN KYOTO, AND HE'S A FERVENT SUPPORTER OF THE SHINSENGUMI.
I'M GLAD TO HEAR...
...THERE ARE STILL SUCH PEOPLE IN OSAKA.

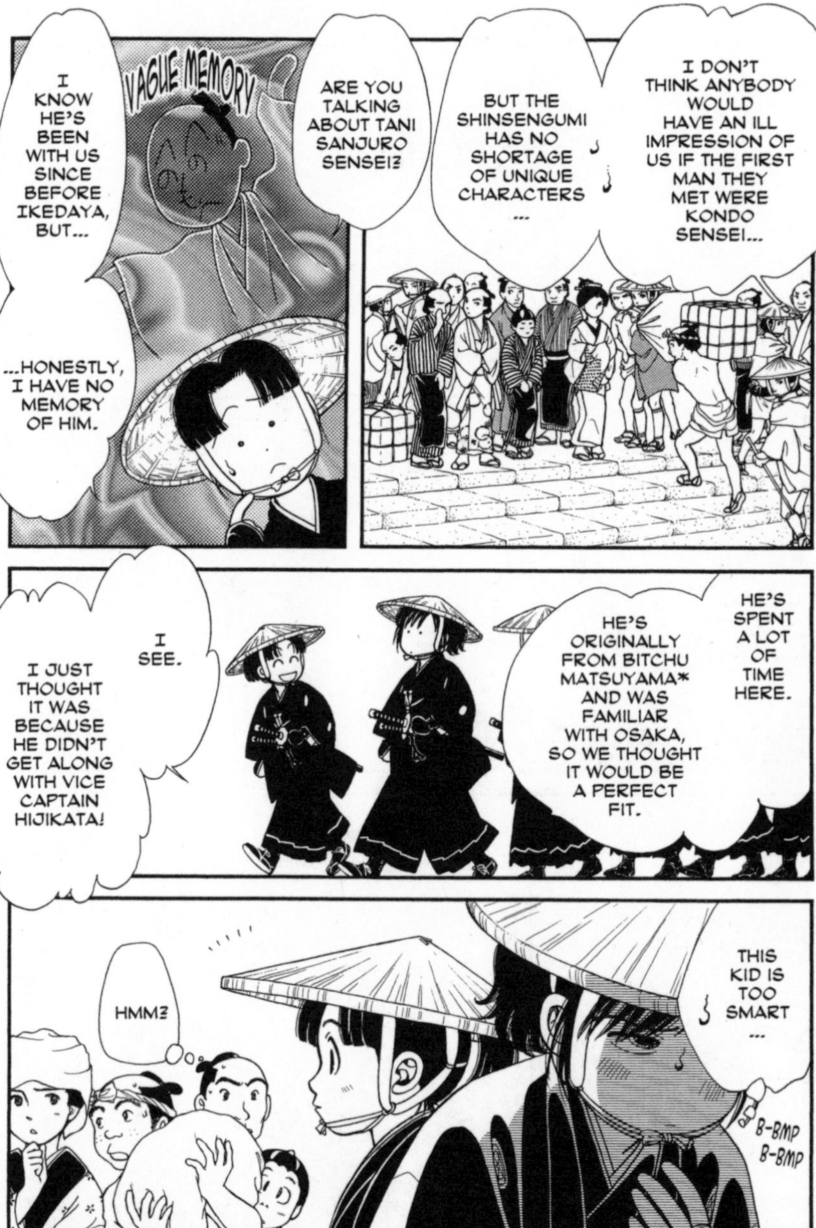
I DON'T THINK ANYBODY WOULD HAVE AN ILL IMPRESSION OF US IF THE FIRST MAN THEY MET WERE KONDO SENSEI...
BUT THE SHINSENGUMI HAS NO SHORTAGE OF UNIQUE CHARACTERS ...
ARE YOU TALKING ABOUT TANI SANJURO SENSEI?
VAGUE MEMORY
I KNOW HE'S BEEN WITH US SINCE BEFORE IKEDAYA, BUT...
...HONESTLY, I HAVE NO MEMORY OF HIM.
HE'S SPENT A LOT OF TIME HERE.
HE'S ORIGINALLY FROM BITCHU MATSUYAMA* AND WAS FAMILIAR WITH OSAKA, SO WE THOUGHT IT WOULD BE A PERFECT FIT.
I SEE.
I JUST THOUGHT IT WAS BECAUSE HE DIDN'T GET ALONG WITH VICE CAPTAIN HIJIKATA!
THIS KID IS TOO SMART ...
B-BMP B-BMP
HMM?

*Present-day Takahashi in the Okayama prefecture

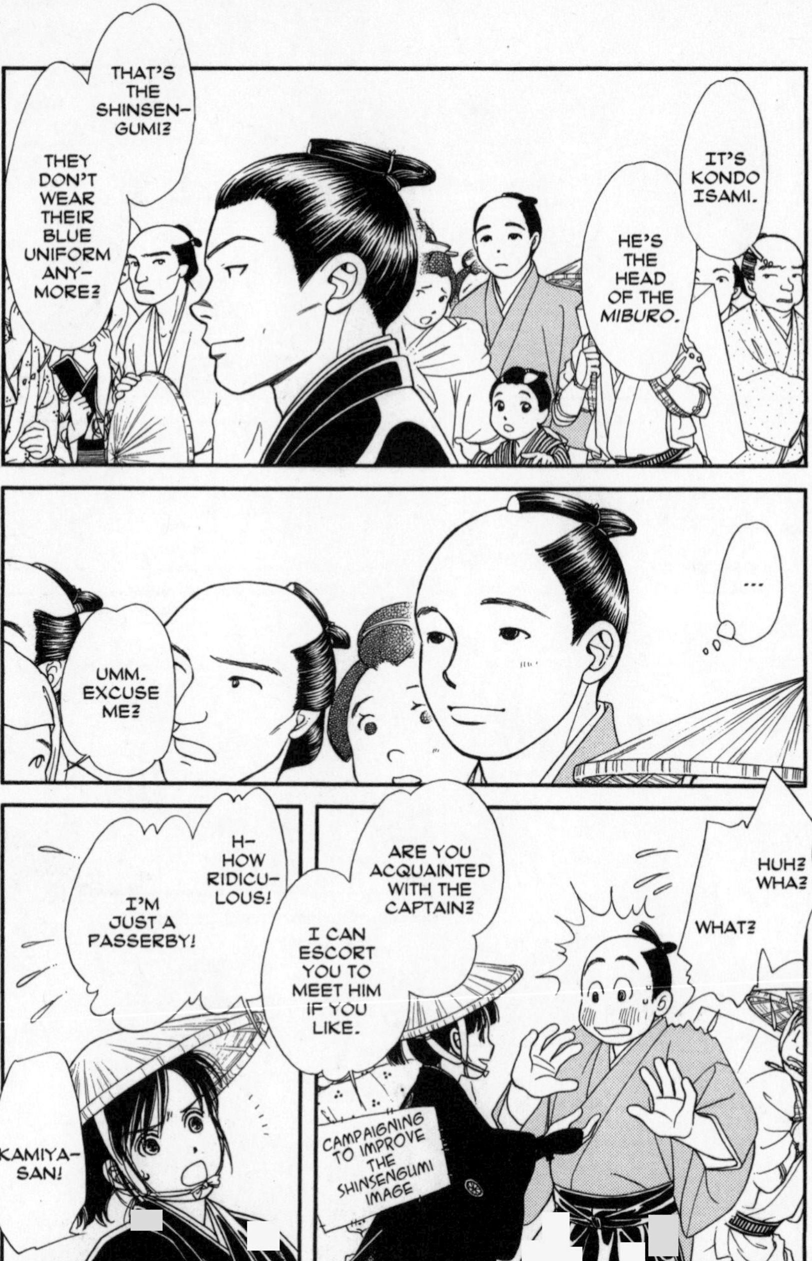
THAT'S THE SHINSEN-GUMI?
THEY DON'T WEAR THEIR BLUE UNIFORM ANY-MORE?
IT'S KONDO ISAMI.
HE'S THE HEAD OF THE *MIBURO*.
...
UMM. EXCUSE ME?
ARE YOU ACQUAINTED WITH THE CAPTAIN?
I CAN ESCORT YOU TO MEET HIM IF YOU LIKE.
HUH? WHA?
WHAT?
CAMPAIGNING TO IMPROVE THE SHINSENGUMI IMAGE
H-HOW RIDICU-LOUS!
I'M JUST A PASSERBY!
KAMIYA-SAN!

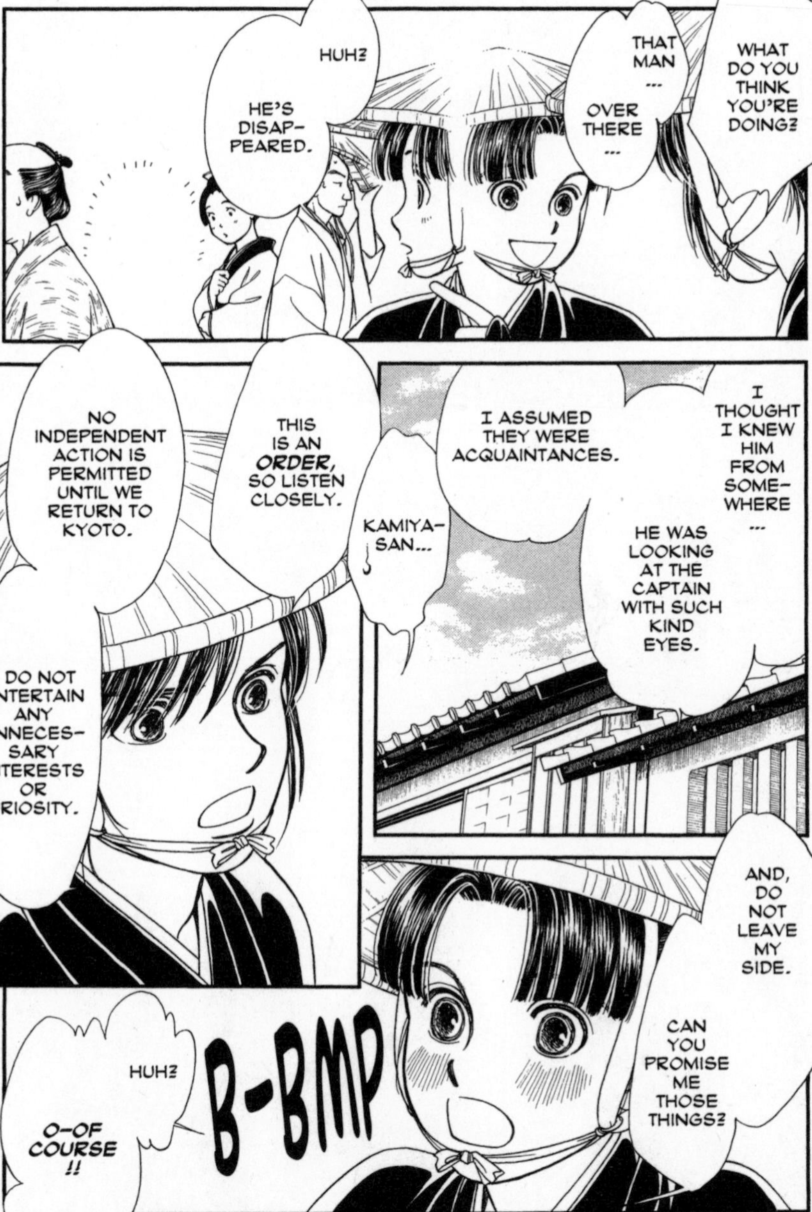
WHAT DO YOU THINK YOU'RE DOING?
THAT MAN ... OVER THERE ...
HUH?
HE'S DISAPPEARED.
I THOUGHT I KNEW HIM FROM SOMEWHERE ...
HE WAS LOOKING AT THE CAPTAIN WITH SUCH KIND EYES.
I ASSUMED THEY WERE ACQUAINTANCES.
KAMIYA-SAN...
THIS IS AN ***ORDER,*** SO LISTEN CLOSELY.
NO INDEPENDENT ACTION IS PERMITTED UNTIL WE RETURN TO KYOTO.
DO NOT ENTERTAIN ANY UNNECESSARY INTERESTS OR CURIOSITY.
AND, DO NOT LEAVE MY SIDE.
CAN YOU PROMISE ME THOSE THINGS?
B-BMP
HUH?
O-OF COURSE !!

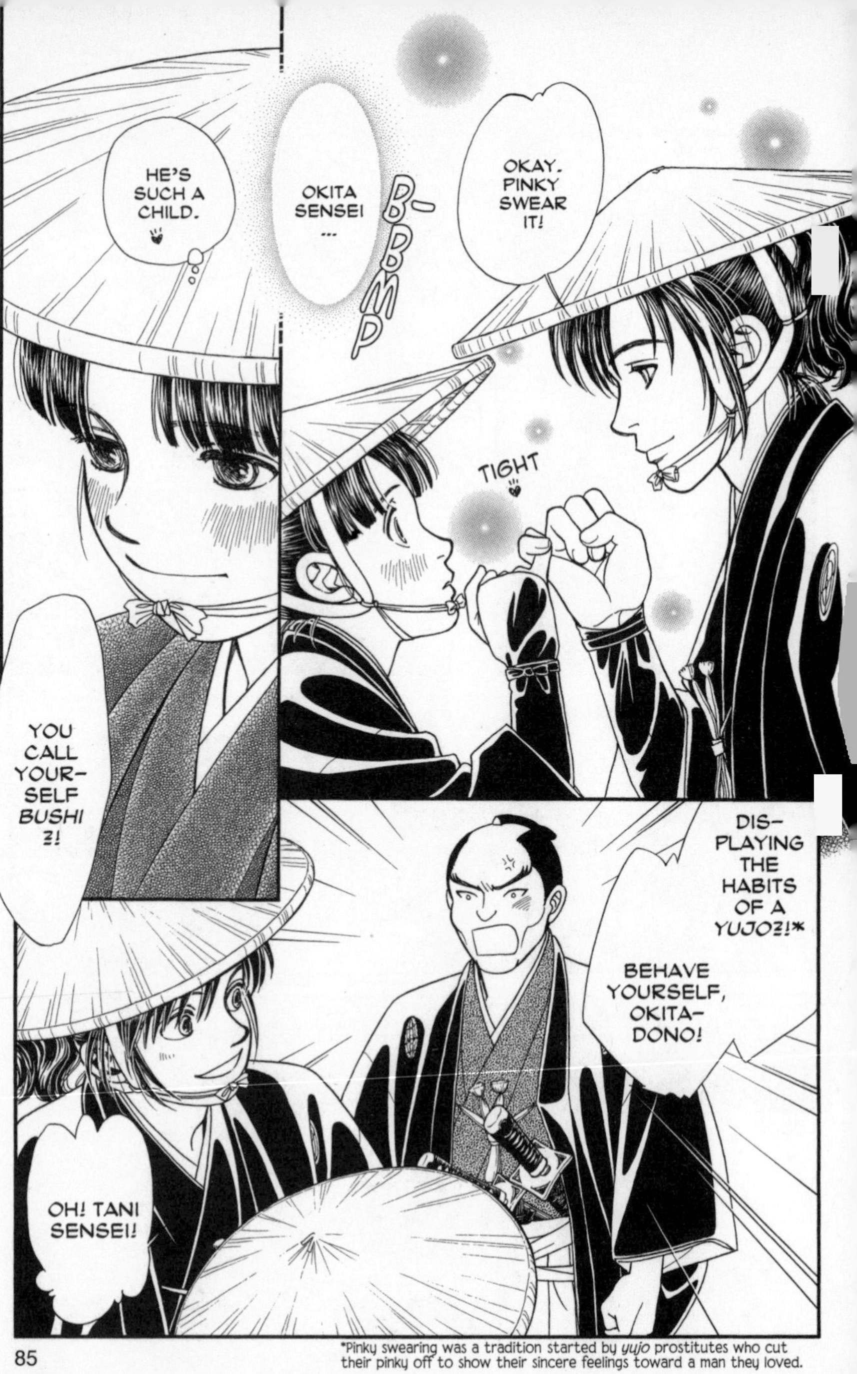
OKAY. PINKY SWEAR IT!
B-BBMP
OKITA SENSEI...
TIGHT
HE'S SUCH A CHILD.
DIS-PLAYING THE HABITS OF A *YUJO*?!*
BEHAVE YOURSELF, OKITA-DONO!
YOU CALL YOURSELF *BUSHI*?!
OH! TANI SENSEI!

*Pinky swearing was a tradition started by *yujo* prostitutes who cut their pinky off to show their sincere feelings toward a man they loved.

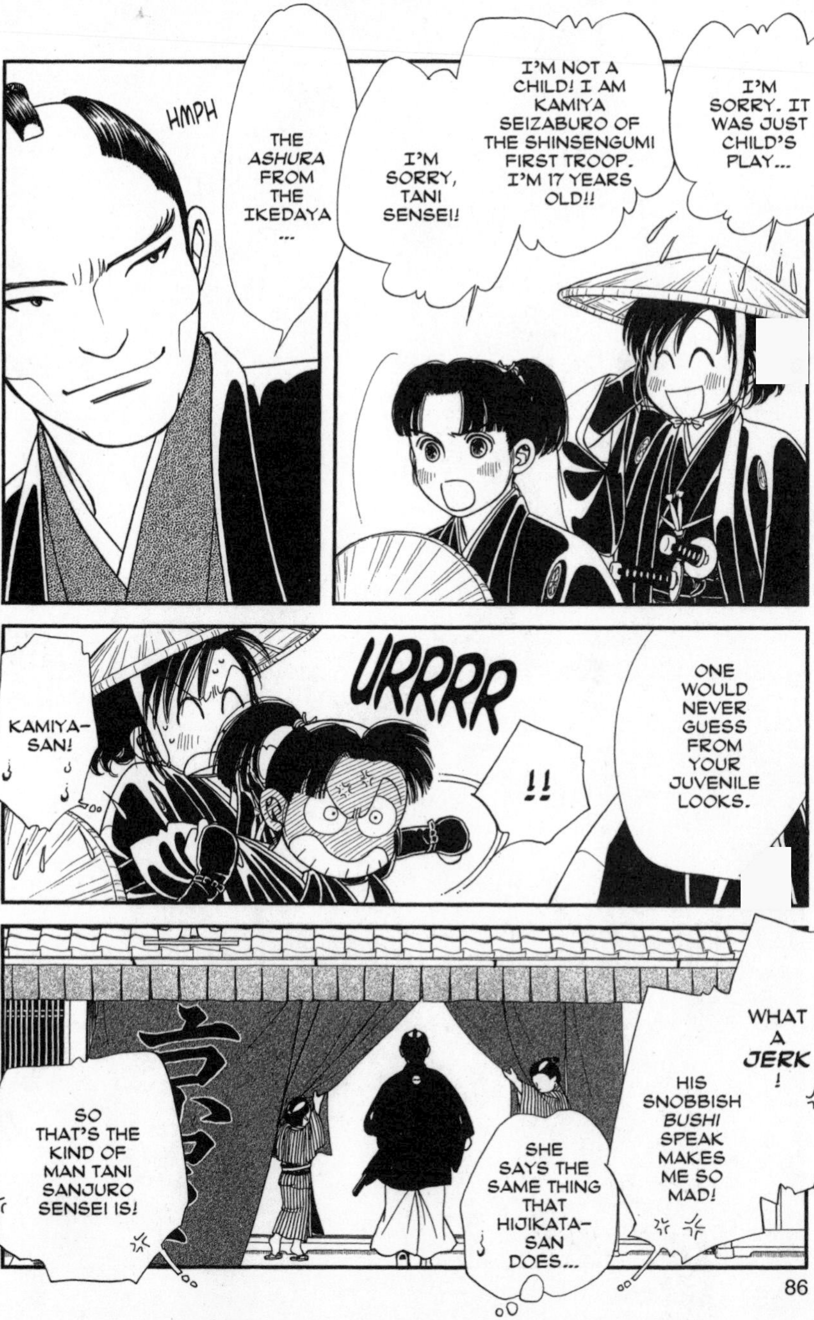
I'M SORRY. IT WAS JUST CHILD'S PLAY...
I'M NOT A CHILD! I AM KAMIYA SEIZABURO OF THE SHINSENGUMI FIRST TROOP. I'M 17 YEARS OLD!!
I'M SORRY, TANI SENSEI!!
THE ASHURA FROM THE IKEDAYA ...
HMPH
ONE WOULD NEVER GUESS FROM YOUR JUVENILE LOOKS.
!!
URRRR
KAMIYA-SAN!
WHAT A JERK!
HIS SNOBBISH BUSHI SPEAK MAKES ME SO MAD!
SHE SAYS THE SAME THING THAT HIJIKATA-SAN DOES...
SO THAT'S THE KIND OF MAN TANI SANJURO SENSEI IS!

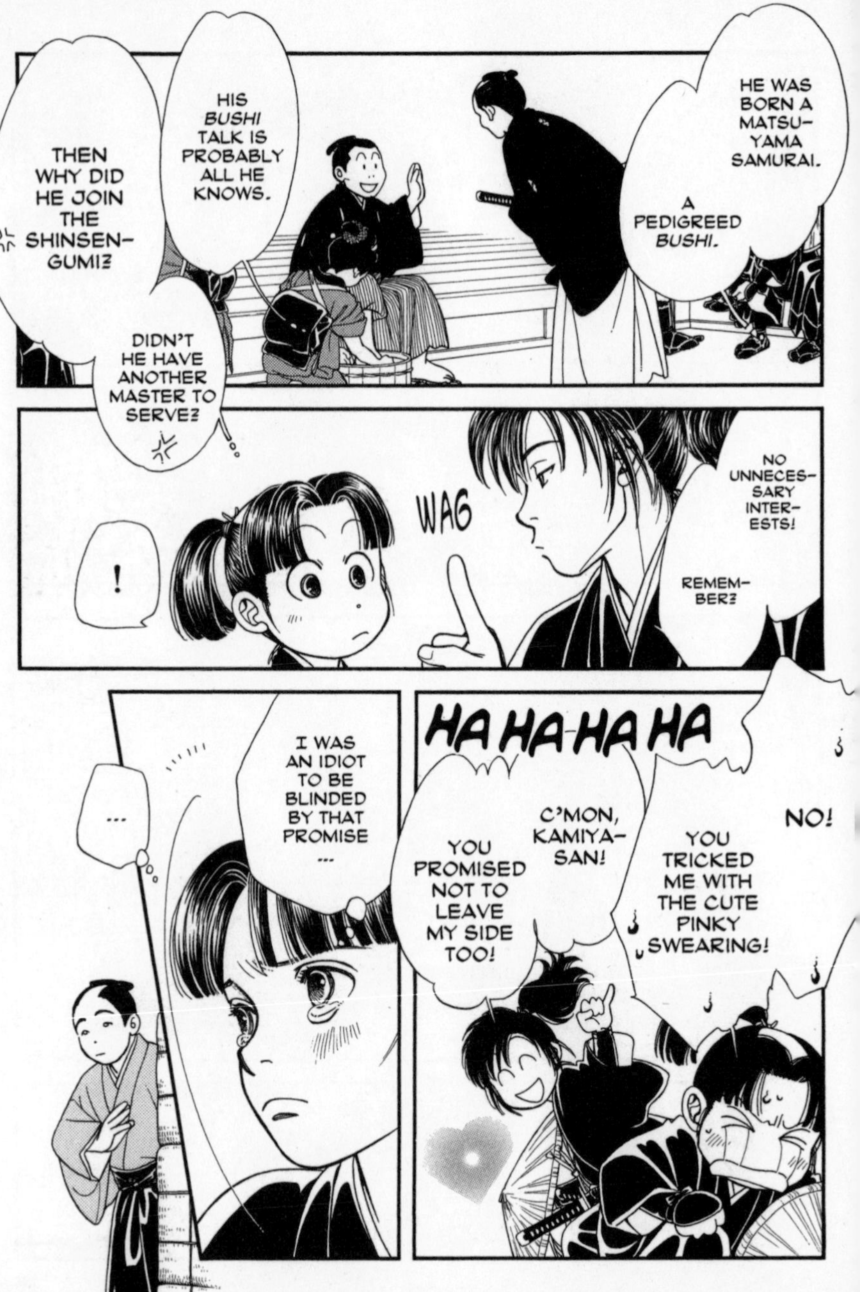
HE WAS BORN A MATSU-YAMA SAMURAI.
A PEDIGREED *BUSHI*.
HIS *BUSHI* TALK IS PROBABLY ALL HE KNOWS.
THEN WHY DID HE JOIN THE SHINSEN-GUMI?
DIDN'T HE HAVE ANOTHER MASTER TO SERVE?
NO UNNECES-SARY INTER-ESTS!
REMEM-BER?
WAG
!
NO!
YOU TRICKED ME WITH THE CUTE PINKY SWEARING!
HA HA-HA HA
C'MON, KAMIYA-SAN!
YOU PROMISED NOT TO LEAVE MY SIDE TOO!
I WAS AN IDIOT TO BE BLINDED BY THAT PROMISE ...
...

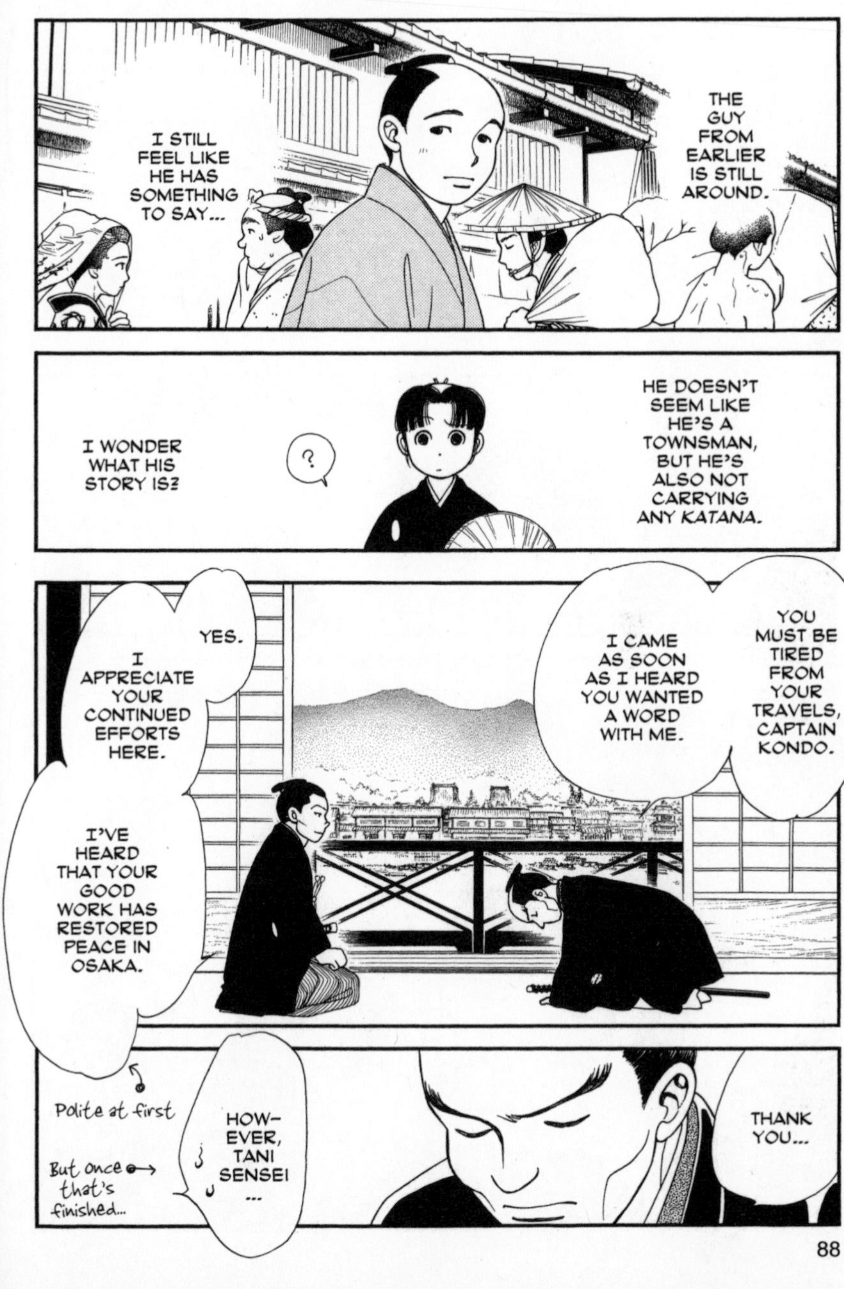
THE GUY FROM EARLIER IS STILL AROUND.
I STILL FEEL LIKE HE HAS SOMETHING TO SAY...
HE DOESN'T SEEM LIKE HE'S A TOWNSMAN, BUT HE'S ALSO NOT CARRYING ANY *KATANA*.
?
I WONDER WHAT HIS STORY IS?
YOU MUST BE TIRED FROM YOUR TRAVELS, CAPTAIN KONDO.
I CAME AS SOON AS I HEARD YOU WANTED A WORD WITH ME.
YES.
I APPRECIATE YOUR CONTINUED EFFORTS HERE.
I'VE HEARD THAT YOUR GOOD WORK HAS RESTORED PEACE IN OSAKA.
THANK YOU...
HOW-EVER, TANI SENSEI...
Polite at first
But once that's finished...

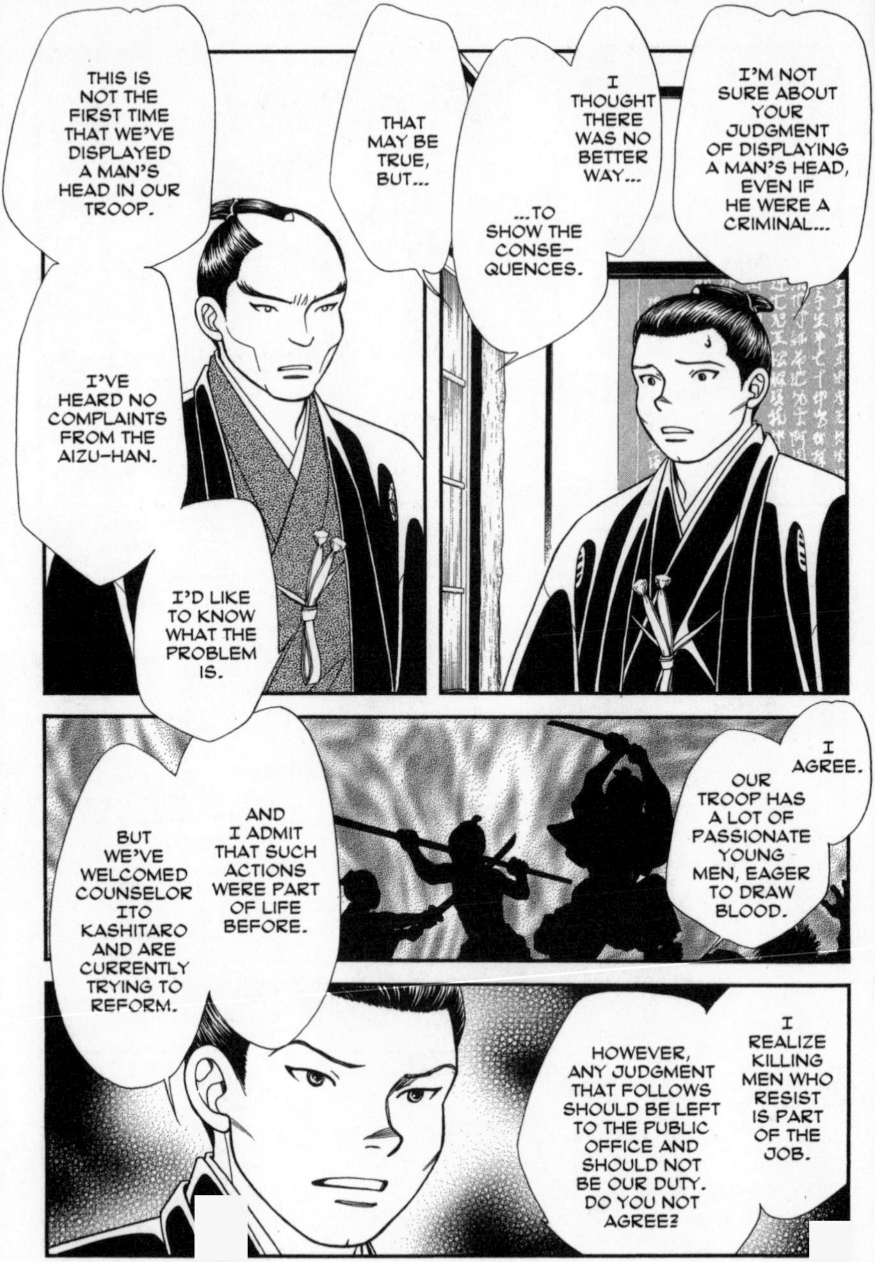
I'M NOT SURE ABOUT YOUR JUDGMENT OF DISPLAYING A MAN'S HEAD, EVEN IF HE WERE A CRIMINAL...
I THOUGHT THERE WAS NO BETTER WAY...
...TO SHOW THE CONSE-QUENCES.
THAT MAY BE TRUE, BUT...
THIS IS NOT THE FIRST TIME THAT WE'VE DISPLAYED A MAN'S HEAD IN OUR TROOP.
I'VE HEARD NO COMPLAINTS FROM THE AIZU-HAN.
I'D LIKE TO KNOW WHAT THE PROBLEM IS.
I AGREE.
OUR TROOP HAS A LOT OF PASSIONATE YOUNG MEN, EAGER TO DRAW BLOOD.
AND I ADMIT THAT SUCH ACTIONS WERE PART OF LIFE BEFORE.
BUT WE'VE WELCOMED COUNSELOR ITO KASHITARO AND ARE CURRENTLY TRYING TO REFORM.
I REALIZE KILLING MEN WHO RESIST IS PART OF THE JOB.
HOWEVER, ANY JUDGMENT THAT FOLLOWS SHOULD BE LEFT TO THE PUBLIC OFFICE AND SHOULD NOT BE OUR DUTY. DO YOU NOT AGREE?

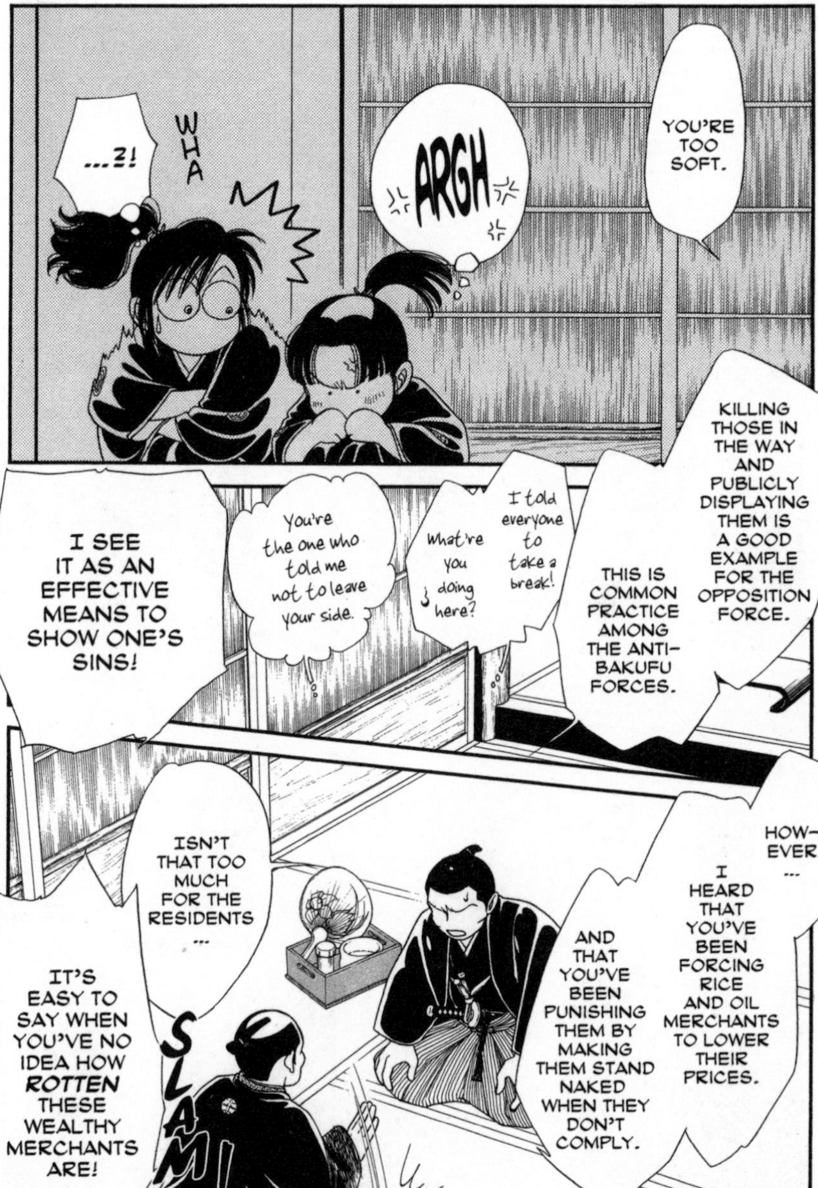
YOU'RE TOO SOFT.
ARGH
WHA
...?!
KILLING THOSE IN THE WAY AND PUBLICLY DISPLAYING THEM IS A GOOD EXAMPLE FOR THE OPPOSITION FORCE.
THIS IS COMMON PRACTICE AMONG THE ANTI-BAKUFU FORCES.
I told everyone to take a break!
What're you doing here?
You're the one who told me not to leave your side.
I SEE IT AS AN EFFECTIVE MEANS TO SHOW ONE'S SINS!
HOW-EVER ...
I HEARD THAT YOU'VE BEEN FORCING RICE AND OIL MERCHANTS TO LOWER THEIR PRICES.
AND THAT YOU'VE BEEN PUNISHING THEM BY MAKING THEM STAND NAKED WHEN THEY DON'T COMPLY.
ISN'T THAT TOO MUCH FOR THE RESIDENTS ...
IT'S EASY TO SAY WHEN YOU'VE NO IDEA HOW ROTTEN THESE WEALTHY MERCHANTS ARE!
SLAM!

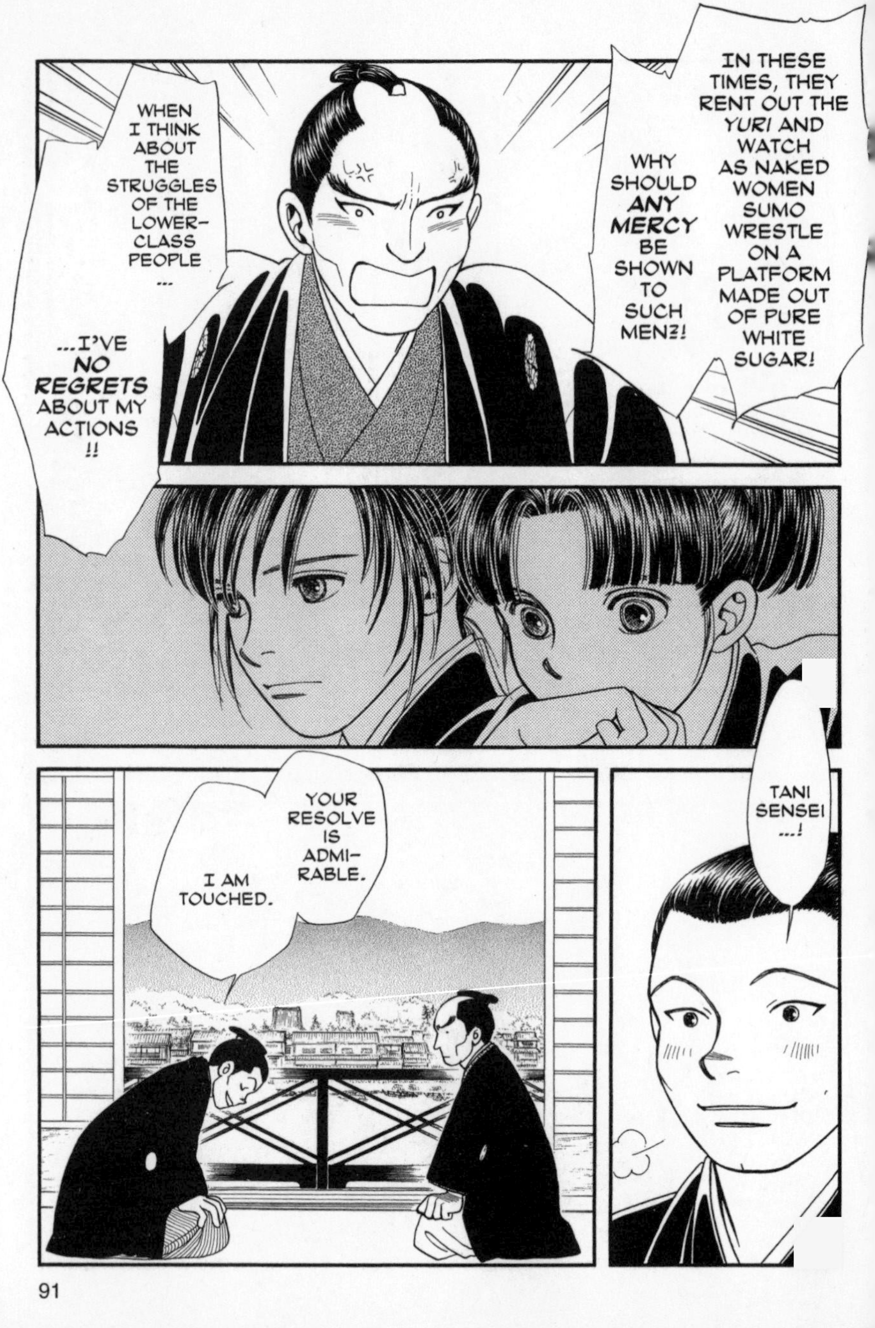
IN THESE TIMES, THEY RENT OUT THE *YURI* AND WATCH AS NAKED WOMEN SUMO WRESTLE ON A PLATFORM MADE OUT OF PURE WHITE SUGAR!
WHY SHOULD **ANY MERCY** BE SHOWN TO SUCH MEN?!
WHEN I THINK ABOUT THE STRUGGLES OF THE LOWER-CLASS PEOPLE...
...I'VE **NO REGRETS** ABOUT MY ACTIONS!!
TANI SENSEI...!
YOUR RESOLVE IS ADMIRABLE.
I AM TOUCHED.

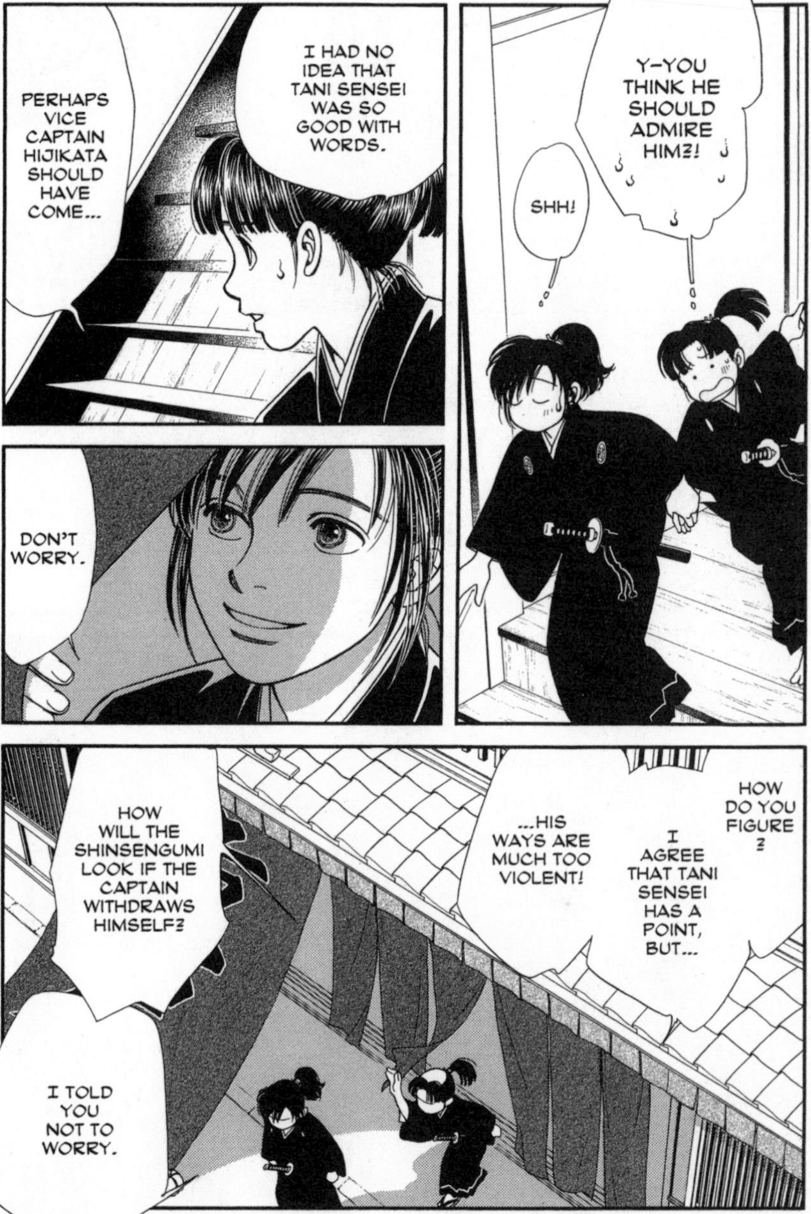
Y-YOU THINK HE SHOULD ADMIRE HIM?!
SHH!
I HAD NO IDEA THAT TANI SENSEI WAS SO GOOD WITH WORDS.
PERHAPS VICE CAPTAIN HIJIKATA SHOULD HAVE COME...
DON'T WORRY.
HOW DO YOU FIGURE?
I AGREE THAT TANI SENSEI HAS A POINT, BUT...
...HIS WAYS ARE MUCH TOO VIOLENT!
HOW WILL THE SHINSENGUMI LOOK IF THE CAPTAIN WITHDRAWS HIMSELF?
I TOLD YOU NOT TO WORRY.

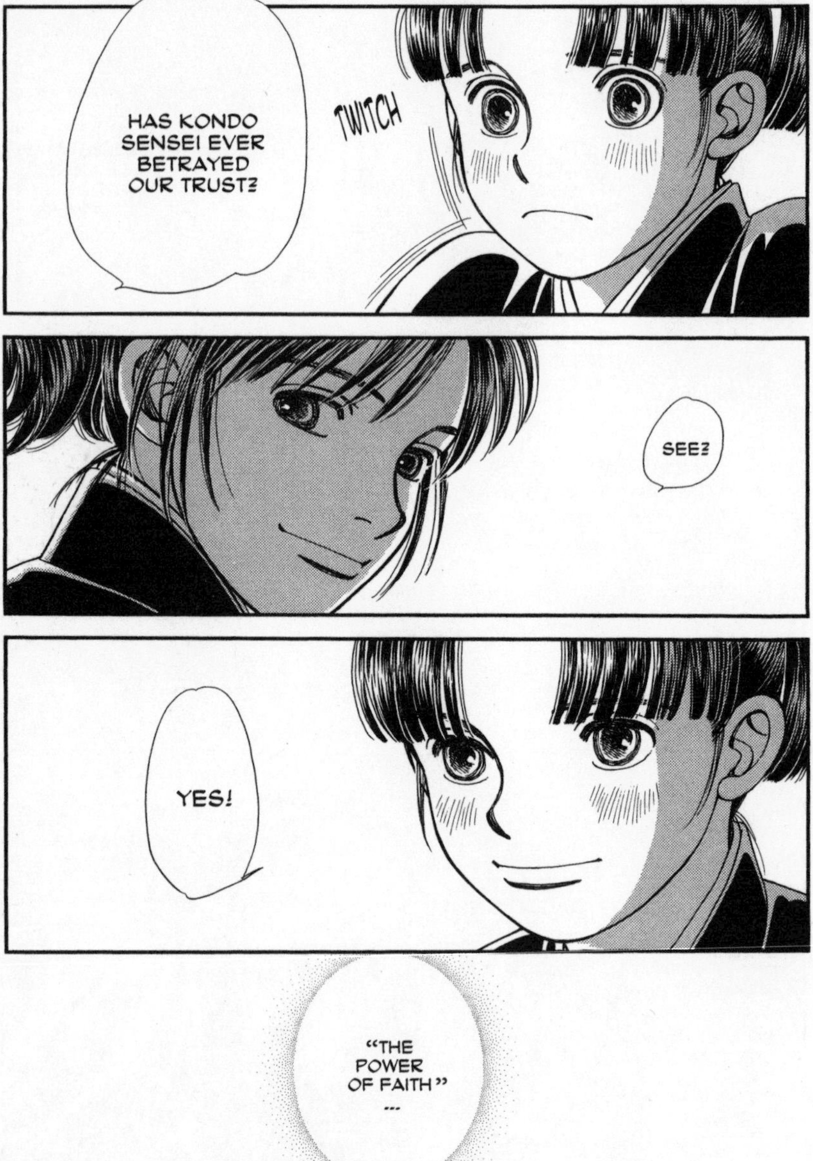
TWITCH
HAS KONDO SENSEI EVER BETRAYED OUR TRUST?
SEE?
YES!
"THE POWER OF FAITH" ...

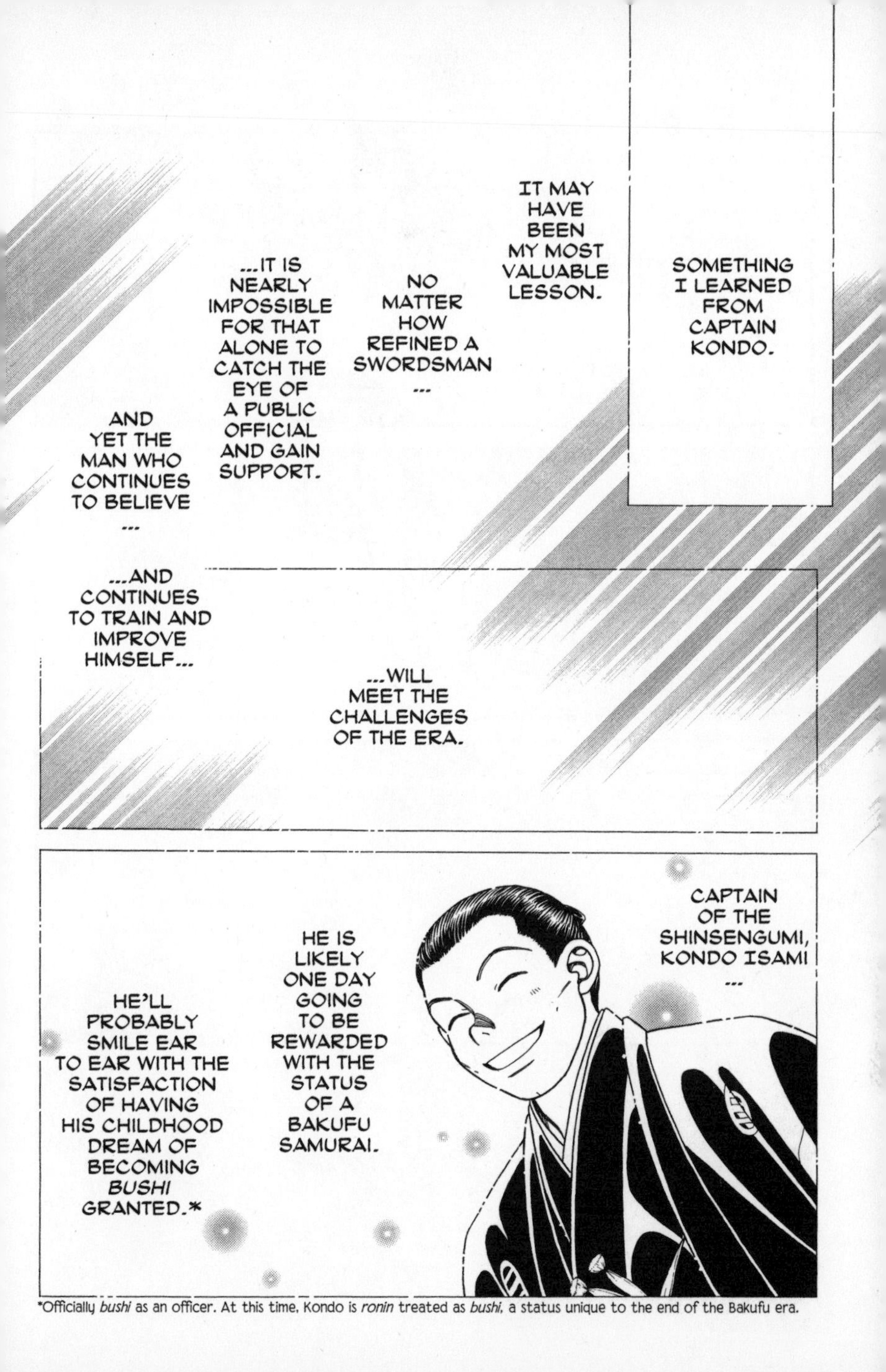
SOMETHING I LEARNED FROM CAPTAIN KONDO.
IT MAY HAVE BEEN MY MOST VALUABLE LESSON.
NO MATTER HOW REFINED A SWORDSMAN ...
...IT IS NEARLY IMPOSSIBLE FOR THAT ALONE TO CATCH THE EYE OF A PUBLIC OFFICIAL AND GAIN SUPPORT.
AND YET THE MAN WHO CONTINUES TO BELIEVE ...
...AND CONTINUES TO TRAIN AND IMPROVE HIMSELF...
...WILL MEET THE CHALLENGES OF THE ERA.
CAPTAIN OF THE SHINSENGUMI, KONDO ISAMI ...
HE IS LIKELY ONE DAY GOING TO BE REWARDED WITH THE STATUS OF A BAKUFU SAMURAI.
HE'LL PROBABLY SMILE EAR TO EAR WITH THE SATISFACTION OF HAVING HIS CHILDHOOD DREAM OF BECOMING *BUSHI* GRANTED.*

*Officially *bushi* as an officer. At this time, Kondo is *ronin* treated as *bushi*, a status unique to the end of the Bakufu era.

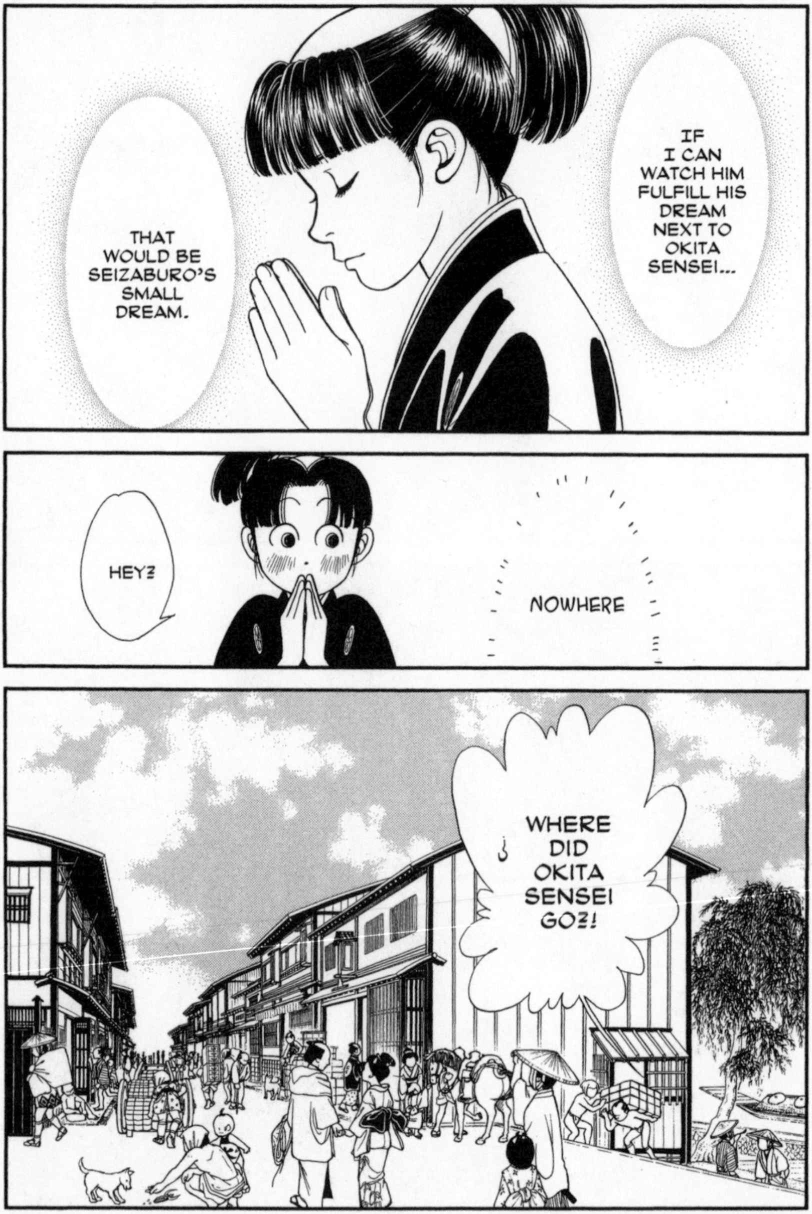
IF I CAN WATCH HIM FULFILL HIS DREAM NEXT TO OKITA SENSEI...
THAT WOULD BE SEIZABURO'S SMALL DREAM.
NOWHERE
HEY?!
WHERE DID OKITA SENSEI GO?!

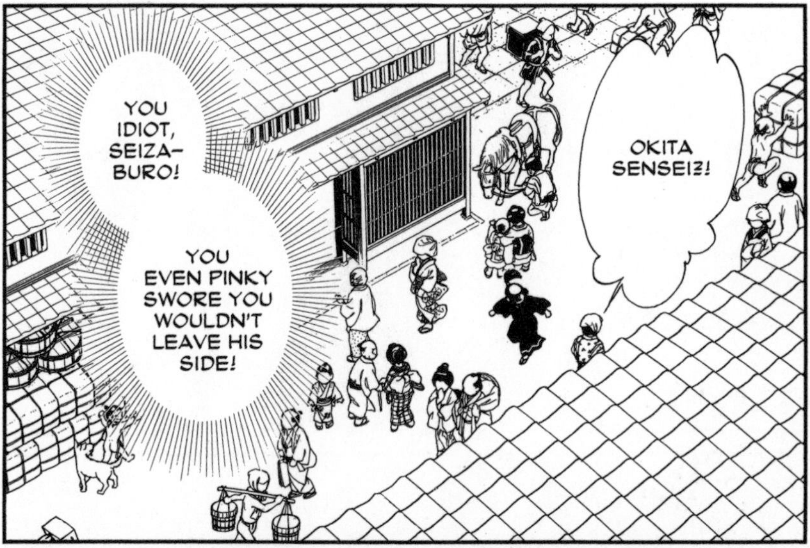
OKITA SENSEI!?
YOU IDIOT, SEIZABURO!
YOU EVEN PINKY SWORE YOU WOULDN'T LEAVE HIS SIDE!

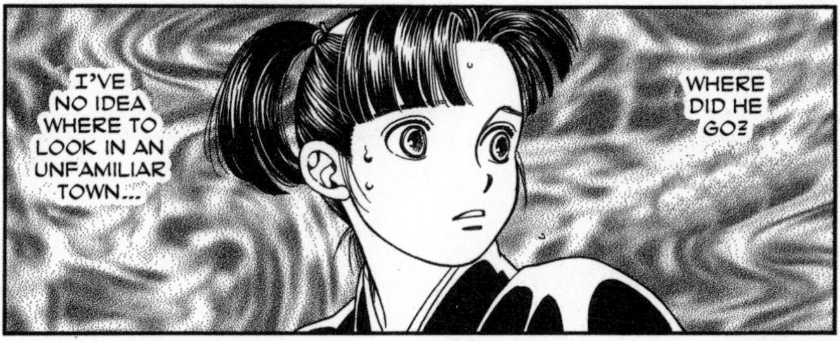
WHERE DID HE GO?
I'VE NO IDEA WHERE TO LOOK IN AN UNFAMILIAR TOWN...

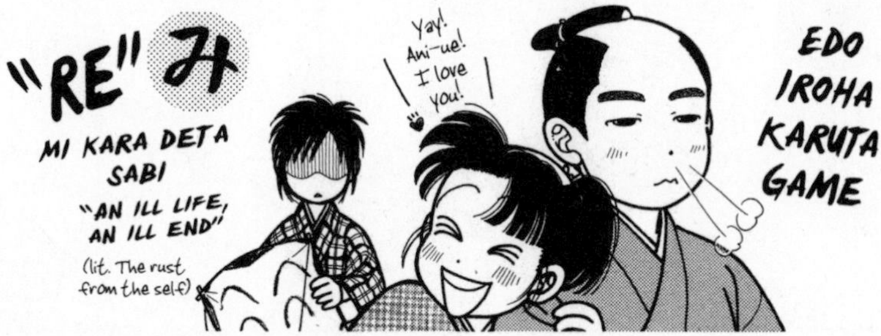
EDO IROHA KARUTA GAME
Yay! Ani-ue! I love you!
"RE" み
MI KARA DETA SABI
"AN ILL LIFE, AN ILL END"
(lit. The rust from the self)

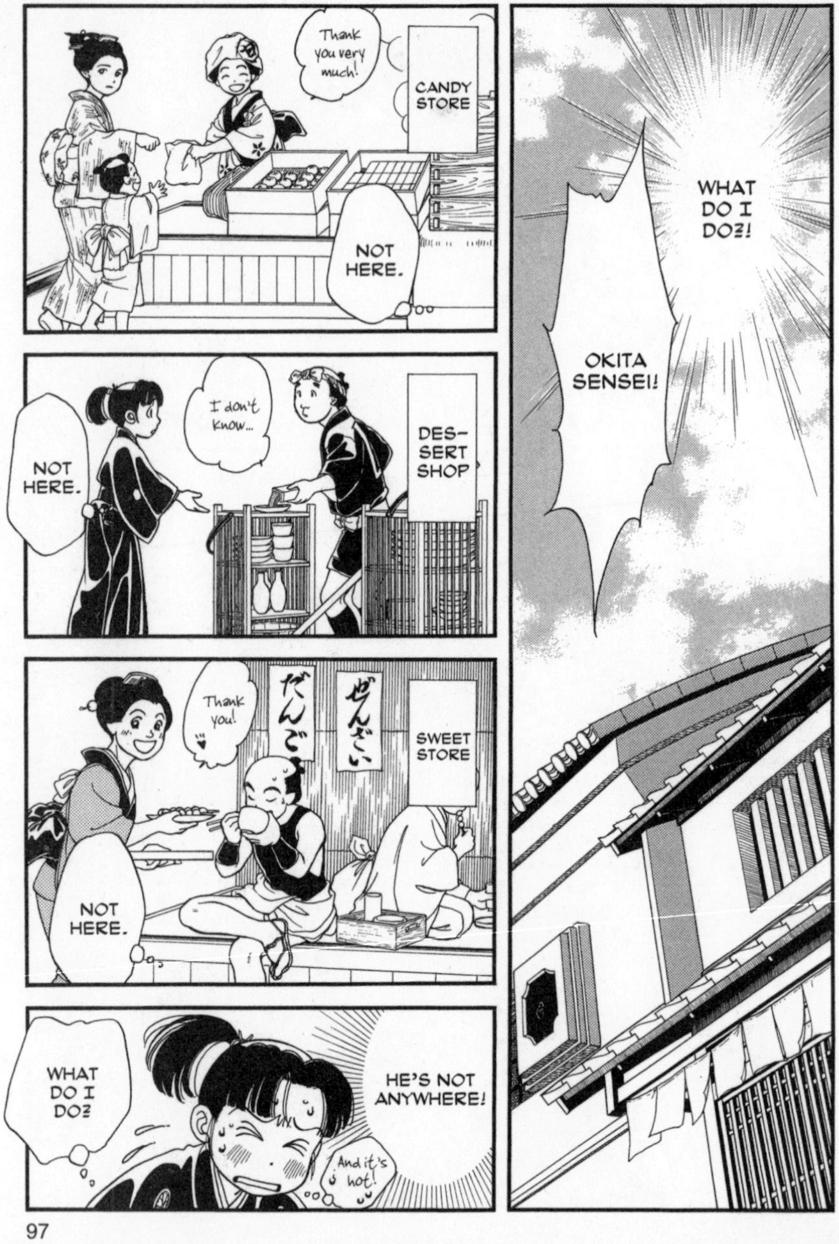
WHAT DO I DO?!
OKITA SENSEI!
CANDY STORE
Thank you very much!
NOT HERE.
DES-SERT SHOP
I don't know...
NOT HERE.
SWEET STORE
ぜんざい
だんご
Thank you!
NOT HERE.
HE'S NOT ANYWHERE!
And it's hot!
WHAT DO I DO?

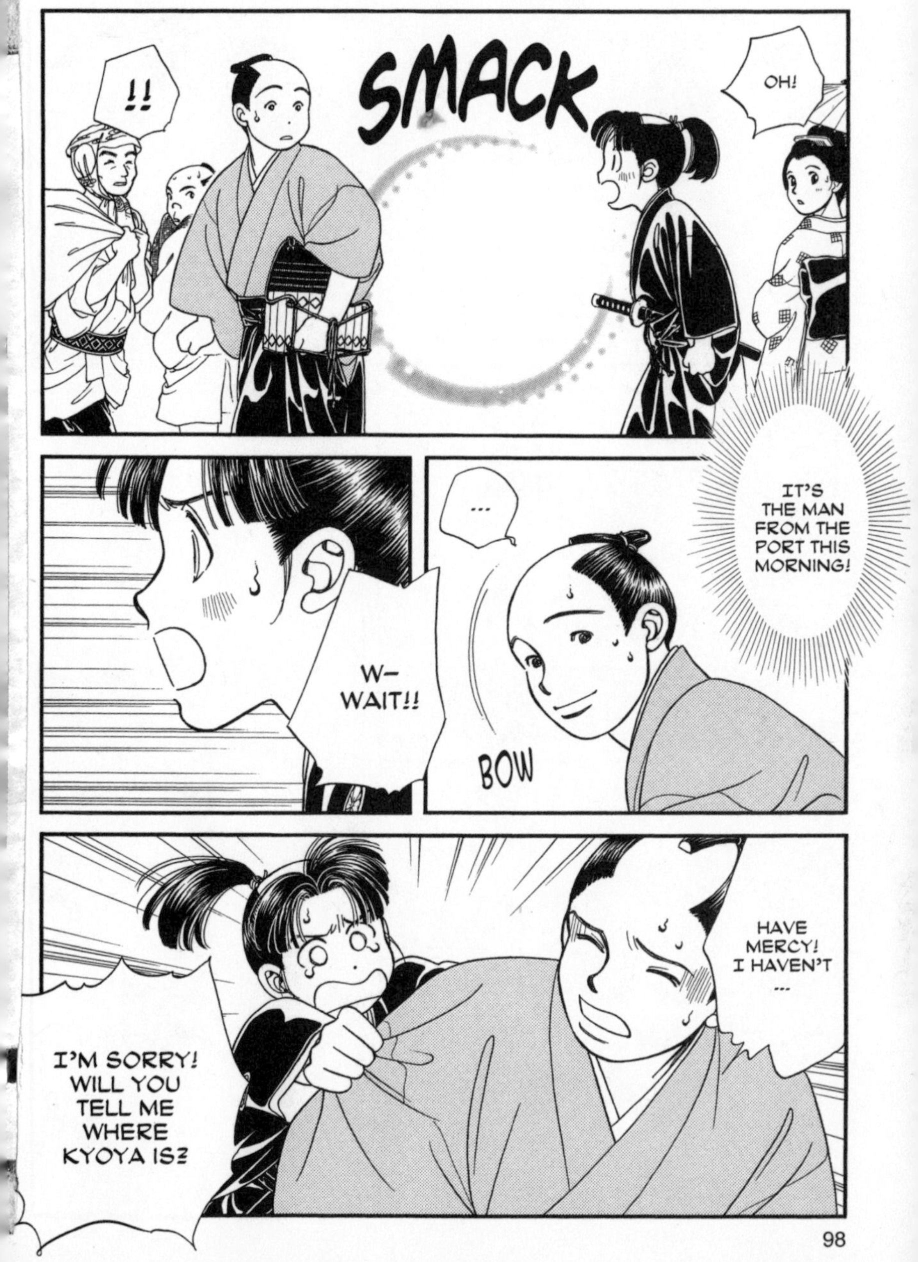
OH!
SMACK
!!
IT'S THE MAN FROM THE PORT THIS MORNING!
...
BOW
W-WAIT!!
HAVE MERCY! I HAVEN'T ...
I'M SORRY! WILL YOU TELL ME WHERE KYOYA IS?

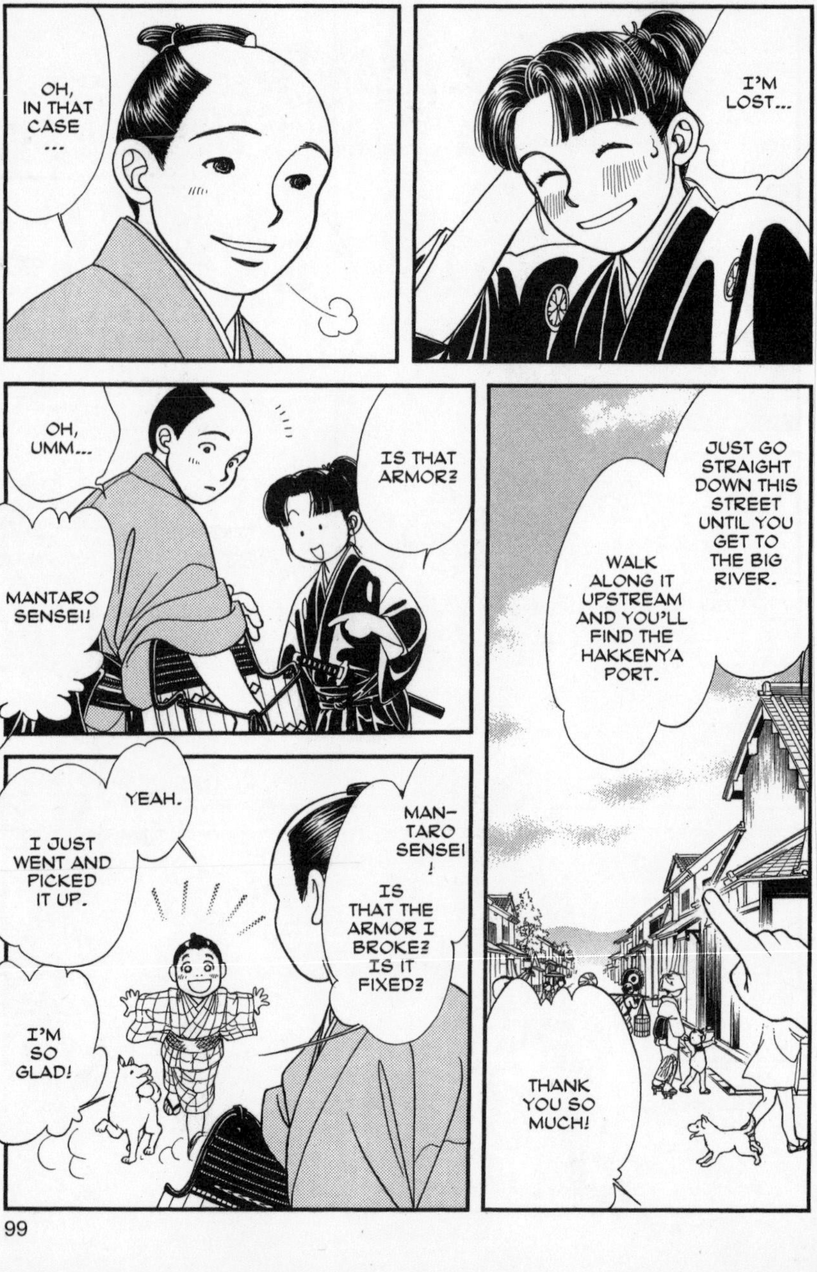
I'M LOST...
OH, IN THAT CASE ...
JUST GO STRAIGHT DOWN THIS STREET UNTIL YOU GET TO THE BIG RIVER.
WALK ALONG IT UPSTREAM AND YOU'LL FIND THE HAKKENYA PORT.
THANK YOU SO MUCH!
IS THAT ARMOR?
OH, UMM...
MANTARO SENSEI!
MANTARO SENSEI! IS THAT THE ARMOR I BROKE? IS IT FIXED?
YEAH.
I JUST WENT AND PICKED IT UP.
I'M SO GLAD!

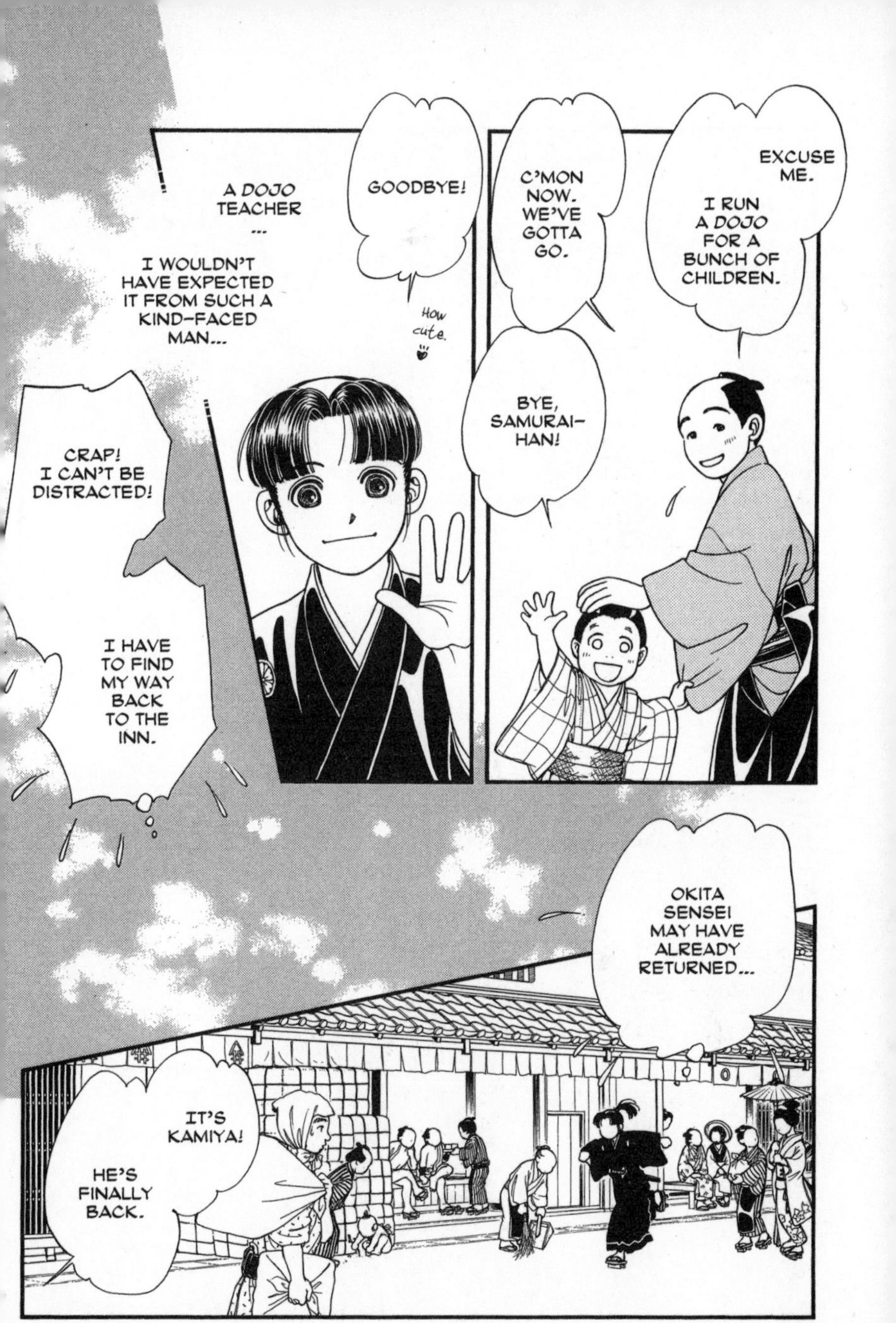
EXCUSE ME.
I RUN A DOJO FOR A BUNCH OF CHILDREN.
C'MON NOW. WE'VE GOTTA GO.
BYE, SAMURAI-HAN!
GOODBYE!
How cute.
A DOJO TEACHER ...
I WOULDN'T HAVE EXPECTED IT FROM SUCH A KIND-FACED MAN...
CRAP! I CAN'T BE DISTRACTED!
I HAVE TO FIND MY WAY BACK TO THE INN.
OKITA SENSEI MAY HAVE ALREADY RETURNED...
IT'S KAMIYA!
HE'S FINALLY BACK.

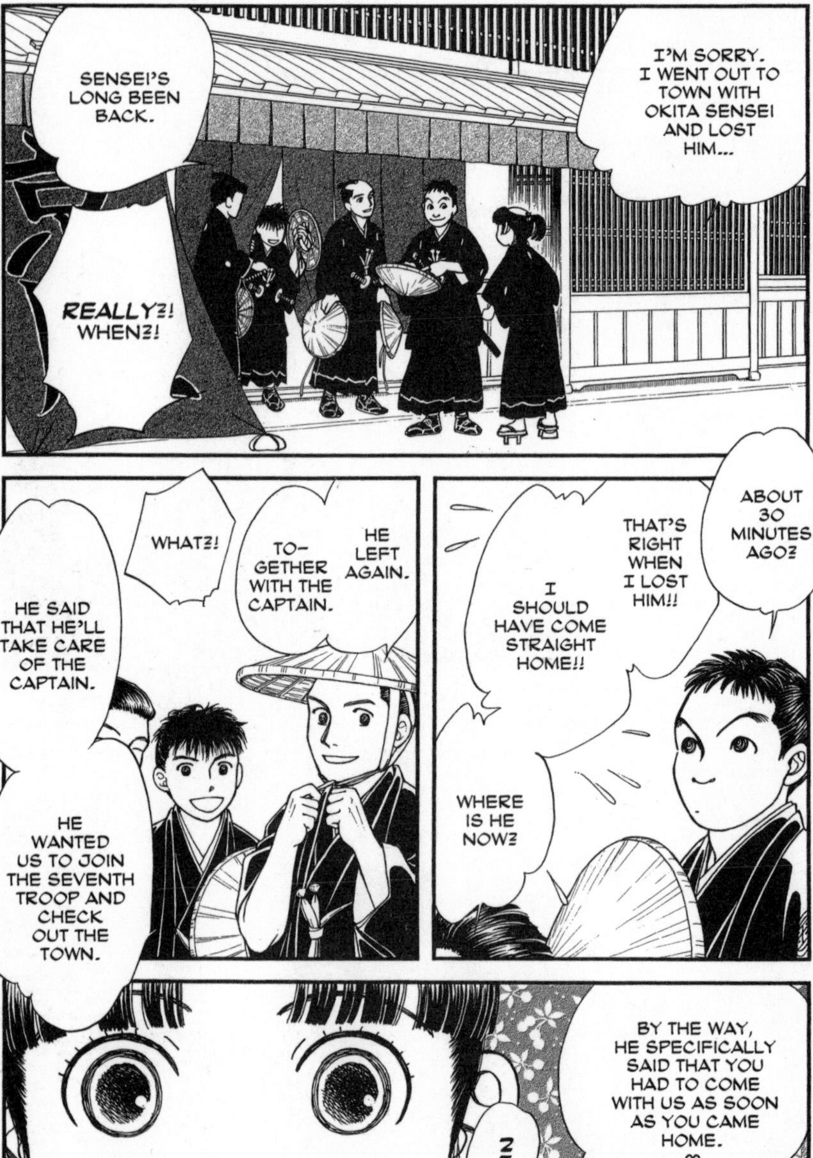
I'M SORRY. I WENT OUT TO TOWN WITH OKITA SENSEI AND LOST HIM...
SENSEI'S LONG BEEN BACK.
REALLY?! WHEN?!
ABOUT 30 MINUTES AGO?
THAT'S RIGHT WHEN I LOST HIM!!
I SHOULD HAVE COME STRAIGHT HOME!!
WHERE IS HE NOW?
HE LEFT AGAIN.
TO-GETHER WITH THE CAPTAIN.
WHAT?!
HE SAID THAT HE'LL TAKE CARE OF THE CAPTAIN.
HE WANTED US TO JOIN THE SEVENTH TROOP AND CHECK OUT THE TOWN.
BY THE WAY, HE SPECIFICALLY SAID THAT YOU HAD TO COME WITH US AS SOON AS YOU CAME HOME. ♡
?

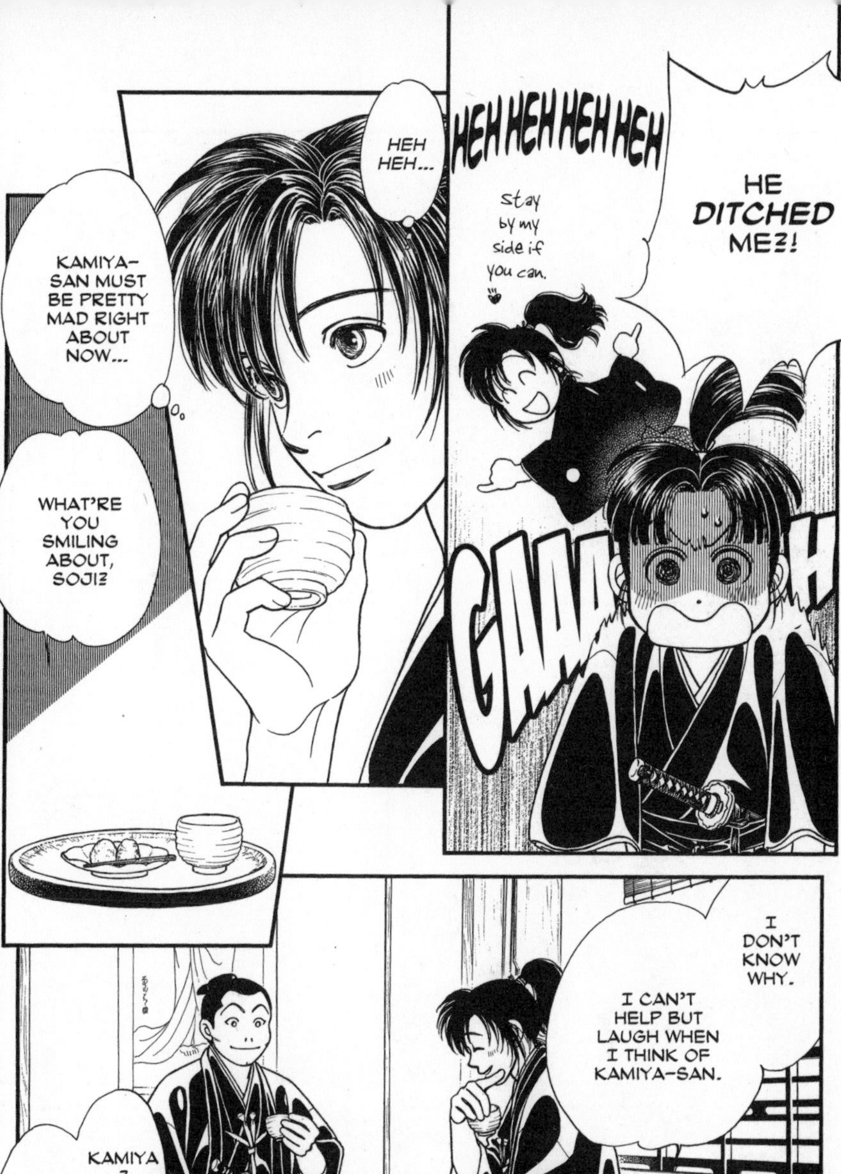
HEH HEH HEH HEH
stay by my side if you can.
HE DITCHED ME?!
HEH HEH...
KAMIYA-SAN MUST BE PRETTY MAD RIGHT ABOUT NOW...
WHAT'RE YOU SMILING ABOUT, SOJI?
I DON'T KNOW WHY.
I CAN'T HELP BUT LAUGH WHEN I THINK OF KAMIYA-SAN.
KAMIYA?
HE IS QUITE THE CHARACTER.

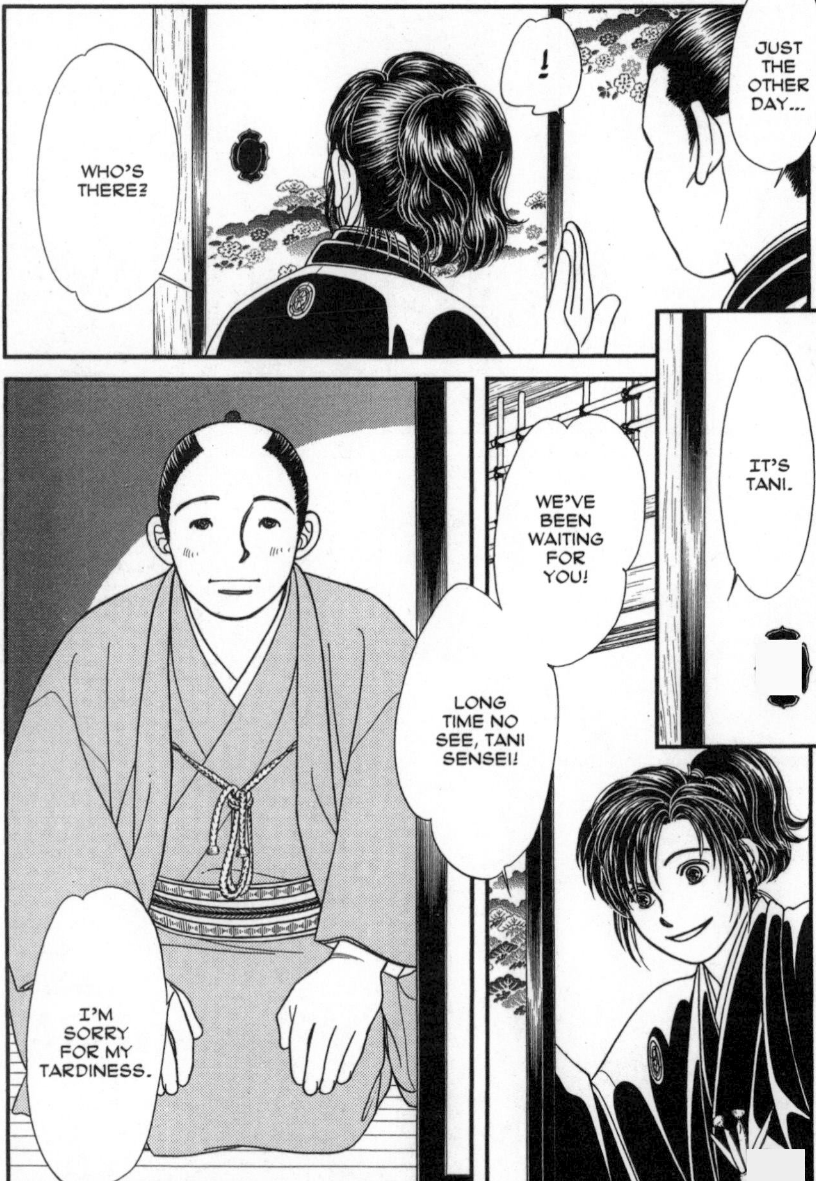
JUST THE OTHER DAY...
!
WHO'S THERE?
IT'S TANI.
WE'VE BEEN WAITING FOR YOU!
LONG TIME NO SEE, TANI SENSEI!
I'M SORRY FOR MY TARDINESS.

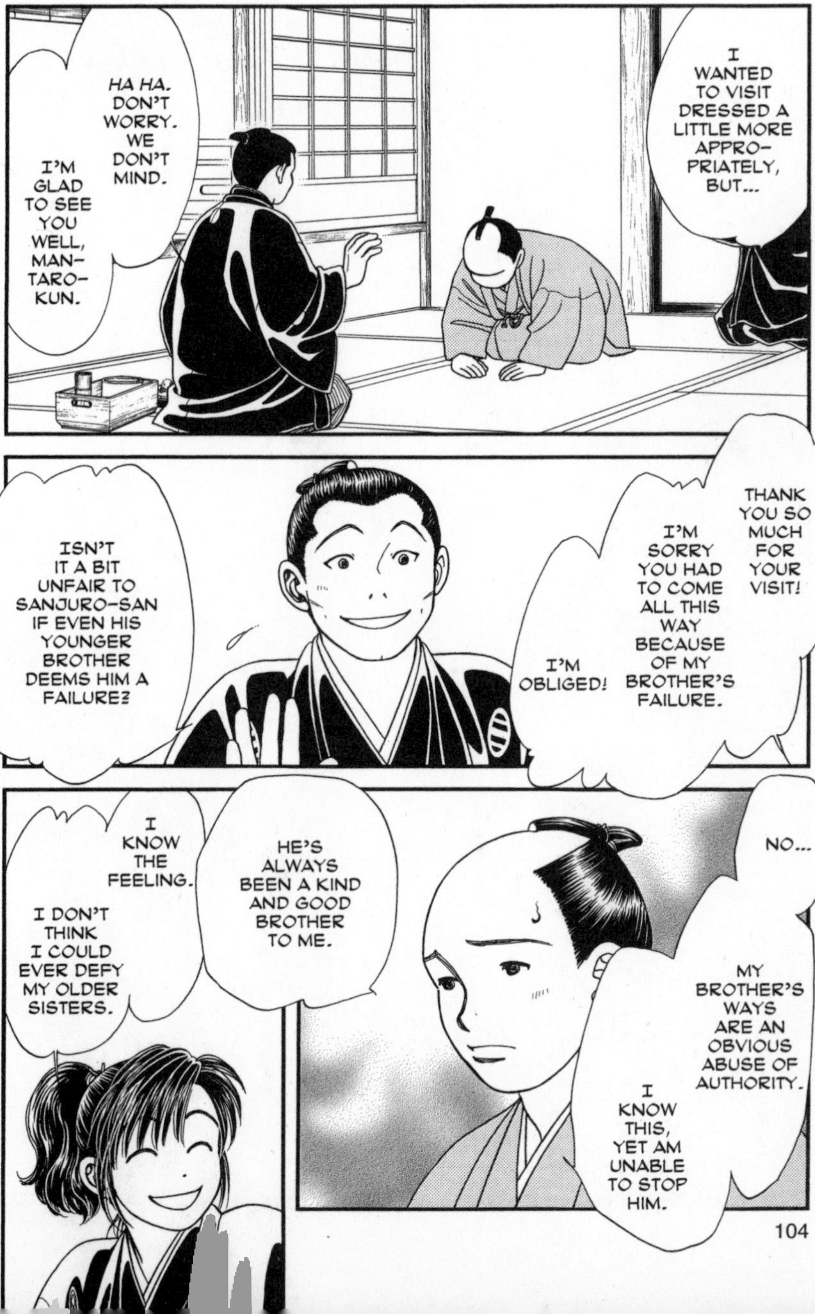
I WANTED TO VISIT DRESSED A LITTLE MORE APPRO-PRIATELY, BUT...
HA HA. DON'T WORRY. WE DON'T MIND.
I'M GLAD TO SEE YOU WELL, MAN-TARO-KUN.
THANK YOU SO MUCH FOR YOUR VISIT!
I'M SORRY YOU HAD TO COME ALL THIS WAY BECAUSE OF MY BROTHER'S FAILURE.
I'M OBLIGED!
ISN'T IT A BIT UNFAIR TO SANJURO-SAN IF EVEN HIS YOUNGER BROTHER DEEMS HIM A FAILURE?
NO...
MY BROTHER'S WAYS ARE AN OBVIOUS ABUSE OF AUTHORITY.
I KNOW THIS, YET AM UNABLE TO STOP HIM.
HE'S ALWAYS BEEN A KIND AND GOOD BROTHER TO ME.
I KNOW THE FEELING.
I DON'T THINK I COULD EVER DEFY MY OLDER SISTERS.

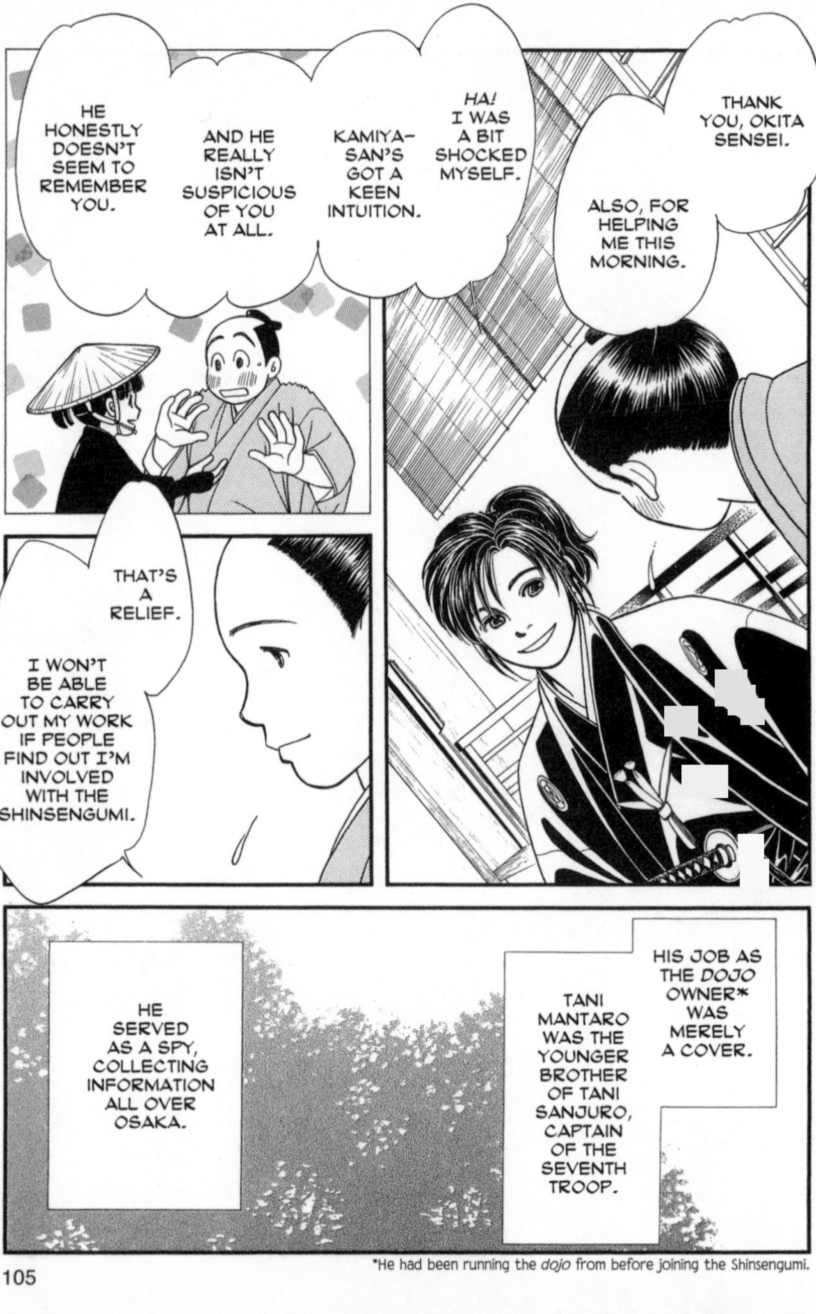
THANK YOU, OKITA SENSEI.
ALSO, FOR HELPING ME THIS MORNING.
HA! I WAS A BIT SHOCKED MYSELF.
KAMIYA-SAN'S GOT A KEEN INTUITION.
AND HE REALLY ISN'T SUSPICIOUS OF YOU AT ALL.
HE HONESTLY DOESN'T SEEM TO REMEMBER YOU.
THAT'S A RELIEF.
I WON'T BE ABLE TO CARRY OUT MY WORK IF PEOPLE FIND OUT I'M INVOLVED WITH THE SHINSENGUMI.
HIS JOB AS THE *DOJO* OWNER* WAS MERELY A COVER.
TANI MANTARO WAS THE YOUNGER BROTHER OF TANI SANJURO, CAPTAIN OF THE SEVENTH TROOP.
HE SERVED AS A SPY, COLLECTING INFORMATION ALL OVER OSAKA.

*He had been running the *dojo* from before joining the Shinsengumi.

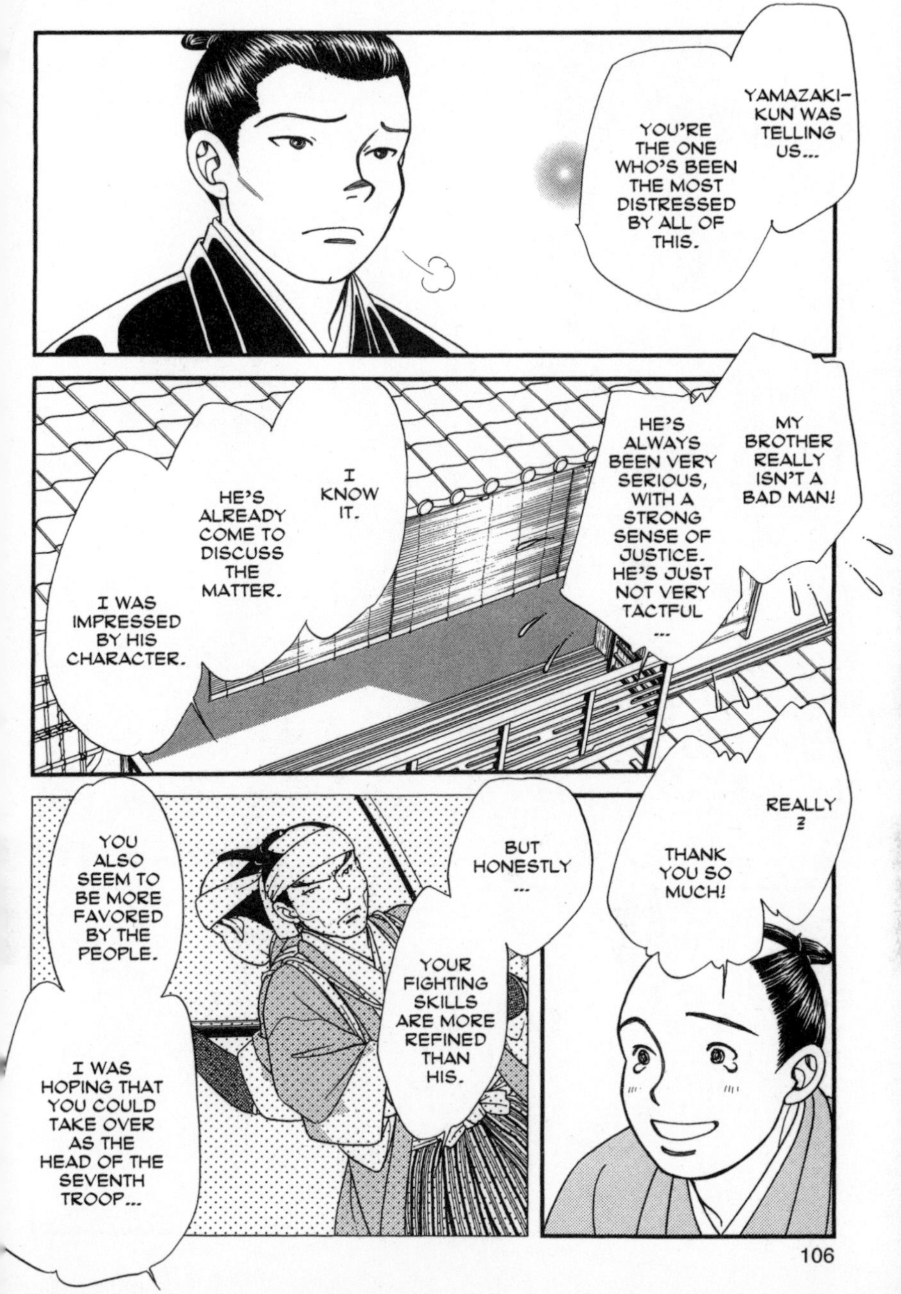

YAMAZAKI-KUN WAS TELLING US...
YOU'RE THE ONE WHO'S BEEN THE MOST DISTRESSED BY ALL OF THIS.
MY BROTHER REALLY ISN'T A BAD MAN!
HE'S ALWAYS BEEN VERY SERIOUS, WITH A STRONG SENSE OF JUSTICE. HE'S JUST NOT VERY TACTFUL ...
I KNOW IT.
HE'S ALREADY COME TO DISCUSS THE MATTER.
I WAS IMPRESSED BY HIS CHARACTER.
REALLY?
THANK YOU SO MUCH!
BUT HONESTLY ...
YOUR FIGHTING SKILLS ARE MORE REFINED THAN HIS.
YOU ALSO SEEM TO BE MORE FAVORED BY THE PEOPLE.
I WAS HOPING THAT YOU COULD TAKE OVER AS THE HEAD OF THE SEVENTH TROOP...

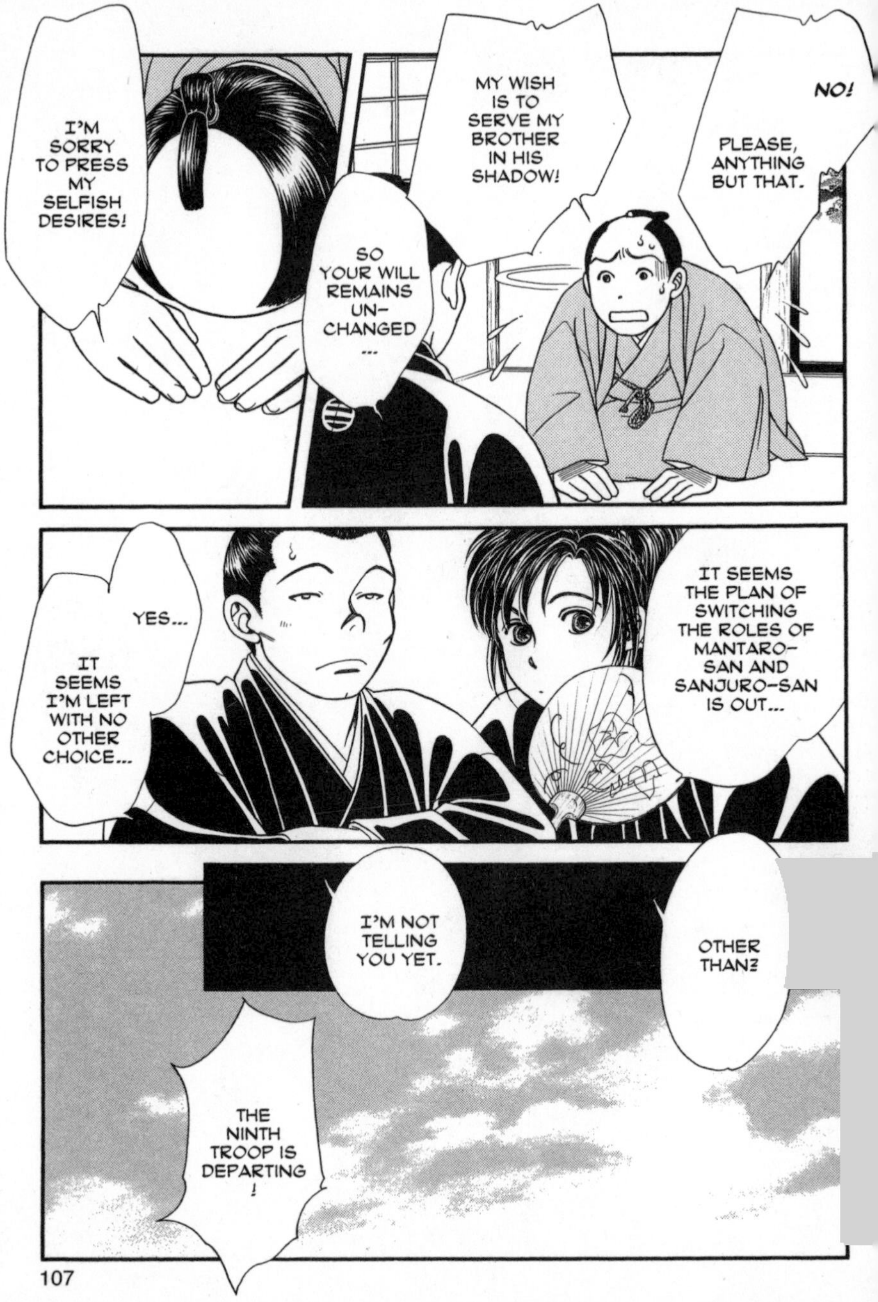
NO!
PLEASE, ANYTHING BUT THAT.
MY WISH IS TO SERVE MY BROTHER IN HIS SHADOW!
SO YOUR WILL REMAINS UN-CHANGED...
I'M SORRY TO PRESS MY SELFISH DESIRES!
IT SEEMS THE PLAN OF SWITCHING THE ROLES OF MANTARO-SAN AND SANJURO-SAN IS OUT...
YES...
IT SEEMS I'M LEFT WITH NO OTHER CHOICE...
OTHER THAN?
I'M NOT TELLING YOU YET.
THE NINTH TROOP IS DEPARTING!

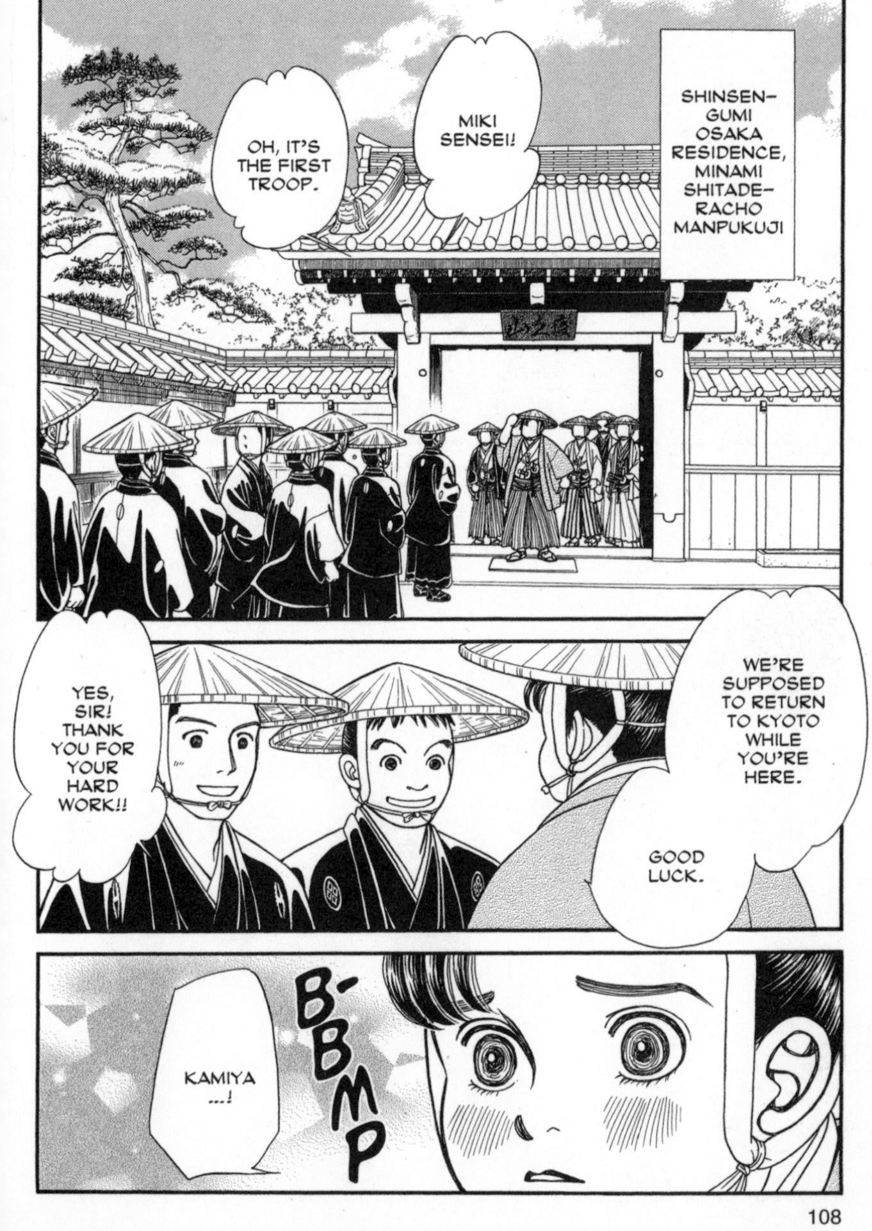
SHINSEN-GUMI OSAKA RESIDENCE, MINAMI SHITADE-RACHO MANPUKUJI
MIKI SENSEI!
OH, IT'S THE FIRST TROOP.
WE'RE SUPPOSED TO RETURN TO KYOTO WHILE YOU'RE HERE.
GOOD LUCK.
YES, SIR! THANK YOU FOR YOUR HARD WORK!!
B-BMP
KAMIYA ...!

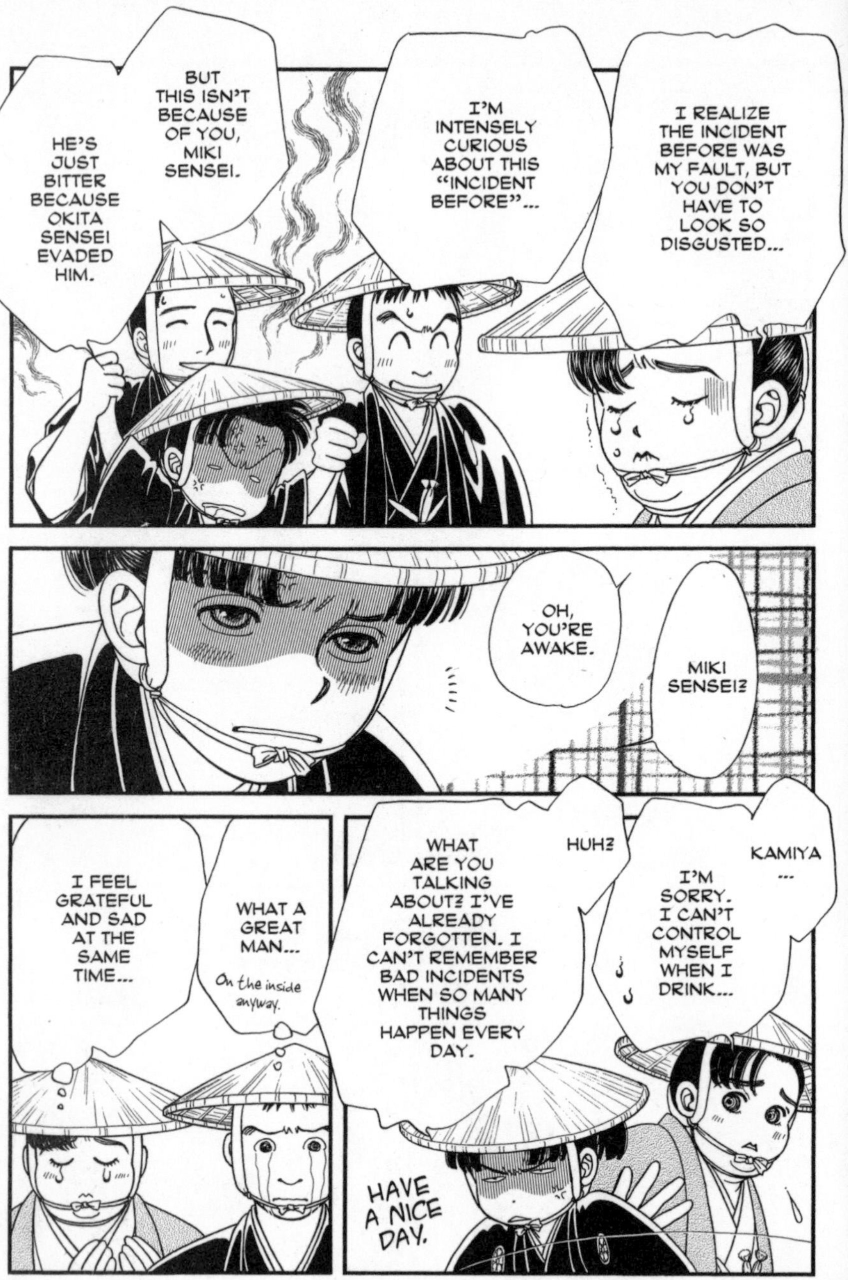
I REALIZE THE INCIDENT BEFORE WAS MY FAULT, BUT YOU DON'T HAVE TO LOOK SO DISGUSTED...
I'M INTENSELY CURIOUS ABOUT THIS "INCIDENT BEFORE"...
BUT THIS ISN'T BECAUSE OF YOU, MIKI SENSEI.
HE'S JUST BITTER BECAUSE OKITA SENSEI EVADED HIM.
MIKI SENSEI!?
OH, YOU'RE AWAKE.
KAMIYA...
I'M SORRY. I CAN'T CONTROL MYSELF WHEN I DRINK...
HUH?
WHAT ARE YOU TALKING ABOUT? I'VE ALREADY FORGOTTEN. I CAN'T REMEMBER BAD INCIDENTS WHEN SO MANY THINGS HAPPEN EVERY DAY.
HAVE A NICE DAY.
WHAT A GREAT MAN...
On the inside anyway.
I FEEL GRATEFUL AND SAD AT THE SAME TIME...

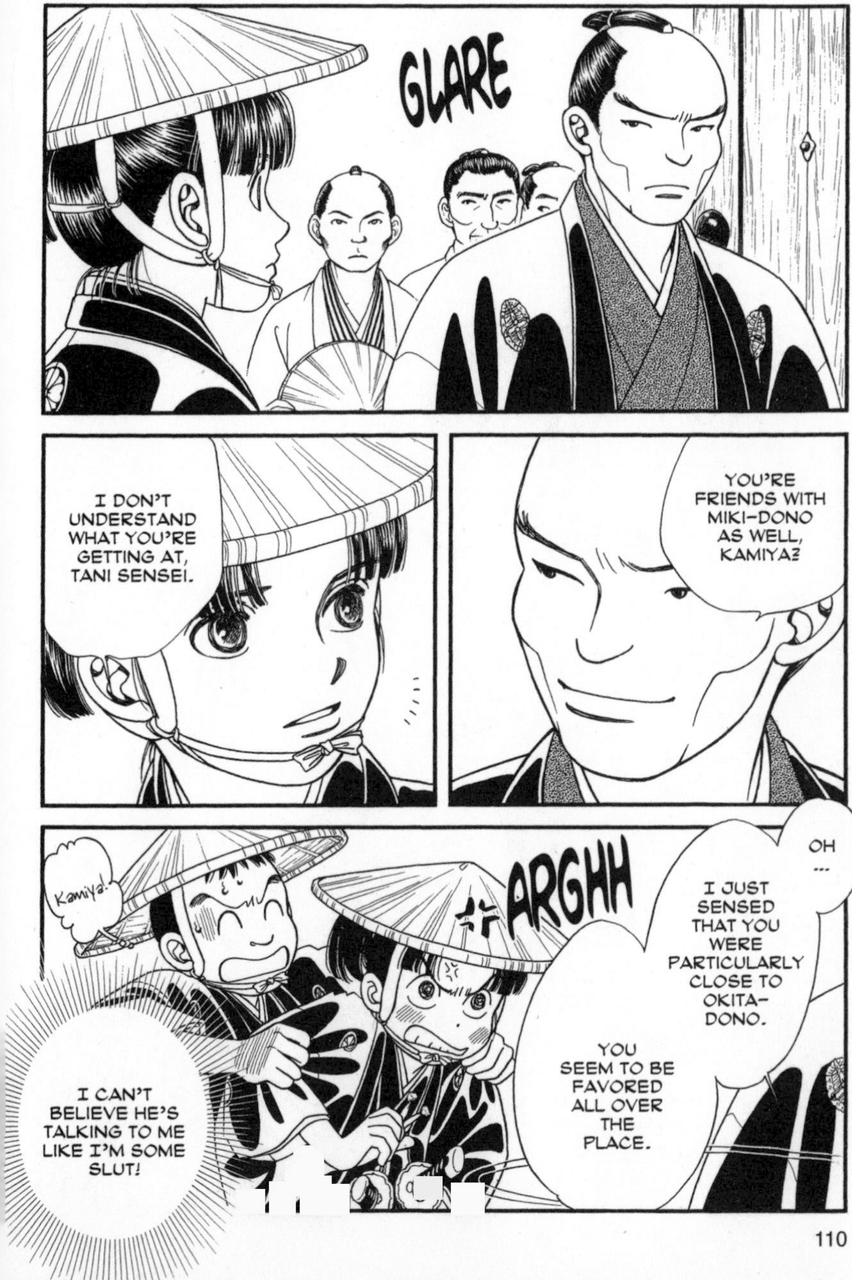
GLARE
YOU'RE FRIENDS WITH MIKI-DONO AS WELL, KAMIYA?
I DON'T UNDERSTAND WHAT YOU'RE GETTING AT, TANI SENSEI.
OH ... I JUST SENSED THAT YOU WERE PARTICULARLY CLOSE TO OKITA-DONO.
YOU SEEM TO BE FAVORED ALL OVER THE PLACE.
ARGHH
Kamiya!
I CAN'T BELIEVE HE'S TALKING TO ME LIKE I'M SOME SLUT!

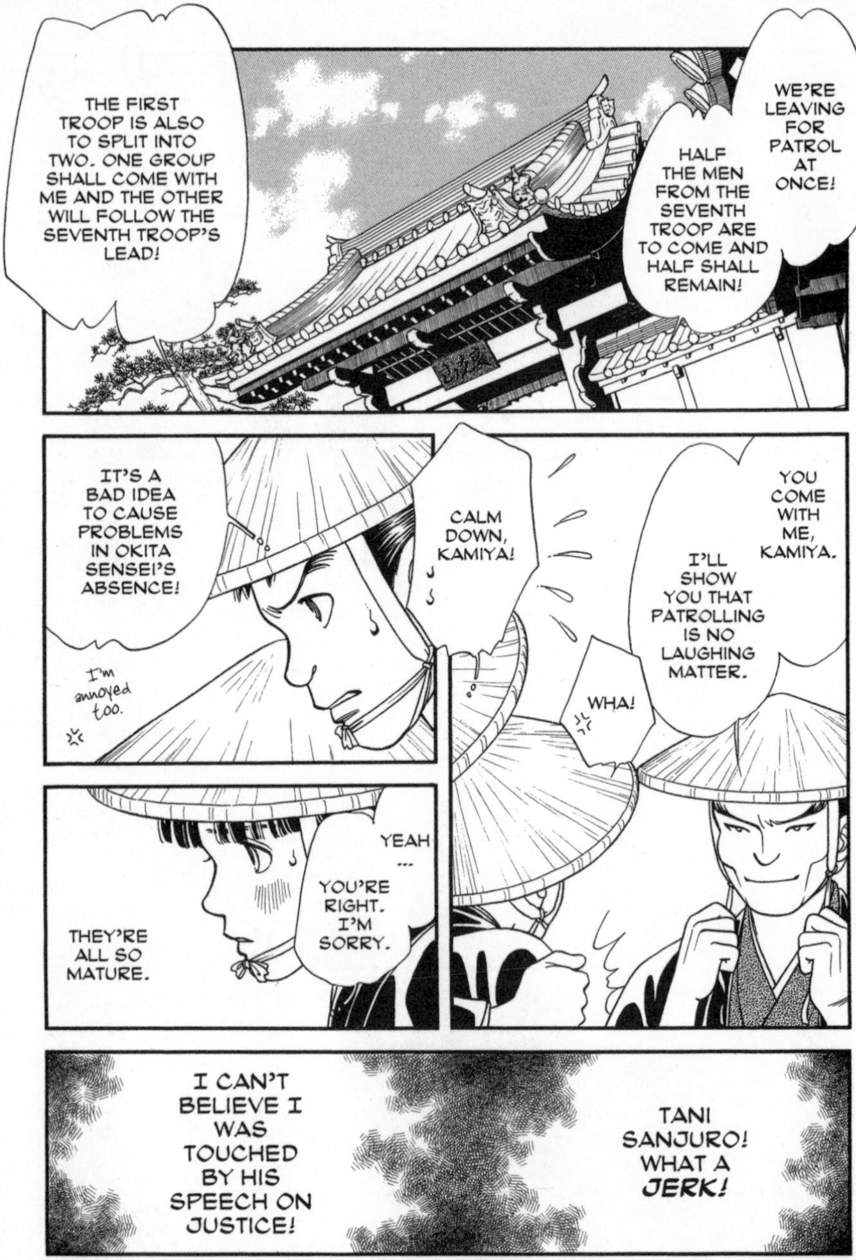
WE'RE LEAVING FOR PATROL AT ONCE!
HALF THE MEN FROM THE SEVENTH TROOP ARE TO COME AND HALF SHALL REMAIN!
THE FIRST TROOP IS ALSO TO SPLIT INTO TWO. ONE GROUP SHALL COME WITH ME AND THE OTHER WILL FOLLOW THE SEVENTH TROOP'S LEAD!
YOU COME WITH ME, KAMIYA.
I'LL SHOW YOU THAT PATROLLING IS NO LAUGHING MATTER.
WHA!
CALM DOWN, KAMIYA!
IT'S A BAD IDEA TO CAUSE PROBLEMS IN OKITA SENSEI'S ABSENCE!
I'm annoyed too.
YEAH...
YOU'RE RIGHT. I'M SORRY.
THEY'RE ALL SO MATURE.
TANI SANJURO! WHAT A *JERK!*
I CAN'T BELIEVE I WAS TOUCHED BY HIS SPEECH ON JUSTICE!

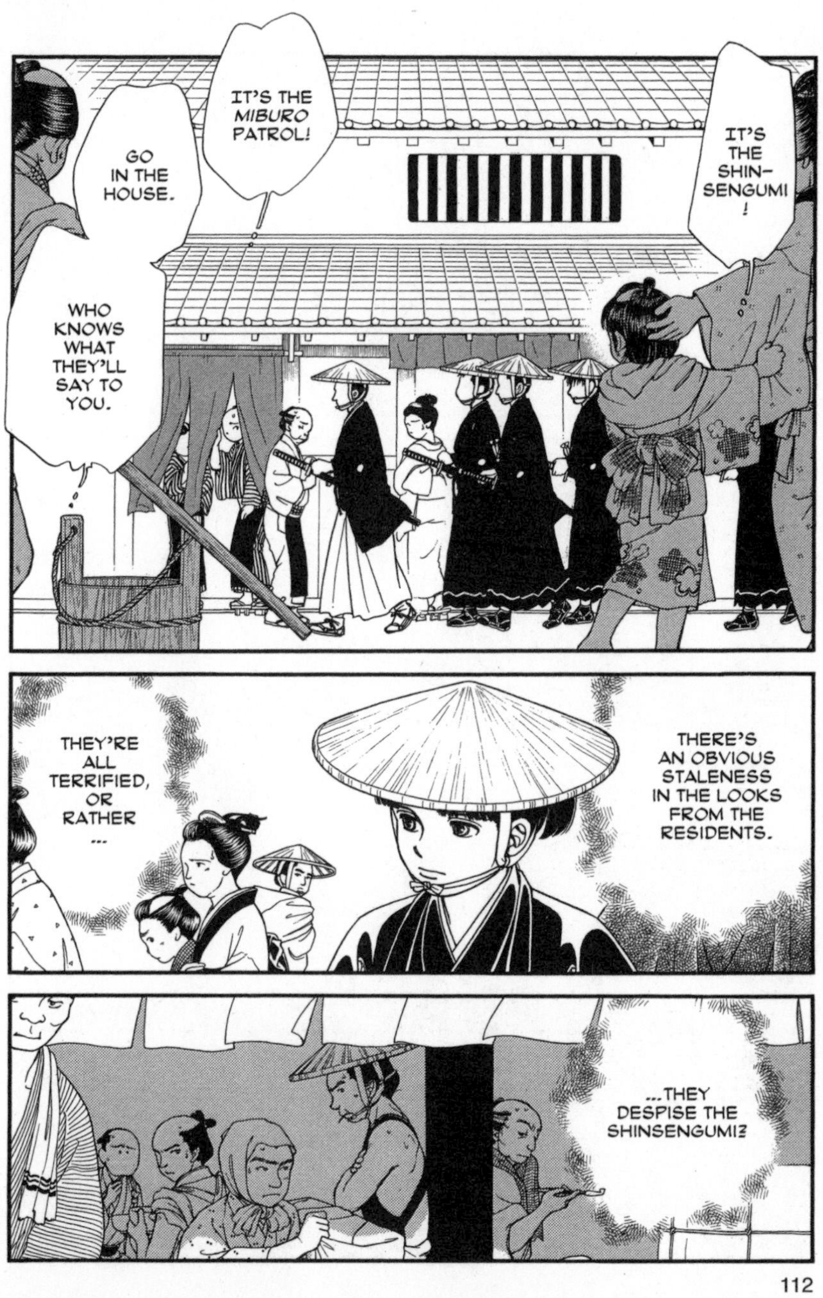
IT'S THE SHIN-SENGUMI!
IT'S THE MIBURO PATROL!
GO IN THE HOUSE.
WHO KNOWS WHAT THEY'LL SAY TO YOU.
THERE'S AN OBVIOUS STALENESS IN THE LOOKS FROM THE RESIDENTS.
THEY'RE ALL TERRIFIED, OR RATHER...
...THEY DESPISE THE SHINSENGUMI?

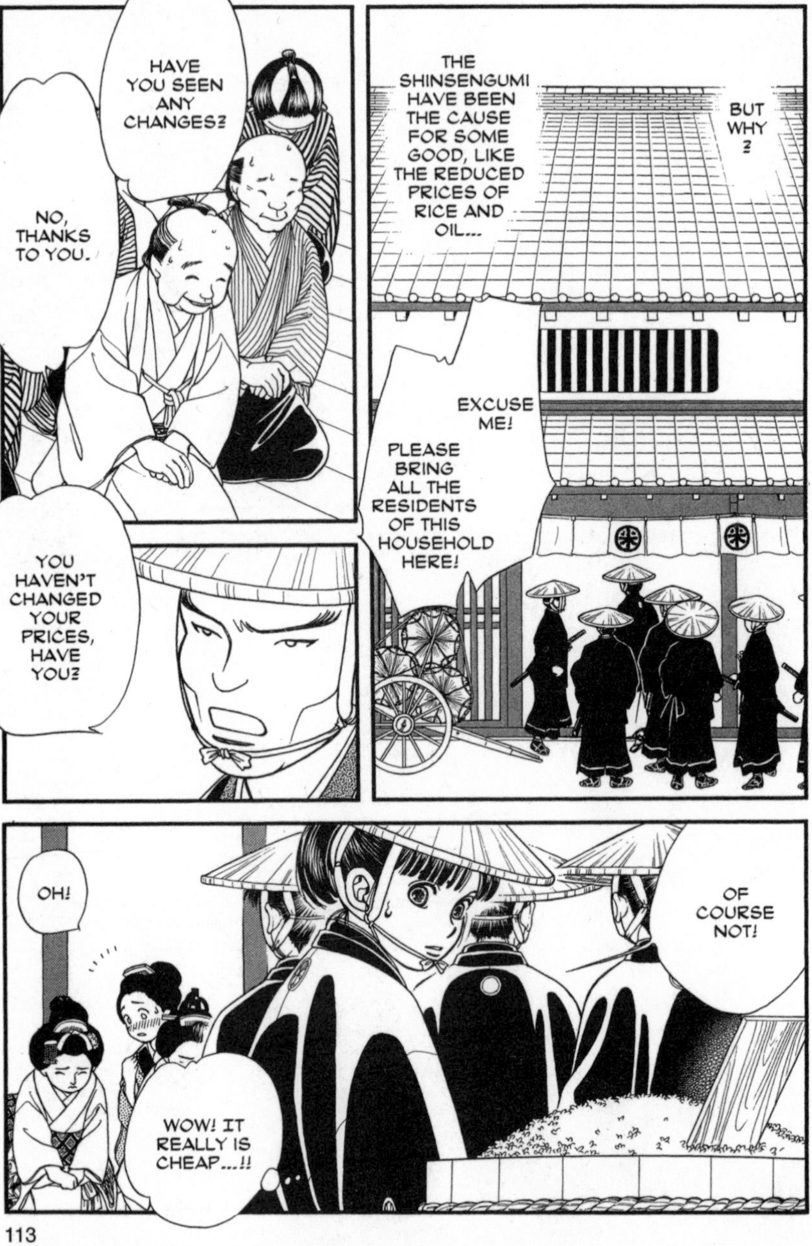
THE SHINSENGUMI HAVE BEEN THE CAUSE FOR SOME GOOD, LIKE THE REDUCED PRICES OF RICE AND OIL...
BUT WHY?
EXCUSE ME!
PLEASE BRING ALL THE RESIDENTS OF THIS HOUSEHOLD HERE!
HAVE YOU SEEN ANY CHANGES?
NO, THANKS TO YOU.
YOU HAVEN'T CHANGED YOUR PRICES, HAVE YOU?
OF COURSE NOT!
OH!
WOW! IT REALLY IS CHEAP...!!

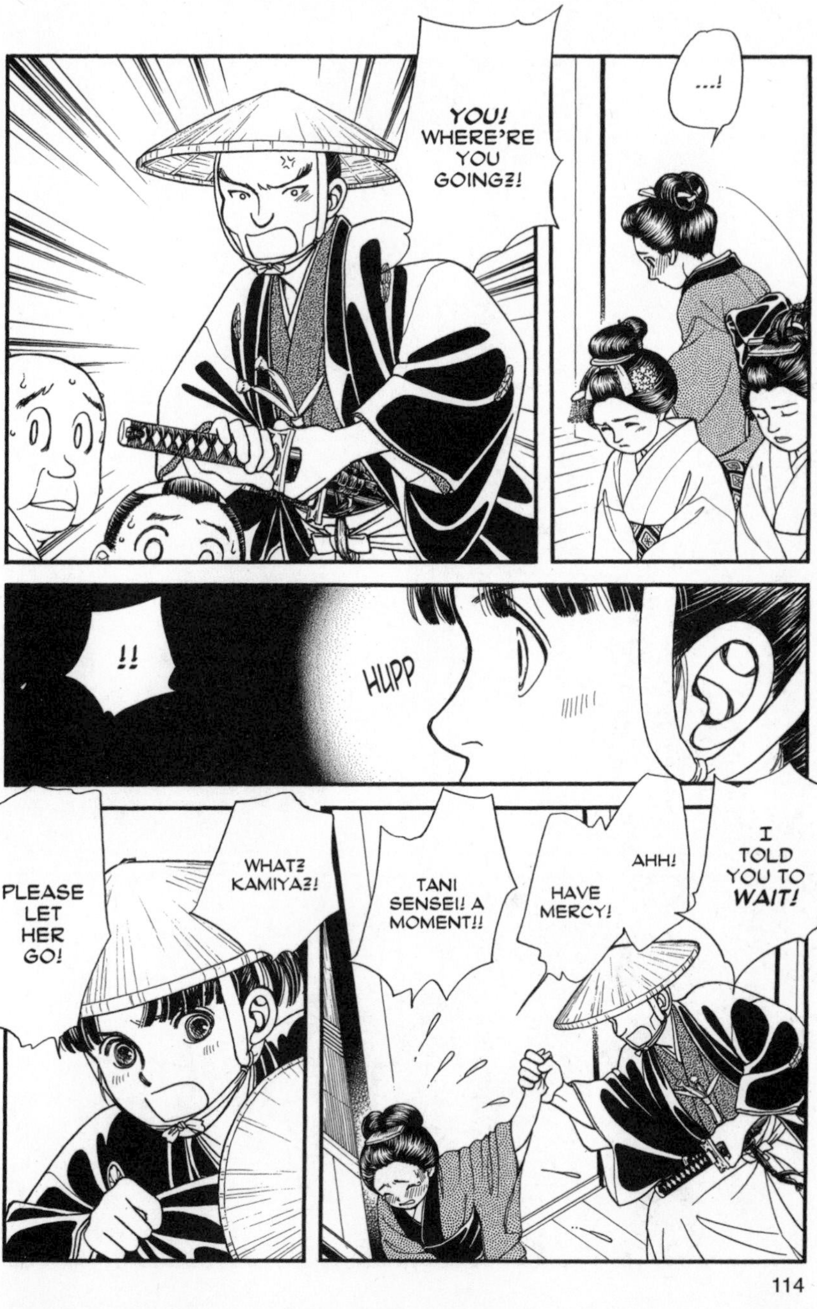
...!
YOU! WHERE'RE YOU GOING?!
HUPP
!!
I TOLD YOU TO *WAIT!*
AHH!
HAVE MERCY!
TANI SENSEI! A MOMENT!!
WHAT? KAMIYA?!
PLEASE LET HER GO!

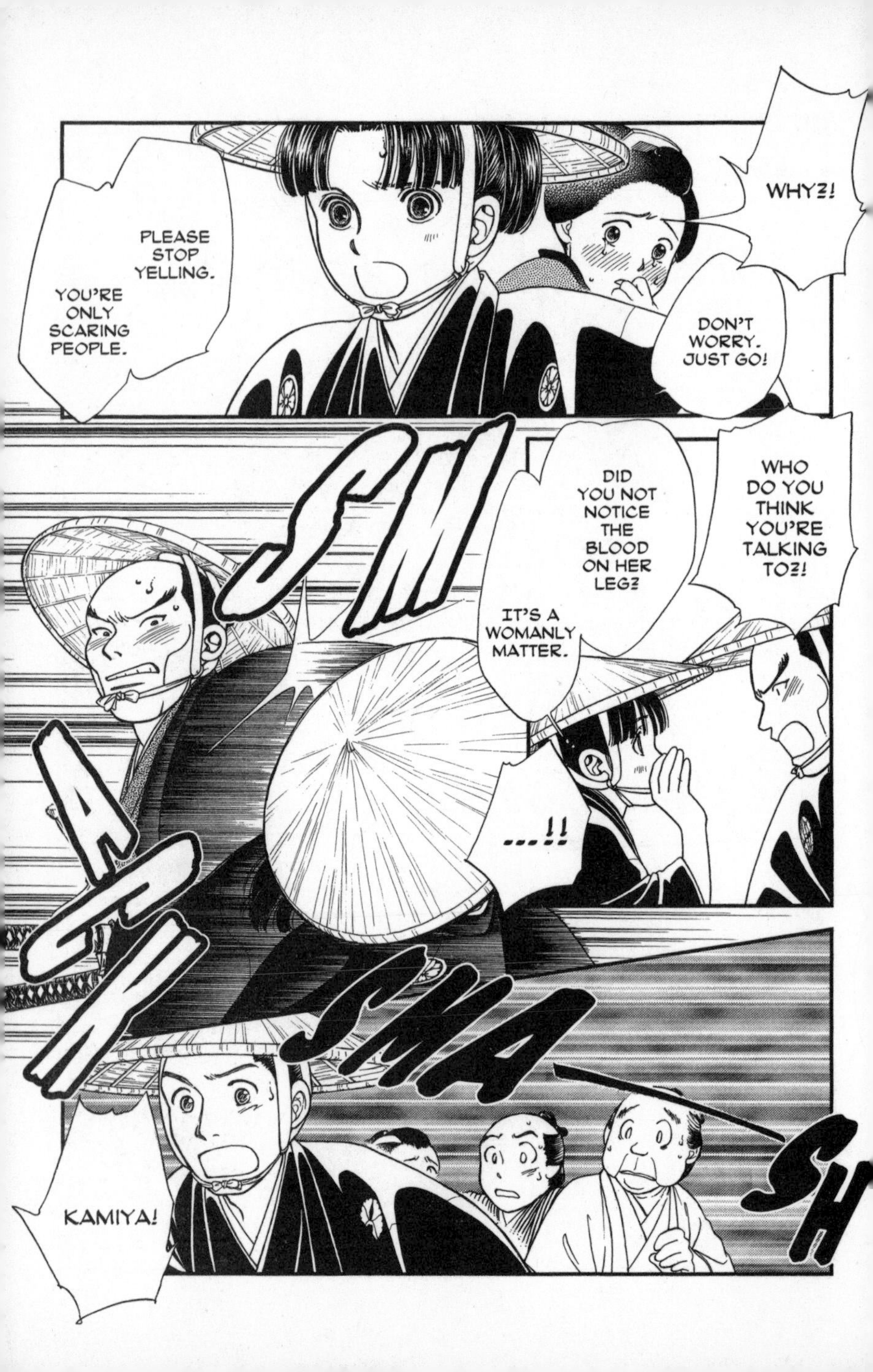
WHY?!
DON'T WORRY. JUST GO!
PLEASE STOP YELLING.
YOU'RE ONLY SCARING PEOPLE.
WHO DO YOU THINK YOU'RE TALKING TO?!
DID YOU NOT NOTICE THE BLOOD ON HER LEG?
IT'S A WOMANLY MATTER.
...!!
SM
ACK
SMA
SH
KAMIYA!

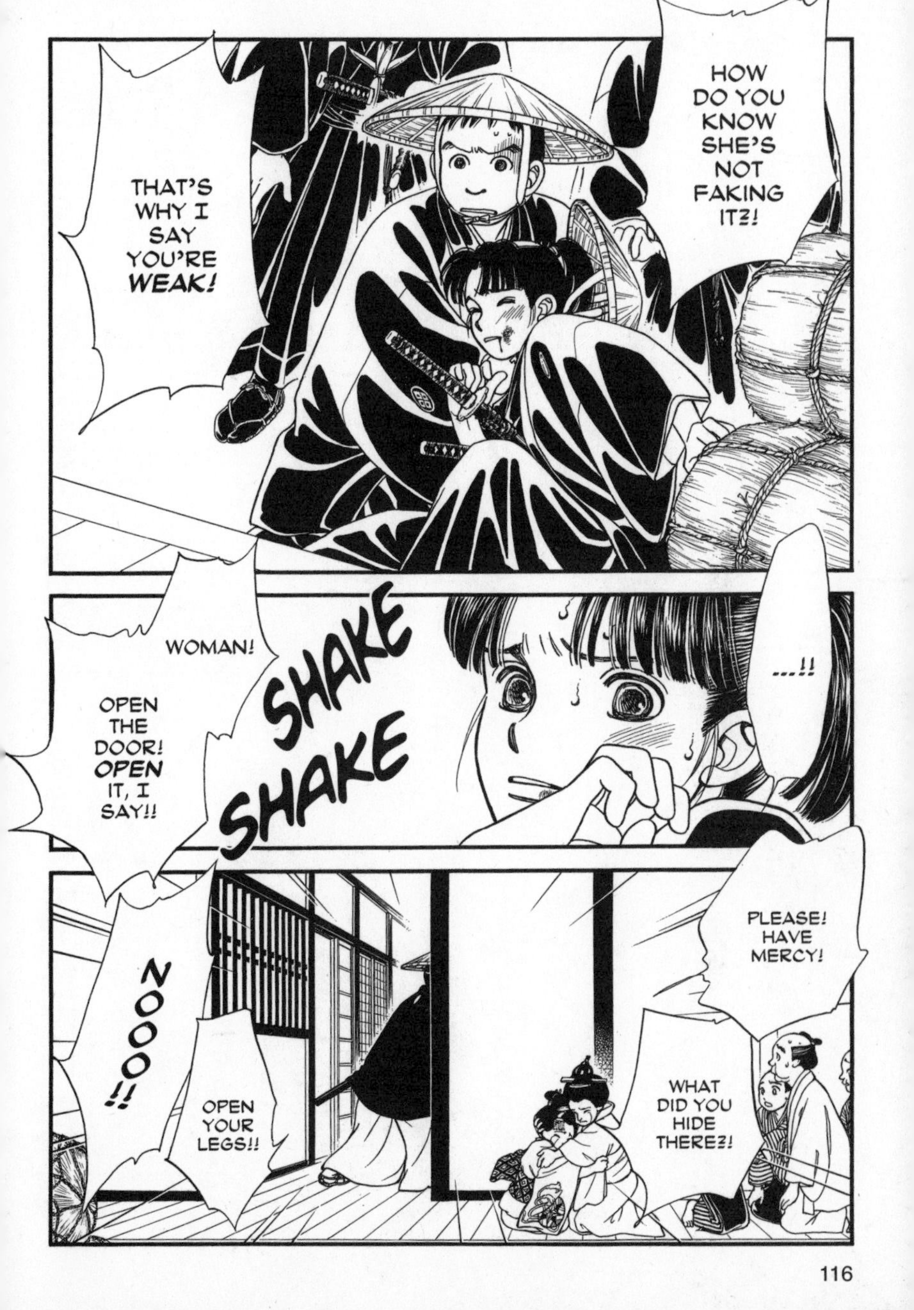
HOW DO YOU KNOW SHE'S NOT FAKING IT?!
THAT'S WHY I SAY YOU'RE WEAK!
...!!
SHAKE SHAKE
WOMAN!
OPEN THE DOOR! OPEN IT, I SAY!!
PLEASE! HAVE MERCY!
WHAT DID YOU HIDE THERE?!
OPEN YOUR LEGS!!
NOOOO!!

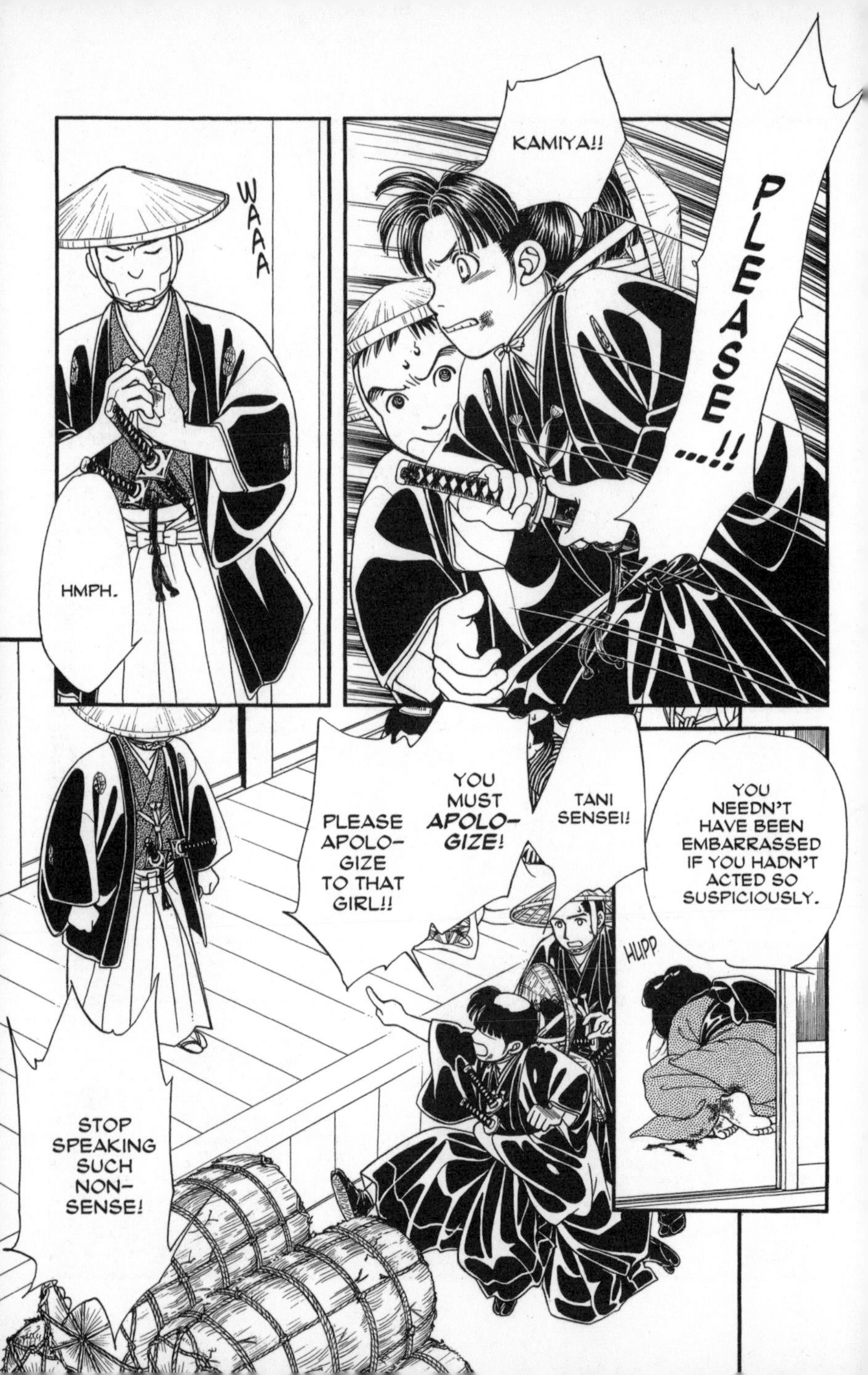
KAMIYA!!
PLEASE ...!!
WAAA
HMPH.
YOU NEEDN'T HAVE BEEN EMBARRASSED IF YOU HADN'T ACTED SO SUSPICIOUSLY.
HUPP
TANI SENSEI!
YOU MUST APOLOGIZE!
PLEASE APOLOGIZE TO THAT GIRL!!
STOP SPEAKING SUCH NONSENSE!

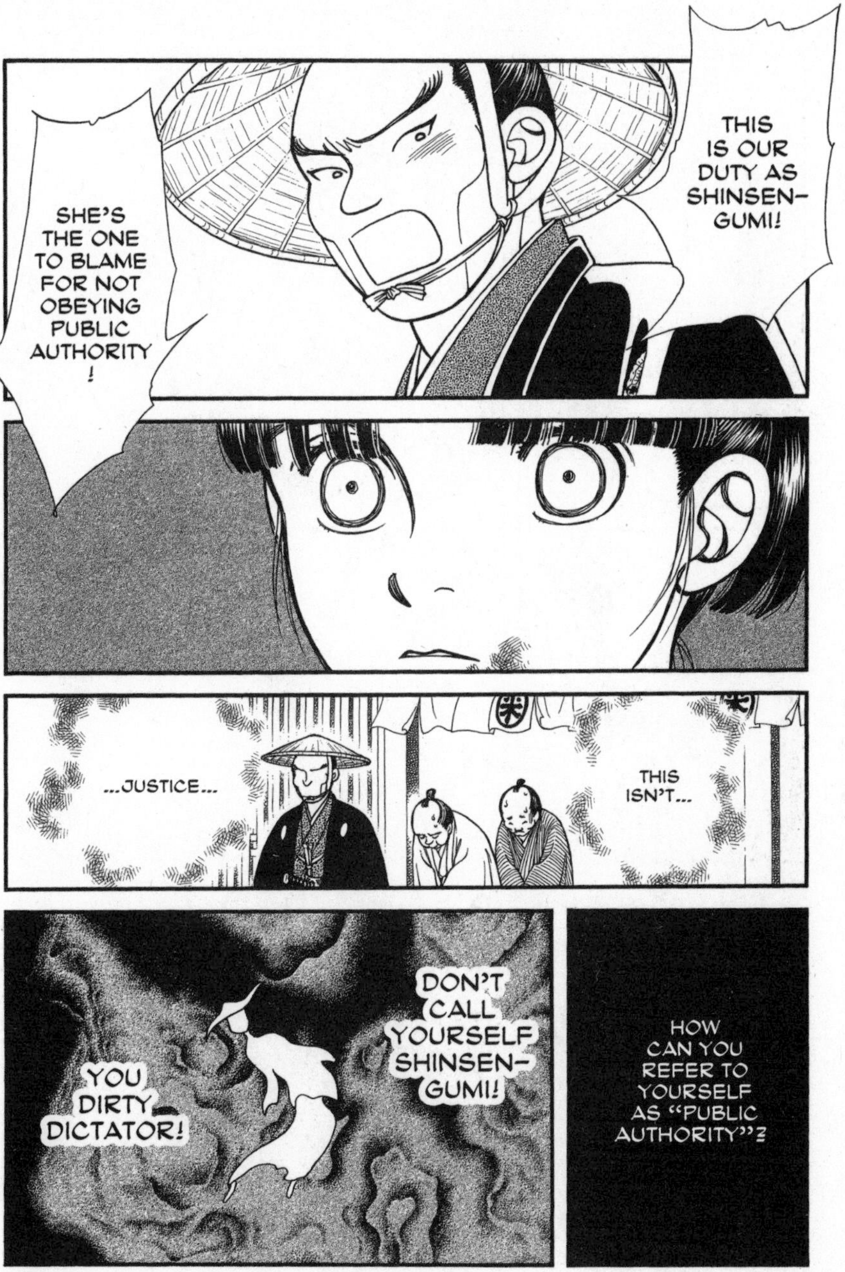
THIS IS OUR DUTY AS SHINSEN-GUMI!
SHE'S THE ONE TO BLAME FOR NOT OBEYING PUBLIC AUTHORITY!
THIS ISN'T...
...JUSTICE...
HOW CAN YOU REFER TO YOURSELF AS "PUBLIC AUTHORITY"?
DON'T CALL YOURSELF SHINSEN-GUMI!
YOU DIRTY DICTATOR!

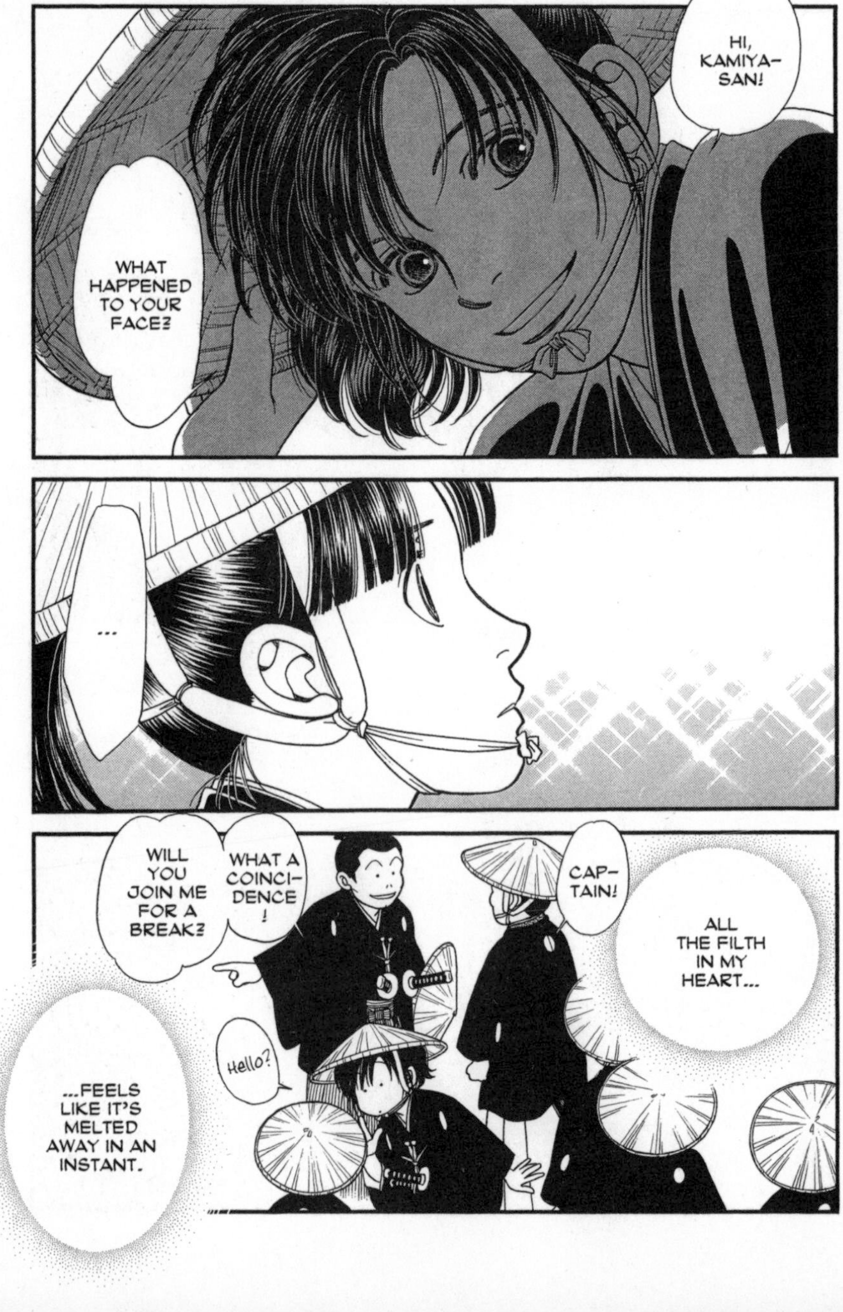
HI, KAMIYA-SAN!
WHAT HAPPENED TO YOUR FACE?
...
CAP-TAIN!
ALL THE FILTH IN MY HEART...
WHAT A COINCI-DENCE!
WILL YOU JOIN ME FOR A BREAK?
Hello?
...FEELS LIKE IT'S MELTED AWAY IN AN INSTANT.

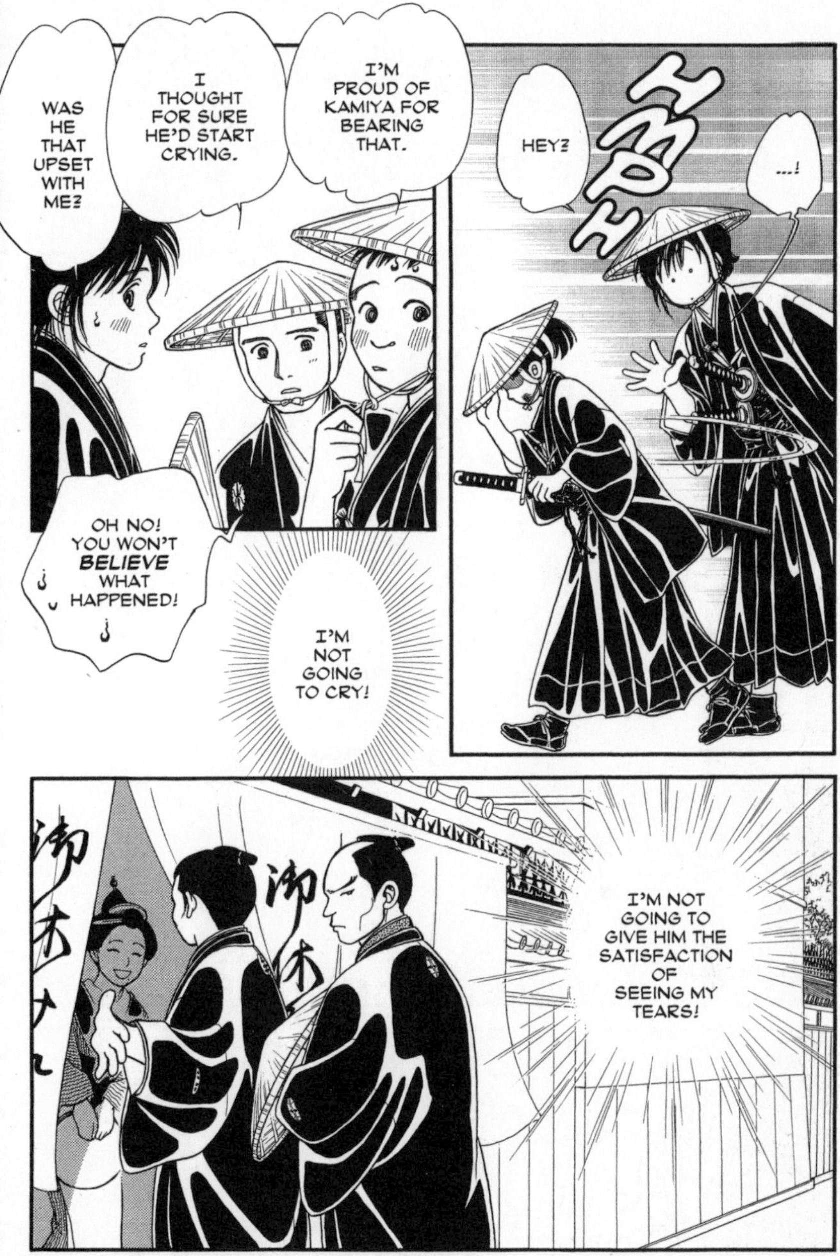
...!
HMPH
HEY?
I'M PROUD OF KAMIYA FOR BEARING THAT.
I THOUGHT FOR SURE HE'D START CRYING.
WAS HE THAT UPSET WITH ME?
OH NO! YOU WON'T BELIEVE WHAT HAPPENED!
I'M NOT GOING TO CRY!
I'M NOT GOING TO GIVE HIM THE SATISFACTION OF SEEING MY TEARS!

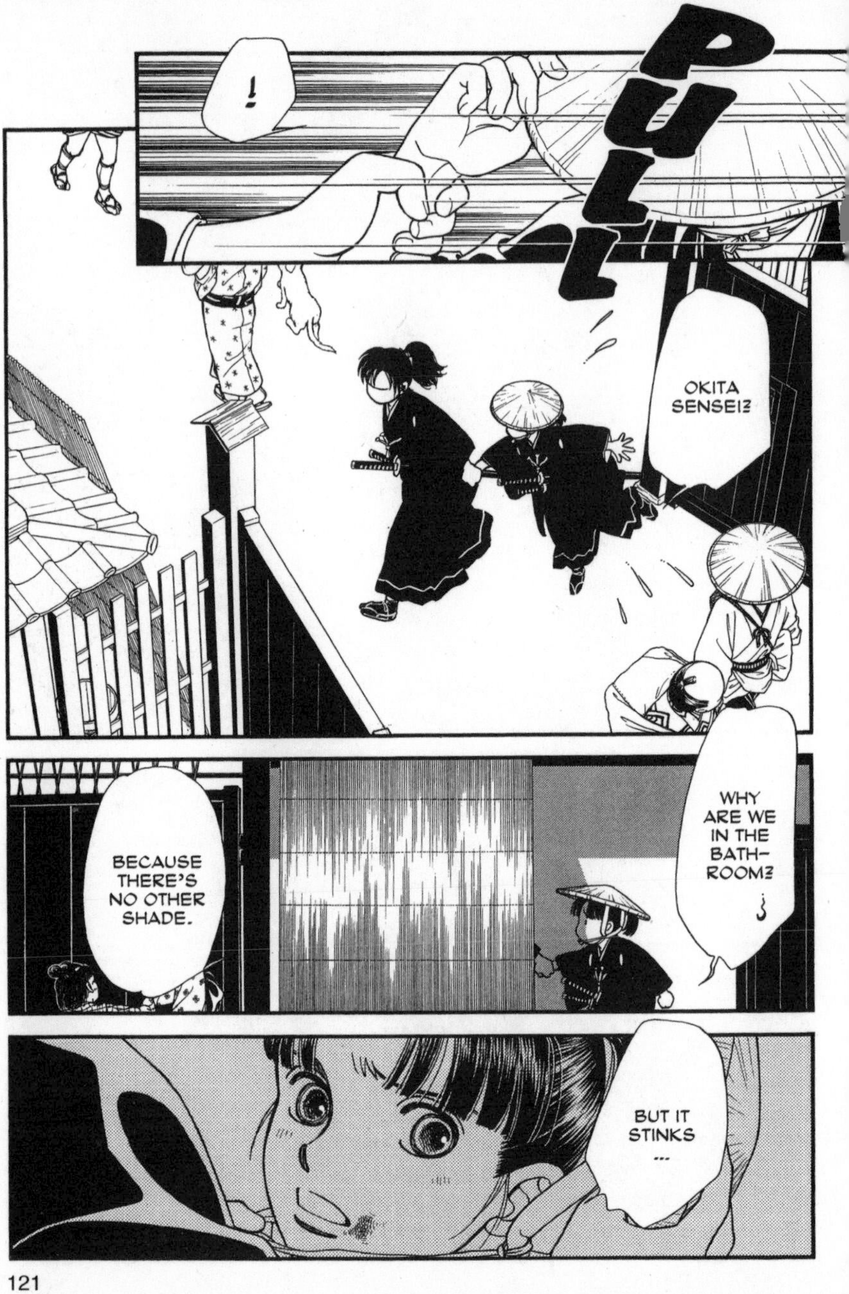
PULL
!
OKITA SENSEI?
WHY ARE WE IN THE BATHROOM?
BECAUSE THERE'S NO OTHER SHADE.
BUT IT STINKS...

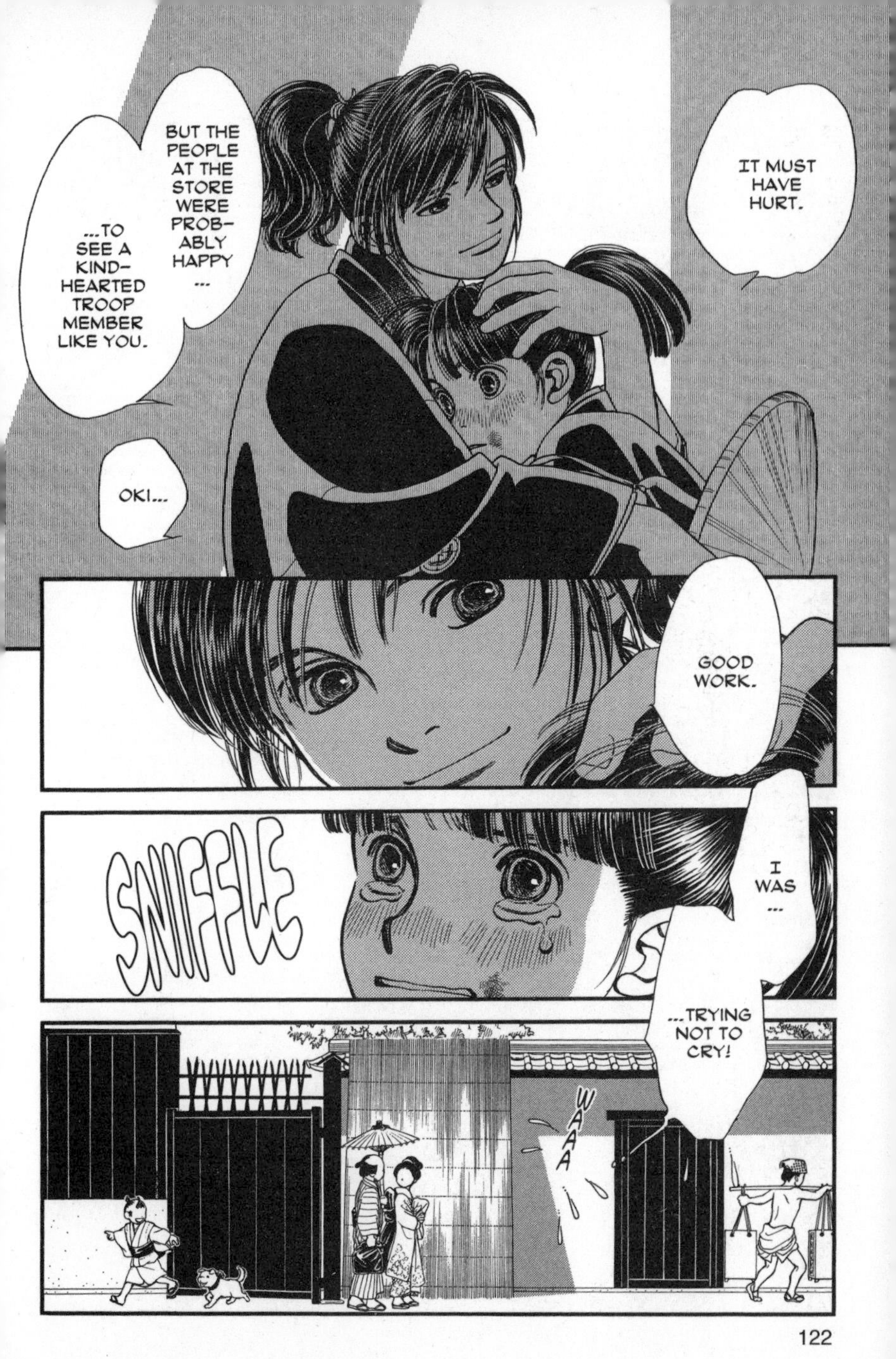
IT MUST HAVE HURT.
BUT THE PEOPLE AT THE STORE WERE PROBABLY HAPPY...
...TO SEE A KIND-HEARTED TROOP MEMBER LIKE YOU.
OKI...
GOOD WORK.
I WAS...
SNIFFLE
...TRYING NOT TO CRY!
WAAAA

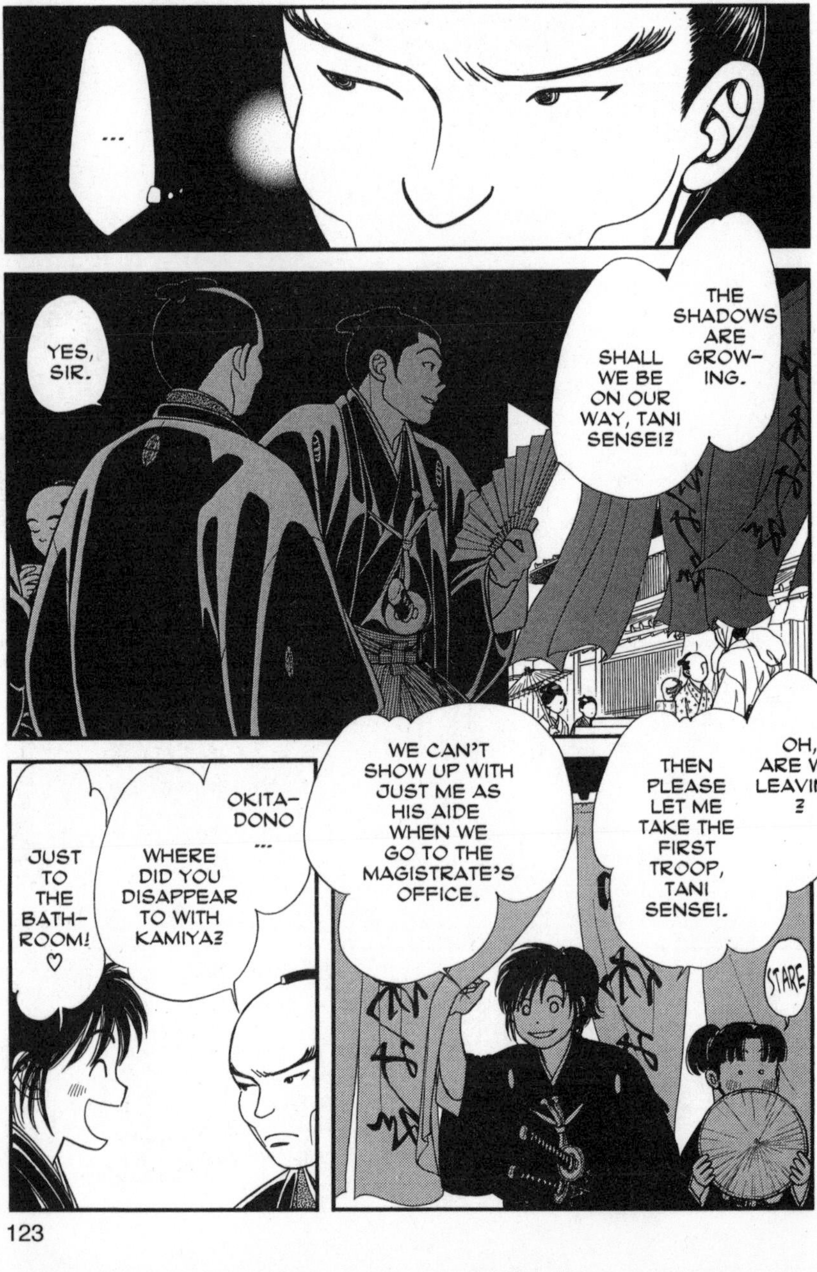
...
THE SHADOWS ARE GROWING.
SHALL WE BE ON OUR WAY, TANI SENSEI?
YES, SIR.
OH, ARE WE LEAVING?
THEN PLEASE LET ME TAKE THE FIRST TROOP, TANI SENSEI.
STARE
WE CAN'T SHOW UP WITH JUST ME AS HIS AIDE WHEN WE GO TO THE MAGISTRATE'S OFFICE.
OKITA-DONO...
WHERE DID YOU DISAPPEAR TO WITH KAMIYA?
JUST TO THE BATHROOM! ♡

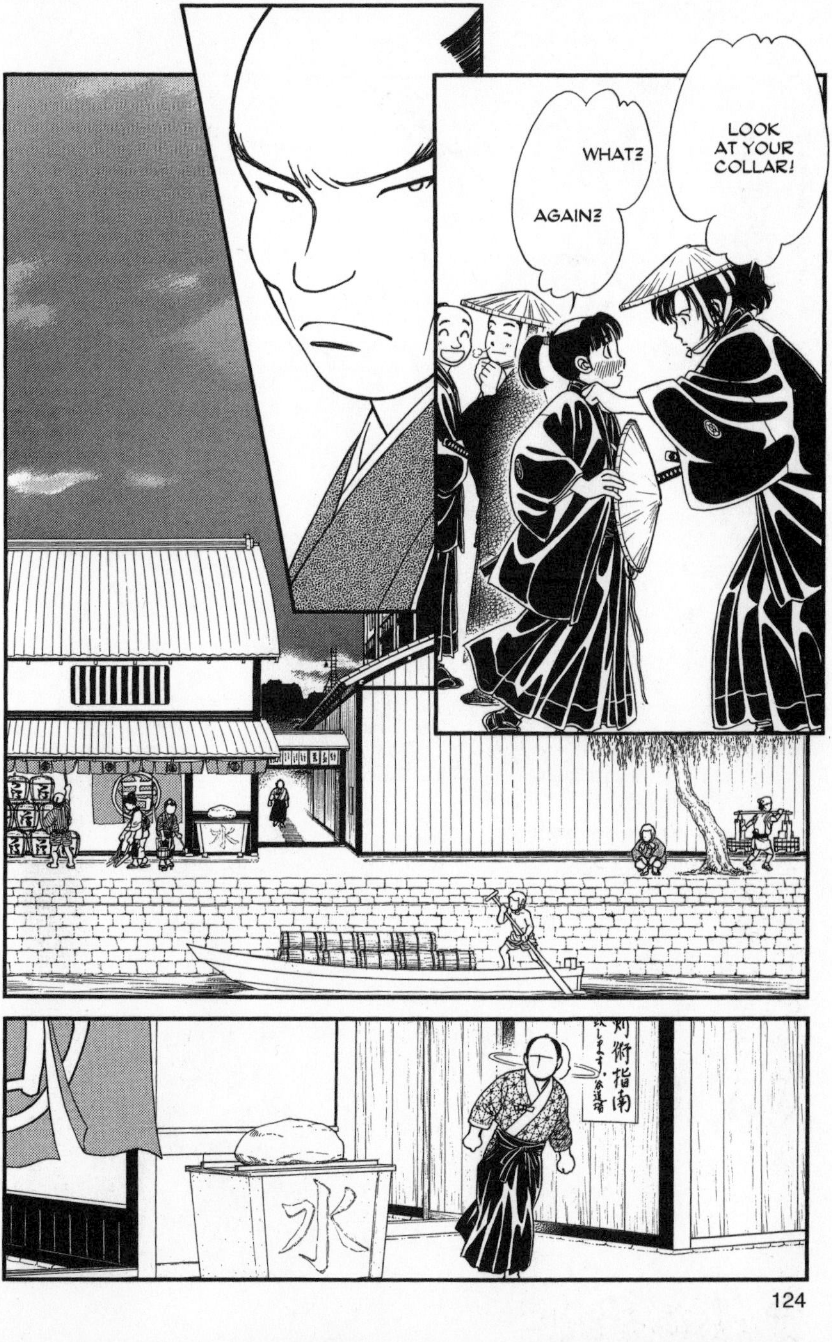
LOOK AT YOUR COLLAR!
WHAT? AGAIN?

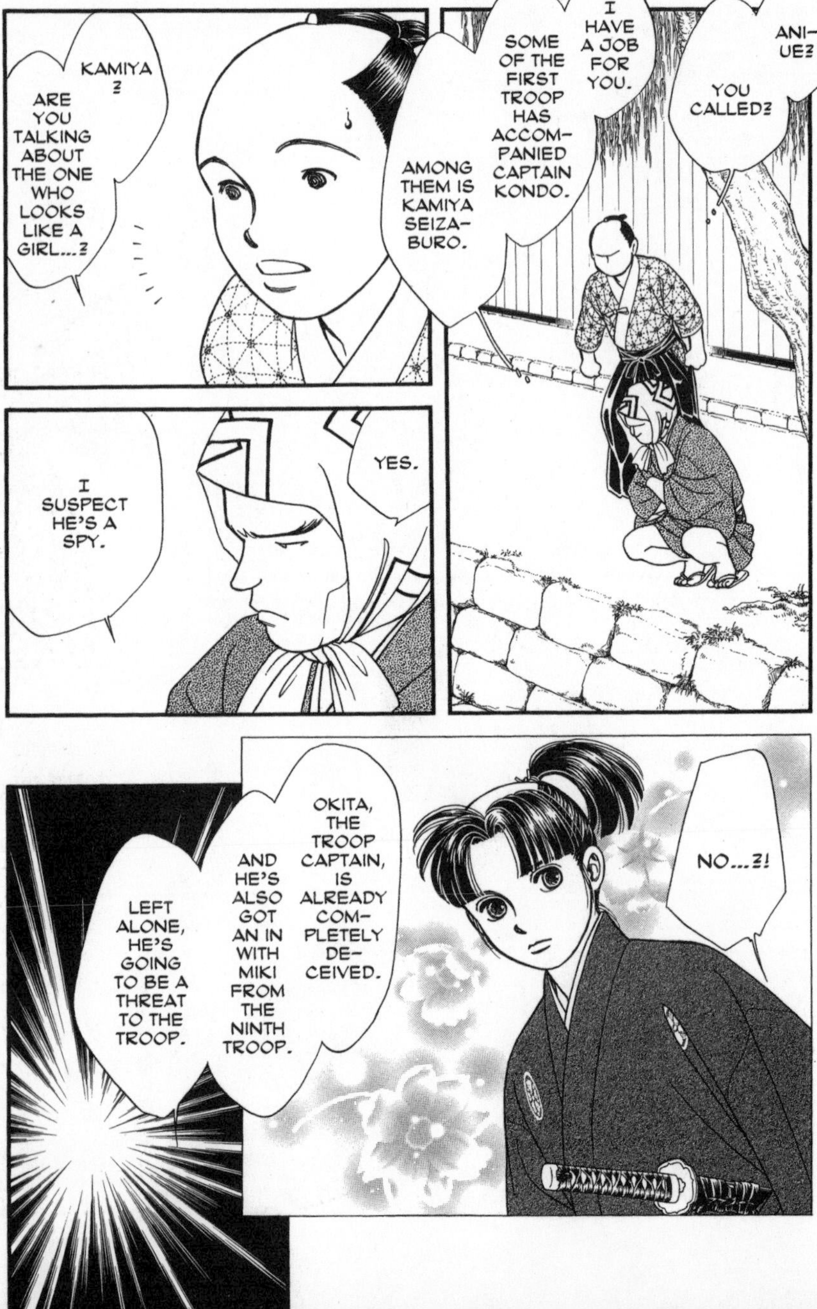
ANI-UE?
YOU CALLED?
I HAVE A JOB FOR YOU.
SOME OF THE FIRST TROOP HAS ACCOMPANIED CAPTAIN KONDO.
AMONG THEM IS KAMIYA SEIZABURO.
KAMIYA?
ARE YOU TALKING ABOUT THE ONE WHO LOOKS LIKE A GIRL...?
YES.
I SUSPECT HE'S A SPY.
NO...?!
OKITA, THE TROOP CAPTAIN, IS ALREADY COMPLETELY DECEIVED.
AND HE'S ALSO GOT AN IN WITH MIKI FROM THE NINTH TROOP.
LEFT ALONE, HE'S GOING TO BE A THREAT TO THE TROOP.

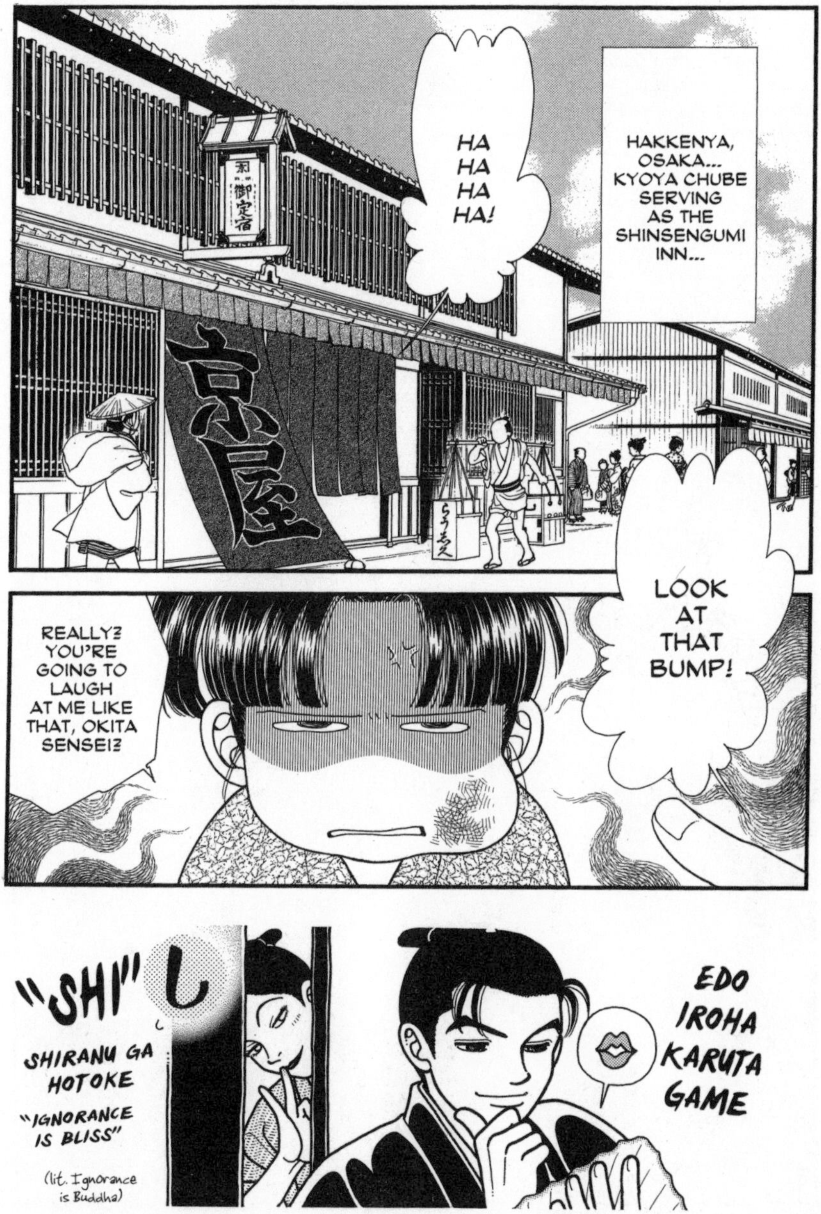
HAKKENYA, OSAKA... KYOYA CHUBE SERVING AS THE SHINSENGUMI INN...
HA HA HA HA!
京屋
LOOK AT THAT BUMP!
REALLY!? YOU'RE GOING TO LAUGH AT ME LIKE THAT, OKITA SENSEI!?
EDO IROHA KARUTA GAME
"SHI" し
SHIRANU GA HOTOKE
"IGNORANCE IS BLISS"
(lit. Ignorance is Buddha)

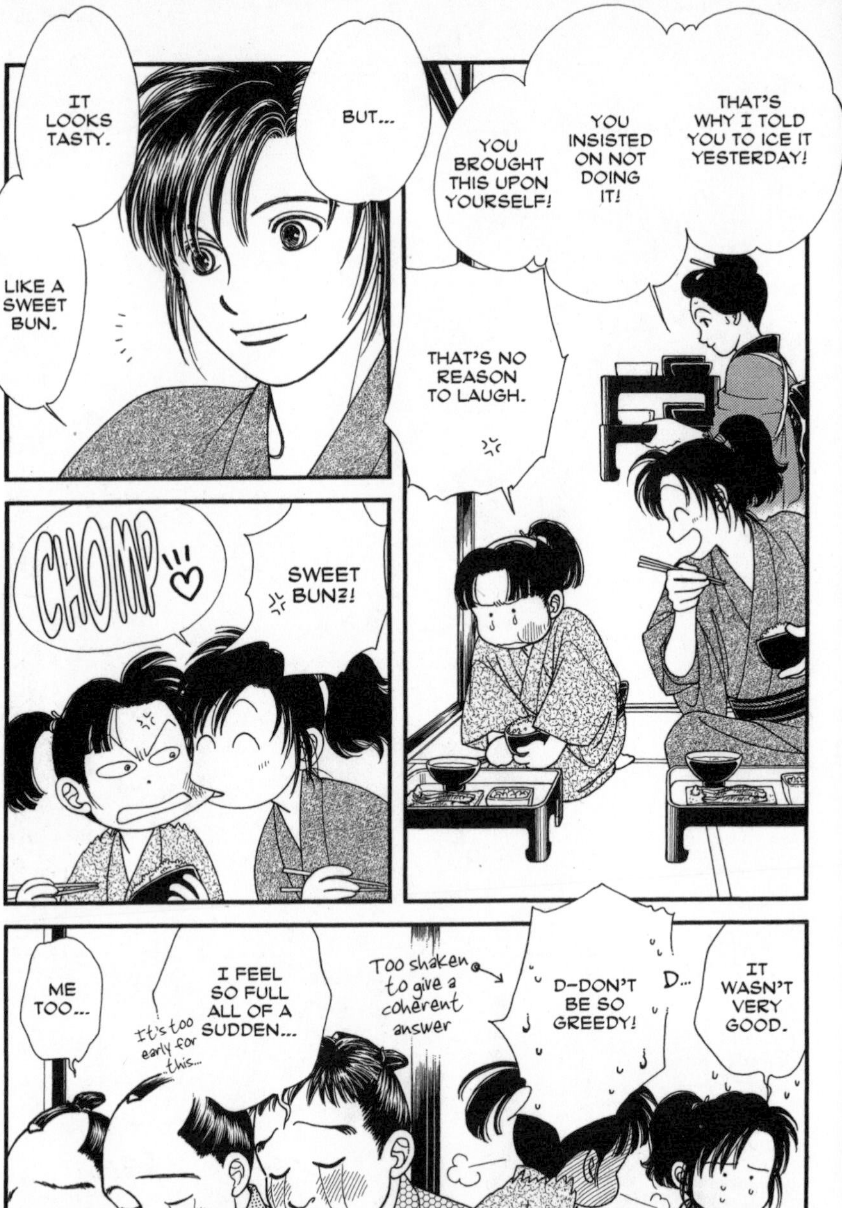
THAT'S WHY I TOLD YOU TO ICE IT YESTERDAY!
YOU INSISTED ON NOT DOING IT!
YOU BROUGHT THIS UPON YOURSELF!
THAT'S NO REASON TO LAUGH.
BUT...
IT LOOKS TASTY.
LIKE A SWEET BUN.
SWEET BUN?!
CHOMP
IT WASN'T VERY GOOD.
D...
D-DON'T BE SO GREEDY!
Too shaken to give a coherent answer
I FEEL SO FULL ALL OF A SUDDEN...
It's too early for this...
ME TOO...

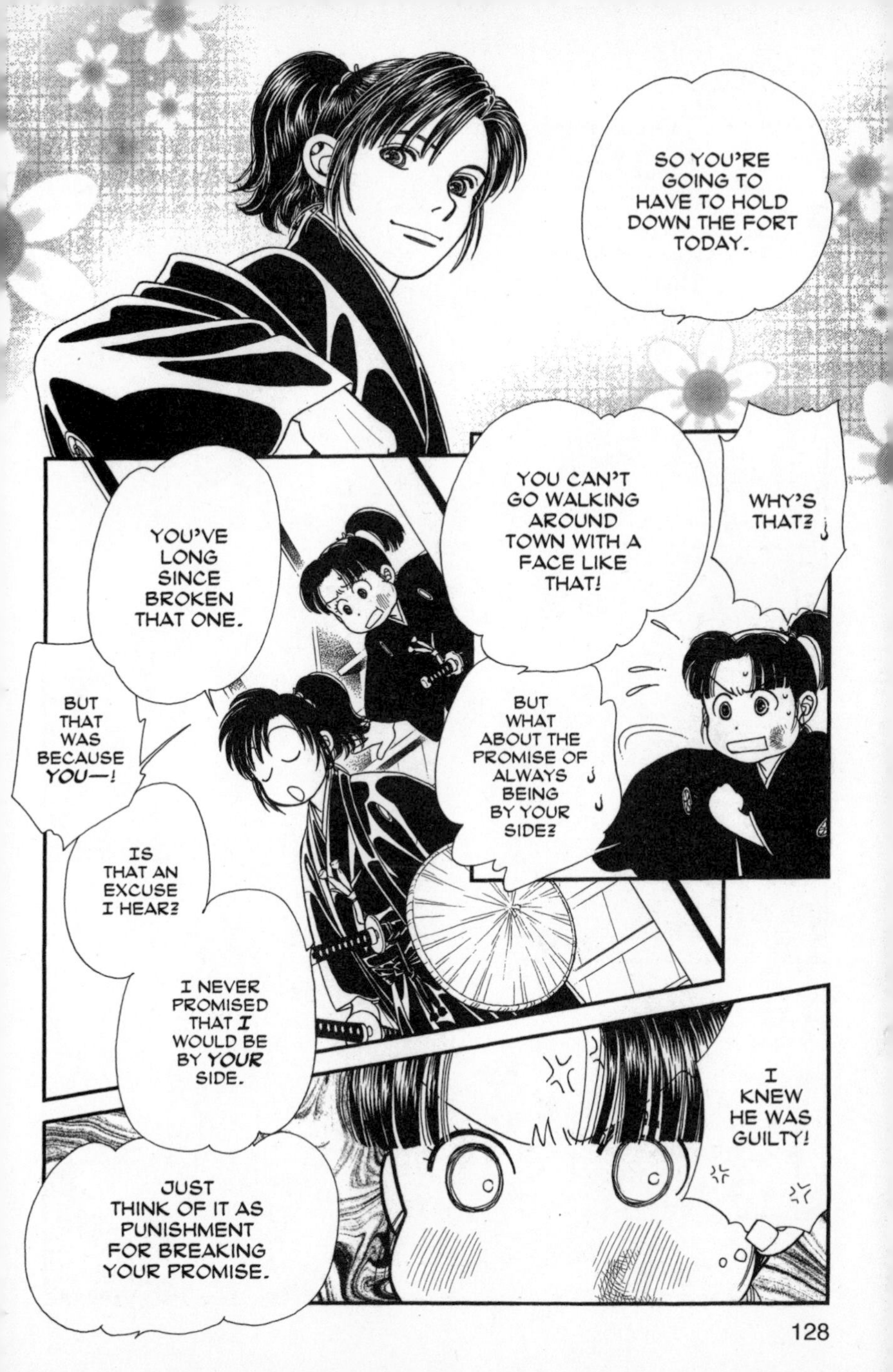
SO YOU'RE GOING TO HAVE TO HOLD DOWN THE FORT TODAY.
WHY'S THAT?
YOU CAN'T GO WALKING AROUND TOWN WITH A FACE LIKE THAT!
BUT WHAT ABOUT THE PROMISE OF ALWAYS BEING BY YOUR SIDE?
YOU'VE LONG SINCE BROKEN THAT ONE.
BUT THAT WAS BECAUSE *YOU*—!
IS THAT AN EXCUSE I HEAR?
I NEVER PROMISED THAT *I* WOULD BE BY *YOUR* SIDE.
I KNEW HE WAS GUILTY!
JUST THINK OF IT AS PUNISHMENT FOR BREAKING YOUR PROMISE.

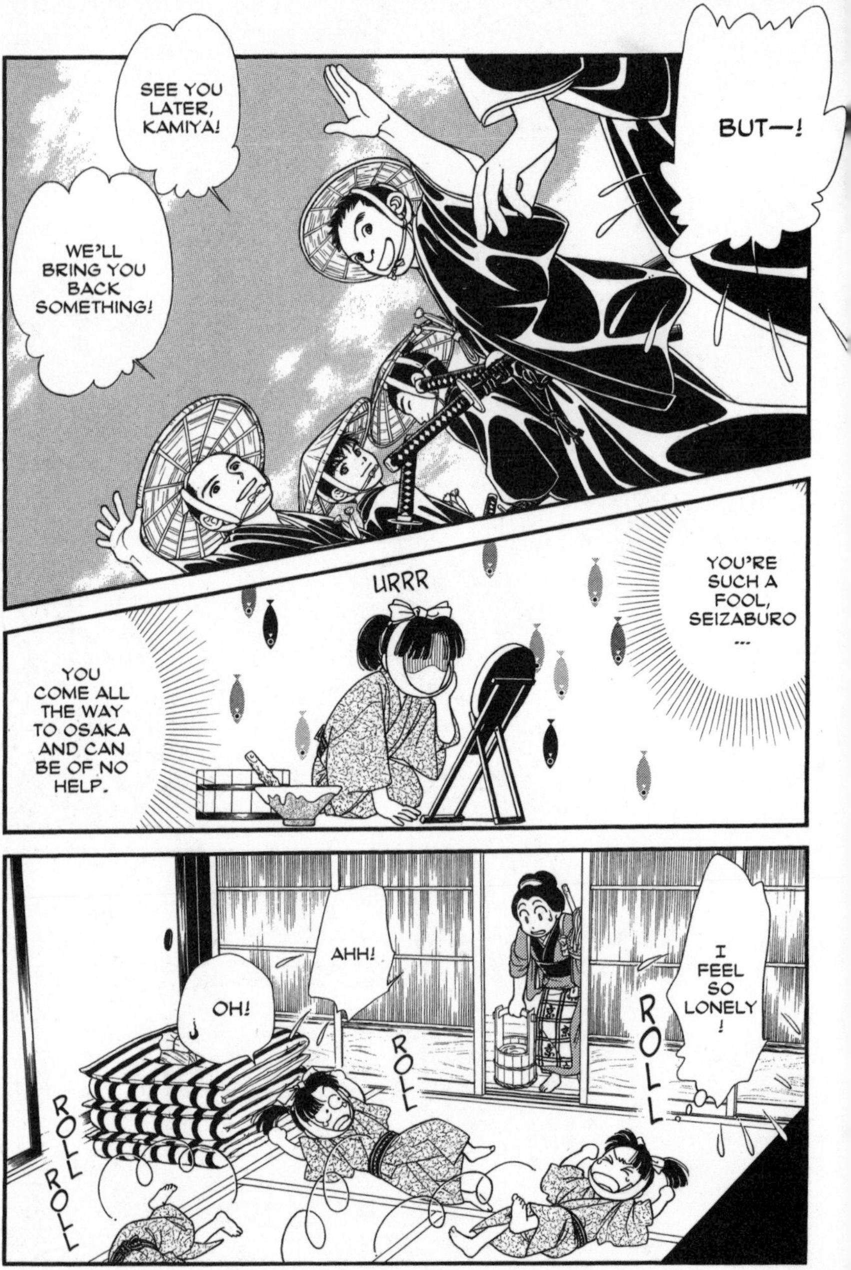
BUT—!
SEE YOU LATER, KAMIYA!
WE'LL BRING YOU BACK SOMETHING!
YOU'RE SUCH A FOOL, SEIZABURO ...
URRR
YOU COME ALL THE WAY TO OSAKA AND CAN BE OF NO HELP.
I FEEL SO LONELY!
ROLL
ROLL
AHH!
OH!
ROLL
ROLL

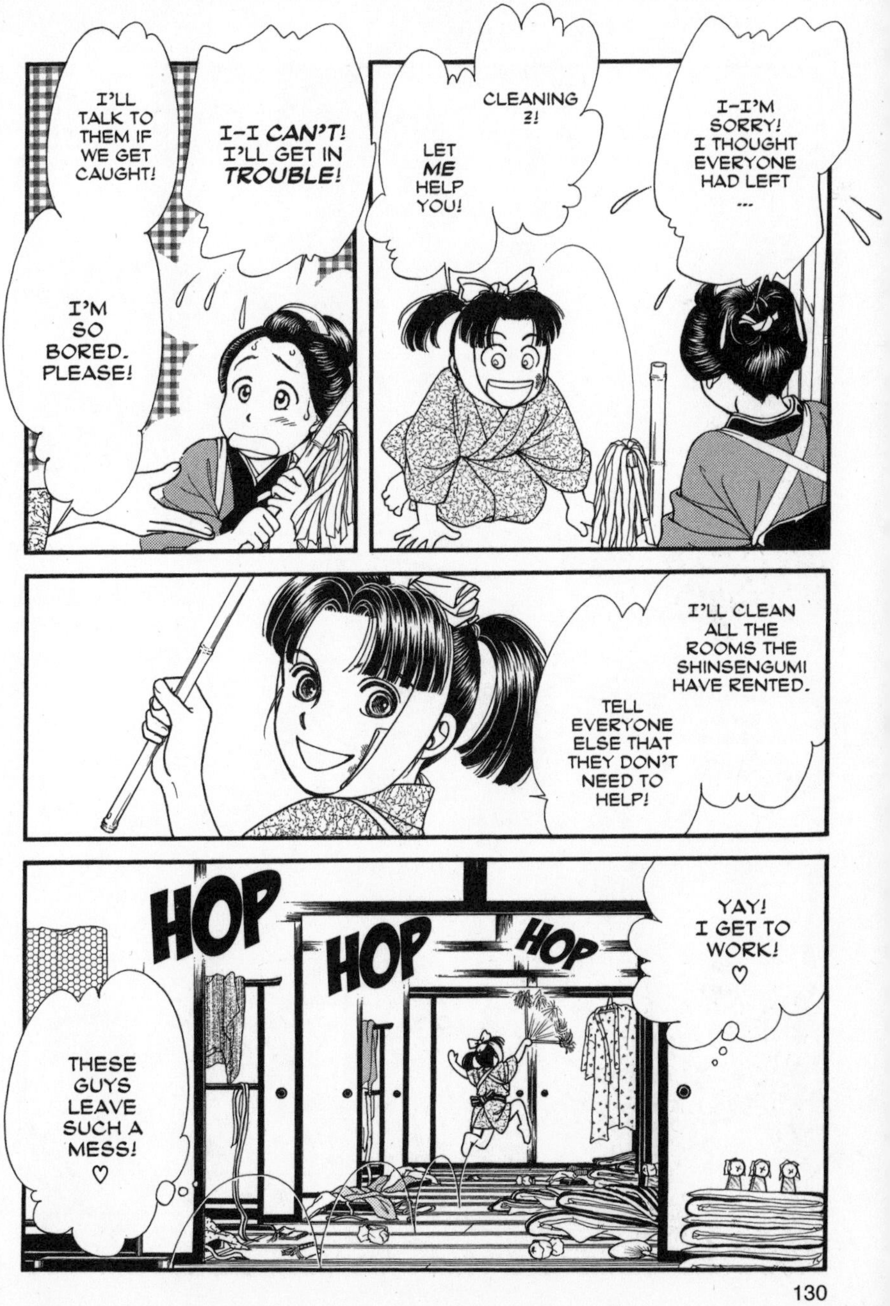
I-I'M SORRY! I THOUGHT EVERYONE HAD LEFT ...
CLEANING ?!
LET ME HELP YOU!
I-I CAN'T! I'LL GET IN TROUBLE!
I'LL TALK TO THEM IF WE GET CAUGHT!
I'M SO BORED. PLEASE!
I'LL CLEAN ALL THE ROOMS THE SHINSENGUMI HAVE RENTED.
TELL EVERYONE ELSE THAT THEY DON'T NEED TO HELP!
YAY! I GET TO WORK! ♡
HOP
HOP
HOP
THESE GUYS LEAVE SUCH A MESS! ♡

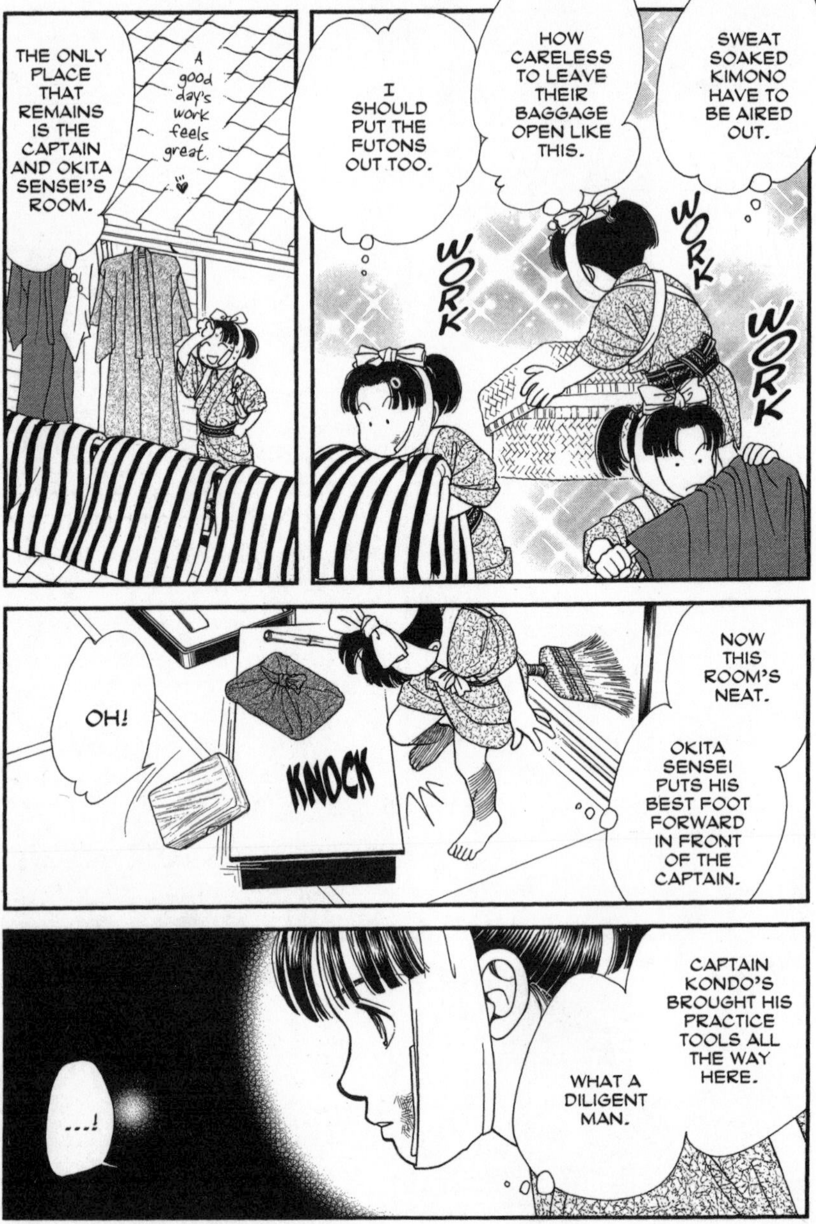
SWEAT SOAKED KIMONO HAVE TO BE AIRED OUT.
WORK
WORK
HOW CARELESS TO LEAVE THEIR BAGGAGE OPEN LIKE THIS.
WORK
I SHOULD PUT THE FUTONS OUT TOO.
A good day's work feels great.
THE ONLY PLACE THAT REMAINS IS THE CAPTAIN AND OKITA SENSEI'S ROOM.
NOW THIS ROOM'S NEAT.
OKITA SENSEI PUTS HIS BEST FOOT FORWARD IN FRONT OF THE CAPTAIN.
KNOCK
OH!
CAPTAIN KONDO'S BROUGHT HIS PRACTICE TOOLS ALL THE WAY HERE.
WHAT A DILIGENT MAN.
...!

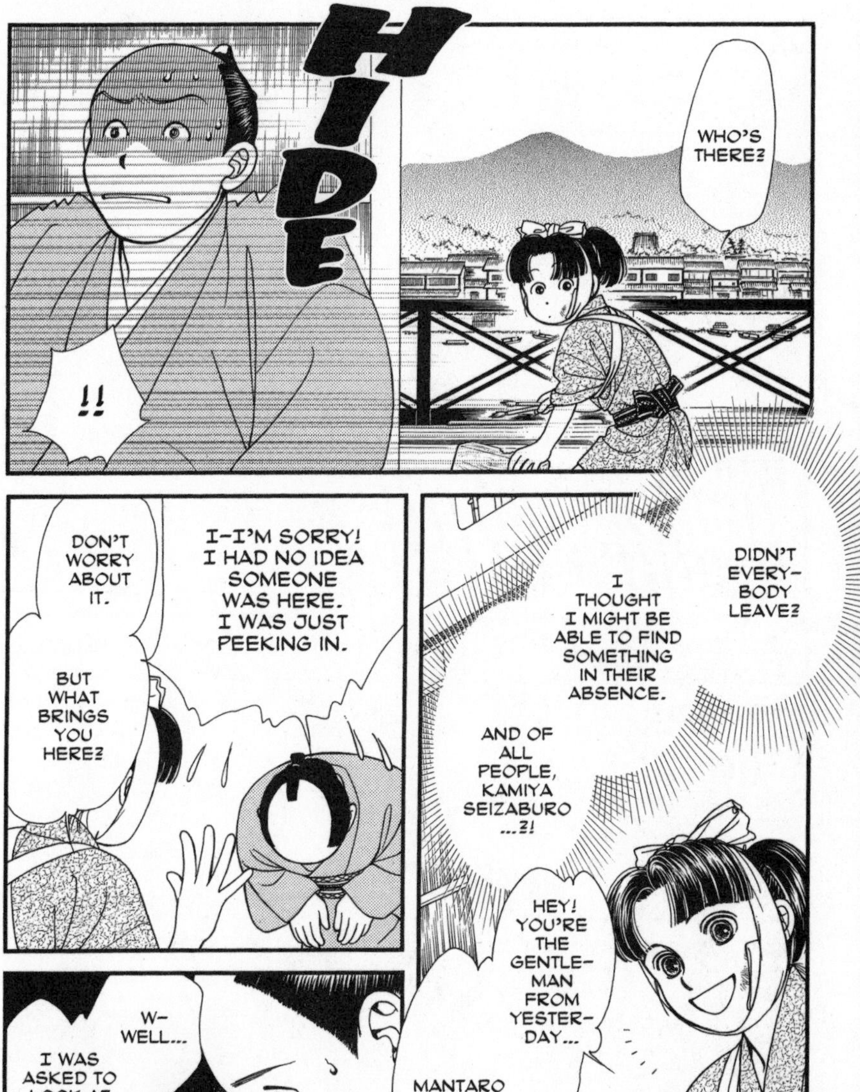
WHO'S THERE?
HIDE
!!
DIDN'T EVERYBODY LEAVE?
I THOUGHT I MIGHT BE ABLE TO FIND SOMETHING IN THEIR ABSENCE.
AND OF ALL PEOPLE, KAMIYA SEIZABURO ...?!
HEY! YOU'RE THE GENTLEMAN FROM YESTERDAY...
MANTARO SENSEI, RIGHT?
I-I'M SORRY! I HAD NO IDEA SOMEONE WAS HERE. I WAS JUST PEEKING IN.
DON'T WORRY ABOUT IT.
BUT WHAT BRINGS YOU HERE?
W-WELL...
I WAS ASKED TO LOOK AT SOME INNS FOR A FRIEND TRAVELING FROM FAR AWAY.

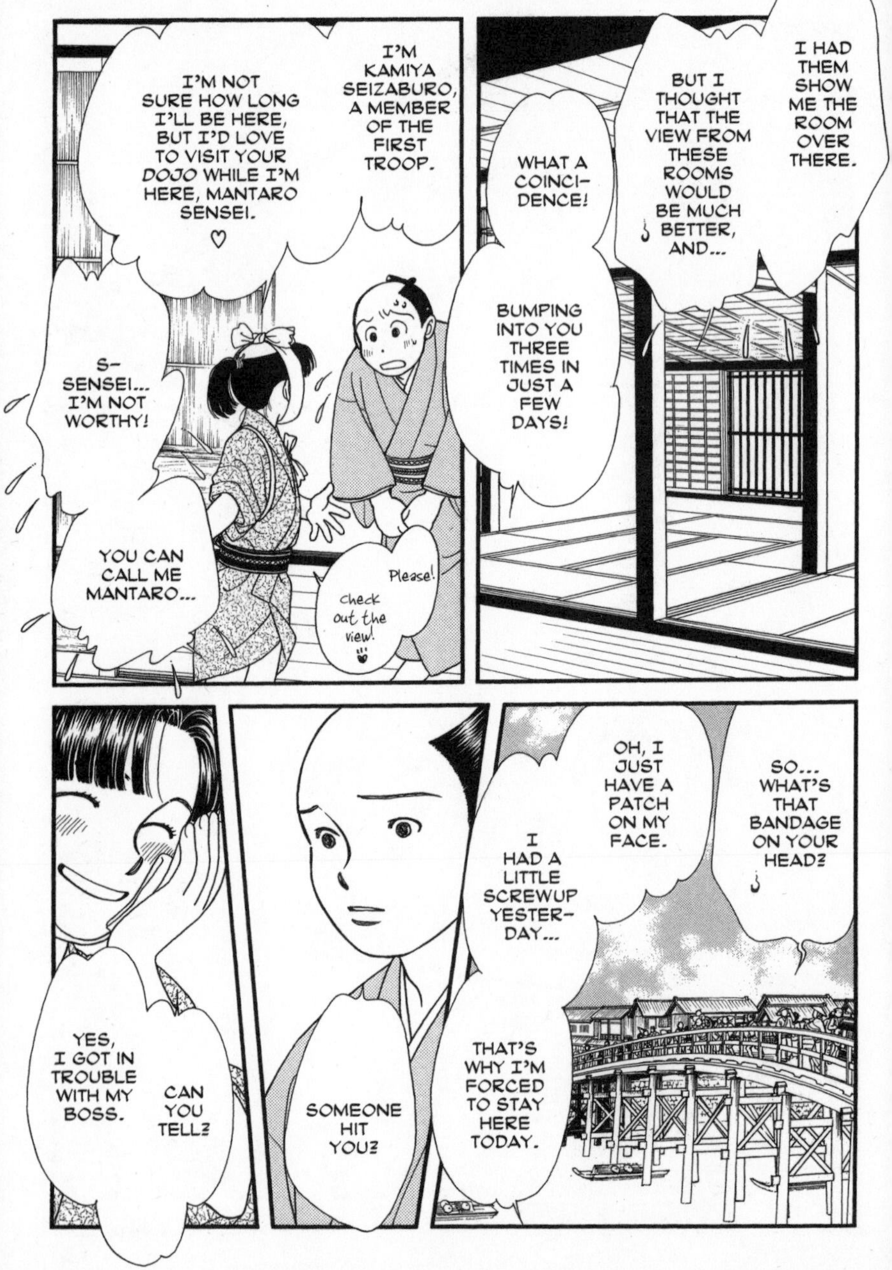
I HAD THEM SHOW ME THE ROOM OVER THERE.
BUT I THOUGHT THAT THE VIEW FROM THESE ROOMS WOULD BE MUCH BETTER, AND...
WHAT A COINCI-DENCE!
BUMPING INTO YOU THREE TIMES IN JUST A FEW DAYS!
I'M KAMIYA SEIZABURO, A MEMBER OF THE FIRST TROOP.
I'M NOT SURE HOW LONG I'LL BE HERE, BUT I'D LOVE TO VISIT YOUR *DOJO* WHILE I'M HERE, MANTARO SENSEI. ♡
S-SENSEI... I'M NOT WORTHY!
YOU CAN CALL ME MANTARO...
Please!
Check out the view!
SO... WHAT'S THAT BANDAGE ON YOUR HEAD?
OH, I JUST HAVE A PATCH ON MY FACE.
I HAD A LITTLE SCREWUP YESTER-DAY...
THAT'S WHY I'M FORCED TO STAY HERE TODAY.
SOMEONE HIT YOU?
YES, I GOT IN TROUBLE WITH MY BOSS.
CAN YOU TELL?

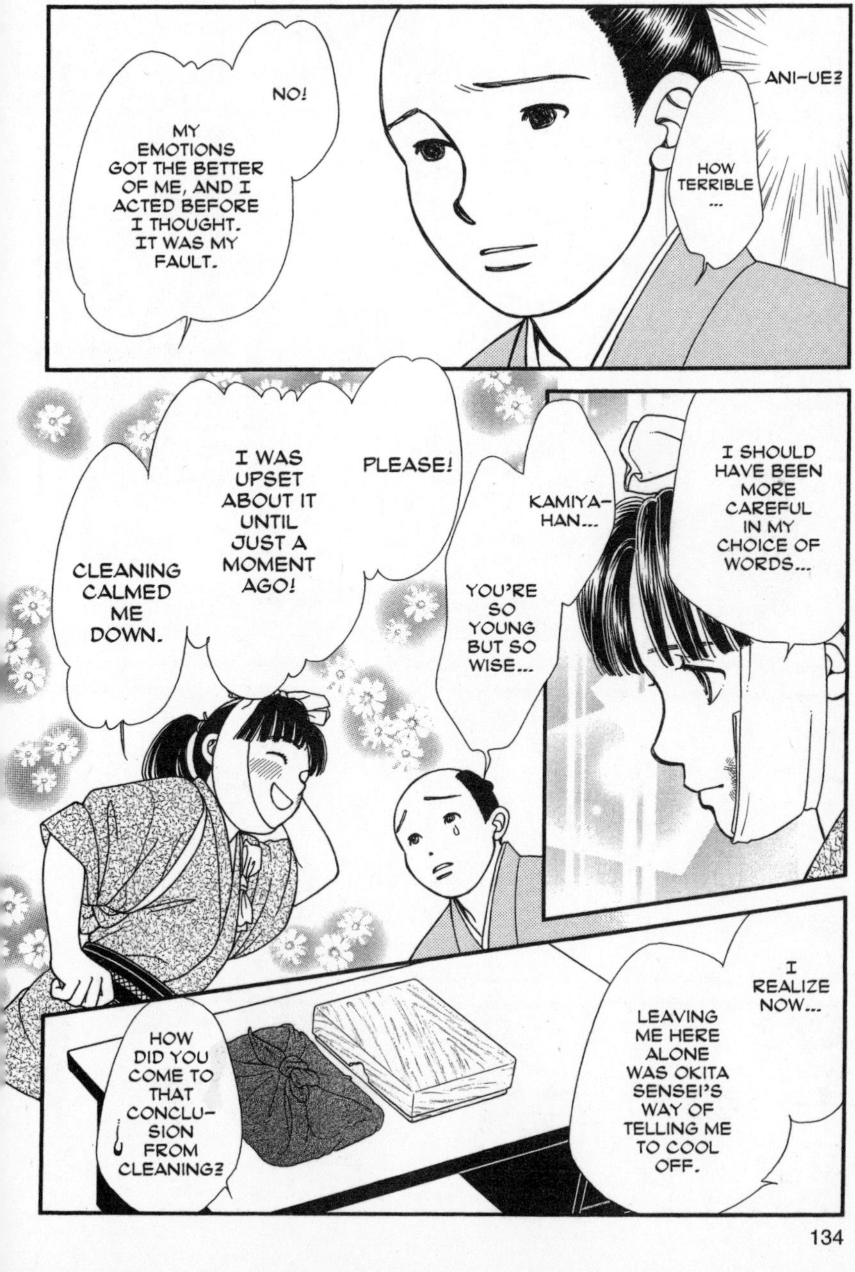
ANI-UE?
HOW TERRIBLE...
NO!
MY EMOTIONS GOT THE BETTER OF ME, AND I ACTED BEFORE I THOUGHT. IT WAS MY FAULT.
I SHOULD HAVE BEEN MORE CAREFUL IN MY CHOICE OF WORDS...
KAMIYA-HAN...
YOU'RE SO YOUNG BUT SO WISE...
PLEASE!
I WAS UPSET ABOUT IT UNTIL JUST A MOMENT AGO!
CLEANING CALMED ME DOWN.
I REALIZE NOW...
LEAVING ME HERE ALONE WAS OKITA SENSEI'S WAY OF TELLING ME TO COOL OFF.
HOW DID YOU COME TO THAT CONCLUSION FROM CLEANING?

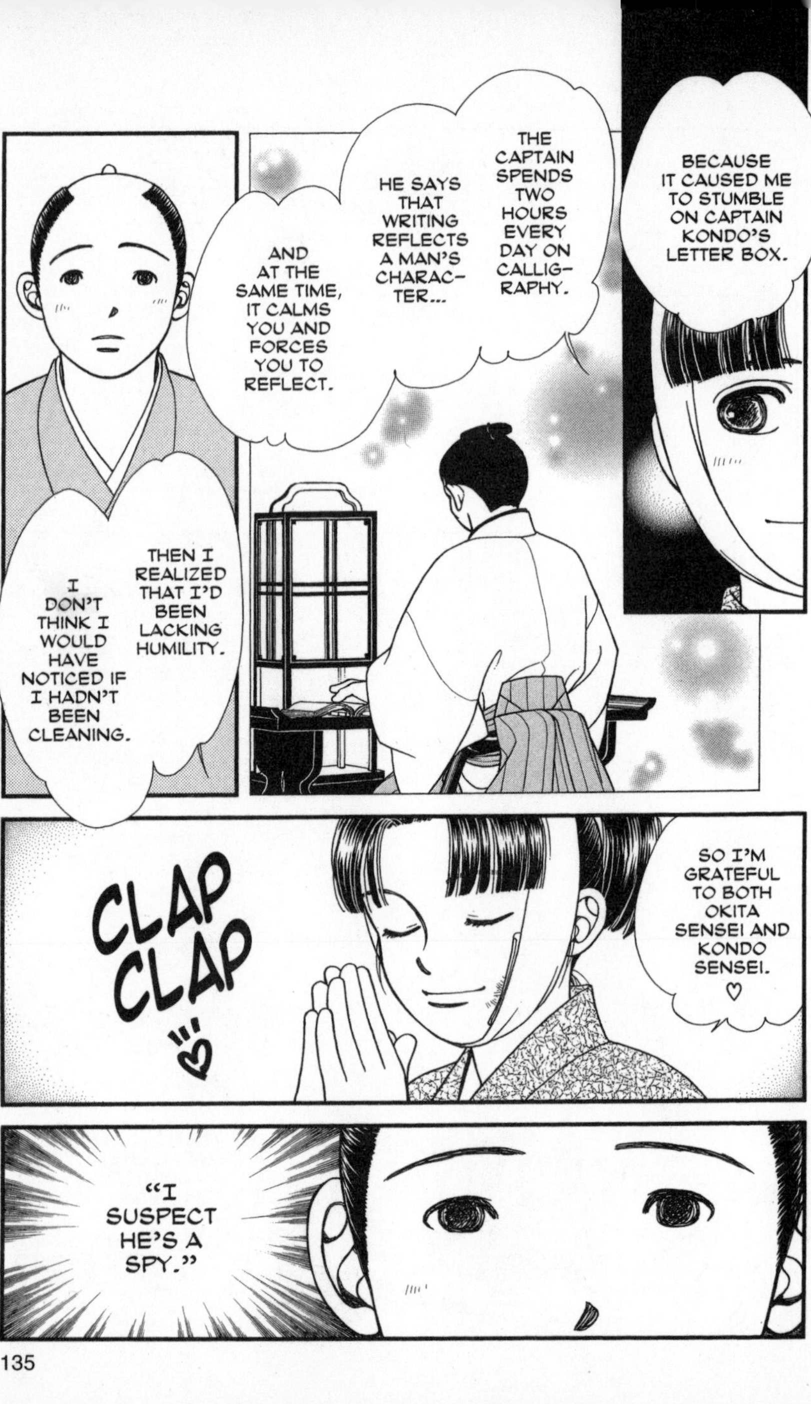
BECAUSE IT CAUSED ME TO STUMBLE ON CAPTAIN KONDO'S LETTER BOX.
THE CAPTAIN SPENDS TWO HOURS EVERY DAY ON CALLIG-RAPHY.
HE SAYS THAT WRITING REFLECTS A MAN'S CHARAC-TER...
AND AT THE SAME TIME, IT CALMS YOU AND FORCES YOU TO REFLECT.
THEN I REALIZED THAT I'D BEEN LACKING HUMILITY.
I DON'T THINK I WOULD HAVE NOTICED IF I HADN'T BEEN CLEANING.
SO I'M GRATEFUL TO BOTH OKITA SENSEI AND KONDO SENSEI. ♡
CLAP CLAP
"I SUSPECT HE'S A SPY."

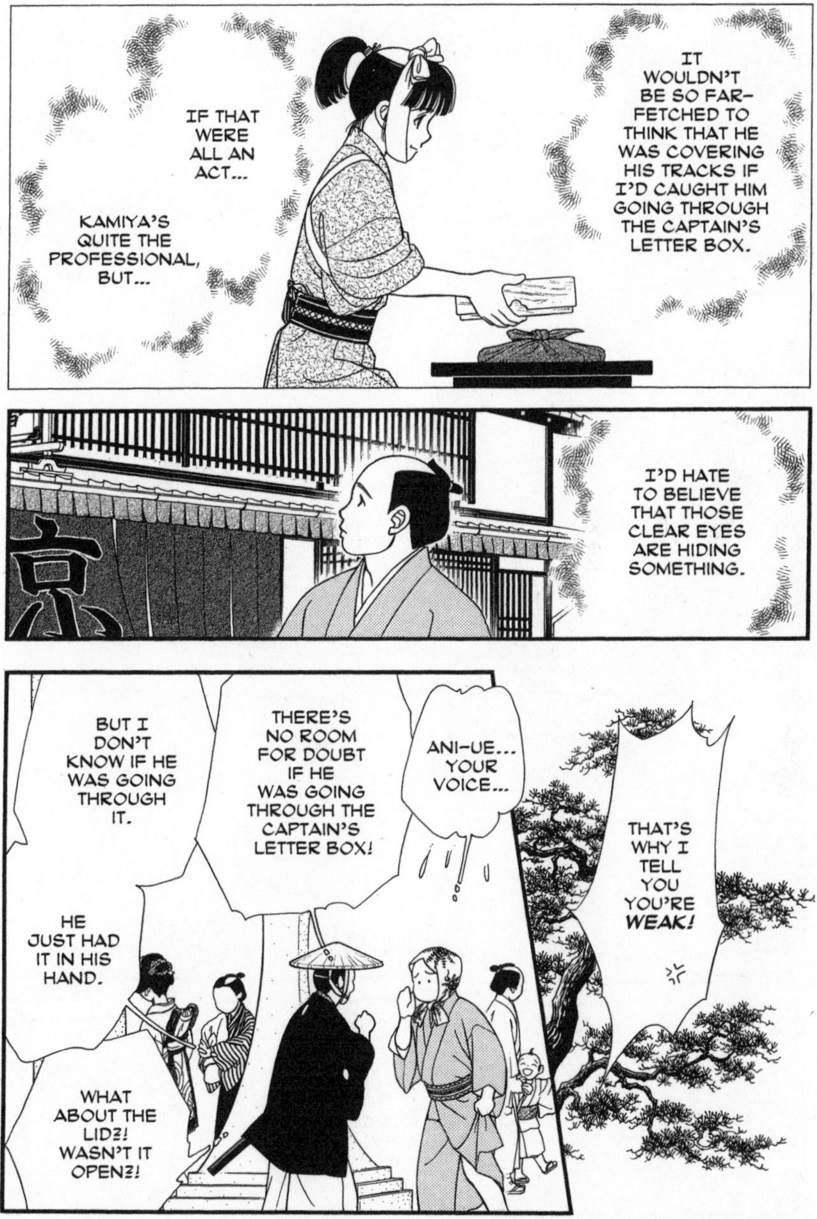
IT WOULDN'T BE SO FAR-FETCHED TO THINK THAT HE WAS COVERING HIS TRACKS IF I'D CAUGHT HIM GOING THROUGH THE CAPTAIN'S LETTER BOX.
IF THAT WERE ALL AN ACT...
KAMIYA'S QUITE THE PROFESSIONAL, BUT...
I'D HATE TO BELIEVE THAT THOSE CLEAR EYES ARE HIDING SOMETHING.
THAT'S WHY I TELL YOU YOU'RE *WEAK!*
ANI-UE... YOUR VOICE...
THERE'S NO ROOM FOR DOUBT IF HE WAS GOING THROUGH THE CAPTAIN'S LETTER BOX!
BUT I DON'T KNOW IF HE WAS GOING THROUGH IT.
HE JUST HAD IT IN HIS HAND.
WHAT ABOUT THE LID?! WASN'T IT OPEN?!

YES...
SO KAMIYA IS ALONE IN THE INN?
HMPH
ANI-UE? WHAT ARE YOU...?!
I'M JUST GOING TO TALK TO HIM.
YOU CAN GO NOW.
BUT DON'T DO ANYTHING VIOLENT...
YOU'RE UNDER KAMIYA'S SPELL TOO, MANTARO!
ANI-UE ...!

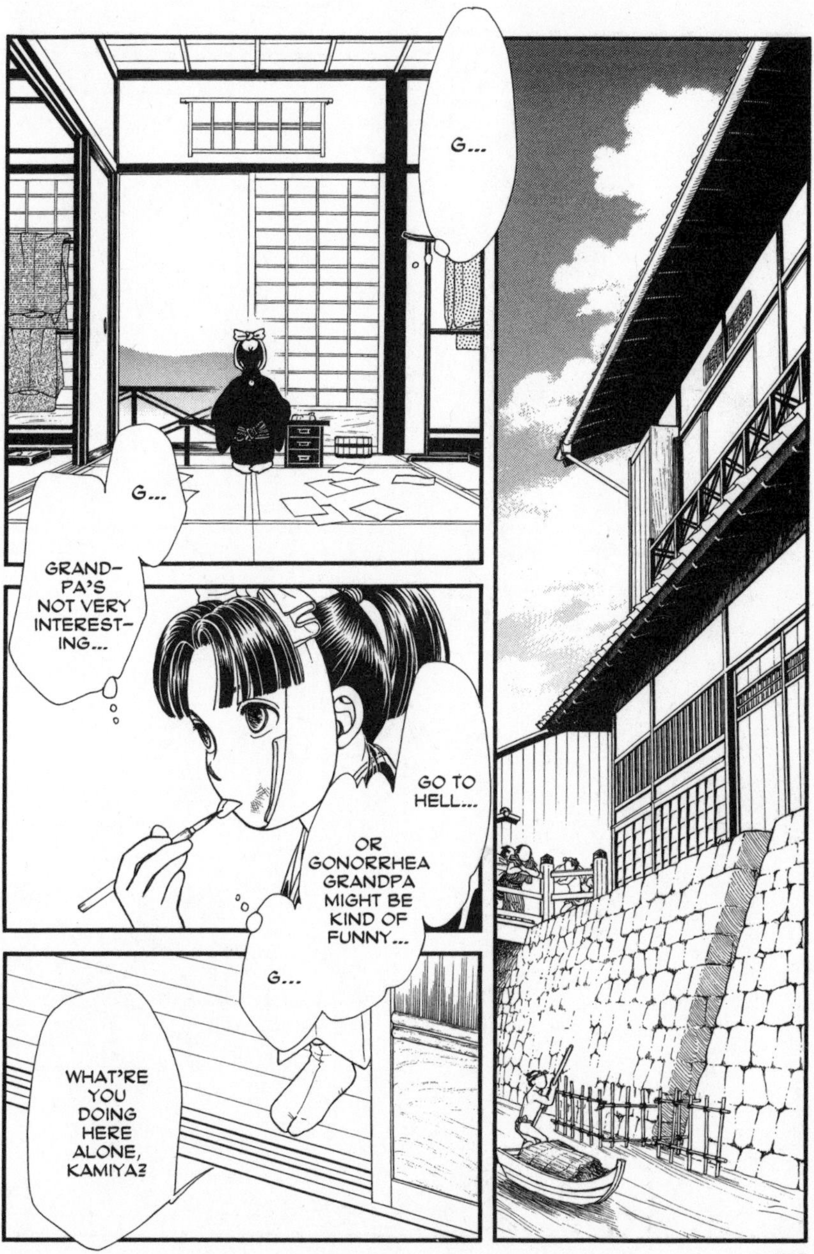
G...
G...
GRAND-PA'S NOT VERY INTEREST-ING...
GO TO HELL...
OR GONORRHEA GRANDPA MIGHT BE KIND OF FUNNY...
G...
WHAT'RE YOU DOING HERE ALONE, KAMIYA?

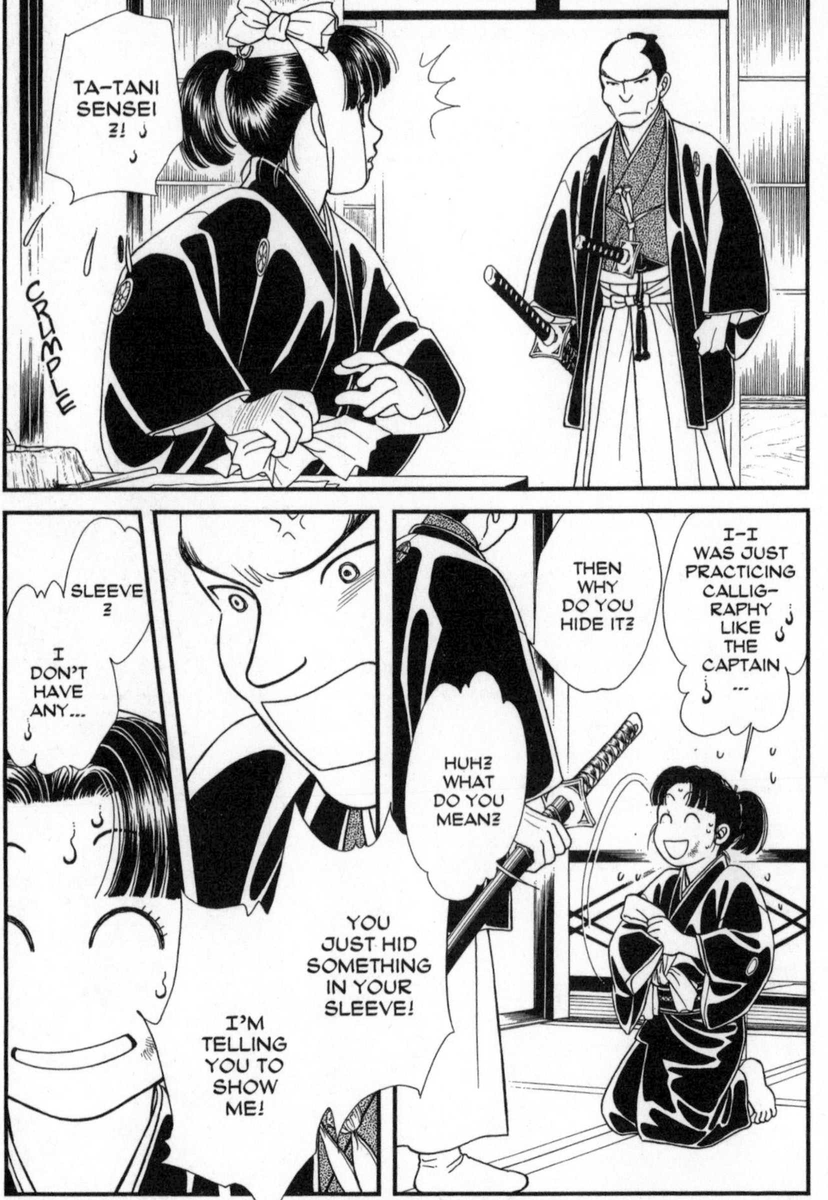

TA-TANI SENSEI ?!
CRUMPLE
I-I WAS JUST PRACTICING CALLIGRAPHY LIKE THE CAPTAIN...
THEN WHY DO YOU HIDE IT?
HUH? WHAT DO YOU MEAN?
YOU JUST HID SOMETHING IN YOUR SLEEVE!
I'M TELLING YOU TO SHOW ME!
SLEEVE?
I DON'T HAVE ANY...

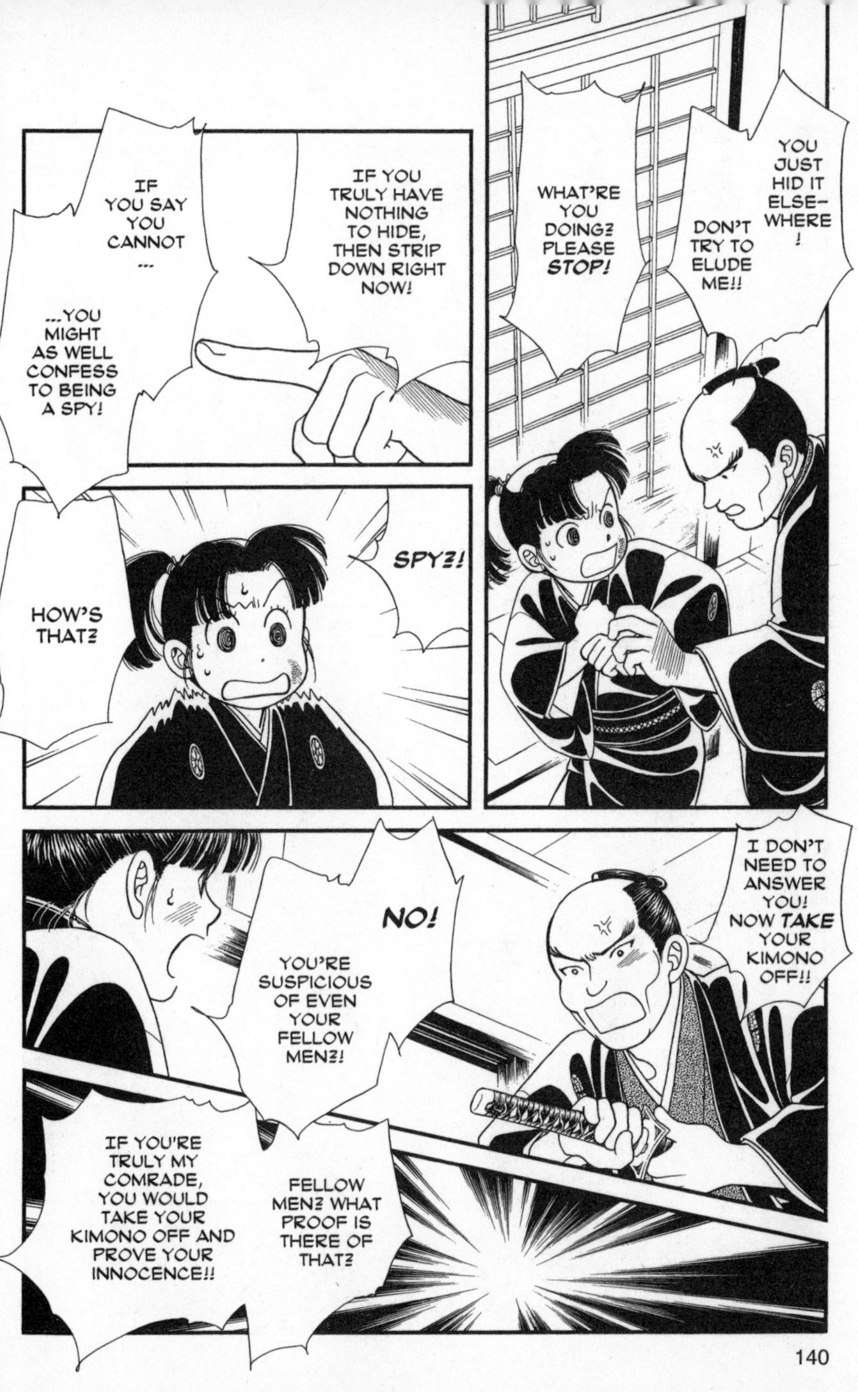
YOU JUST HID IT ELSEWHERE!
DON'T TRY TO ELUDE ME!!
WHAT'RE YOU DOING? PLEASE *STOP!*
IF YOU TRULY HAVE NOTHING TO HIDE, THEN STRIP DOWN RIGHT NOW!
IF YOU SAY YOU CANNOT...
...YOU MIGHT AS WELL CONFESS TO BEING A SPY!
SPY?!
HOW'S THAT?
I DON'T NEED TO ANSWER YOU! NOW *TAKE* YOUR KIMONO OFF!!
NO!
YOU'RE SUSPICIOUS OF EVEN YOUR FELLOW MEN?!
FELLOW MEN? WHAT PROOF IS THERE OF THAT?
IF YOU'RE TRULY MY COMRADE, YOU WOULD TAKE YOUR KIMONO OFF AND PROVE YOUR INNOCENCE!!

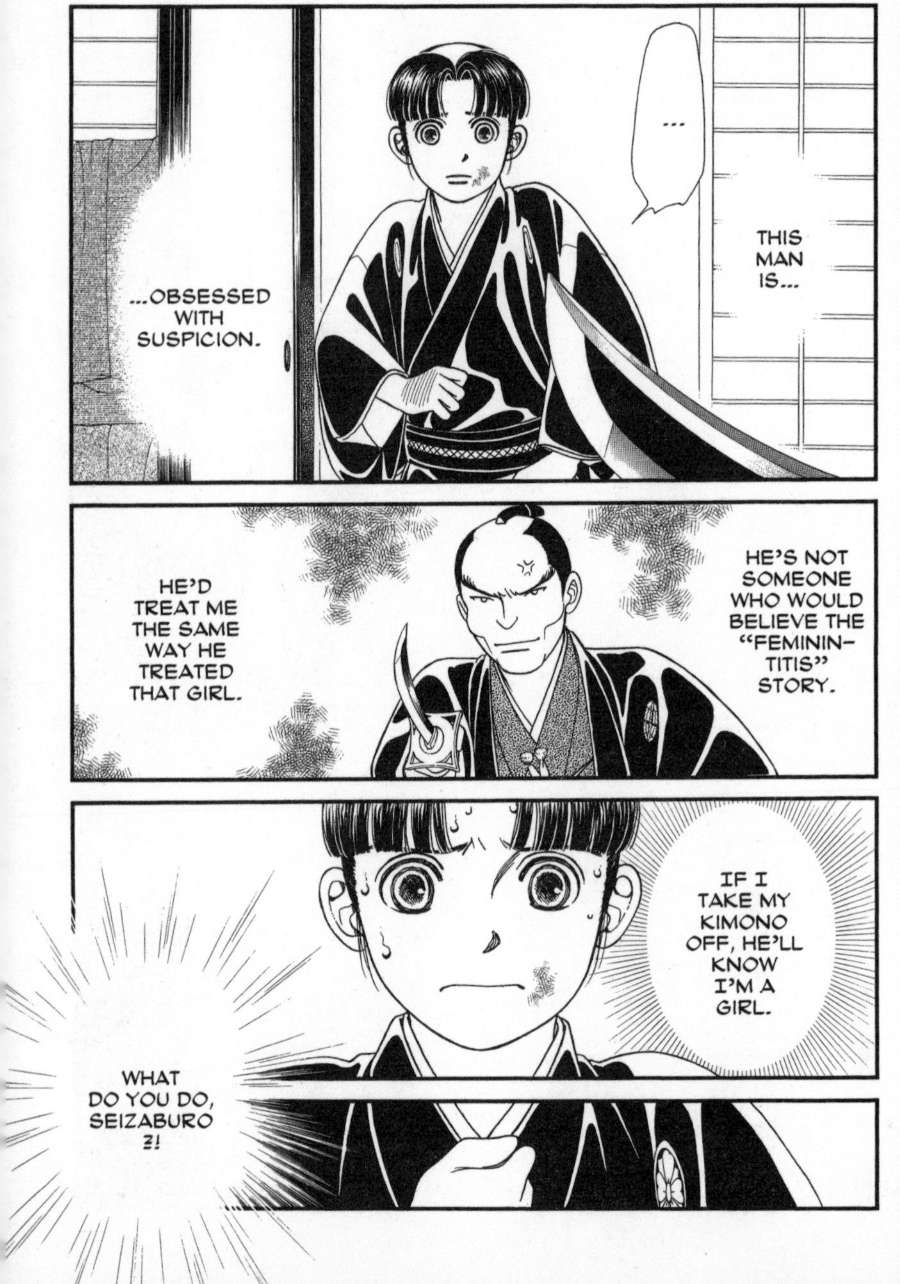
...
THIS MAN IS...
...OBSESSED WITH SUSPICION.
HE'S NOT SOMEONE WHO WOULD BELIEVE THE "FEMININ-TITIS" STORY.
HE'D TREAT ME THE SAME WAY HE TREATED THAT GIRL.
IF I TAKE MY KIMONO OFF, HE'LL KNOW I'M A GIRL.
WHAT DO YOU DO, SEIZABURO?!

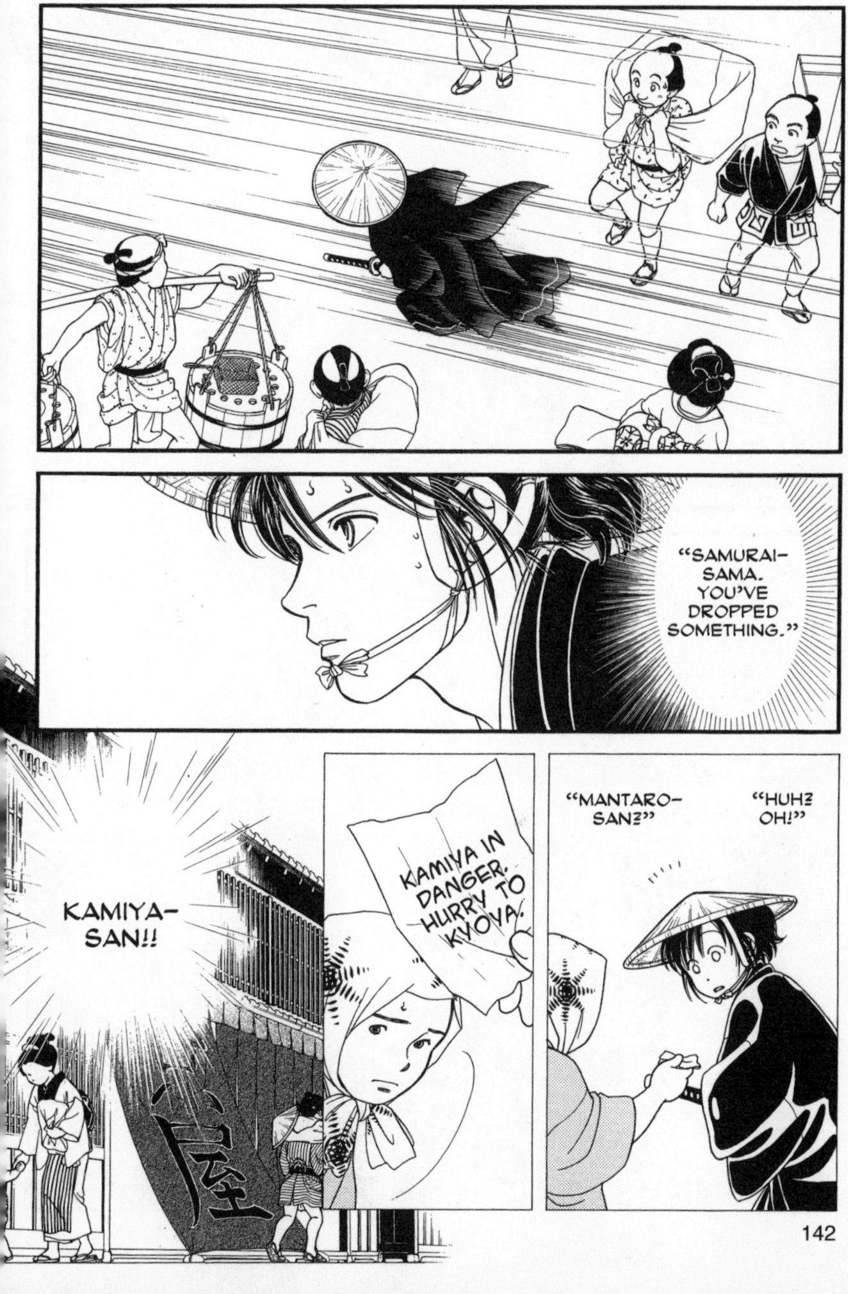
"SAMURAI-SAMA. YOU'VE DROPPED SOMETHING."
"HUH? OH!"
"MANTARO-SAN?"
KAMIYA IN DANGER. HURRY TO KYOYA.
KAMIYA-SAN!!

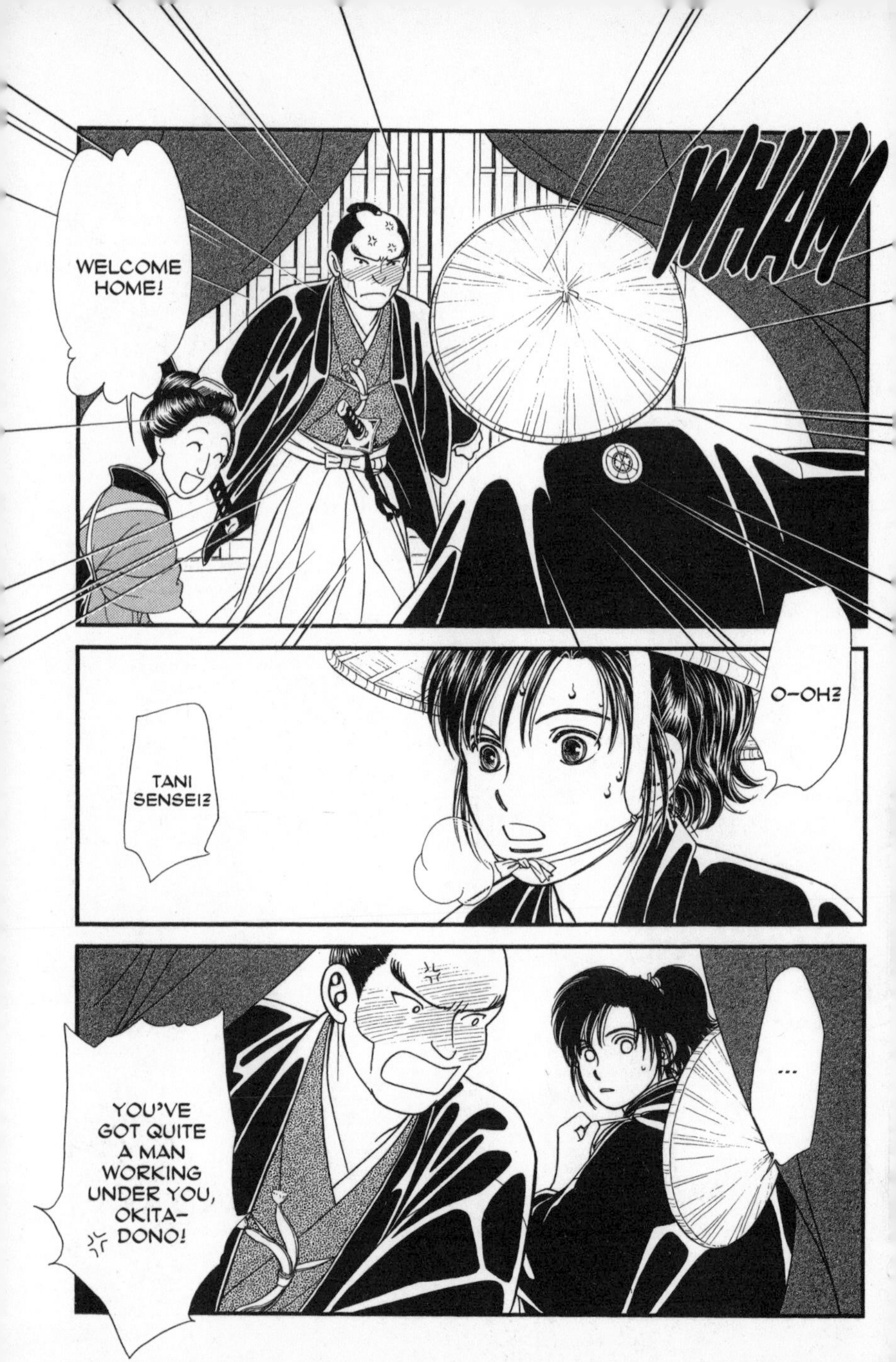
WHAM
WELCOME HOME!
O-OH?
TANI SENSEI!?
...
YOU'VE GOT QUITE A MAN WORKING UNDER YOU, OKITA-DONO!

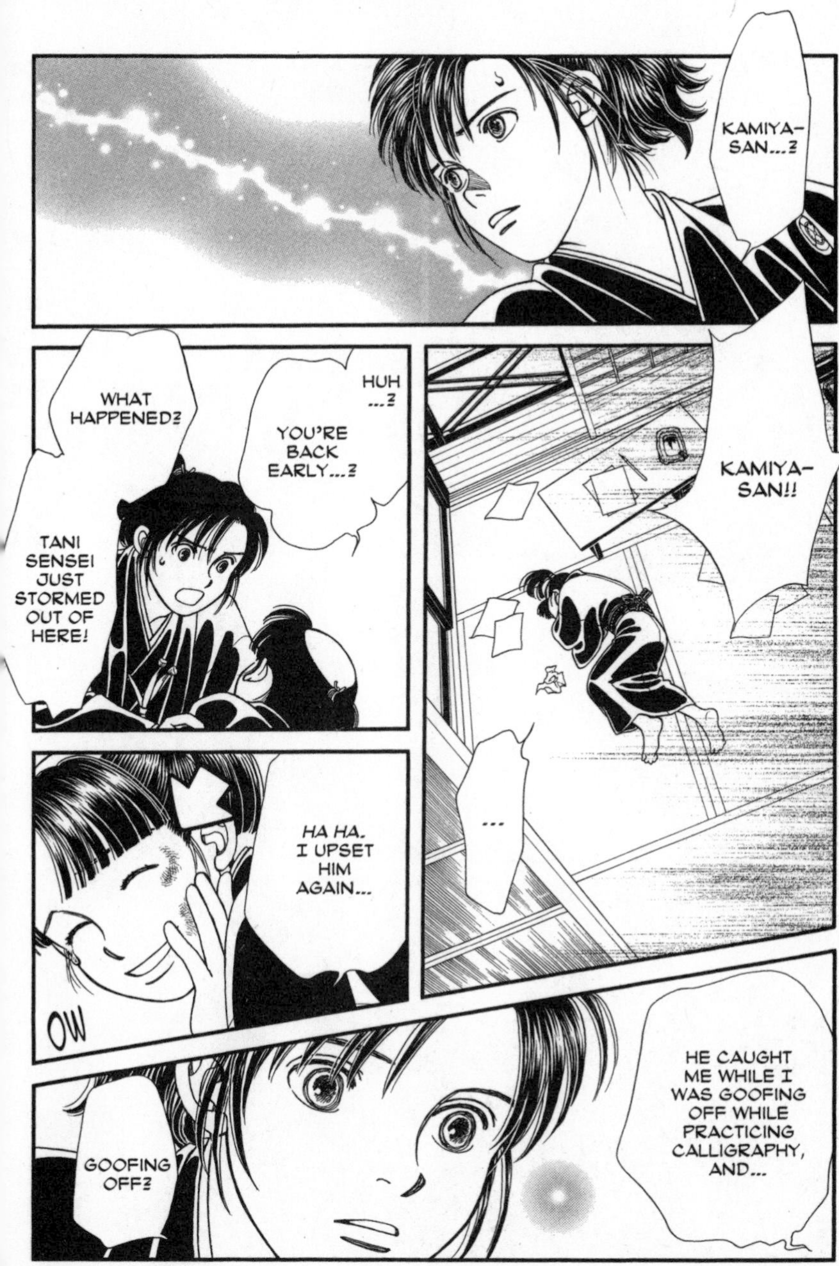
KAMIYA-SAN...?
KAMIYA-SAN!!
...
HUH ...?
YOU'RE BACK EARLY...?
WHAT HAPPENED?
TANI SENSEI JUST STORMED OUT OF HERE!
HA HA. I UPSET HIM AGAIN...
OW
HE CAUGHT ME WHILE I WAS GOOFING OFF WHILE PRACTICING CALLIGRAPHY, AND...
GOOFING OFF?

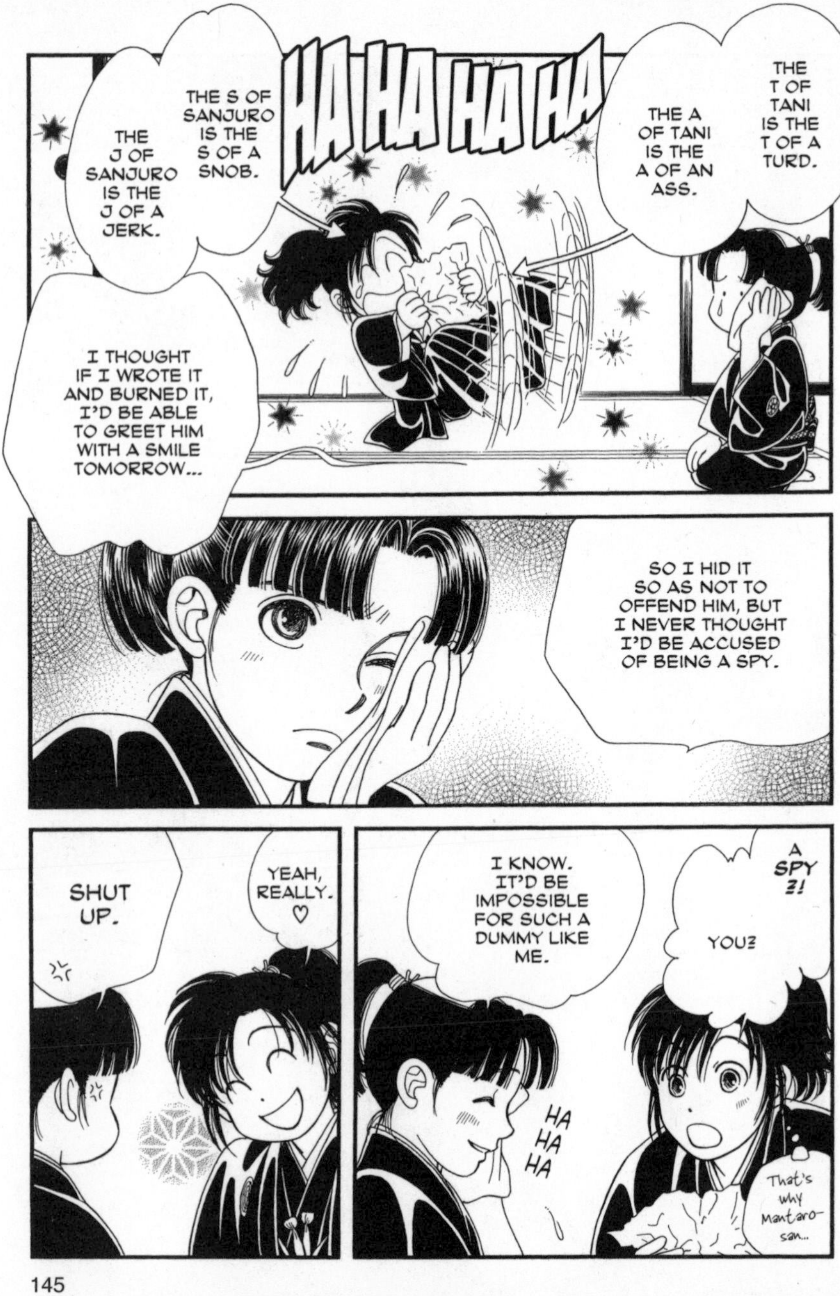
THE T OF TANI IS THE T OF A TURD.
THE A OF TANI IS THE A OF AN ASS.
HA HA HA HA
THE S OF SANJURO IS THE S OF A SNOB.
THE J OF SANJURO IS THE J OF A JERK.
I THOUGHT IF I WROTE IT AND BURNED IT, I'D BE ABLE TO GREET HIM WITH A SMILE TOMORROW...
SO I HID IT SO AS NOT TO OFFEND HIM, BUT I NEVER THOUGHT I'D BE ACCUSED OF BEING A SPY.
A SPY?!
YOU?
That's why Mantaro-san...
I KNOW. IT'D BE IMPOSSIBLE FOR SUCH A DUMMY LIKE ME.
HA HA HA
YEAH, REALLY. ♡
SHUT UP.

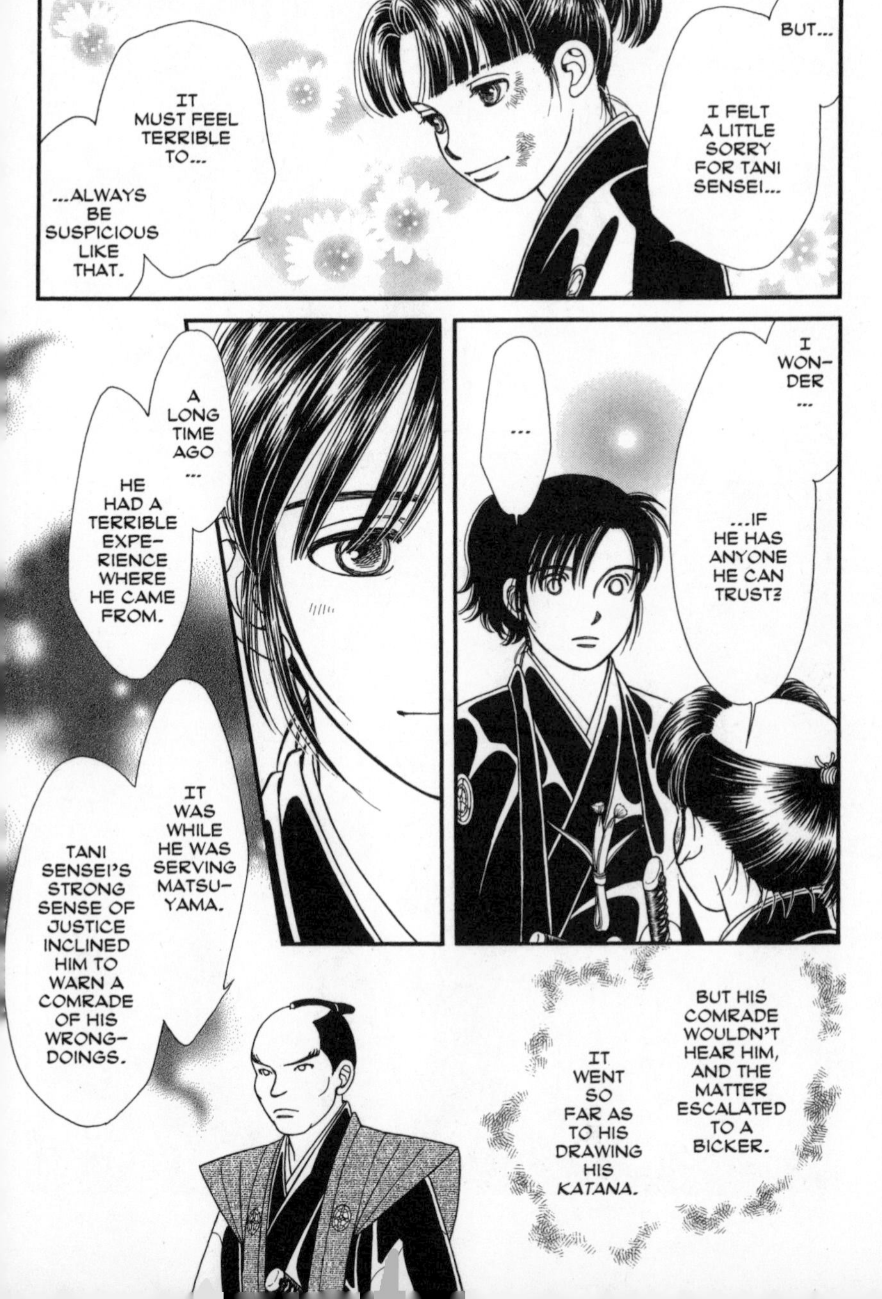
BUT...
I FELT A LITTLE SORRY FOR TANI SENSEI...
IT MUST FEEL TERRIBLE TO...
...ALWAYS BE SUSPICIOUS LIKE THAT.
I WONDER...
...IF HE HAS ANYONE HE CAN TRUST?
...
A LONG TIME AGO...
HE HAD A TERRIBLE EXPERIENCE WHERE HE CAME FROM.
IT WAS WHILE HE WAS SERVING MATSUYAMA.
TANI SENSEI'S STRONG SENSE OF JUSTICE INCLINED HIM TO WARN A COMRADE OF HIS WRONGDOINGS.
BUT HIS COMRADE WOULDN'T HEAR HIM, AND THE MATTER ESCALATED TO A BICKER.
IT WENT SO FAR AS TO HIS DRAWING HIS KATANA.

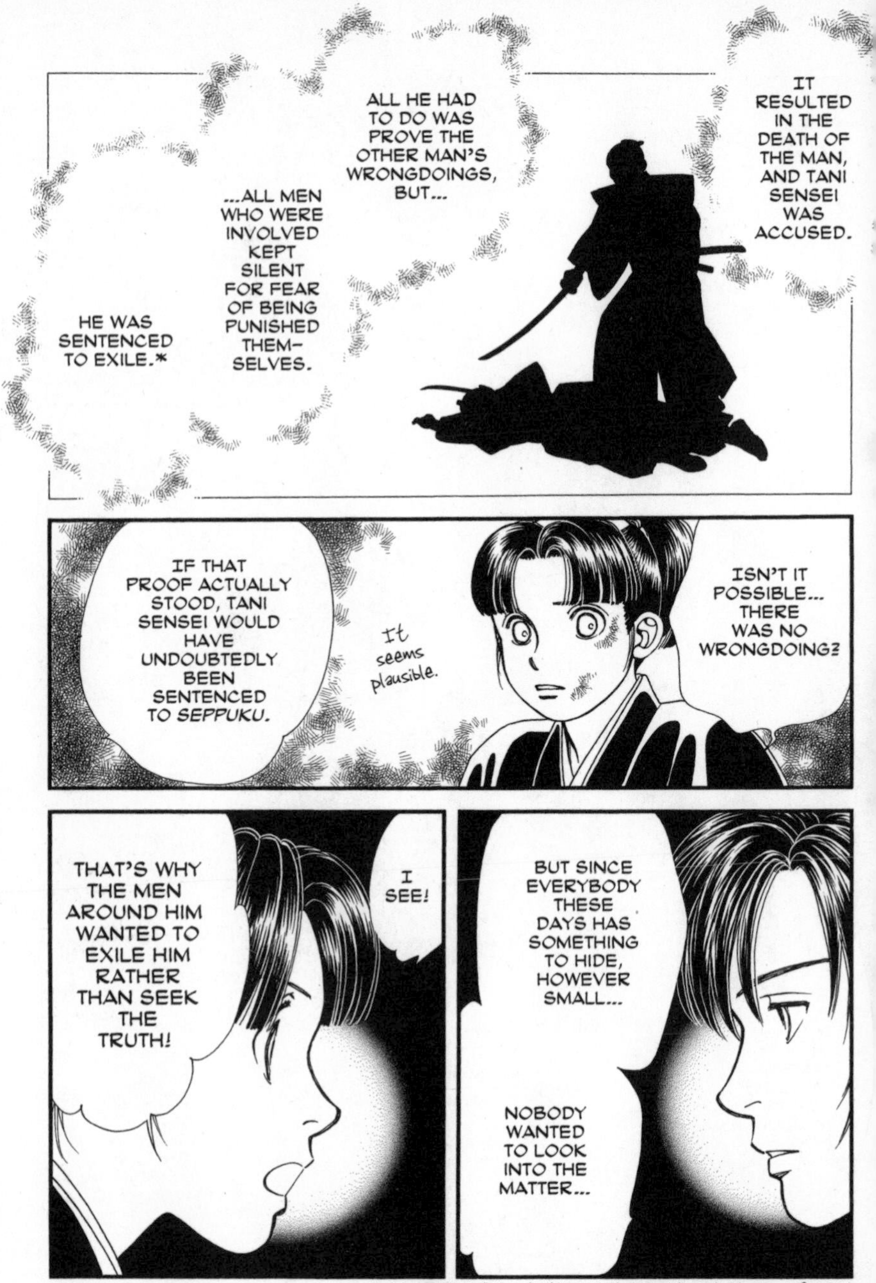
IT RESULTED IN THE DEATH OF THE MAN, AND TANI SENSEI WAS ACCUSED.
ALL HE HAD TO DO WAS PROVE THE OTHER MAN'S WRONGDOINGS, BUT...
...ALL MEN WHO WERE INVOLVED KEPT SILENT FOR FEAR OF BEING PUNISHED THEM-SELVES.
HE WAS SENTENCED TO EXILE.*
ISN'T IT POSSIBLE... THERE WAS NO WRONGDOING?
It seems plausible.
IF THAT PROOF ACTUALLY STOOD, TANI SENSEI WOULD HAVE UNDOUBTEDLY BEEN SENTENCED TO *SEPPUKU*.
BUT SINCE EVERYBODY THESE DAYS HAS SOMETHING TO HIDE, HOWEVER SMALL...
NOBODY WANTED TO LOOK INTO THE MATTER...
I SEE!
THAT'S WHY THE MEN AROUND HIM WANTED TO EXILE HIM RATHER THAN SEEK THE TRUTH!

*Being exiled as *bushi* meant that your household was confiscated. The distance of exile was determined on a case-by-case basis.

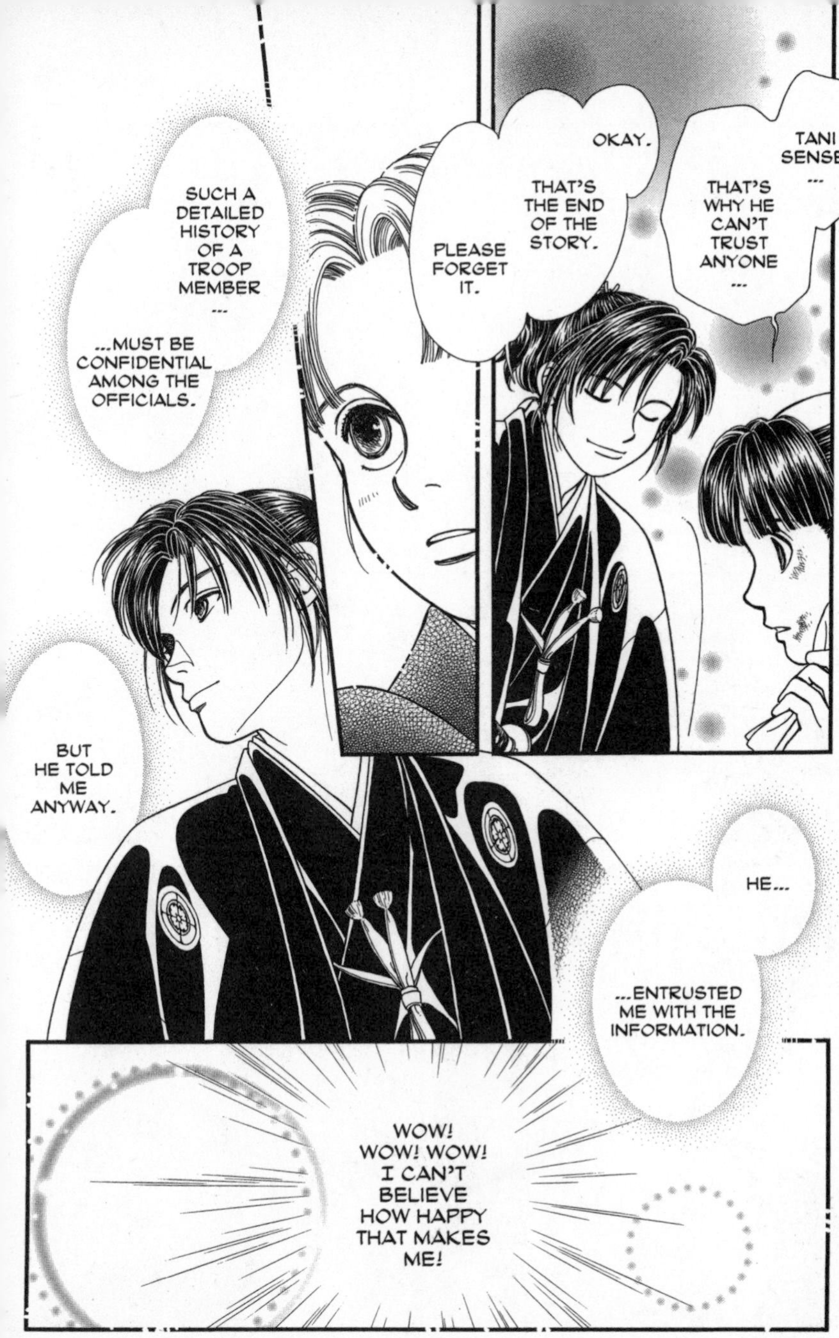
TANI SENSEI...
THAT'S WHY HE CAN'T TRUST ANYONE...
OKAY.
THAT'S THE END OF THE STORY.
PLEASE FORGET IT.
SUCH A DETAILED HISTORY OF A TROOP MEMBER...
...MUST BE CONFIDENTIAL AMONG THE OFFICIALS.
BUT HE TOLD ME ANYWAY.
HE...
...ENTRUSTED ME WITH THE INFORMATION.
WOW! WOW! WOW! I CAN'T BELIEVE HOW HAPPY THAT MAKES ME!

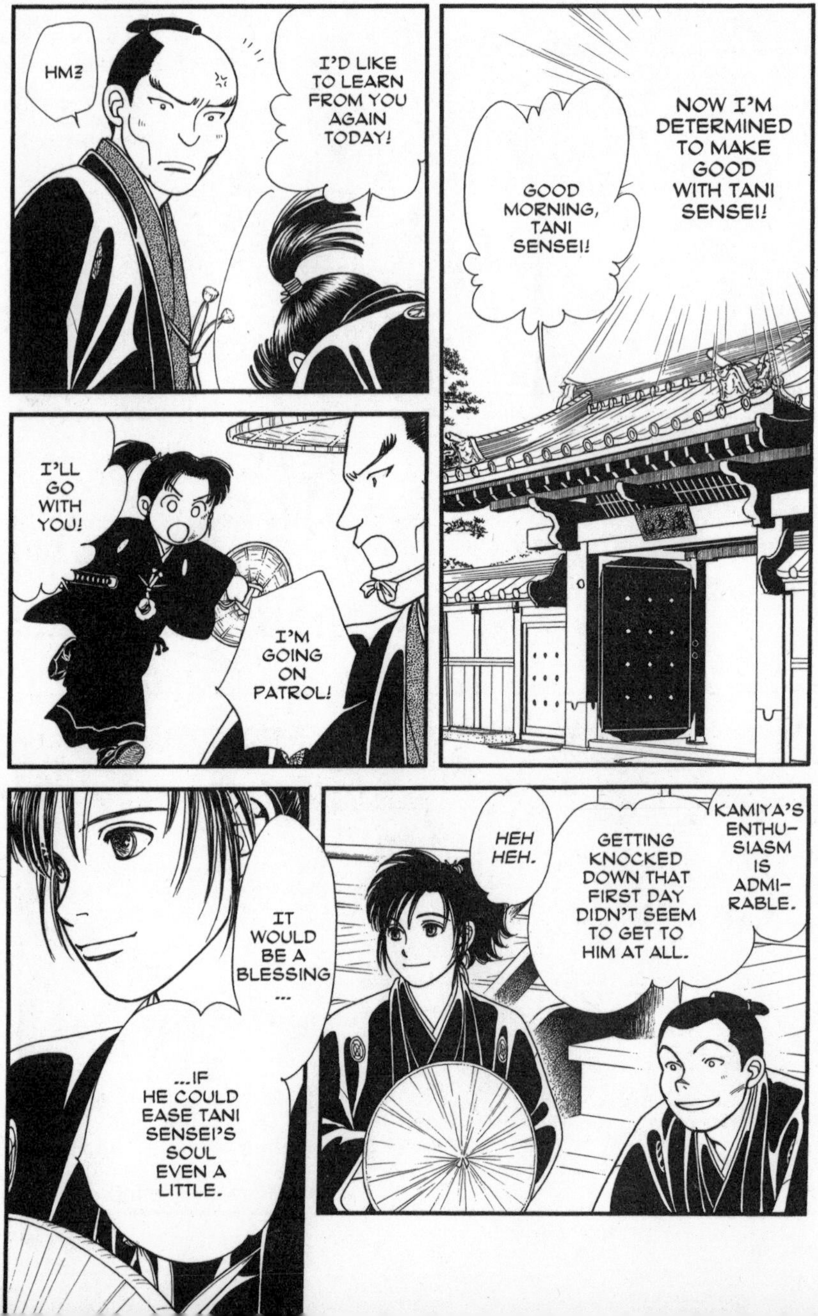
NOW I'M DETERMINED TO MAKE GOOD WITH TANI SENSEI!
GOOD MORNING, TANI SENSEI!
I'D LIKE TO LEARN FROM YOU AGAIN TODAY!
HM?
I'M GOING ON PATROL!
I'LL GO WITH YOU!
KAMIYA'S ENTHUSIASM IS ADMIRABLE.
GETTING KNOCKED DOWN THAT FIRST DAY DIDN'T SEEM TO GET TO HIM AT ALL.
HEH HEH.
IT WOULD BE A BLESSING...
...IF HE COULD EASE TANI SENSEI'S SOUL EVEN A LITTLE.

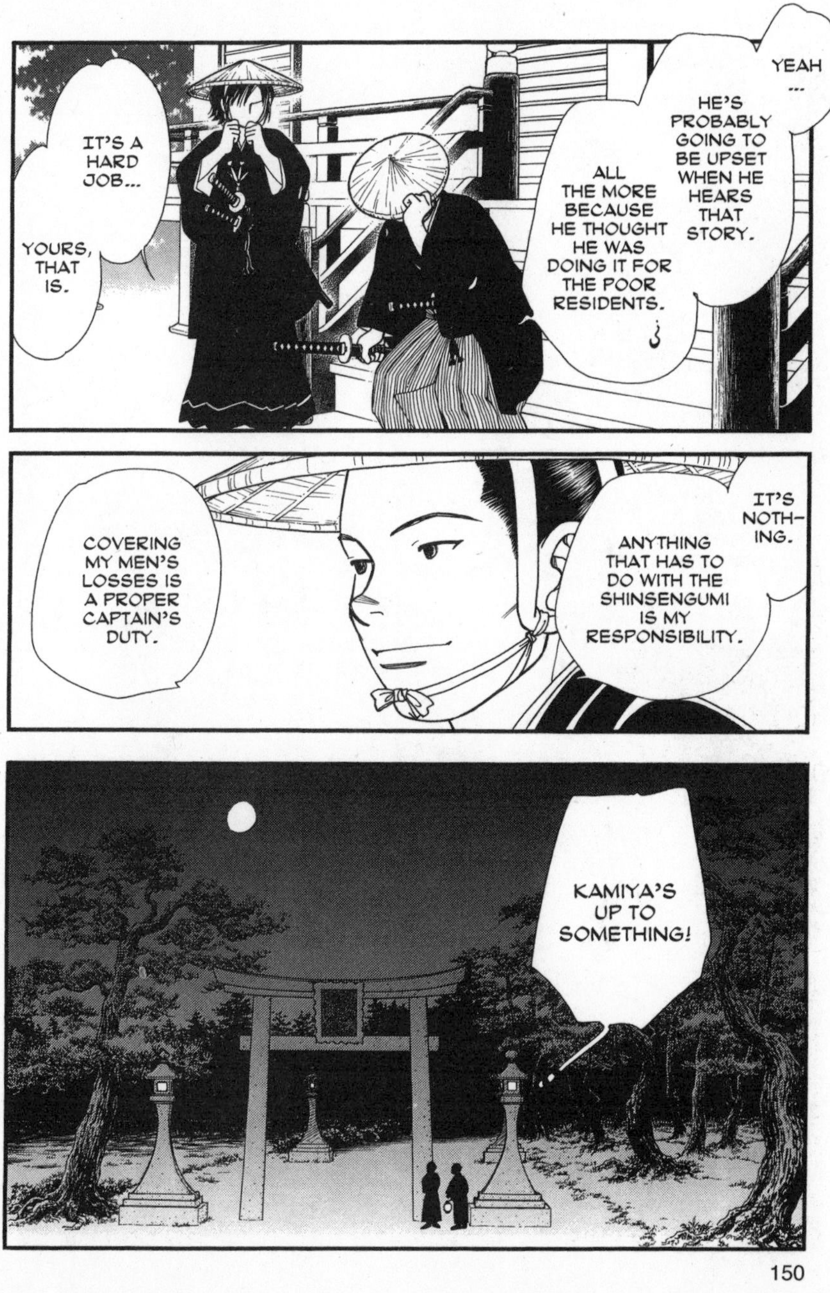
YEAH ...
HE'S PROBABLY GOING TO BE UPSET WHEN HE HEARS THAT STORY.
ALL THE MORE BECAUSE HE THOUGHT HE WAS DOING IT FOR THE POOR RESIDENTS.
IT'S A HARD JOB...
YOURS, THAT IS.
IT'S NOTHING.
ANYTHING THAT HAS TO DO WITH THE SHINSENGUMI IS MY RESPONSIBILITY.
COVERING MY MEN'S LOSSES IS A PROPER CAPTAIN'S DUTY.
KAMIYA'S UP TO SOMETHING!

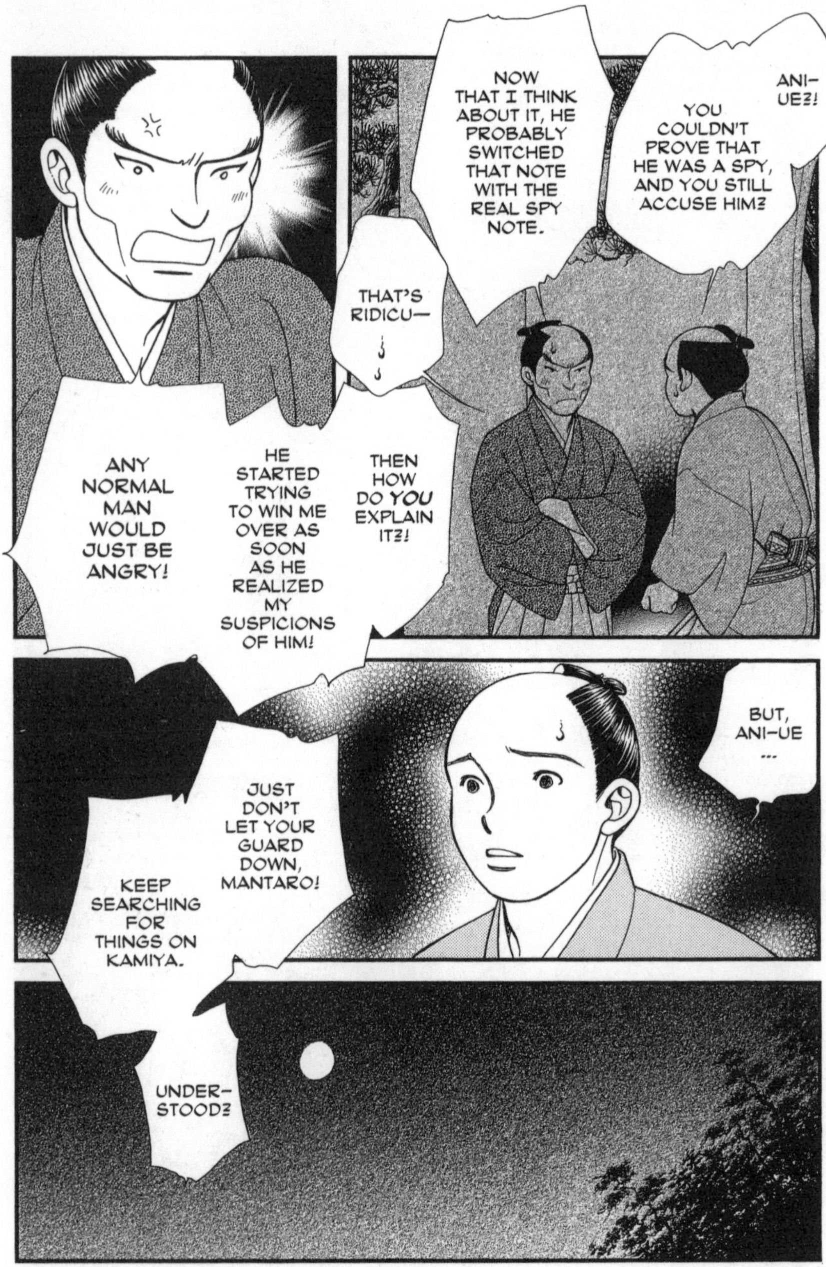

ANI-UE?!
YOU COULDN'T PROVE THAT HE WAS A SPY, AND YOU STILL ACCUSE HIM?
NOW THAT I THINK ABOUT IT, HE PROBABLY SWITCHED THAT NOTE WITH THE REAL SPY NOTE.
THAT'S RIDICU—
THEN HOW DO *YOU* EXPLAIN IT?!
HE STARTED TRYING TO WIN ME OVER AS SOON AS HE REALIZED MY SUSPICIONS OF HIM!
ANY NORMAL MAN WOULD JUST BE ANGRY!
BUT, ANI-UE ...
JUST DON'T LET YOUR GUARD DOWN, MANTARO!
KEEP SEARCHING FOR THINGS ON KAMIYA.
UNDER-STOOD?

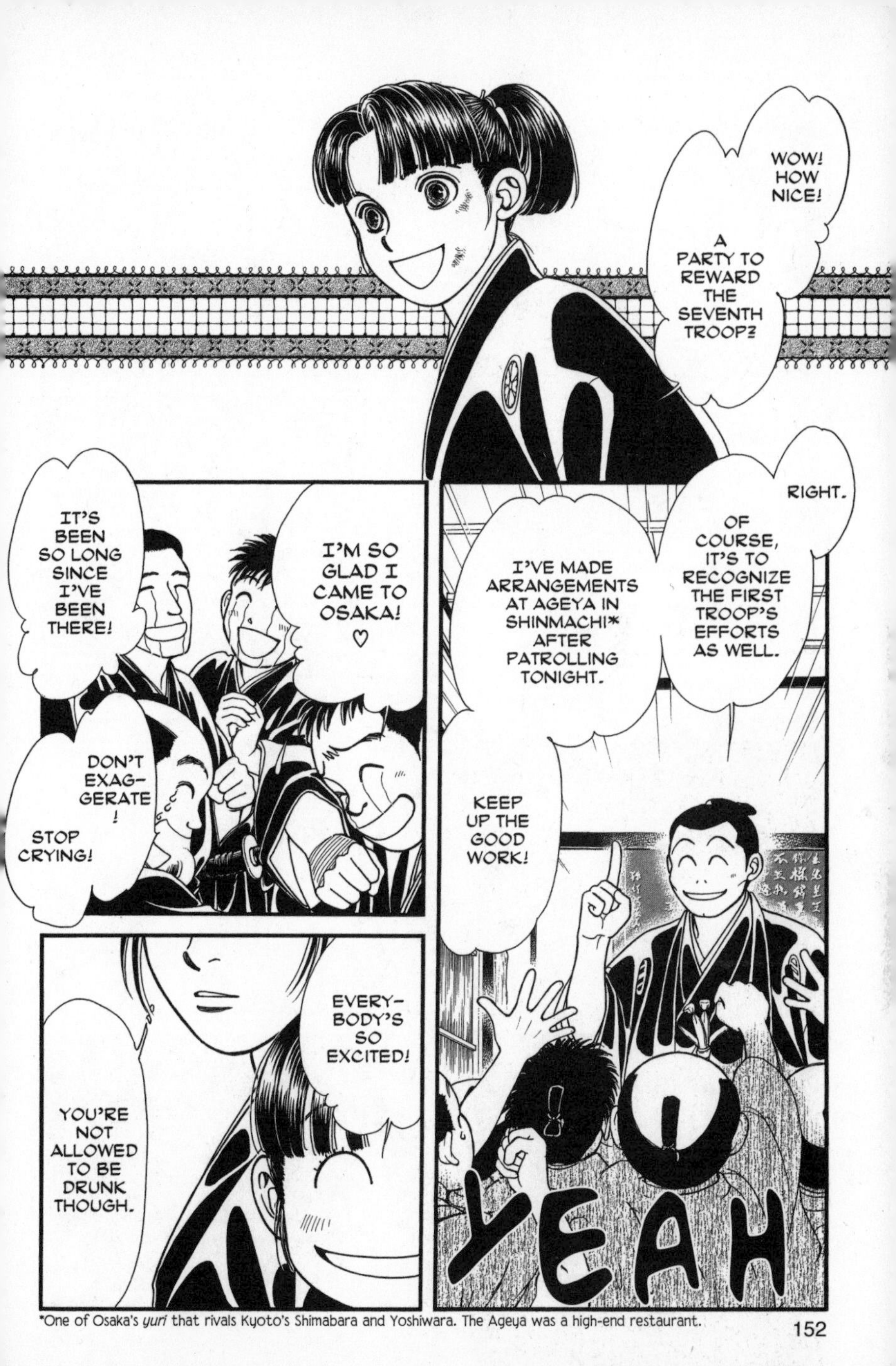
WOW! HOW NICE!
A PARTY TO REWARD THE SEVENTH TROOP?
RIGHT.
OF COURSE, IT'S TO RECOGNIZE THE FIRST TROOP'S EFFORTS AS WELL.
I'VE MADE ARRANGEMENTS AT AGEYA IN SHINMACHI* AFTER PATROLLING TONIGHT.
KEEP UP THE GOOD WORK!
YEAH
I'M SO GLAD I CAME TO OSAKA! ♡
IT'S BEEN SO LONG SINCE I'VE BEEN THERE!
DON'T EXAG-GERATE!
STOP CRYING!
EVERY-BODY'S SO EXCITED!
YOU'RE NOT ALLOWED TO BE DRUNK THOUGH.

*One of Osaka's *yuri* that rivals Kyoto's Shimabara and Yoshiwara. The Ageya was a high-end restaurant.

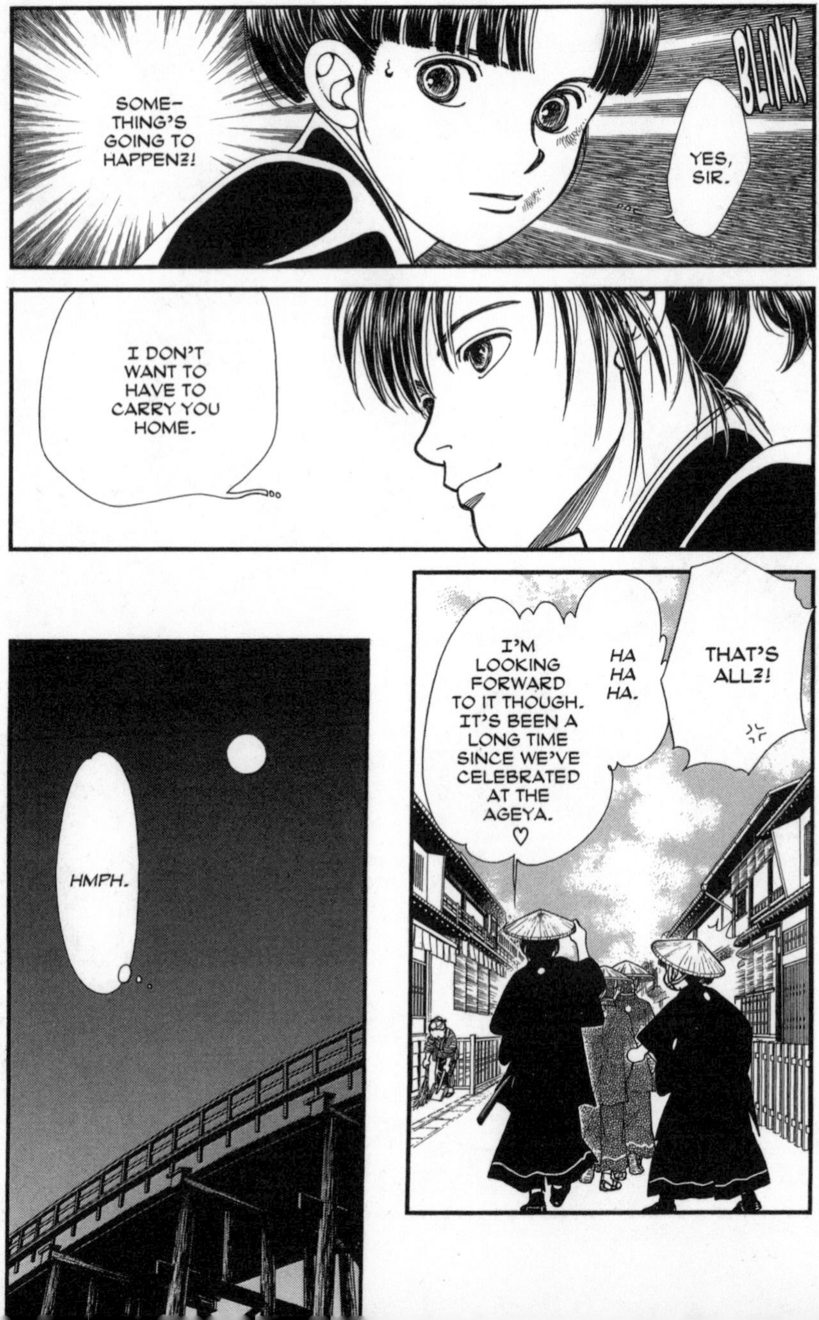
BLINK
YES, SIR.
SOME-THING'S GOING TO HAPPEN?!
I DON'T WANT TO HAVE TO CARRY YOU HOME.
THAT'S ALL?!
HA HA HA.
I'M LOOKING FORWARD TO IT THOUGH. IT'S BEEN A LONG TIME SINCE WE'VE CELEBRATED AT THE AGEYA. ♡
HMPH.

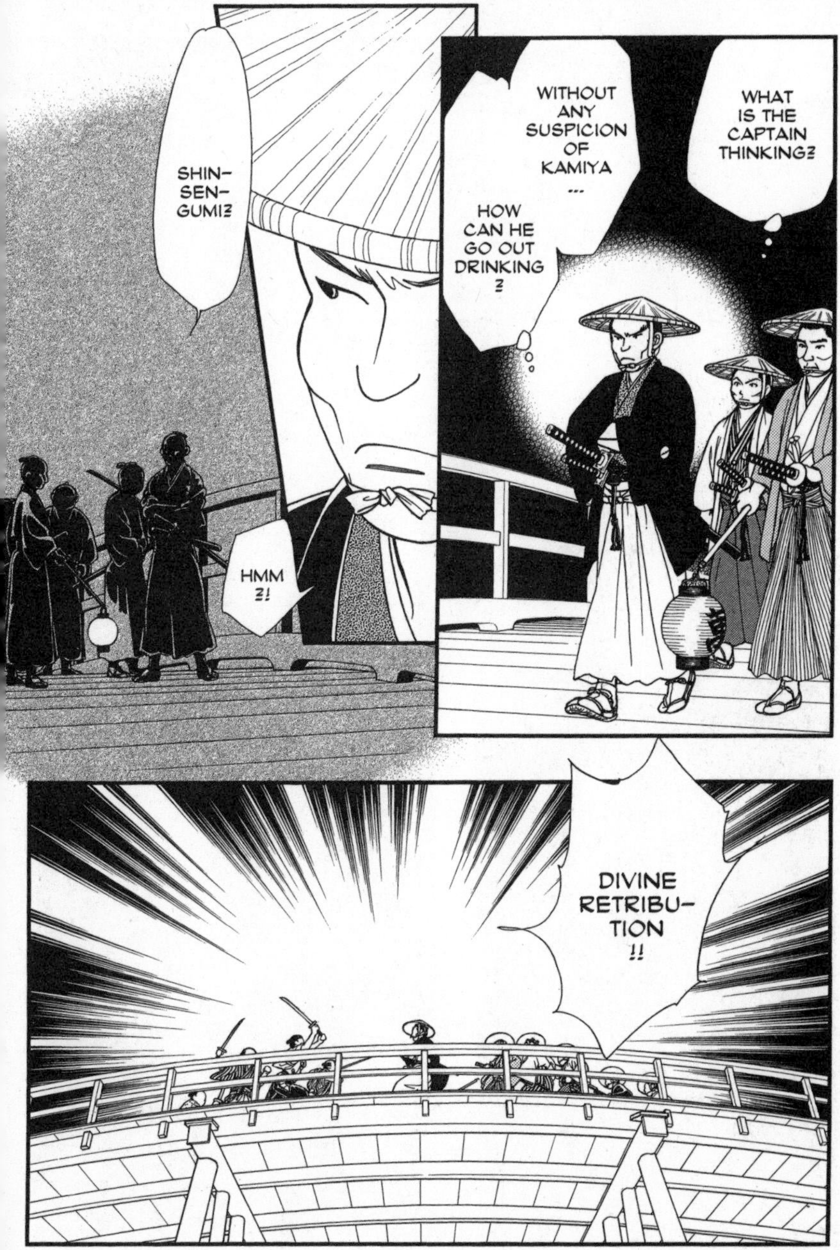
WHAT IS THE CAPTAIN THINKING?
WITHOUT ANY SUSPICION OF KAMIYA ...
HOW CAN HE GO OUT DRINKING?
SHIN-SEN-GUMI?
HMM?!
DIVINE RETRIBU-TION!!

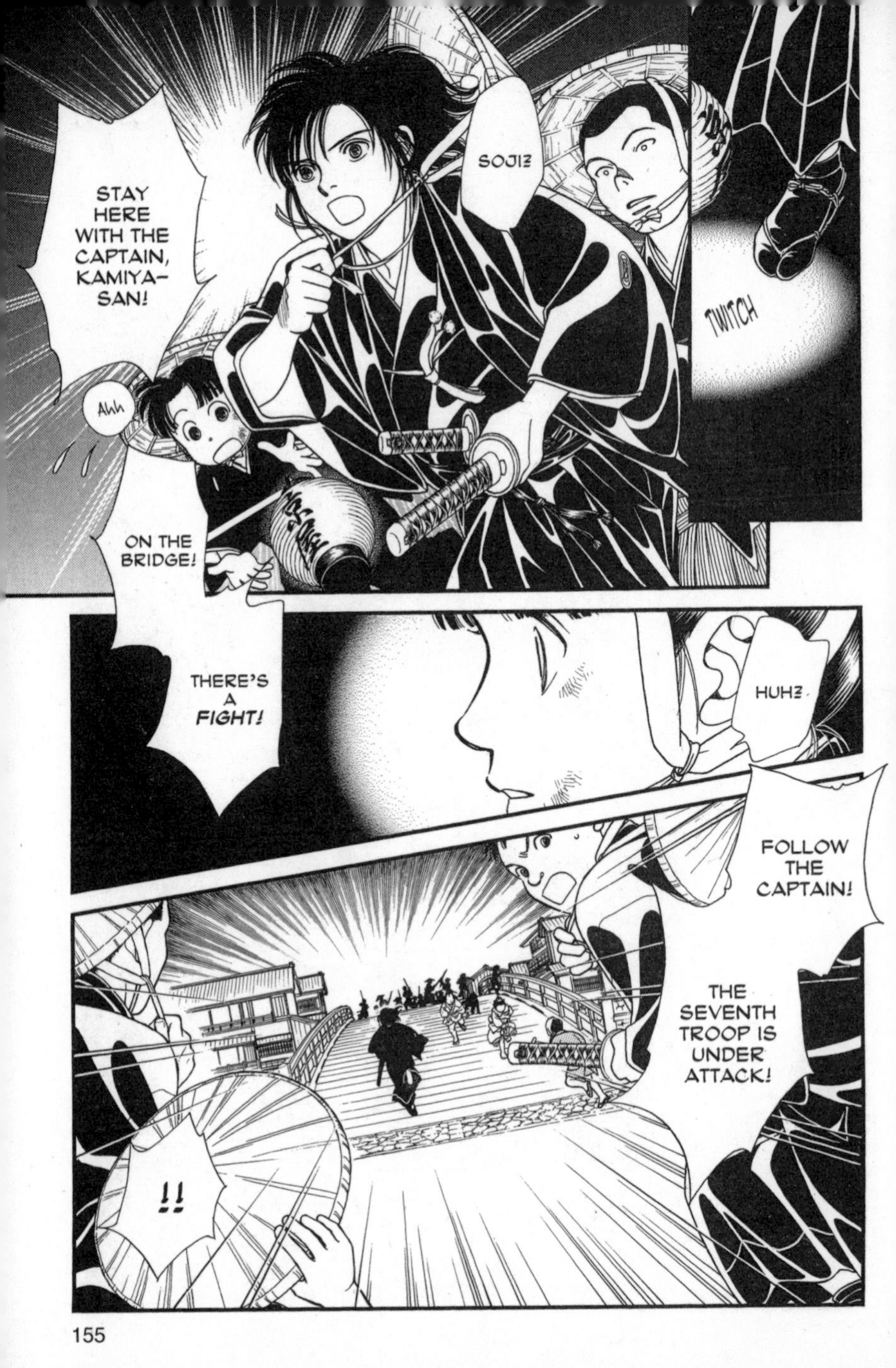
TWITCH
SOJI?
STAY HERE WITH THE CAPTAIN, KAMIYA-SAN!
Ahh
ON THE BRIDGE!
THERE'S A *FIGHT!*
HUH?
FOLLOW THE CAPTAIN!
THE SEVENTH TROOP IS UNDER ATTACK!
!!

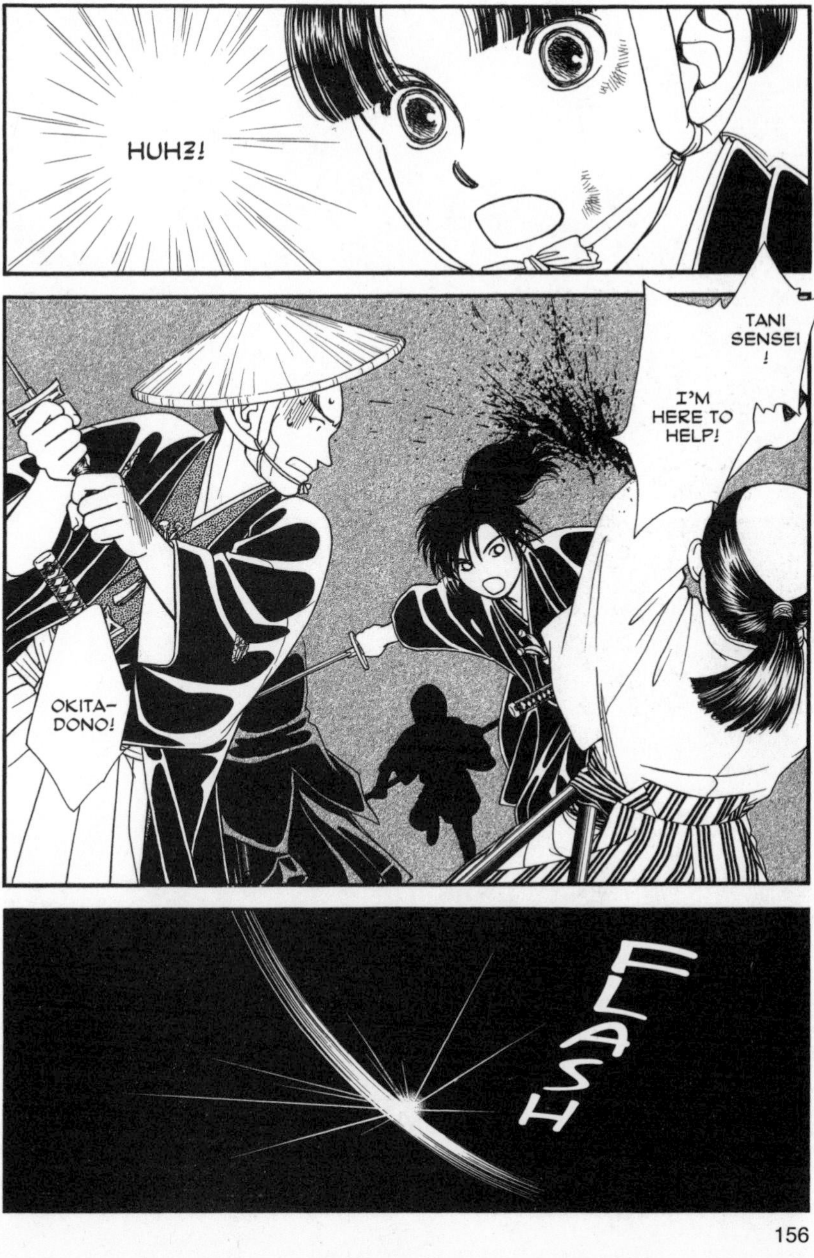
HUH?!
TANI SENSEI!
I'M HERE TO HELP!
OKITA-DONO!
FLASH

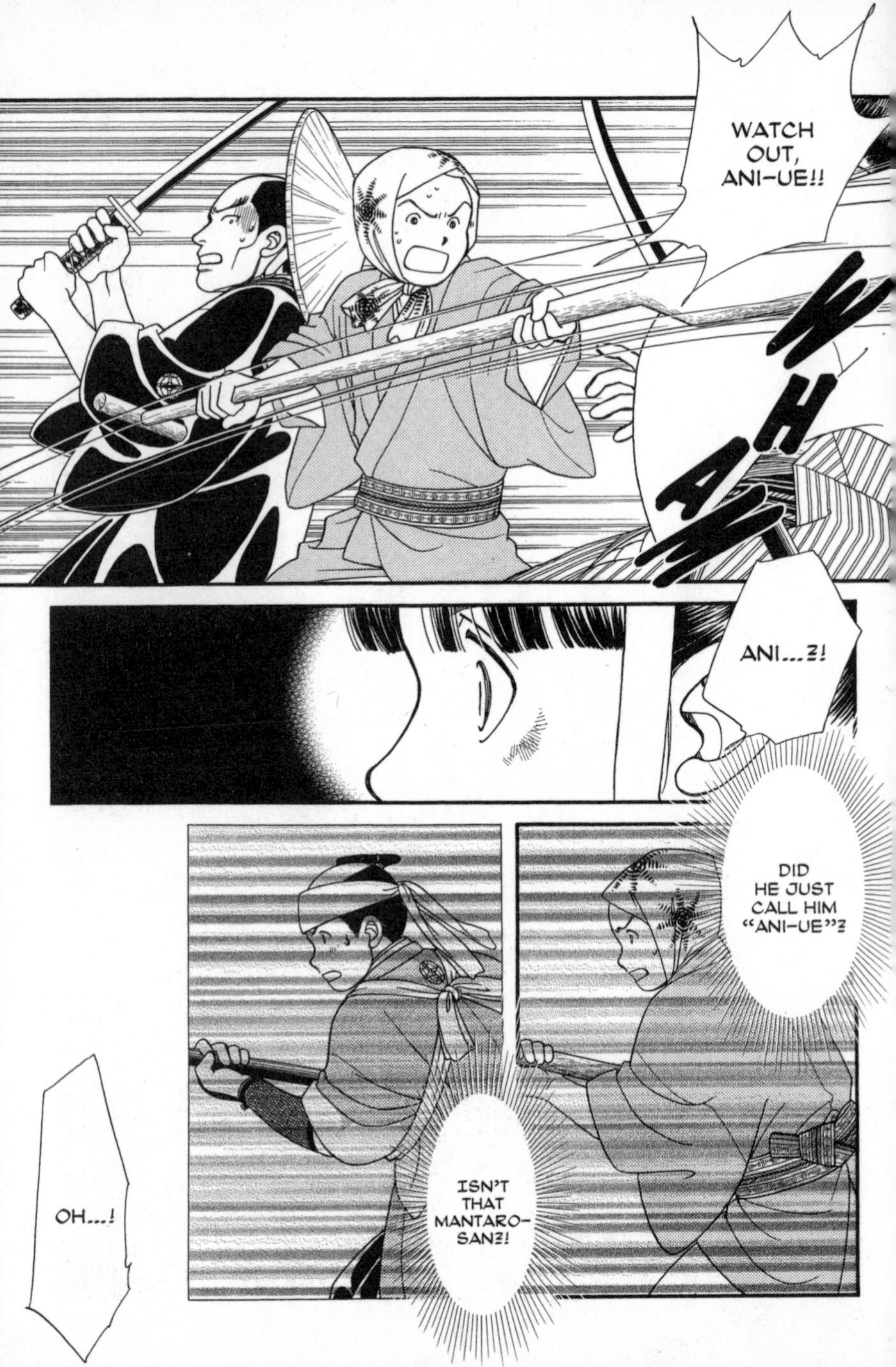
WATCH OUT, ANI-UE!!
WHAM
ANI...?!
DID HE JUST CALL HIM "ANI-UE"?
ISN'T THAT MANTARO-SAN?!
OH...!

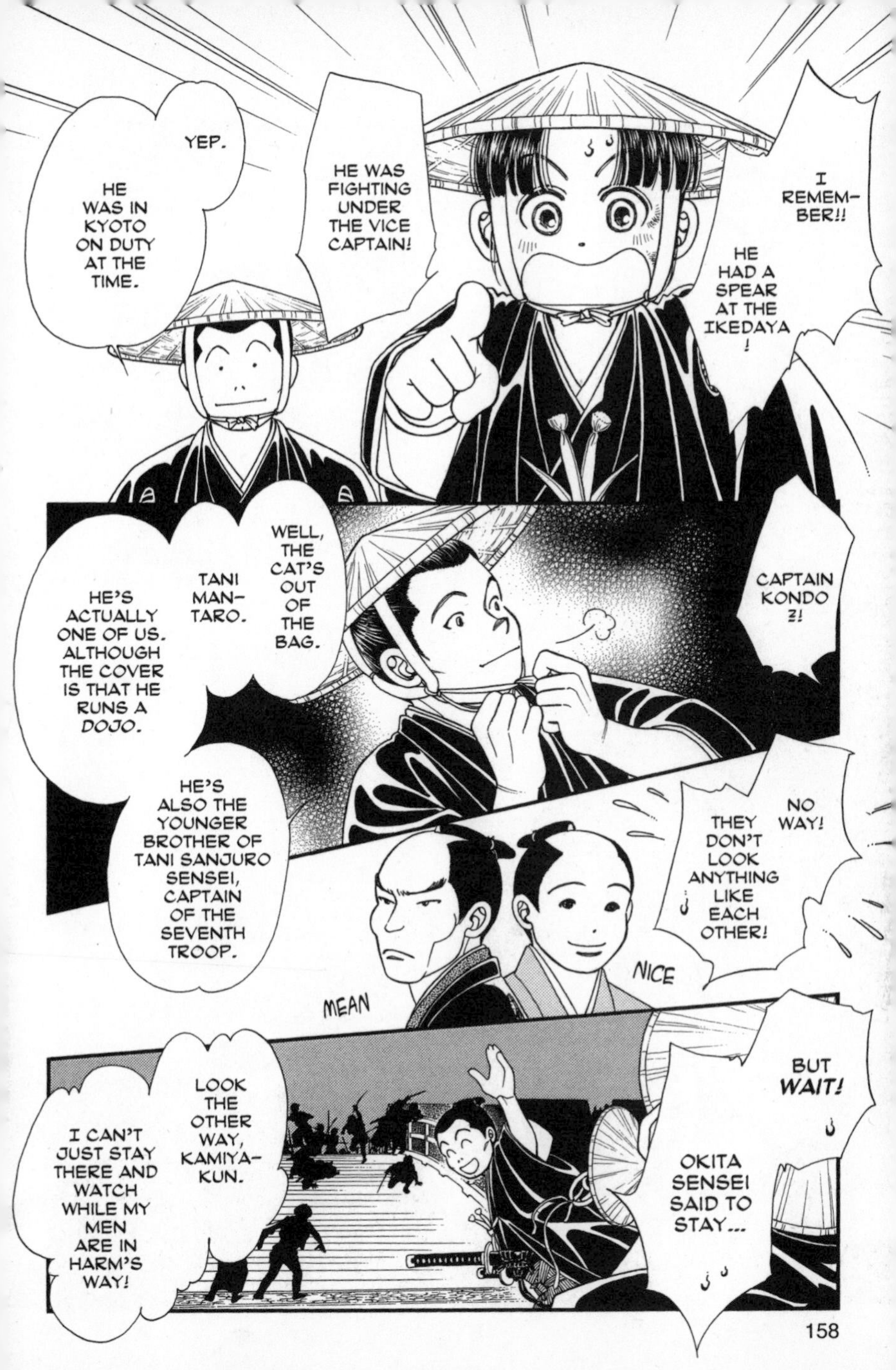
I REMEMBER!!
HE HAD A SPEAR AT THE IKEDAYA!
HE WAS FIGHTING UNDER THE VICE CAPTAIN!
YEP.
HE WAS IN KYOTO ON DUTY AT THE TIME.
CAPTAIN KONDO?!
WELL, THE CAT'S OUT OF THE BAG.
TANI MANTARO.
HE'S ACTUALLY ONE OF US. ALTHOUGH THE COVER IS THAT HE RUNS A *DOJO*.
NO WAY!
THEY DON'T LOOK ANYTHING LIKE EACH OTHER!
NICE
MEAN
HE'S ALSO THE YOUNGER BROTHER OF TANI SANJURO SENSEI, CAPTAIN OF THE SEVENTH TROOP.
BUT **WAIT!**
OKITA SENSEI SAID TO STAY...
LOOK THE OTHER WAY, KAMIYA-KUN.
I CAN'T JUST STAY THERE AND WATCH WHILE MY MEN ARE IN HARM'S WAY!

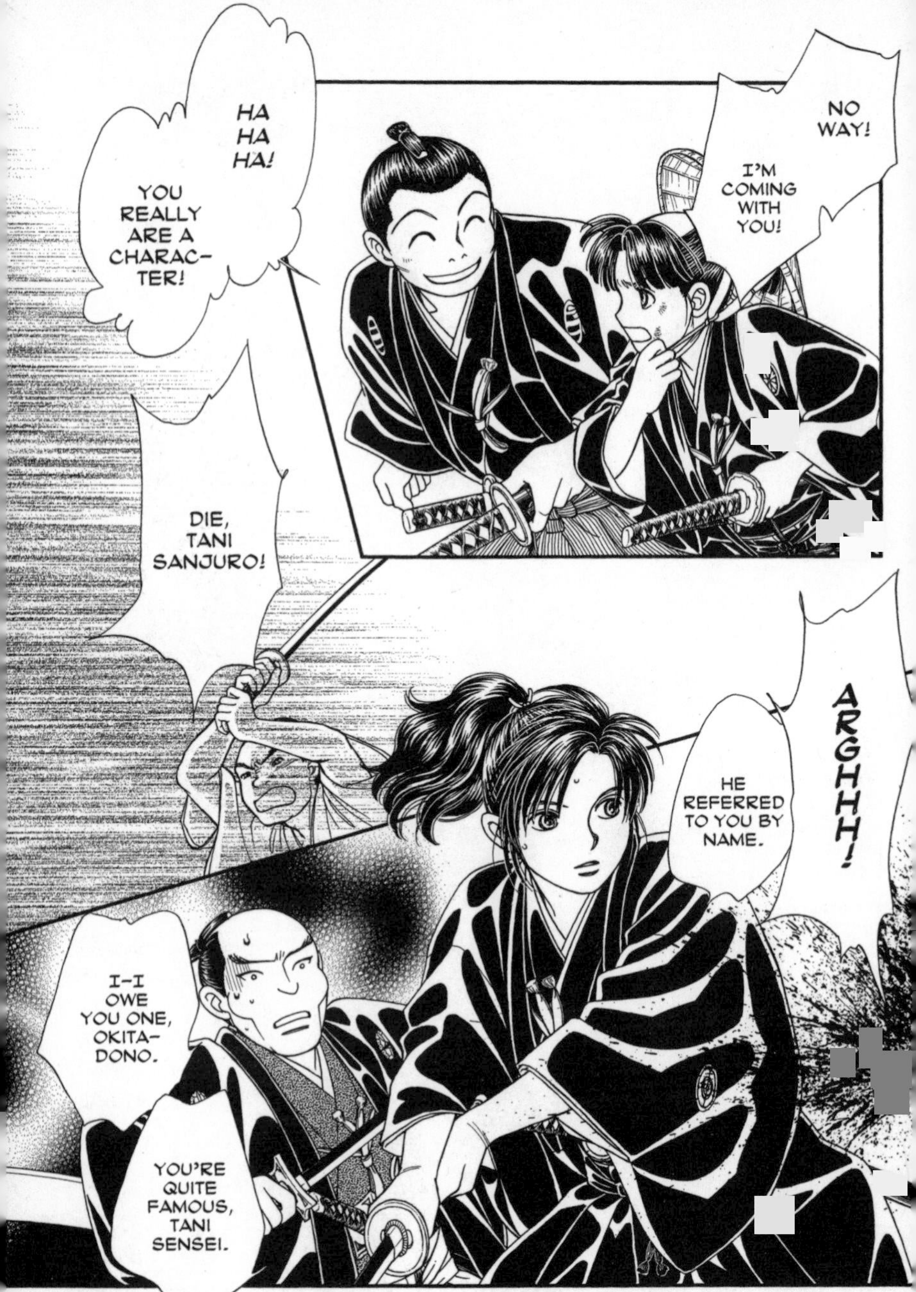
NO WAY!
I'M COMING WITH YOU!
HA HA HA!
YOU REALLY ARE A CHARAC-TER!
DIE, TANI SANJURO!
ARGHHH!
HE REFERRED TO YOU BY NAME.
I-I OWE YOU ONE, OKITA-DONO.
YOU'RE QUITE FAMOUS, TANI SENSEI.

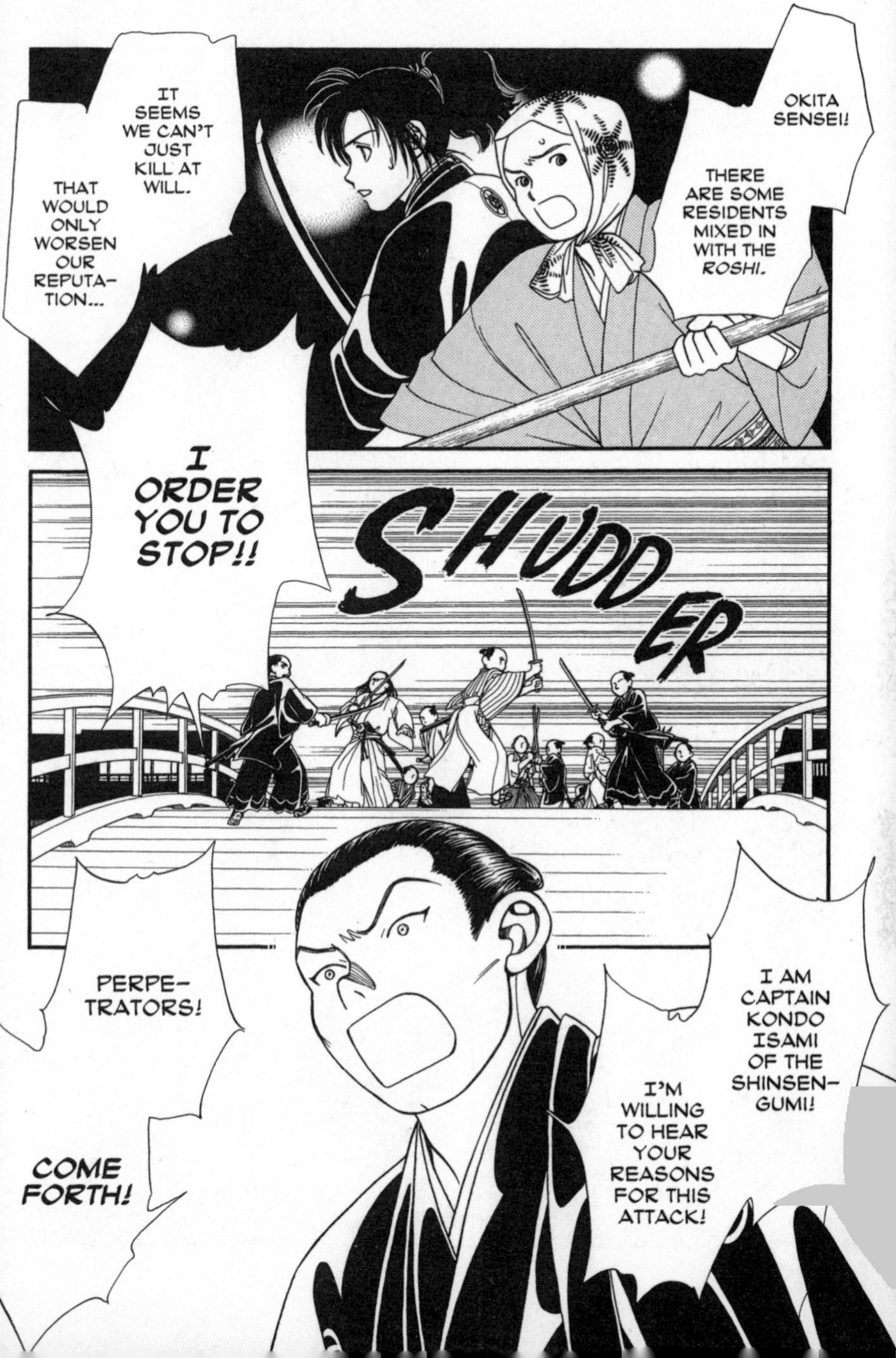
OKITA SENSEI!
THERE ARE SOME RESIDENTS MIXED IN WITH THE *ROSHI*.
IT SEEMS WE CAN'T JUST KILL AT WILL.
THAT WOULD ONLY WORSEN OUR REPUTATION...
SHUDDER
I ORDER YOU TO STOP!!
I AM CAPTAIN KONDO ISAMI OF THE SHINSEN-GUMI!
I'M WILLING TO HEAR YOUR REASONS FOR THIS ATTACK!
PERPETRATORS!
COME FORTH!

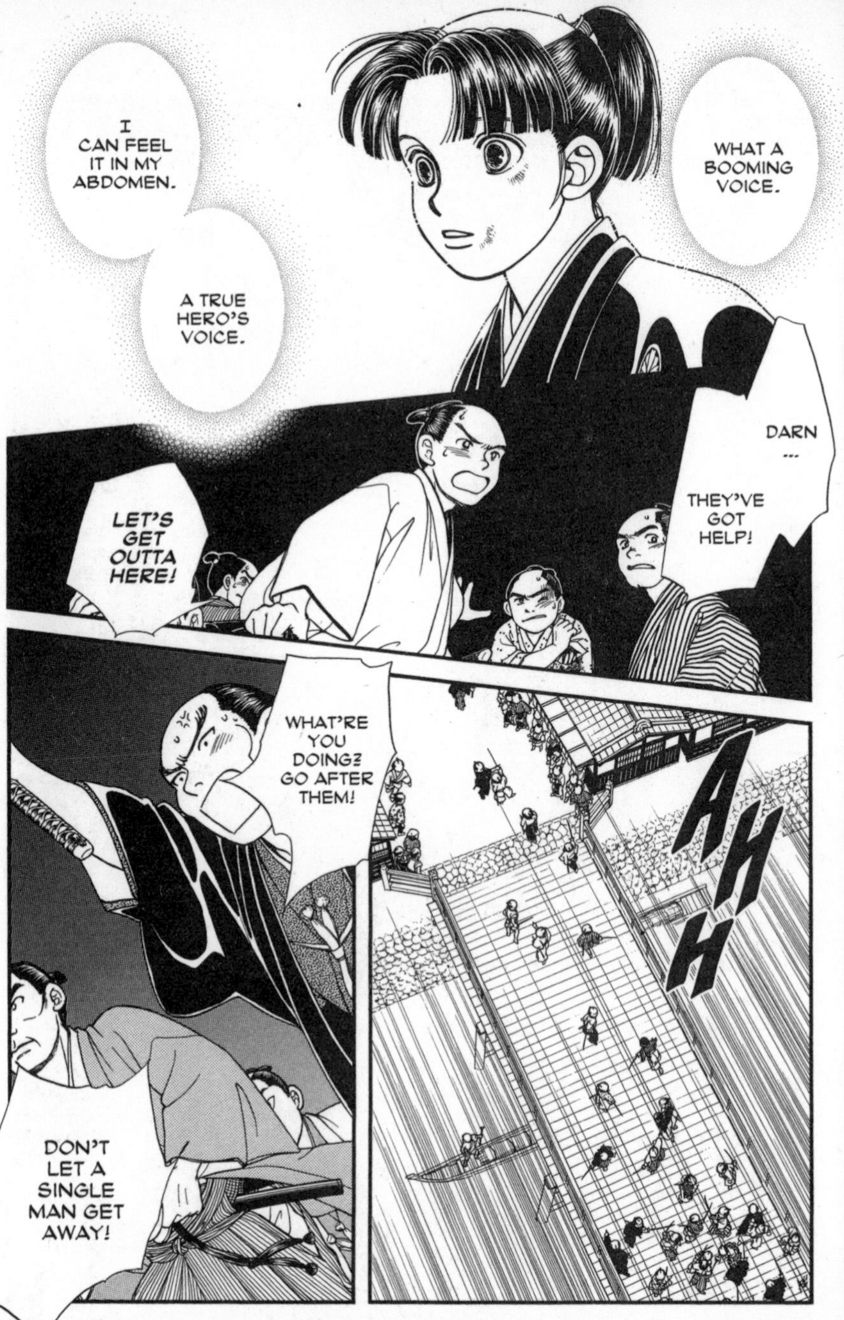
WHAT A BOOMING VOICE.
I CAN FEEL IT IN MY ABDOMEN.
A TRUE HERO'S VOICE.
DARN... THEY'VE GOT HELP!
LET'S GET OUTTA HERE!
AHH
WHAT'RE YOU DOING? GO AFTER THEM!
DON'T LET A SINGLE MAN GET AWAY!

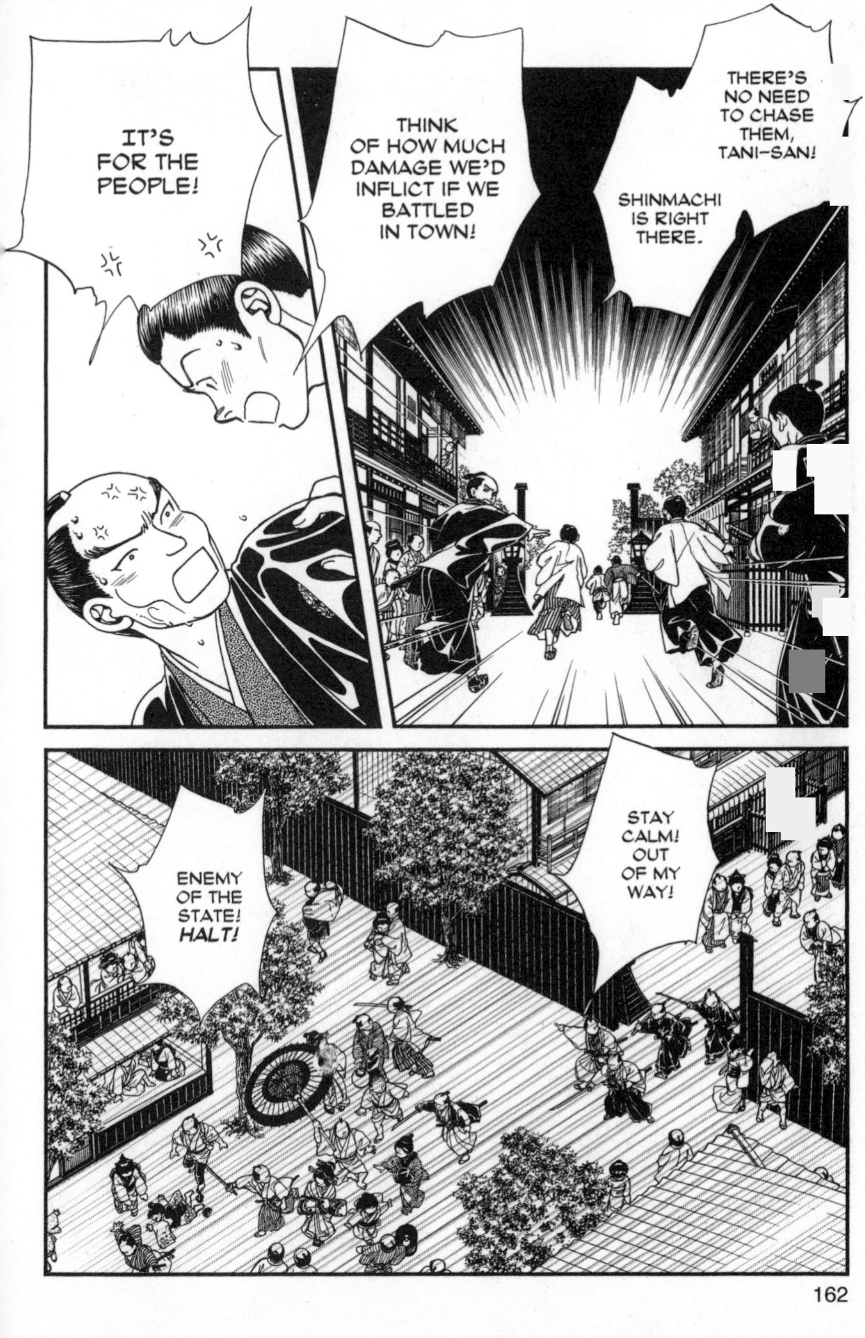
THERE'S NO NEED TO CHASE THEM, TANI-SAN!
SHINMACHI IS RIGHT THERE.
THINK OF HOW MUCH DAMAGE WE'D INFLICT IF WE BATTLED IN TOWN!
IT'S FOR THE PEOPLE!
STAY CALM! OUT OF MY WAY!
ENEMY OF THE STATE! *HALT!*

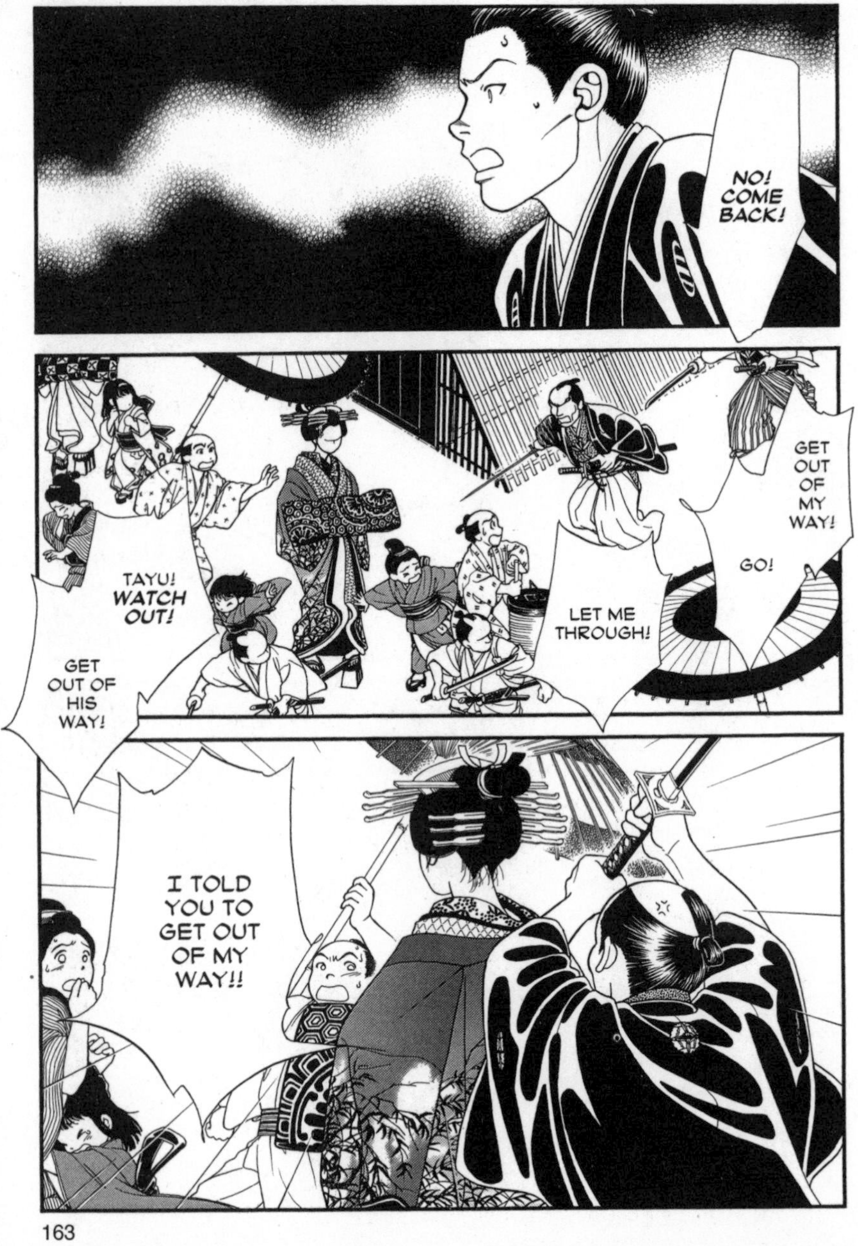
NO! COME BACK!
GET OUT OF MY WAY!
GO!
LET ME THROUGH!
TAYU! WATCH OUT!
GET OUT OF HIS WAY!
I TOLD YOU TO GET OUT OF MY WAY!!

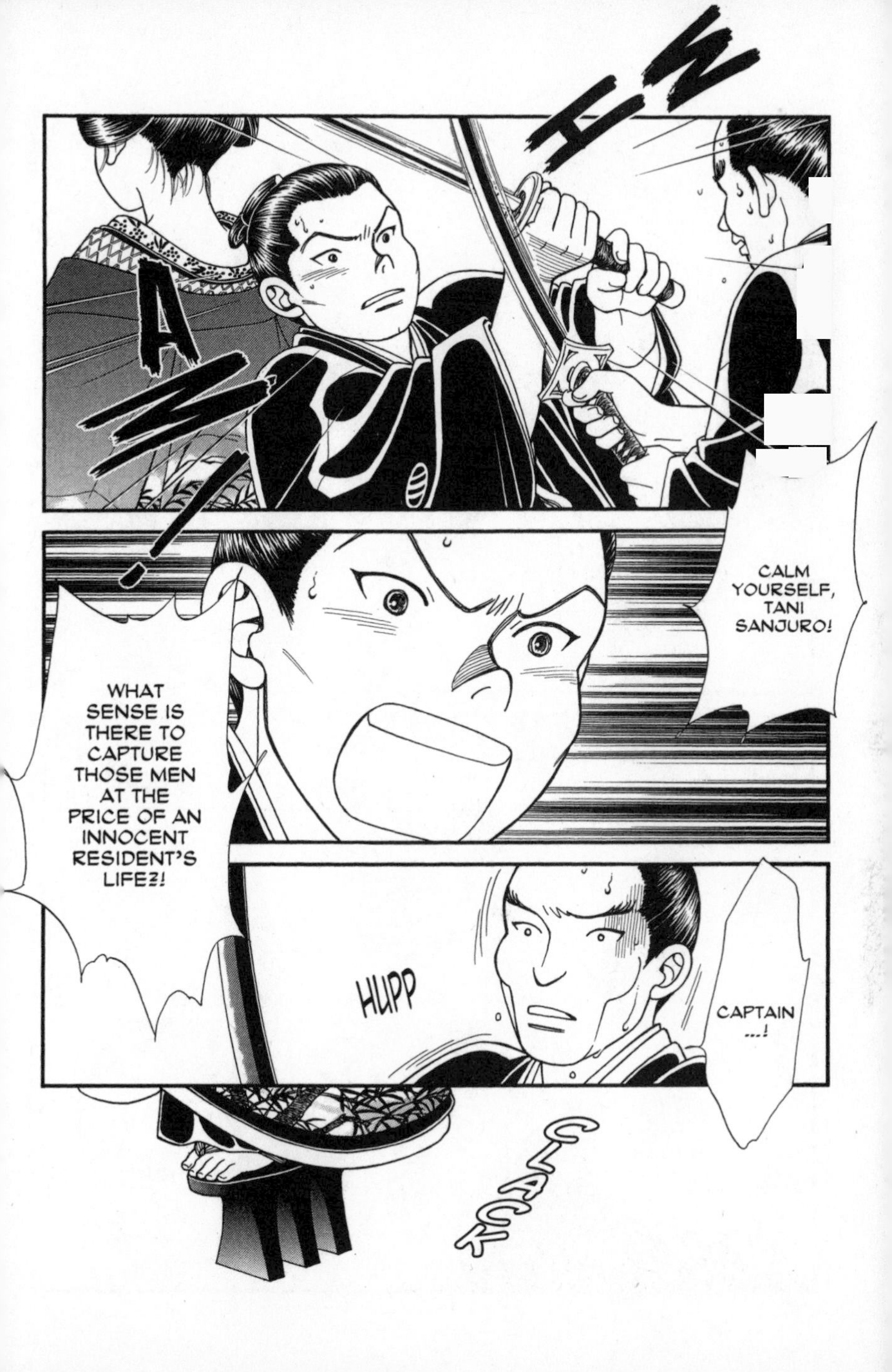
WHAM!
CALM YOURSELF, TANI SANJURO!
WHAT SENSE IS THERE TO CAPTURE THOSE MEN AT THE PRICE OF AN INNOCENT RESIDENT'S LIFE?!
CAPTAIN ...!
HUPP
CLACK

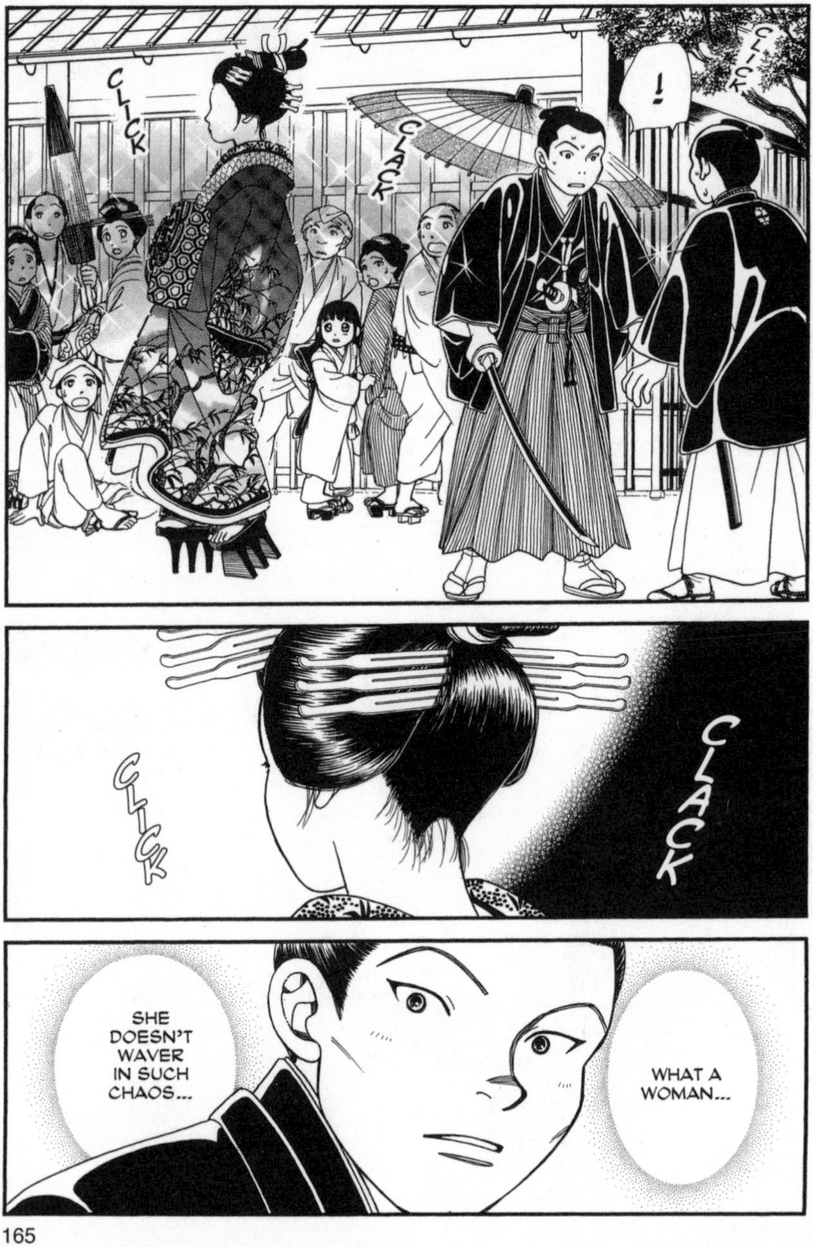
CLICK
!
CLACK
CLICK
CLACK
CLICK
WHAT A WOMAN...
SHE DOESN'T WAVER IN SUCH CHAOS...

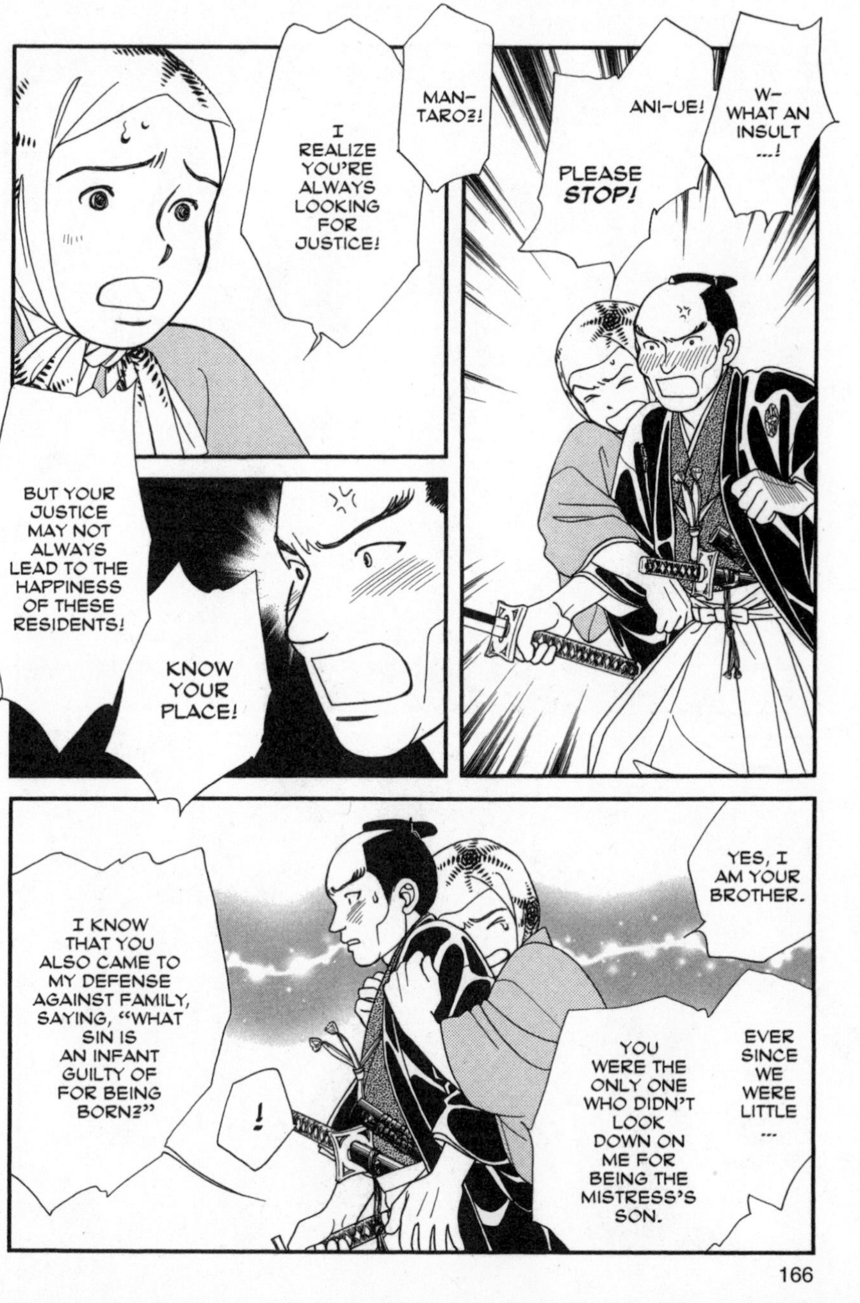
W— WHAT AN INSULT ...!
ANI-UE! PLEASE STOP!
MAN-TARO?!
I REALIZE YOU'RE ALWAYS LOOKING FOR JUSTICE!
BUT YOUR JUSTICE MAY NOT ALWAYS LEAD TO THE HAPPINESS OF THESE RESIDENTS!
KNOW YOUR PLACE!
YES, I AM YOUR BROTHER.
EVER SINCE WE WERE LITTLE ...
YOU WERE THE ONLY ONE WHO DIDN'T LOOK DOWN ON ME FOR BEING THE MISTRESS'S SON.
!
I KNOW THAT YOU ALSO CAME TO MY DEFENSE AGAINST FAMILY, SAYING, "WHAT SIN IS AN INFANT GUILTY OF FOR BEING BORN?"

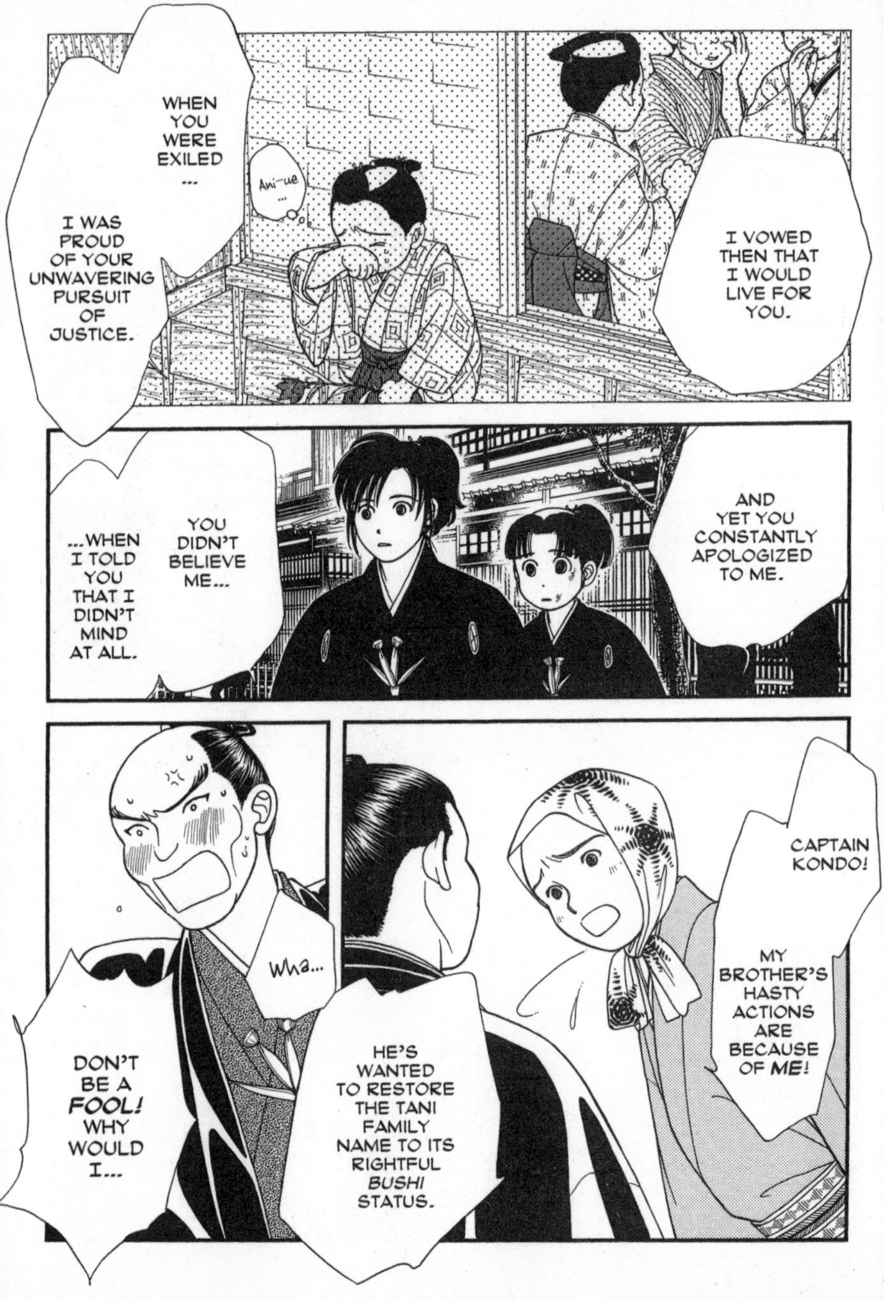
WHEN YOU WERE EXILED ...
I WAS PROUD OF YOUR UNWAVERING PURSUIT OF JUSTICE.
Ani-ue ...
I VOWED THEN THAT I WOULD LIVE FOR YOU.
AND YET YOU CONSTANTLY APOLOGIZED TO ME.
YOU DIDN'T BELIEVE ME...
...WHEN I TOLD YOU THAT I DIDN'T MIND AT ALL.
CAPTAIN KONDO!
MY BROTHER'S HASTY ACTIONS ARE BECAUSE OF *ME*!
HE'S WANTED TO RESTORE THE TANI FAMILY NAME TO ITS RIGHTFUL *BUSHI* STATUS.
Wha...
DON'T BE A ***FOOL!*** WHY WOULD I...

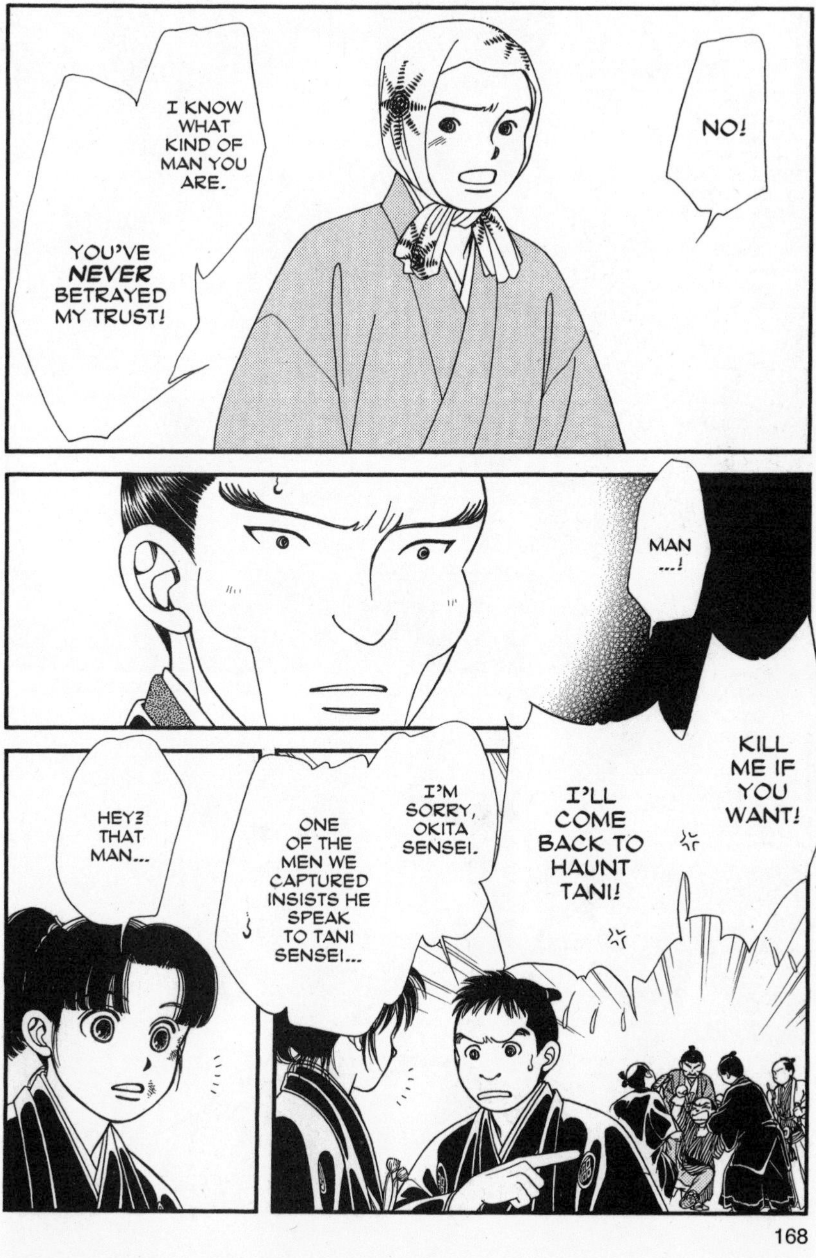
NO!
I KNOW WHAT KIND OF MAN YOU ARE.
YOU'VE *NEVER* BETRAYED MY TRUST!
MAN ...!
KILL ME IF YOU WANT!
I'LL COME BACK TO HAUNT TANI!
I'M SORRY, OKITA SENSEI.
ONE OF THE MEN WE CAPTURED INSISTS HE SPEAK TO TANI SENSEI...
HEY? THAT MAN...

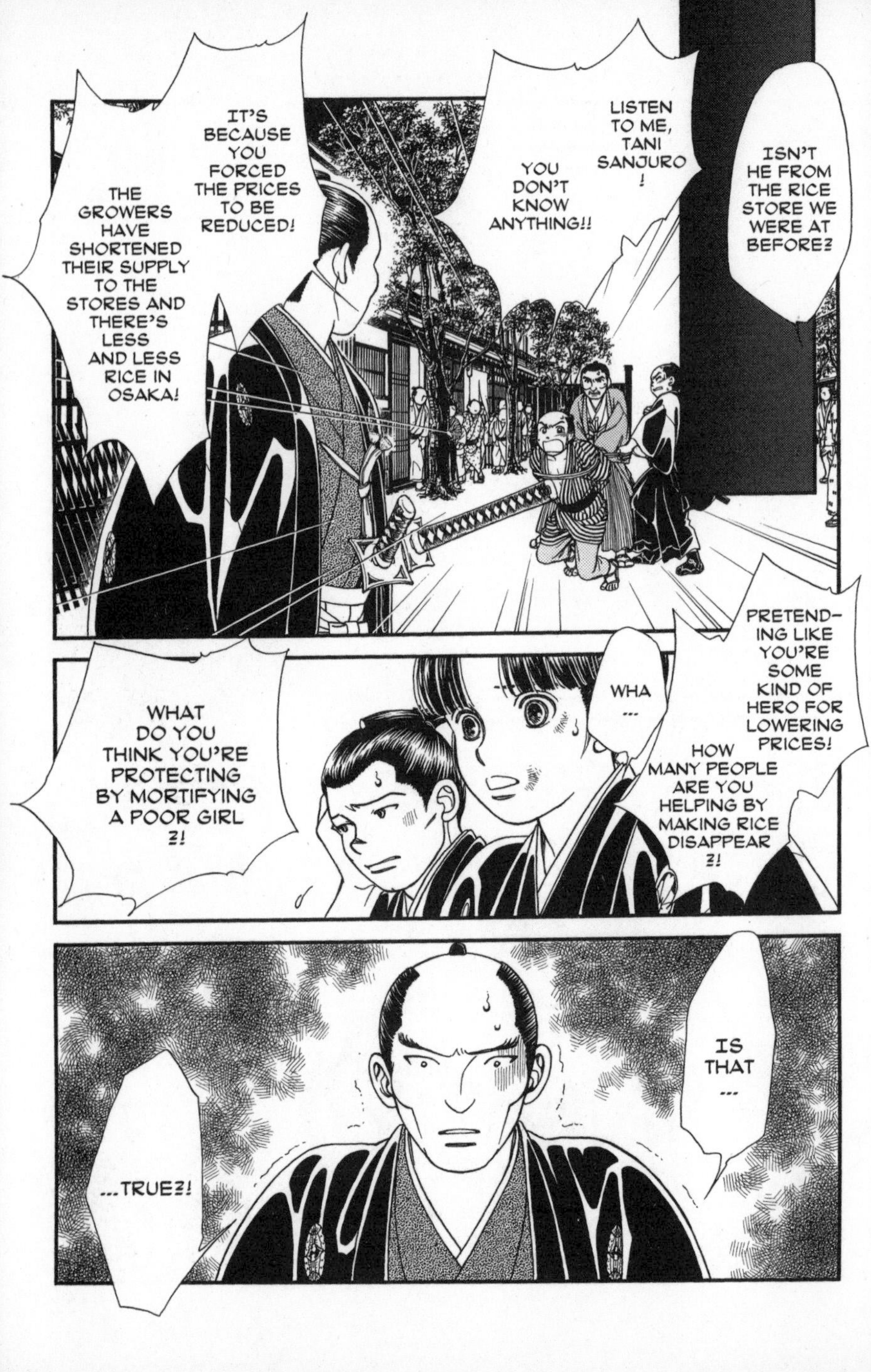
ISN'T HE FROM THE RICE STORE WE WERE AT BEFORE?
LISTEN TO ME, TANI SANJURO!
YOU DON'T KNOW ANYTHING!!
IT'S BECAUSE YOU FORCED THE PRICES TO BE REDUCED!
THE GROWERS HAVE SHORTENED THEIR SUPPLY TO THE STORES AND THERE'S LESS AND LESS RICE IN OSAKA!
PRETENDING LIKE YOU'RE SOME KIND OF HERO FOR LOWERING PRICES!
HOW MANY PEOPLE ARE YOU HELPING BY MAKING RICE DISAPPEAR?!
WHA...
WHAT DO YOU THINK YOU'RE PROTECTING BY MORTIFYING A POOR GIRL?!
IS THAT...
...TRUE?!

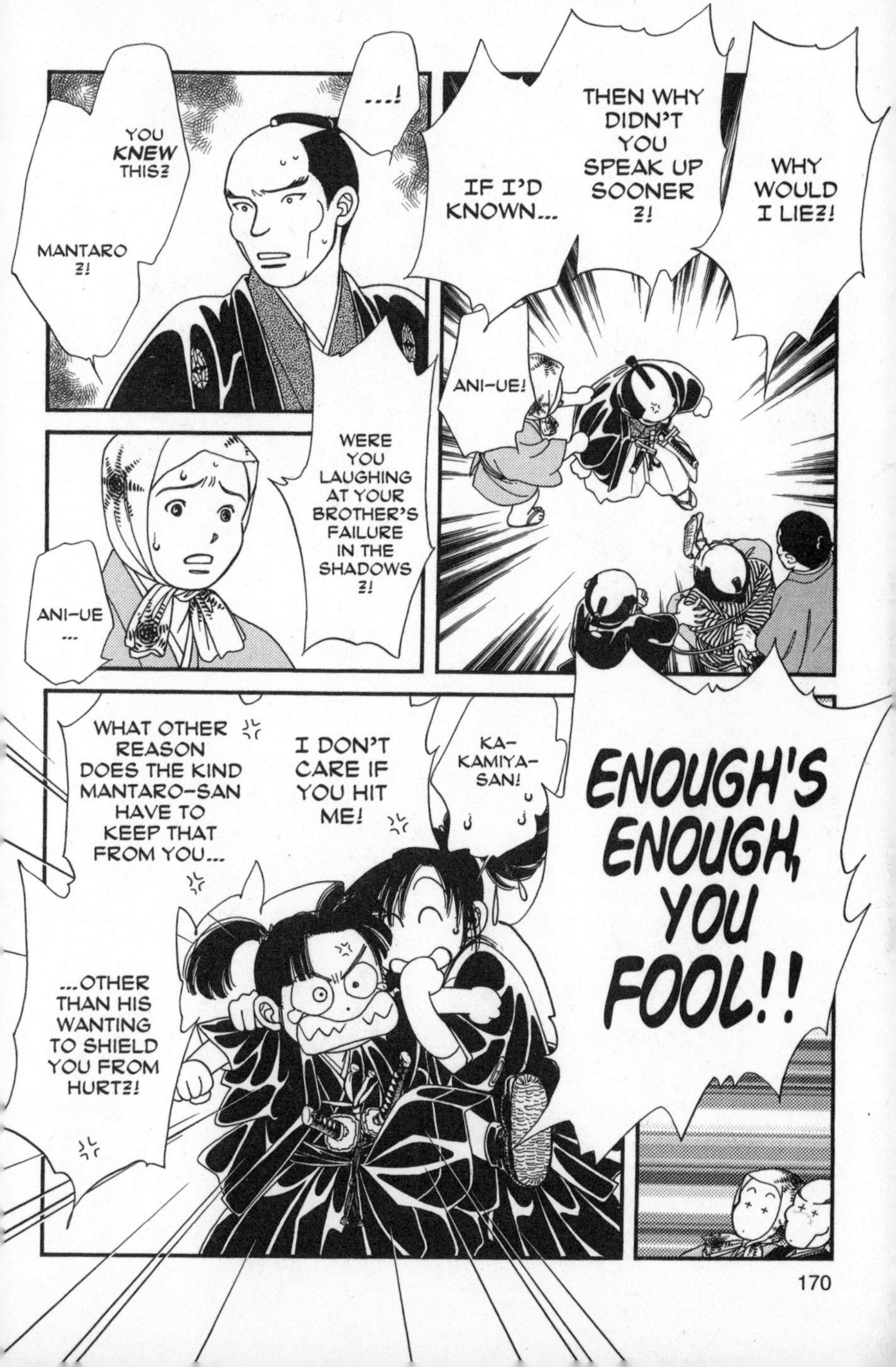
WHY WOULD I LIE?!
THEN WHY DIDN'T YOU SPEAK UP SOONER?!
IF I'D KNOWN...
ANI-UE!
...!
YOU KNEW THIS?
MANTARO?!
WERE YOU LAUGHING AT YOUR BROTHER'S FAILURE IN THE SHADOWS?!
ANI-UE...
ENOUGH'S ENOUGH, YOU FOOL!!
KA-KAMIYA-SAN!
I DON'T CARE IF YOU HIT ME!
WHAT OTHER REASON DOES THE KIND MANTARO-SAN HAVE TO KEEP THAT FROM YOU...
...OTHER THAN HIS WANTING TO SHIELD YOU FROM HURT?!

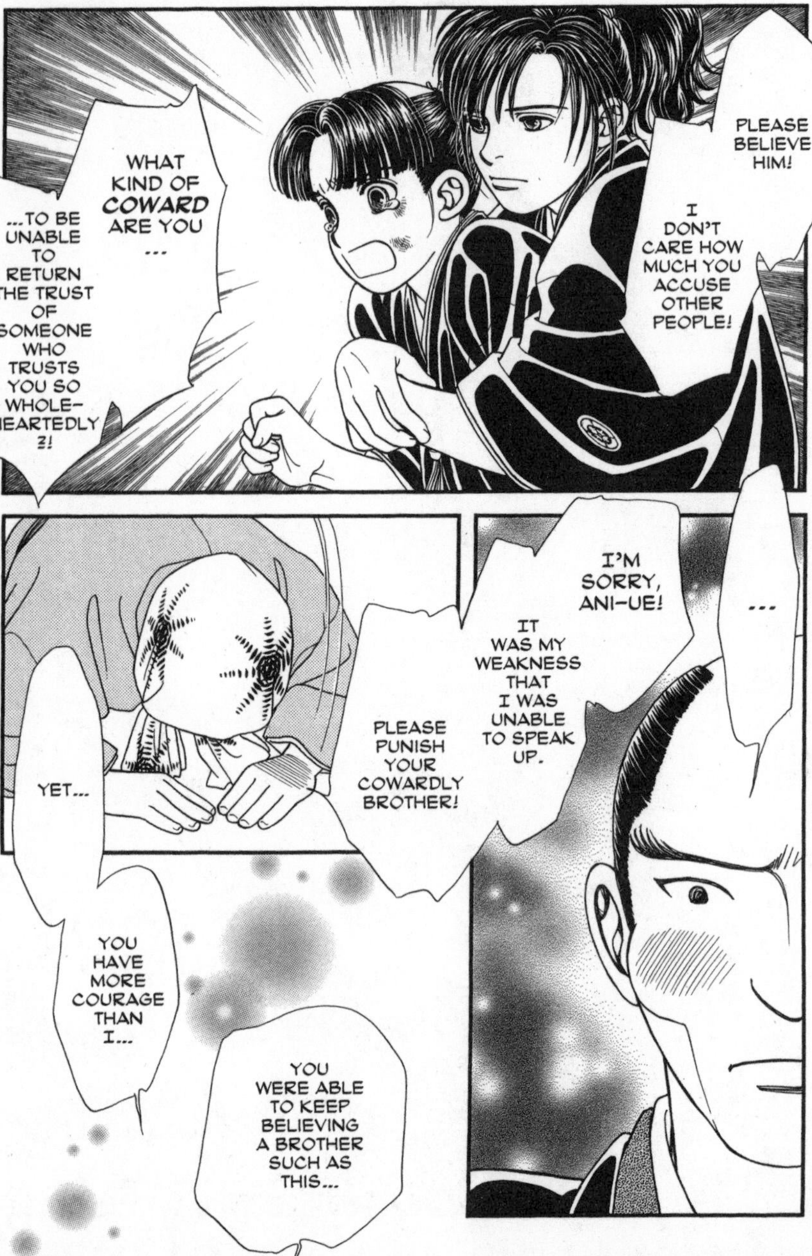
PLEASE BELIEVE HIM!
I DON'T CARE HOW MUCH YOU ACCUSE OTHER PEOPLE!
WHAT KIND OF COWARD ARE YOU ...
...TO BE UNABLE TO RETURN THE TRUST OF SOMEONE WHO TRUSTS YOU SO WHOLE-HEARTEDLY?!
...
I'M SORRY, ANI-UE!
IT WAS MY WEAKNESS THAT I WAS UNABLE TO SPEAK UP.
PLEASE PUNISH YOUR COWARDLY BROTHER!
YET...
YOU HAVE MORE COURAGE THAN I...
YOU WERE ABLE TO KEEP BELIEVING A BROTHER SUCH AS THIS...

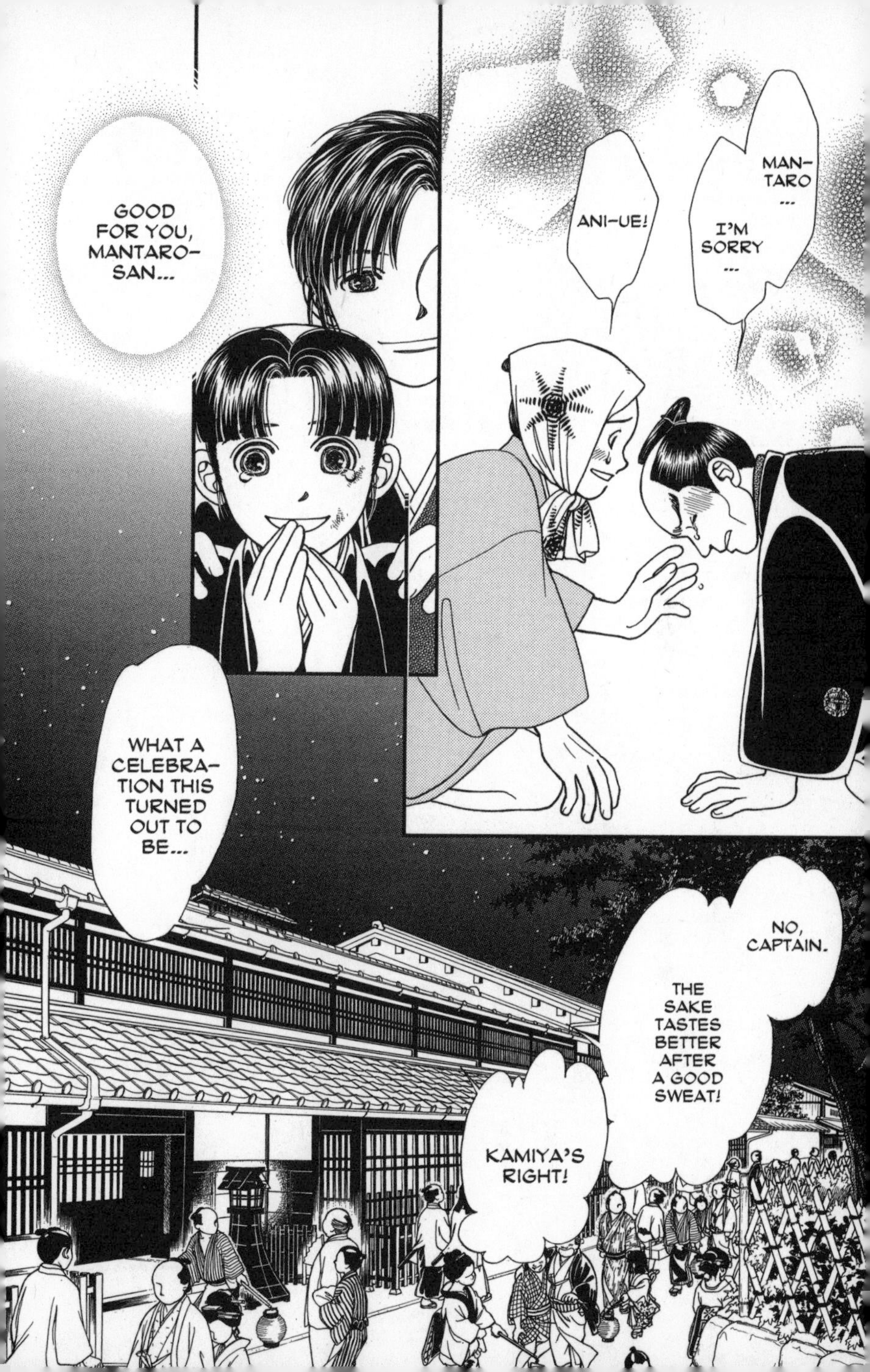
MAN-TARO ... I'M SORRY ...
ANI-UE!
GOOD FOR YOU, MANTARO-SAN...
WHAT A CELEBRATION THIS TURNED OUT TO BE...
NO, CAPTAIN. THE SAKE TASTES BETTER AFTER A GOOD SWEAT!
KAMIYA'S RIGHT!

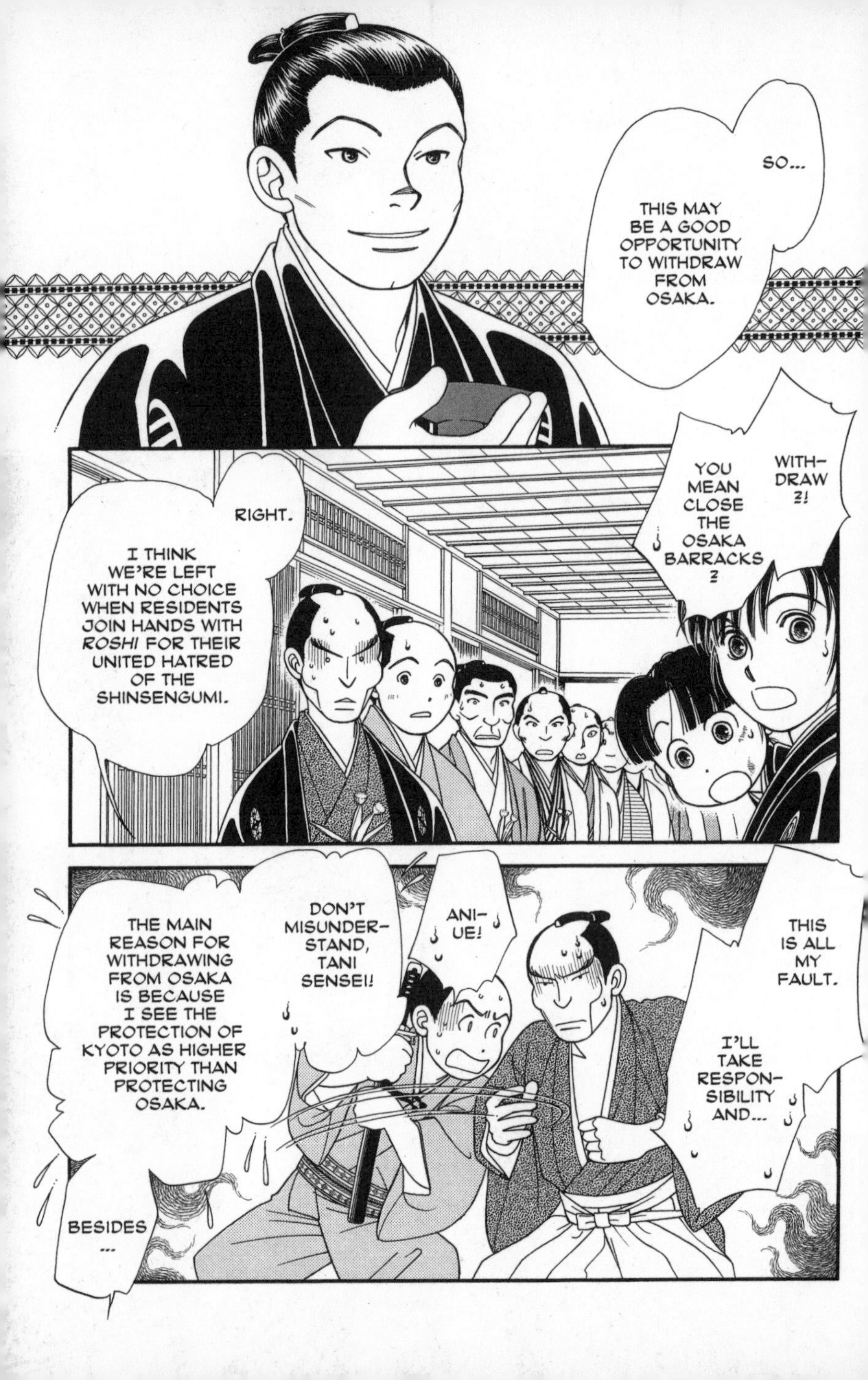
SO...
THIS MAY BE A GOOD OPPORTUNITY TO WITHDRAW FROM OSAKA.
WITH-DRAW?!
YOU MEAN CLOSE THE OSAKA BARRACKS?
RIGHT.
I THINK WE'RE LEFT WITH NO CHOICE WHEN RESIDENTS JOIN HANDS WITH *ROSHI* FOR THEIR UNITED HATRED OF THE SHINSENGUMI.
THIS IS ALL MY FAULT.
I'LL TAKE RESPON-SIBILITY AND...
ANI-UE!
DON'T MISUNDER-STAND, TANI SENSEI!
THE MAIN REASON FOR WITHDRAWING FROM OSAKA IS BECAUSE I SEE THE PROTECTION OF KYOTO AS HIGHER PRIORITY THAN PROTECTING OSAKA.
BESIDES...

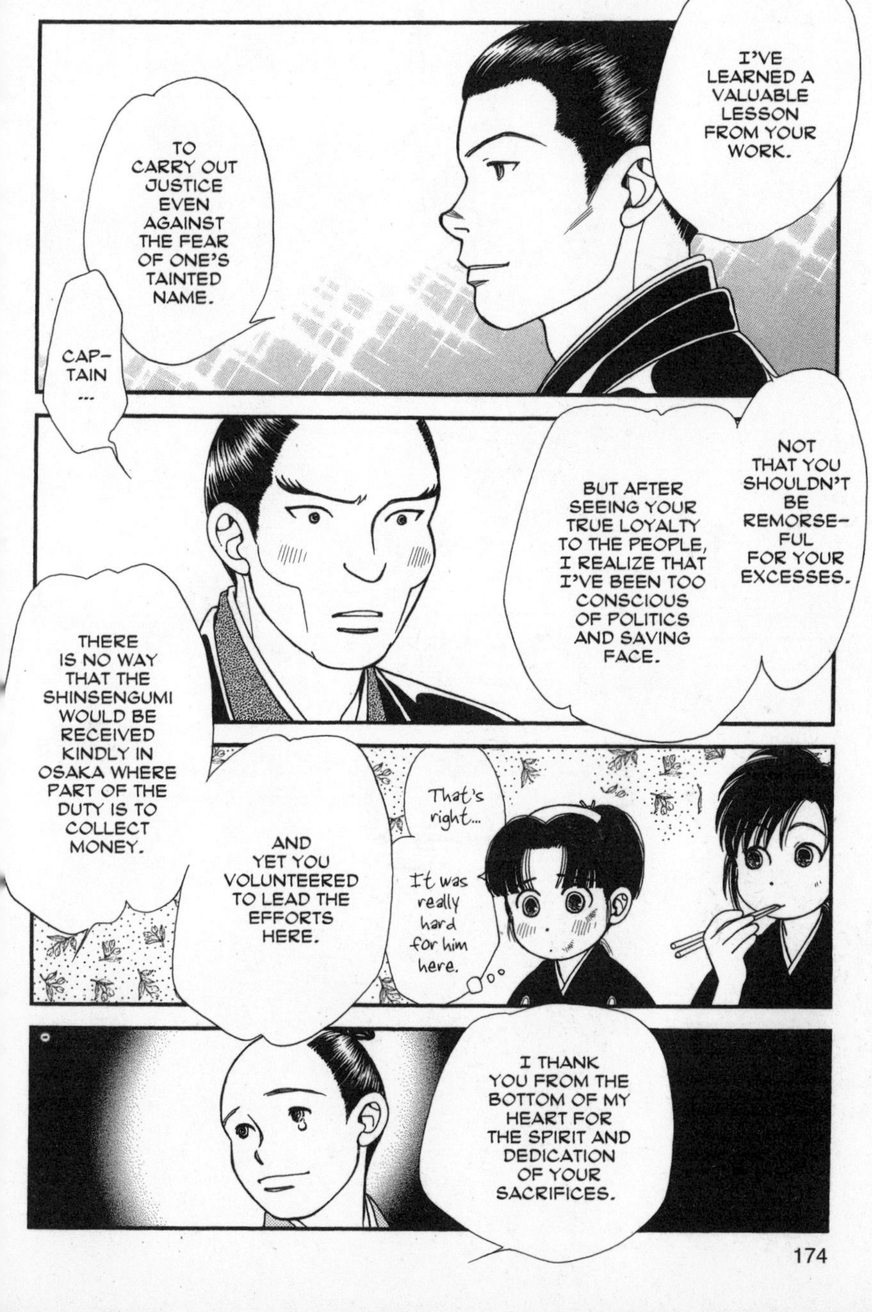

I'VE LEARNED A VALUABLE LESSON FROM YOUR WORK.
TO CARRY OUT JUSTICE EVEN AGAINST THE FEAR OF ONE'S TAINTED NAME.
CAP-TAIN ...
NOT THAT YOU SHOULDN'T BE REMORSE-FUL FOR YOUR EXCESSES.
BUT AFTER SEEING YOUR TRUE LOYALTY TO THE PEOPLE, I REALIZE THAT I'VE BEEN TOO CONSCIOUS OF POLITICS AND SAVING FACE.
THERE IS NO WAY THAT THE SHINSENGUMI WOULD BE RECEIVED KINDLY IN OSAKA WHERE PART OF THE DUTY IS TO COLLECT MONEY.
AND YET YOU VOLUNTEERED TO LEAD THE EFFORTS HERE.
That's right...
It was really hard for him here.
I THANK YOU FROM THE BOTTOM OF MY HEART FOR THE SPIRIT AND DEDICATION OF YOUR SACRIFICES.

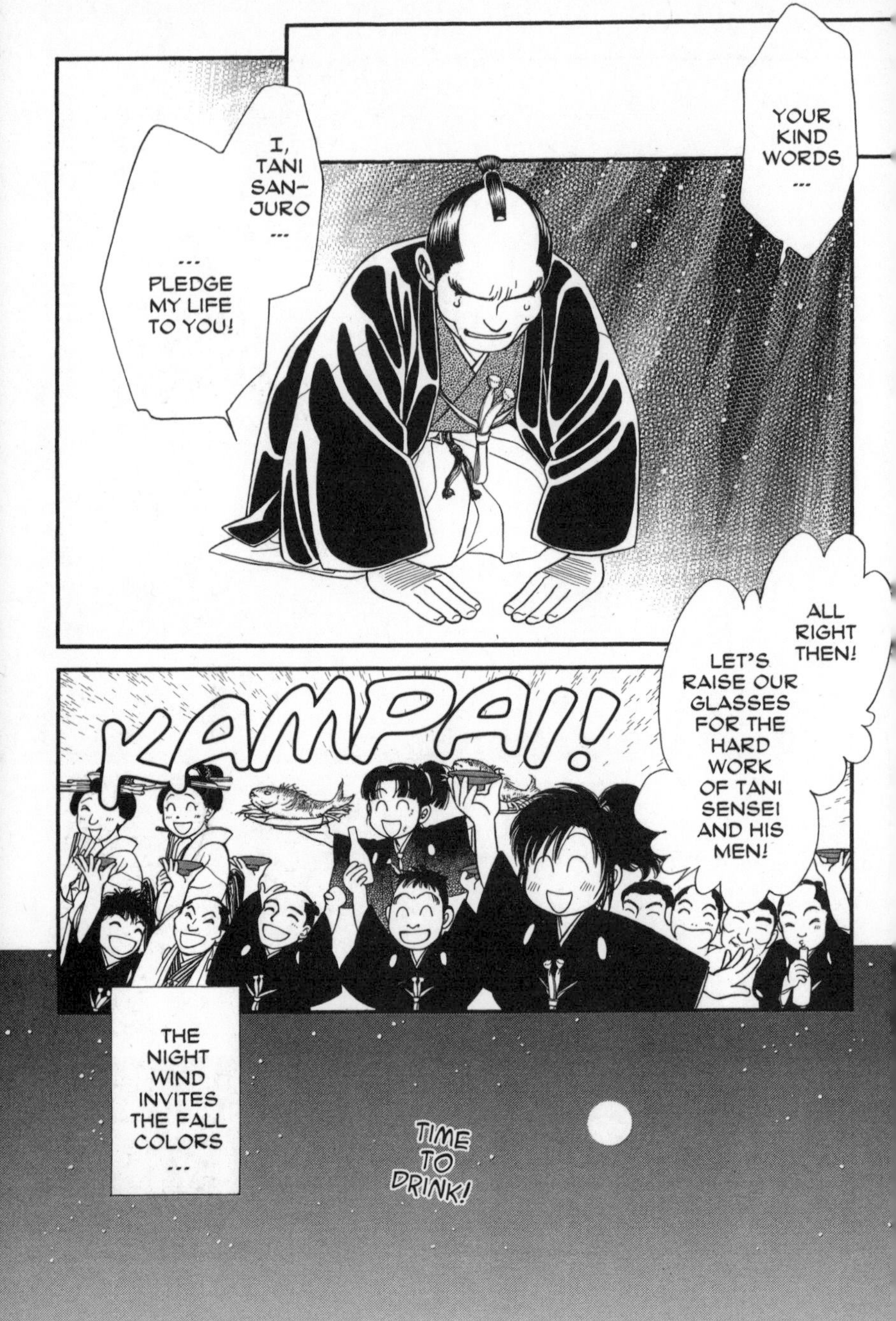
YOUR KIND WORDS ...
I, TANI SAN-JURO ... ... PLEDGE MY LIFE TO YOU!
ALL RIGHT THEN! LET'S RAISE OUR GLASSES FOR THE HARD WORK OF TANI SENSEI AND HIS MEN!
KAMPAI!
THE NIGHT WIND INVITES THE FALL COLORS ...
TIME TO DRINK!

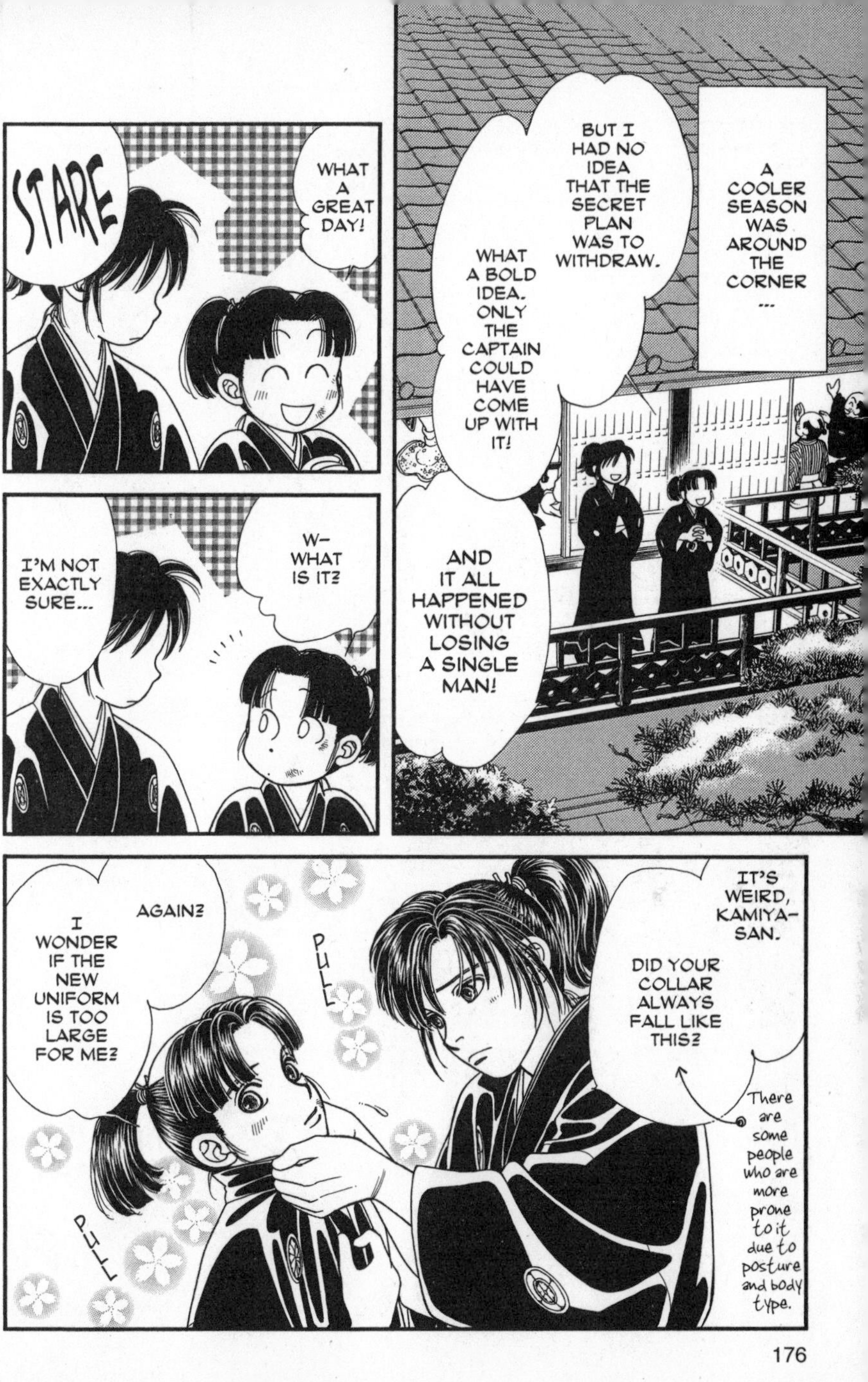
A COOLER SEASON WAS AROUND THE CORNER ...
BUT I HAD NO IDEA THAT THE SECRET PLAN WAS TO WITHDRAW.
WHAT A BOLD IDEA. ONLY THE CAPTAIN COULD HAVE COME UP WITH IT!
AND IT ALL HAPPENED WITHOUT LOSING A SINGLE MAN!
WHAT A GREAT DAY!
STARE
W-WHAT IS IT?
I'M NOT EXACTLY SURE...
IT'S WEIRD, KAMIYA-SAN.
DID YOUR COLLAR ALWAYS FALL LIKE THIS?
There are some people who are more prone to it due to posture and body type.
PULL
AGAIN?
I WONDER IF THE NEW UNIFORM IS TOO LARGE FOR ME?
PULL

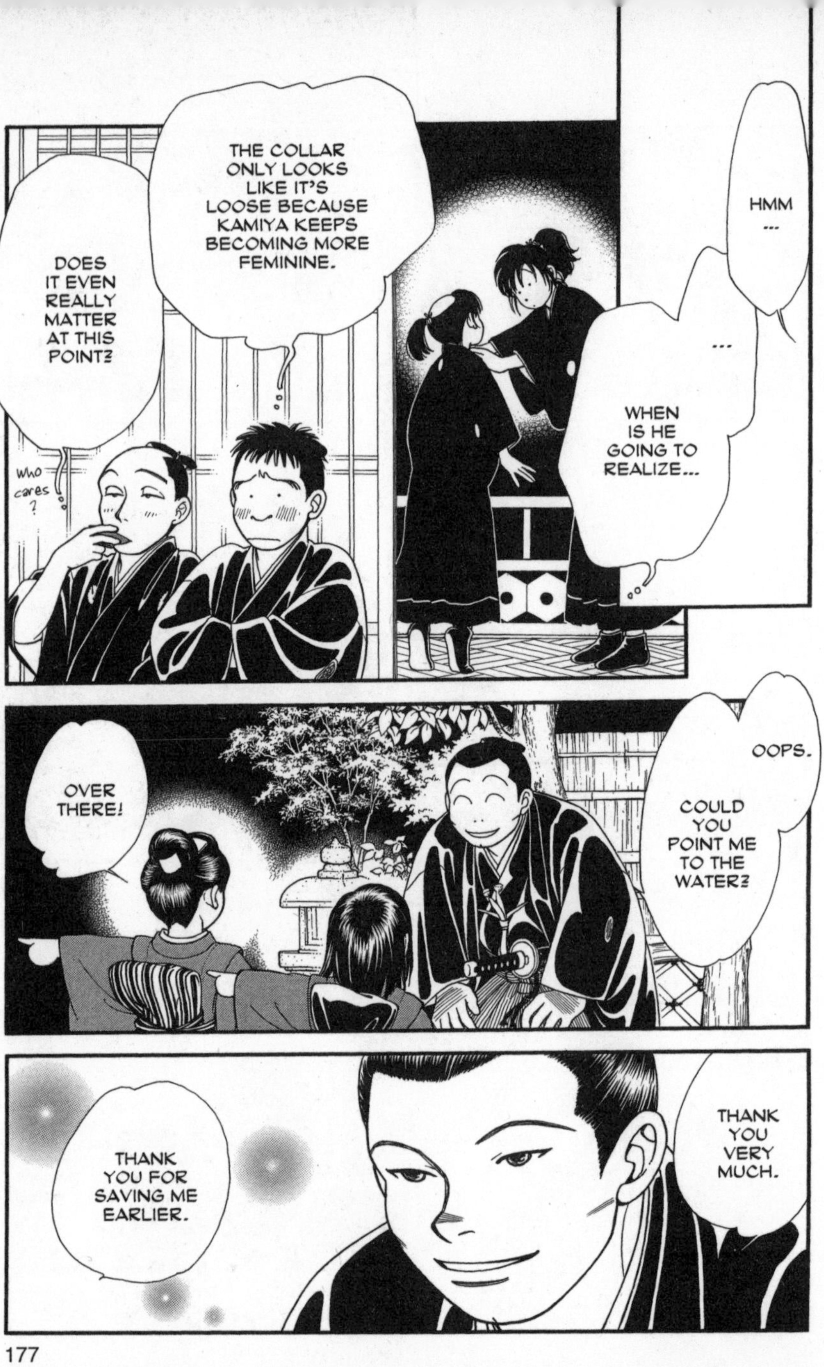
HMM ...
...
WHEN IS HE GOING TO REALIZE...
THE COLLAR ONLY LOOKS LIKE IT'S LOOSE BECAUSE KAMIYA KEEPS BECOMING MORE FEMININE.
DOES IT EVEN REALLY MATTER AT THIS POINT?
Who cares?
OOPS.
COULD YOU POINT ME TO THE WATER?
OVER THERE!
THANK YOU VERY MUCH.
THANK YOU FOR SAVING ME EARLIER.

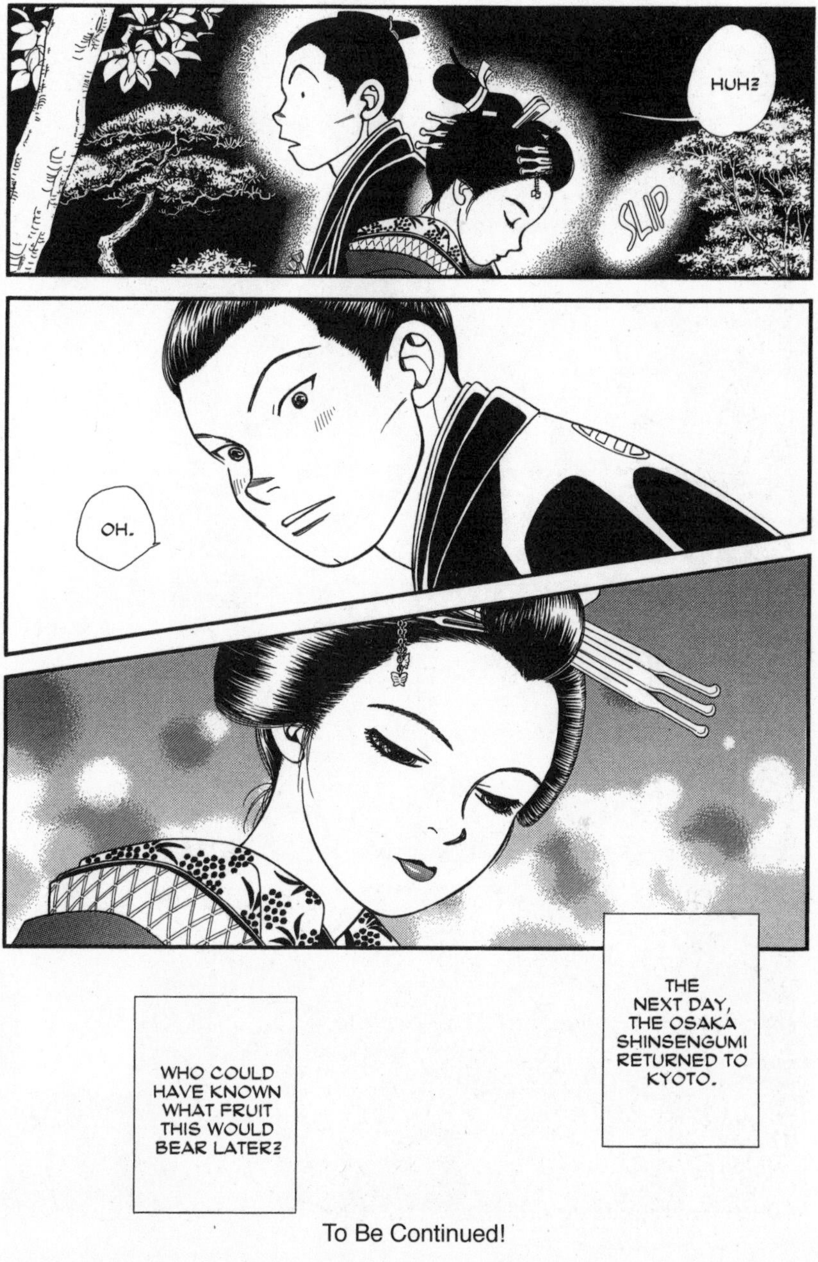
HUH?
SLIP
OH.
THE NEXT DAY, THE OSAKA SHINSENGUMI RETURNED TO KYOTO.
WHO COULD HAVE KNOWN WHAT FRUIT THIS WOULD BEAR LATER?

To Be Continued!

TAEKO WATANABE PRESENTS

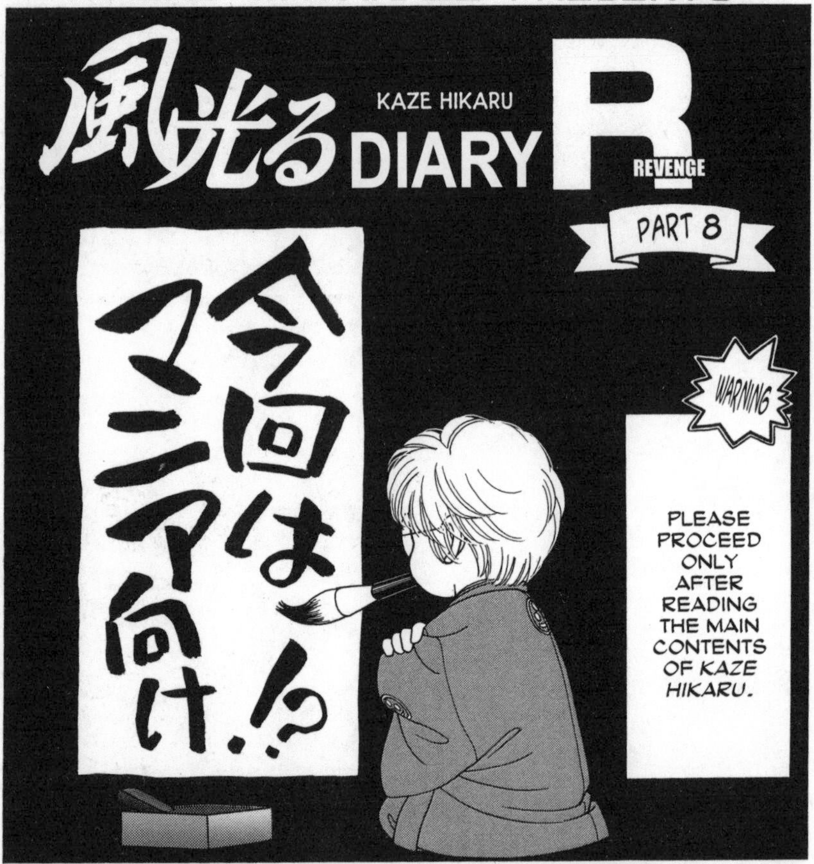
風光る
KAZE HIKARU
DIARY R
REVENGE
PART 8
WARNING
PLEASE PROCEED ONLY AFTER READING THE MAIN CONTENTS OF *KAZE HIKARU*.
今回はマニア向け!?

On sign: This time is for the maniacs?

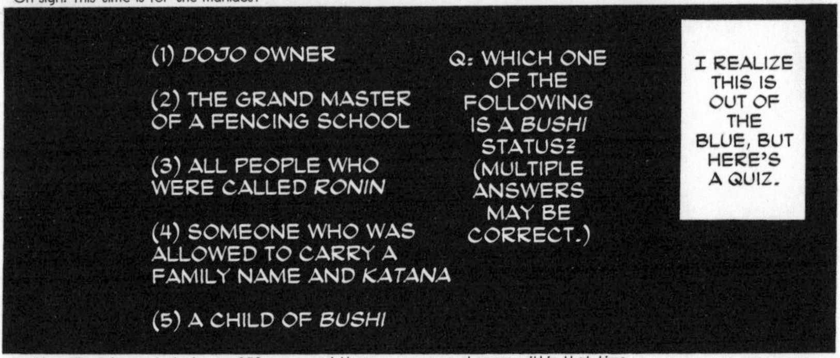
I REALIZE THIS IS OUT OF THE BLUE, BUT HERE'S A QUIZ.
Q: WHICH ONE OF THE FOLLOWING IS A *BUSHI* STATUS? (MULTIPLE ANSWERS MAY BE CORRECT.)
(1) *DOJO* OWNER
(2) THE GRAND MASTER OF A FENCING SCHOOL
(3) ALL PEOPLE WHO WERE CALLED *RONIN*
(4) SOMEONE WHO WAS ALLOWED TO CARRY A FAMILY NAME AND *KATANA*
(5) A CHILD OF *BUSHI*

Caution: The Edo era lasted over 250 years, and there were some changes within that time. Please answer specific to the *Kaze Hikaru* era.

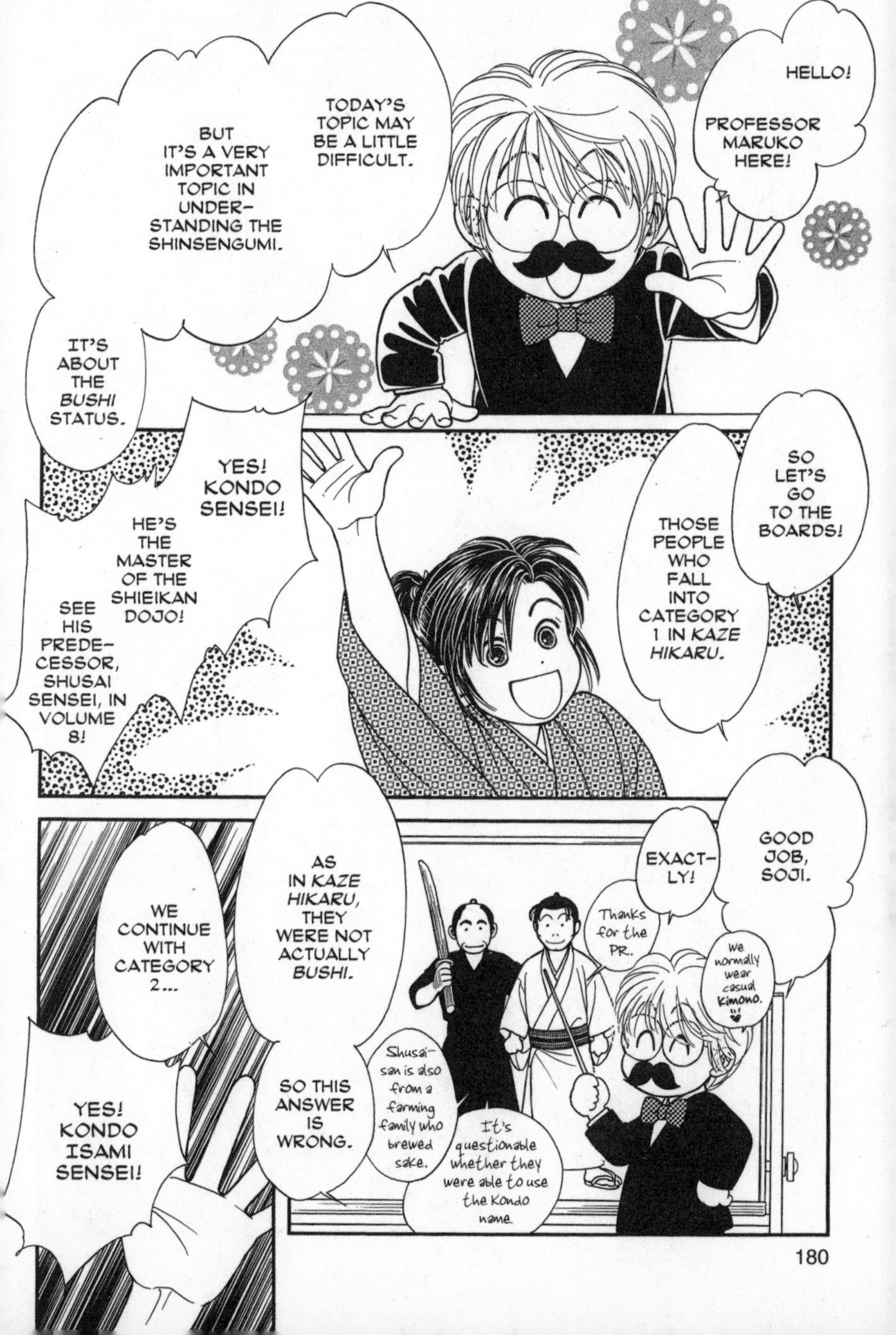
HELLO!
PROFESSOR MARUKO HERE!
TODAY'S TOPIC MAY BE A LITTLE DIFFICULT.
BUT IT'S A VERY IMPORTANT TOPIC IN UNDER-STANDING THE SHINSENGUMI.
IT'S ABOUT THE *BUSHI* STATUS.
SO LET'S GO TO THE BOARDS!
THOSE PEOPLE WHO FALL INTO CATEGORY 1 IN *KAZE HIKARU*.
YES! KONDO SENSEI!
HE'S THE MASTER OF THE SHIEIKAN DOJO!
SEE HIS PREDE-CESSOR, SHUSAI SENSEI, IN VOLUME 8!
GOOD JOB, SOJI.
EXACT-LY!
Thanks for the PR.
We normally wear casual kimono.
AS IN *KAZE HIKARU*, THEY WERE NOT ACTUALLY *BUSHI*.
Shusai-san is also from a farming family who brewed sake.
It's questionable whether they were able to use the Kondo name.
SO THIS ANSWER IS WRONG.
WE CONTINUE WITH CATEGORY 2...
YES! KONDO ISAMI SENSEI!

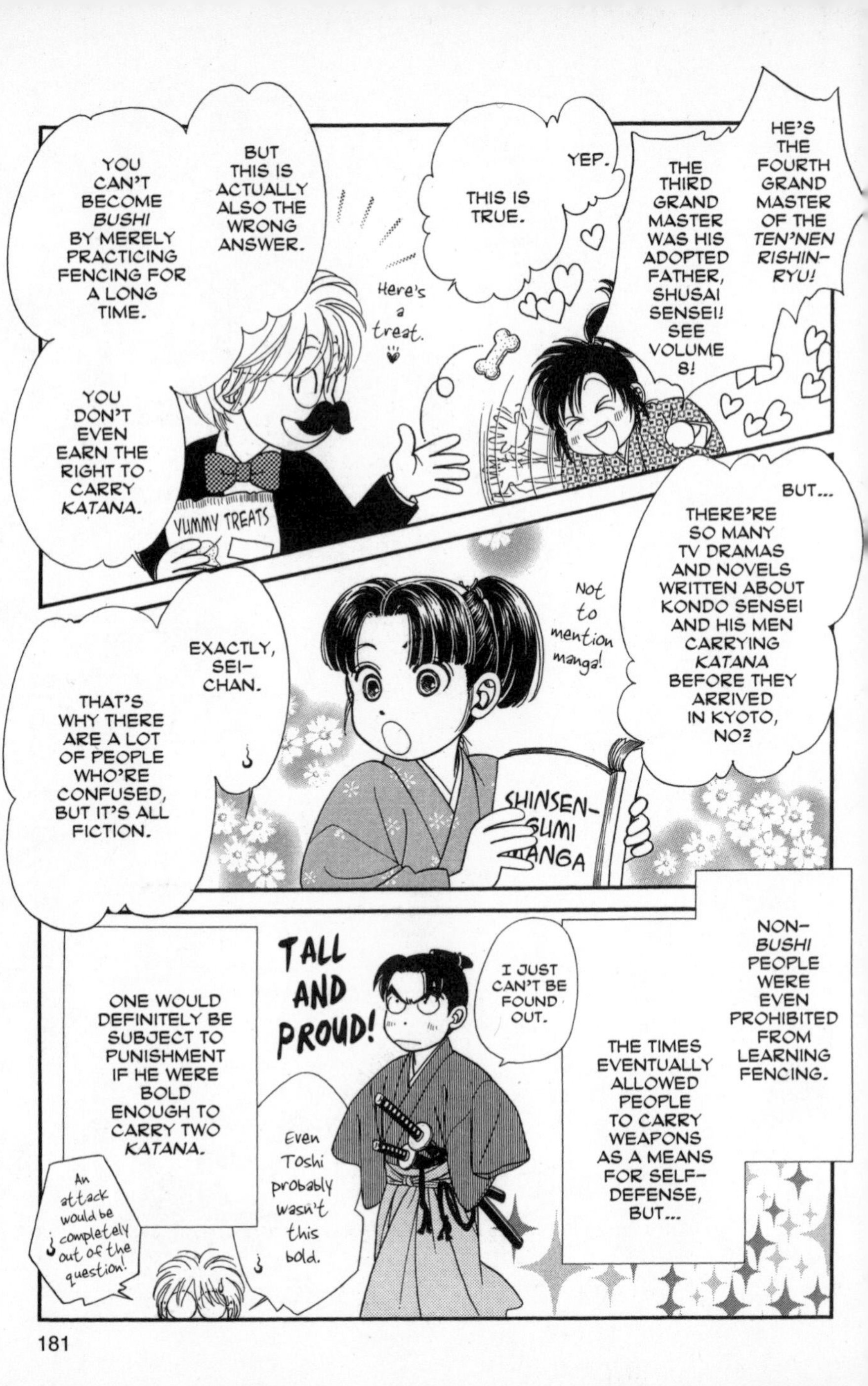

HE'S THE FOURTH GRAND MASTER OF THE *TEN'NEN RISHIN-RYU!*
THE THIRD GRAND MASTER WAS HIS ADOPTED FATHER, SHUSAI SENSEI! SEE VOLUME 8!
YEP.
THIS IS TRUE.
Here's a treat.
BUT THIS IS ACTUALLY ALSO THE WRONG ANSWER.
YOU CAN'T BECOME *BUSHI* BY MERELY PRACTICING FENCING FOR A LONG TIME.
YOU DON'T EVEN EARN THE RIGHT TO CARRY *KATANA.*
YUMMY TREATS
BUT...
THERE'RE SO MANY TV DRAMAS AND NOVELS WRITTEN ABOUT KONDO SENSEI AND HIS MEN CARRYING *KATANA* BEFORE THEY ARRIVED IN KYOTO, NO?
Not to mention manga!
SHINSEN-
EXACTLY, SEI-CHAN.
THAT'S WHY THERE ARE A LOT OF PEOPLE WHO'RE CONFUSED, BUT IT'S ALL FICTION.
NON-*BUSHI* PEOPLE WERE EVEN PROHIBITED FROM LEARNING FENCING.
THE TIMES EVENTUALLY ALLOWED PEOPLE TO CARRY WEAPONS AS A MEANS FOR SELF-DEFENSE, BUT...
I JUST CAN'T BE FOUND OUT.
TALL AND PROUD!
ONE WOULD DEFINITELY BE SUBJECT TO PUNISHMENT IF HE WERE BOLD ENOUGH TO CARRY TWO *KATANA.*
Even Toshi probably wasn't this bold.
An attack would be completely out of the question!

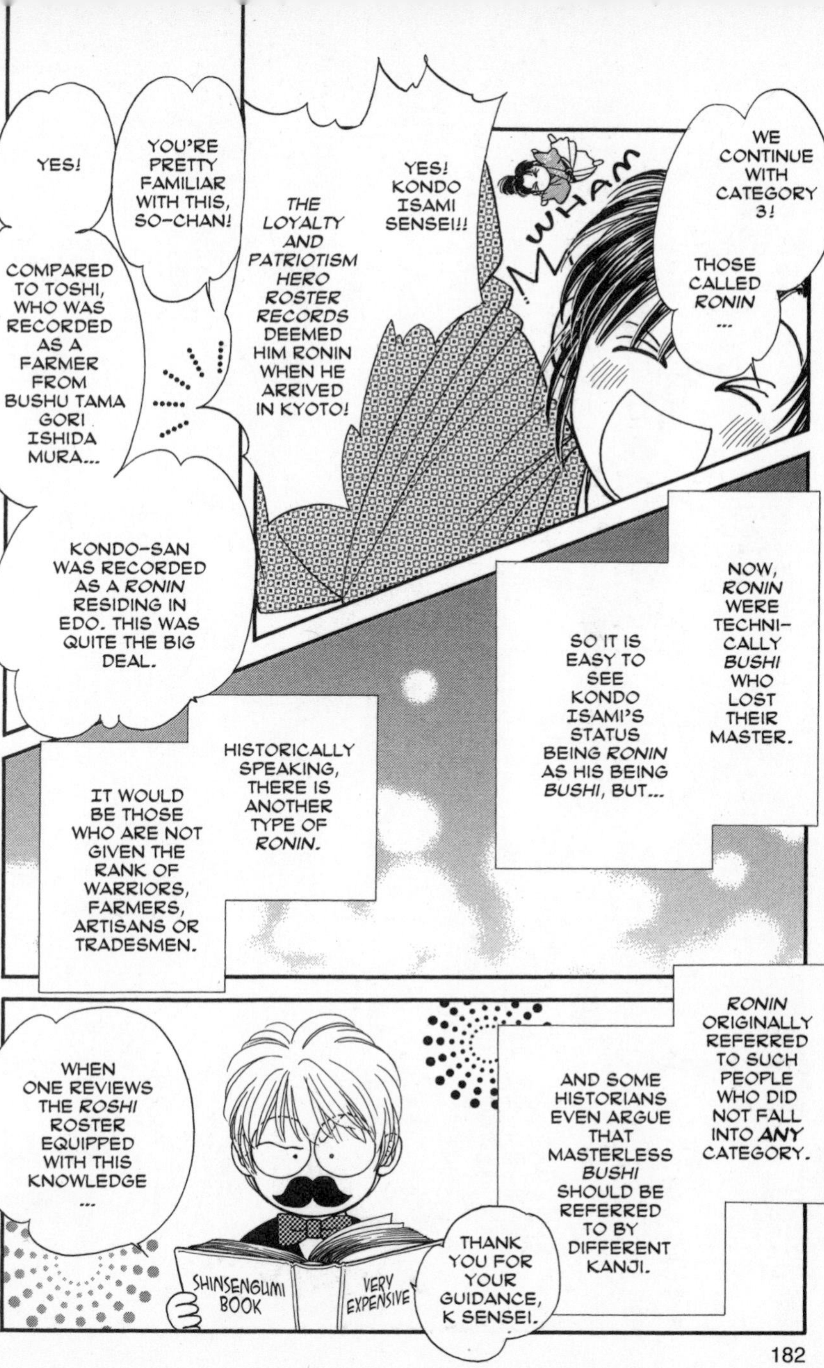
WE CONTINUE WITH CATEGORY 3!
THOSE CALLED RONIN ...
WHAM
YES! KONDO ISAMI SENSEI!!
THE LOYALTY AND PATRIOTISM HERO ROSTER RECORDS DEEMED HIM RONIN WHEN HE ARRIVED IN KYOTO!
YOU'RE PRETTY FAMILIAR WITH THIS, SO-CHAN!
YES!
COMPARED TO TOSHI, WHO WAS RECORDED AS A FARMER FROM BUSHU TAMA GORI ISHIDA MURA...
......
KONDO-SAN WAS RECORDED AS A RONIN RESIDING IN EDO. THIS WAS QUITE THE BIG DEAL.
NOW, RONIN WERE TECHNICALLY BUSHI WHO LOST THEIR MASTER.
SO IT IS EASY TO SEE KONDO ISAMI'S STATUS BEING RONIN AS HIS BEING BUSHI, BUT...
HISTORICALLY SPEAKING, THERE IS ANOTHER TYPE OF RONIN.
IT WOULD BE THOSE WHO ARE NOT GIVEN THE RANK OF WARRIORS, FARMERS, ARTISANS OR TRADESMEN.
RONIN ORIGINALLY REFERRED TO SUCH PEOPLE WHO DID NOT FALL INTO ANY CATEGORY.
AND SOME HISTORIANS EVEN ARGUE THAT MASTERLESS BUSHI SHOULD BE REFERRED TO BY DIFFERENT KANJI.
THANK YOU FOR YOUR GUIDANCE, K SENSEI.
WHEN ONE REVIEWS THE ROSHI ROSTER EQUIPPED WITH THIS KNOWLEDGE ...
SHINSENGUMI BOOK
VERY EXPENSIVE

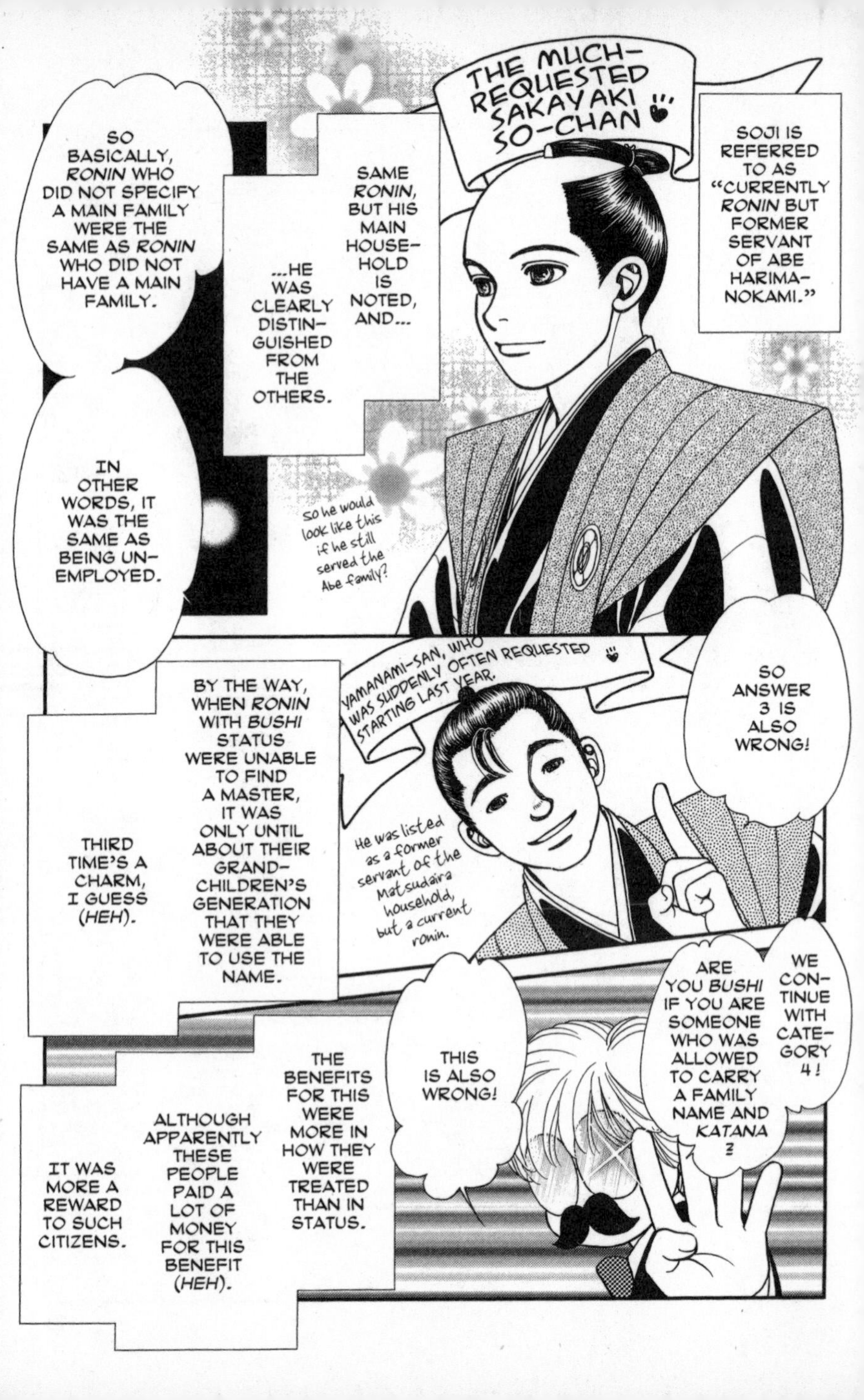
THE MUCH-REQUESTED SAKAYAKI SO-CHAN
SOJI IS REFERRED TO AS "CURRENTLY RONIN BUT FORMER SERVANT OF ABE HARIMA-NOKAMI."
SAME RONIN, BUT HIS MAIN HOUSEHOLD IS NOTED, AND...
...HE WAS CLEARLY DISTINGUISHED FROM THE OTHERS.
so he would look like this if he still served the Abe family?
SO BASICALLY, RONIN WHO DID NOT SPECIFY A MAIN FAMILY WERE THE SAME AS RONIN WHO DID NOT HAVE A MAIN FAMILY.
IN OTHER WORDS, IT WAS THE SAME AS BEING UN-EMPLOYED.
SO ANSWER 3 IS ALSO WRONG!
YAMANAMI-SAN, WHO WAS SUDDENLY OFTEN REQUESTED STARTING LAST YEAR.
He was listed as a former servant of the Matsudaira household, but a current ronin.
BY THE WAY, WHEN RONIN WITH BUSHI STATUS WERE UNABLE TO FIND A MASTER, IT WAS ONLY UNTIL ABOUT THEIR GRAND-CHILDREN'S GENERATION THAT THEY WERE ABLE TO USE THE NAME.
THIRD TIME'S A CHARM, I GUESS (HEH).
WE CONTINUE WITH CATEGORY 4!
ARE YOU BUSHI IF YOU ARE SOMEONE WHO WAS ALLOWED TO CARRY A FAMILY NAME AND KATANA?
THIS IS ALSO WRONG!
THE BENEFITS FOR THIS WERE MORE IN HOW THEY WERE TREATED THAN IN STATUS.
ALTHOUGH APPARENTLY THESE PEOPLE PAID A LOT OF MONEY FOR THIS BENEFIT (HEH).
IT WAS MORE A REWARD TO SUCH CITIZENS.

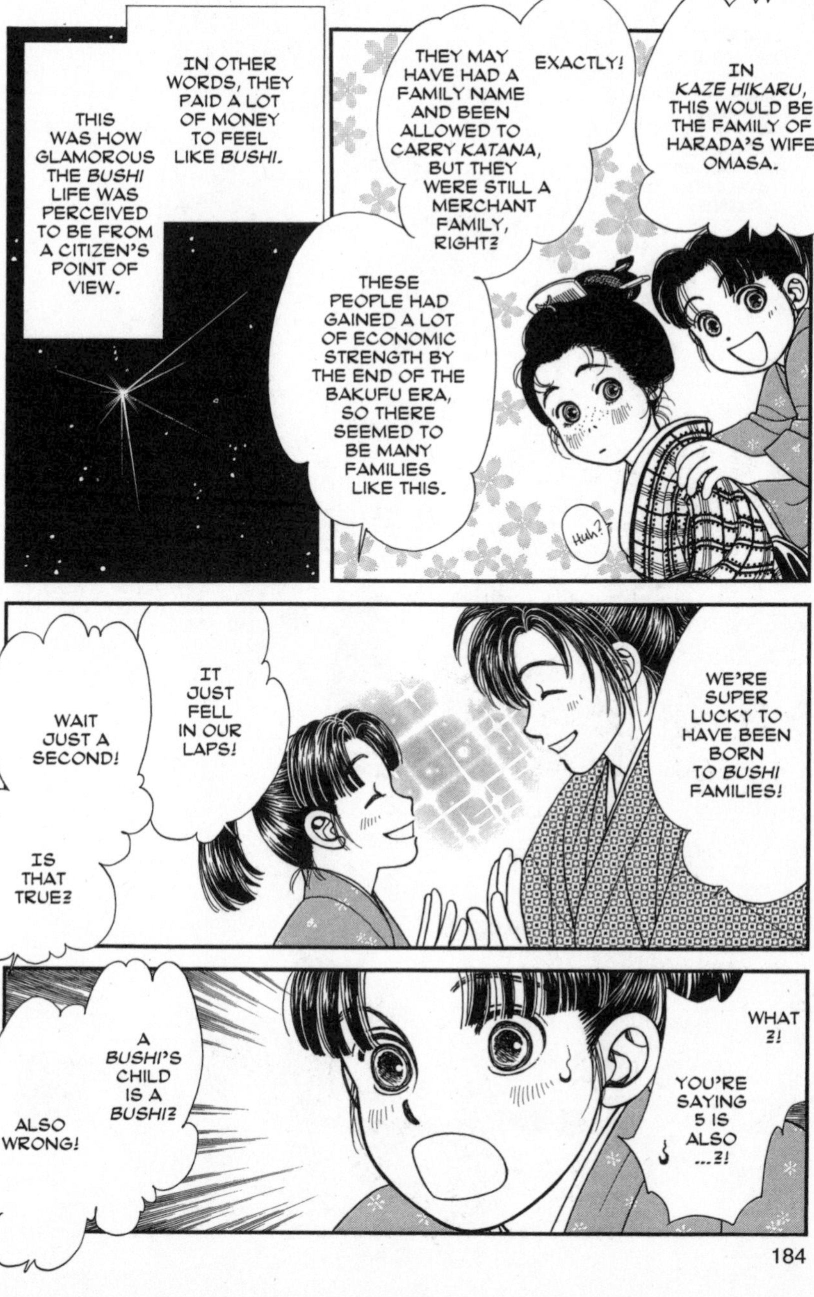
IN KAZE HIKARU, THIS WOULD BE THE FAMILY OF HARADA'S WIFE OMASA.
EXACTLY!
THEY MAY HAVE HAD A FAMILY NAME AND BEEN ALLOWED TO CARRY KATANA, BUT THEY WERE STILL A MERCHANT FAMILY, RIGHT?
THESE PEOPLE HAD GAINED A LOT OF ECONOMIC STRENGTH BY THE END OF THE BAKUFU ERA, SO THERE SEEMED TO BE MANY FAMILIES LIKE THIS.
Huh?
IN OTHER WORDS, THEY PAID A LOT OF MONEY TO FEEL LIKE BUSHI.
THIS WAS HOW GLAMOROUS THE BUSHI LIFE WAS PERCEIVED TO BE FROM A CITIZEN'S POINT OF VIEW.
WE'RE SUPER LUCKY TO HAVE BEEN BORN TO BUSHI FAMILIES!
IT JUST FELL IN OUR LAPS!
WAIT JUST A SECOND!
IS THAT TRUE?!
WHAT?!
YOU'RE SAYING 5 IS ALSO ...?!
A BUSHI'S CHILD IS A BUSHI?!
ALSO WRONG!

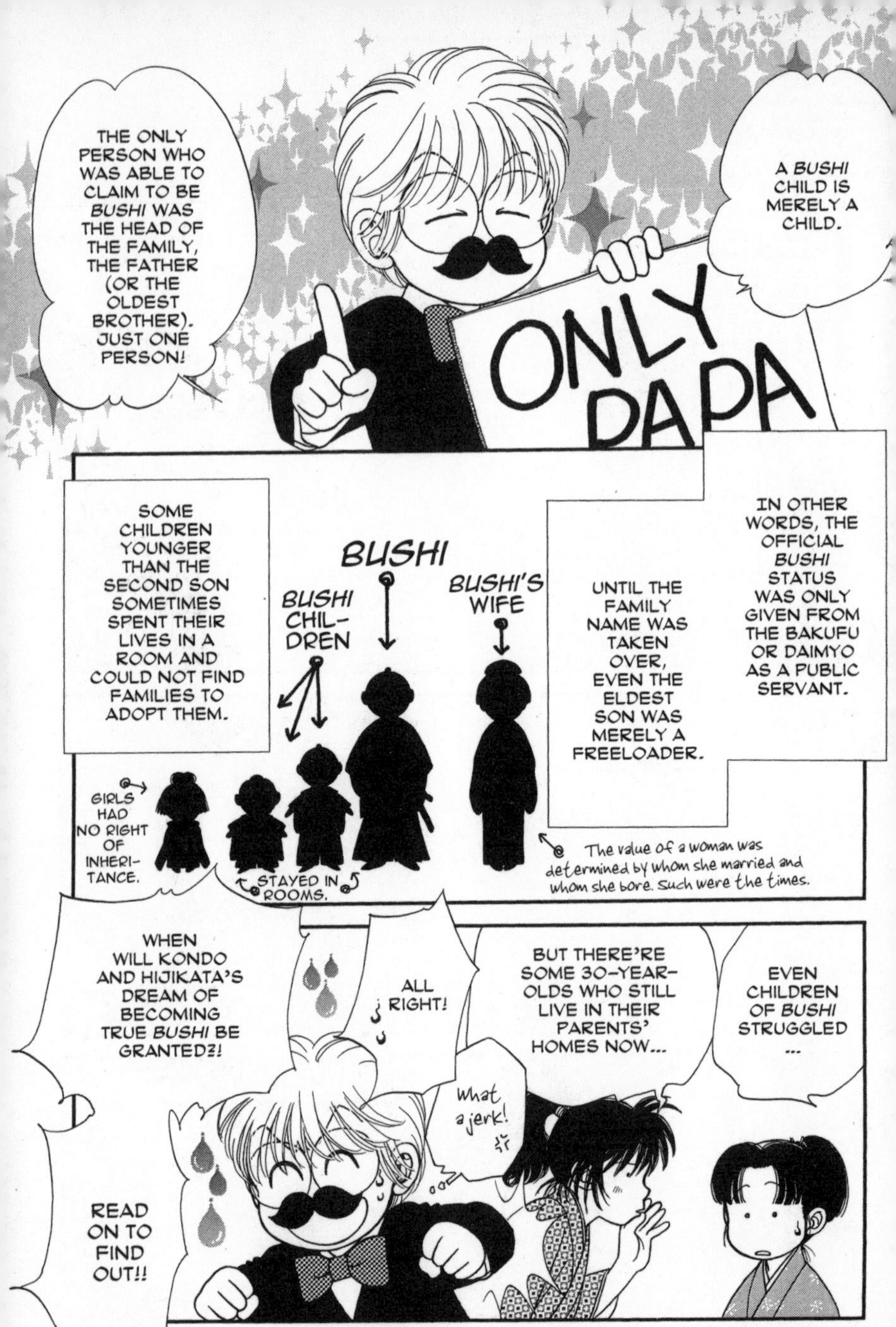

A BUSHI CHILD IS MERELY A CHILD.
THE ONLY PERSON WHO WAS ABLE TO CLAIM TO BE BUSHI WAS THE HEAD OF THE FAMILY, THE FATHER (OR THE OLDEST BROTHER). JUST ONE PERSON!
ONLY PAPA
IN OTHER WORDS, THE OFFICIAL BUSHI STATUS WAS ONLY GIVEN FROM THE BAKUFU OR DAIMYO AS A PUBLIC SERVANT.
UNTIL THE FAMILY NAME WAS TAKEN OVER, EVEN THE ELDEST SON WAS MERELY A FREELOADER.
BUSHI
BUSHI'S WIFE
BUSHI CHILDREN
The value of a woman was determined by whom she married and whom she bore. Such were the times.
STAYED IN ROOMS.
GIRLS HAD NO RIGHT OF INHERITANCE.
SOME CHILDREN YOUNGER THAN THE SECOND SON SOMETIMES SPENT THEIR LIVES IN A ROOM AND COULD NOT FIND FAMILIES TO ADOPT THEM.
EVEN CHILDREN OF BUSHI STRUGGLED ...
BUT THERE'RE SOME 30-YEAR-OLDS WHO STILL LIVE IN THEIR PARENTS' HOMES NOW...
What a jerk!
ALL RIGHT!
WHEN WILL KONDO AND HIJIKATA'S DREAM OF BECOMING TRUE BUSHI BE GRANTED?!
READ ON TO FIND OUT!!

Kaze Hikaru Diary R: The End

Decoding Kaze Hikaru

Kaze Hikaru is a historical drama based in 19th century Japan and thus contains some fairly mystifying terminology. In this glossary we'll break down archaic phrases, terms and other linguistic curiosities for you so that you can move through life with the smug assurance that you are indeed a know-it-all.

First and foremost, because *Kaze Hikaru* is a period story, we kept all character names in their traditional Japanese form—that is, family name followed by first name. For example, the character Okita Soji's family name is Okita and his personal name is Soji.

AKO-ROSHI:
The *ronin* (samurai) of Ako; featured in the immortal Kabuki play *Chushingura* (Loyalty), aka *47 Samurai*.

ANI-UE:
Literally, "brother above"; an honorific for an elder male sibling.

BAKUFU:
Literally, "tent government." Shogunate; the feudal, military government that dominated Japan for more than 200 years.

BUSHI:
A samurai or warrior (part of the compound word *bushido*, which means "way of the warrior").

CHICHI-UE:
An honorific suffix meaning "father above."

DO:
In kendo (a Japanese fencing sport that uses bamboo swords), a short way of describing the offensive single-hit strike *shikake waza ippon uchi*.

-HAN:
The same as the honorific -*san*, pronounced in the dialect of southern Japan.

-KUN:
An honorific suffix that indicates a difference in rank and title. The use of -*kun* is also a way of indicating familiarity and friendliness between students or compatriots.

MEN:
In the context of *Kaze Hikaru*, *men* refers to one of the "points" in kendo. It is a strike to the forehead and is considered a basic move.

MIBU-ROSHI:
A group of warriors that supports the Bakufu.

NE'E-SAN:
Can mean "older sister," "ma'am" or "miss."

NI'I-CHAN:
Short for *oni'i-san* or *oni'i-chan*, meaning older brother.

OKU-SAMA:
This is a polite way to refer to someone's wife. *Oku* means "deep" or "further back" and comes from the fact that wives (in affluent families) stayed hidden away in the back rooms of the house.

ONI:
Literally "ogre," this is Sei's nickname for Vice Captain Hijikata.

RANPO:
Medical science derived from the Dutch.

RONIN:
Masterless samurai.

RYO:
At the time, one *ryo* and two *bu* (four bu equaled roughly one ryo) were enough currency to support a family of five for an entire month.

-SAN:
An honorific suffix that carries the meaning of "Mr." or "Ms."

SENSEI:
A teacher, master or instructor.

SEPPUKU:
A ritualistic suicide that was considered a privilege of the nobility and samurai elite.

SONJO-HA:
Those loyal to the emperor and dedicated to the expulsion of foreigners from the country.

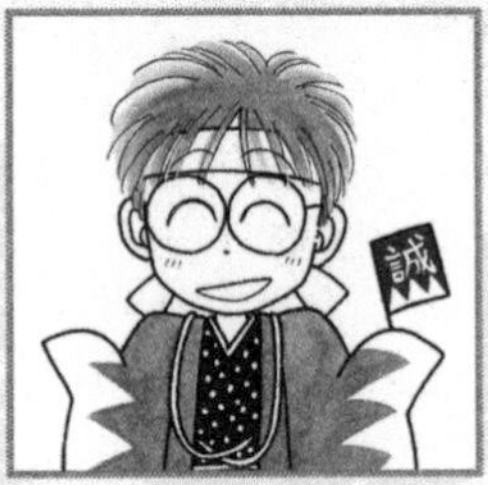
誠

Time flies, and we're about to bust into season five (to say it like the TV show *24*) (heh). I quit while I was ahead with the challenging close-ups, and that may leave some of you curiously anticipating what I'm going to do next. So, what do you think the theme for this cover is? I'll leave you with this hint until volume 18 is released (heh)!

The seasonal word that isn't a hint at all is "East Wind." The kanji is read "kochi." For the Shinsengumi who came from Edo, the east wind of course served as a tailwind. The warm spring wind is often unexpectedly strong, and I feel like it may be indicative of the future of the two. I know... I'm being ambiguous.

Please continue to support Sei in her struggles as a tumultuous blade of grass!

Taeko Watanabe debuted as a manga artist in 1979 with her story *Waka-chan no Netsuai Jidai* (Love Struck Days of Waka). *Kaze Hikaru* is her longest-running series, but she has created a number of other popular series. Watanabe is a two-time winner of the prestigious Shogakukan Manga Award in the girls category—her manga *Hajime-chan ga Ichiban!* (Hajime-chan Is Number One!) claimed the award in 1991, and *Kaze Hikaru* took it in 2003.

Watanabe read hundreds of historical sources to create *Kaze Hikaru*. She is from Tokyo.

KAZE HIKARU VOL. 17
Shojo Beat Edition

STORY AND ART BY
TAEKO WATANABE

© 1997 Taeko WATANABE/Shogakukan
All rights reserved.
Original Japanese edition "KAZE HIKARU" published by SHOGAKUKAN Inc.

Translation & English Adaptation/Mai Ihara
Touch-up Art & Lettering/Rina Mapa
Design/Julie Behn
Editor/Jonathan Tarbox

VP, Production/Alvin Lu
VP, Sales & Product Marketing/Gonzalo Ferreyra
VP, Creative/Linda Espinosa
Publisher/Hyoe Narita

Printed in Canada

Published by VIZ Media, LLC
P.O. Box 77010
San Francisco, CA 94107

10 9 8 7 6 5 4 3 2 1
First printing, May 2010

PARENTAL ADVISORY
KAZE HIKARU is rated T+ for Older Teen and is
recommended for ages 16 and up. This volume
contains realistic violence, alcohol use and sexual
themes.
ratings.viz.com

www.viz.com

www.shojobeat.com

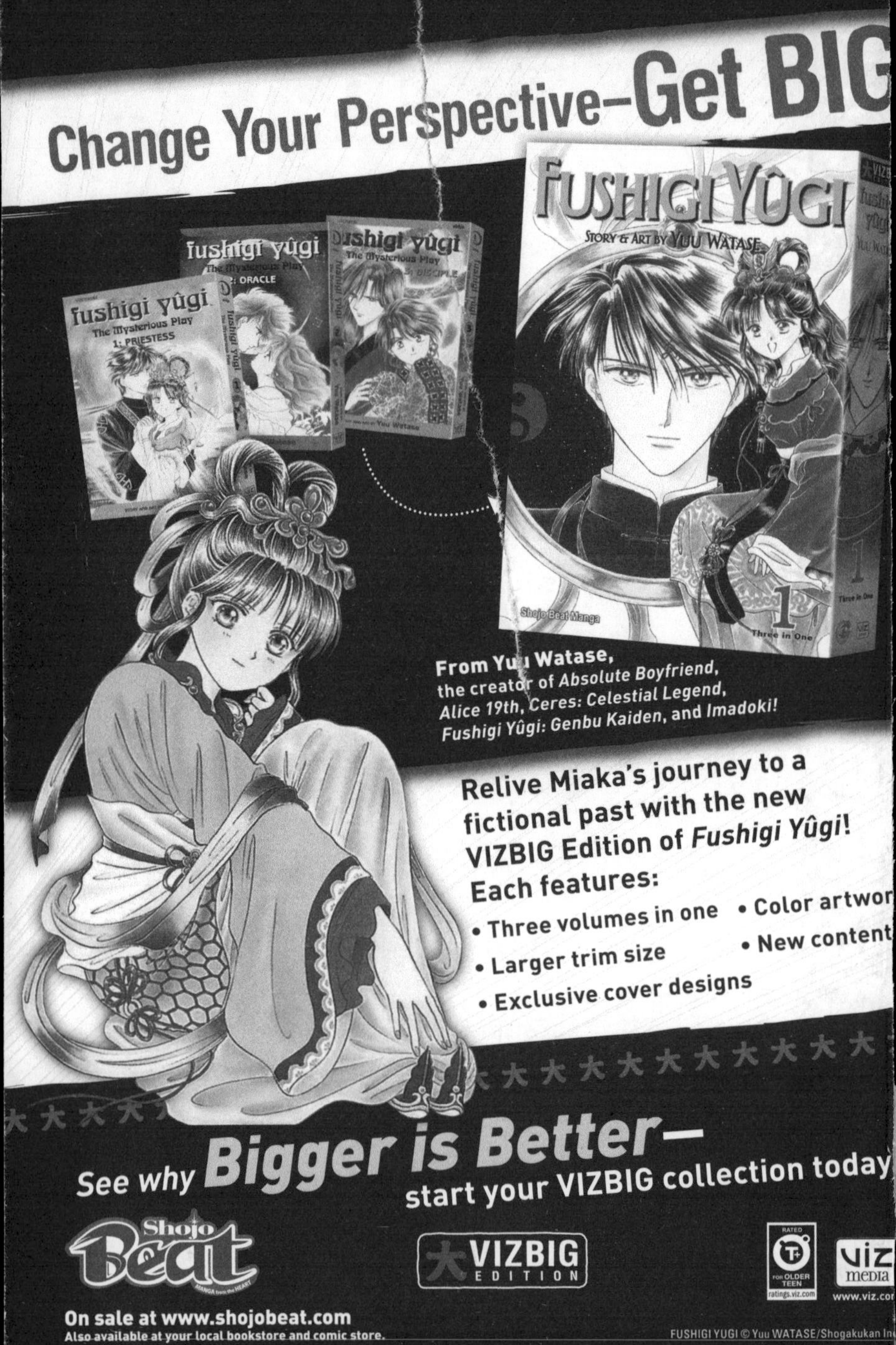

Change Your Perspective–Get BIG
FUSHIGI YÛGI
STORY & ART BY YUU WATASE
fushigi yûgi
The Mysterious Play
1: PRIESTESS
2: ORACLE
3: DISCIPLE
Shojo Beat Manga
1
Three in One
From Yuu Watase,
the creator of Absolute Boyfriend,
Alice 19th, Ceres: Celestial Legend,
Fushigi Yûgi: Genbu Kaiden, and Imadoki!
Relive Miaka's journey to a
fictional past with the new
VIZBIG Edition of Fushigi Yûgi!
Each features:
• Three volumes in one
• Larger trim size
• Exclusive cover designs
• Color artwor
• New content
See why Bigger is Better—
start your VIZBIG collection today
Shojo Beat
VIZBIG EDITION
RATED T+ FOR OLDER TEEN
ratings.viz.com
viz media
www.viz.co
On sale at www.shojobeat.com
Also available at your local bookstore and comic store.
FUSHIGI YUGI © Yuu WATASE/Shogakukan In

Sho

Beat

MANGA from the HEART

OTOMEN

**STORY AND ART BY
AYA KANNO**

VAMPIRE
KNIGHT

**STORY AND ART BY
MATSURI HINO**

Natsume's
BOOK of FRIENDS

**STORY AND ART BY
YUKI MIDORIKAWA**

Want to see more of what you're looking for?

Let your voice be heard!

shojobeat.com/mangasurvey

Help us give you more manga from the heart!